Technology in American Health Care

Technology in American Health Care
Policy Directions for Effective Evaluation and Management

Alan B. Cohen
Ruth S. Hanft

With
   William E. Encinosa
   Stephanie M. Spernak
   Shirley A. Stewart
   Catherine C. White

The University of Michigan Press
Ann Arbor

2007   2006   2005   2004   4   3   2   1

A CIP catalog record for this book is available from the British Library.

Library of Congress Cataloging-in-Publication Data

Cohen, Alan B.
    Technology in American health care : policy directions for effective
evaluation and management / Alan B. Cohen, Ruth S. Hanft ; with William
E. Encinosa . . . [et al.].
        p.   ;   cm.
    Includes bibliographical references and index.
    ISBN 0-472-11326-7 (cloth : alk. paper)
    1. Medical technology—Government policy—United States.   2. Medical
policy—United States.
[DNLM: 1. Biomedical Technology—United States.   2. Health
Policy—United States.   3. Technology Assessment, Biomedical—United
States. W 82 C678t 2003]   I. Hanft, Ruth S., 1929–   II. Title.

R855.5.U6C64   2003
610'.28—dc22   2003021581

Contents

Figures

Tables

Foreword

The delivery of medical and health care in the United States is a vast, complex, social enterprise, and we all need words and ways to describe it for ourselves and to create a common language and ideas we can use together. How policymakers, managers, and the public define health care delivery will shape our agenda for improving it.

Health and medical care can be described in a static structural view as consisting of its components, including patients, doctors, nurses, other health professionals, hospitals, insurance plans, government, and so on. Such descriptions of structure are necessary but not adequate. We have to know how these pieces of the puzzle fit together and relate to each other. For example, how does health insurance coverage define the way patients and doctors relate to each other? Health economics, medical sociology, organization theory, the law, biological science, and other academic disciplines help us to understand the process of care. But even fitting this puzzle together can give a static, one-point-in-time understanding. We need words and theories that will explain the dynamics of change in health care over time.

Medical technology, as described in this book, gives us this third level of understanding. It gives us the words and concepts to understand how health care delivery changes over time as new technologies are created, developed, approved, implemented, and evaluated. These changes involve academic health centers, the drug and device industries, government policies, regulatory agencies, the law, managed care organizations and insurance companies, practitioner use, and patient preferences. To understand this dynamic is to understand change in health care over time.

Alan B. Cohen and Ruth S. Hanft also give the reader ideas, tools, and methods to help guide such change in a beneficial way. Since the 1970s, a group of evaluative methods has been refined and applied to health care technology, including clinical trials, decision models, cost-effectiveness analysis, and information synthesis. These have become the accepted basis for evaluating medical care technologies and are described in this book.

In the absence of such careful analyses, new treatments have been introduced and only later has it been realized that they were useless or even harmful. Good evaluation takes time and effort, a fact that may delay the rapid introduction of truly beneficial treatments.

Approval of a technology at the government, care plan, and provider levels can have vast cost consequences and requires careful managerial attention and an understanding of the evaluative methods described in this book.

Decisions to approve or reject new medical technologies are becoming more difficult. To refuse to reimburse a clearly harmful procedure is relatively easy. It is more difficult when the choice is between good, better, and best, where the best is much more expensive and there is divided and heated opinion about benefits.

We are entering an era when such hard choices are central to medical and health care policy-making and management. This is why the contents of this book are so important.

—Duncan Neuhauser

Preface

In today's turbulent and increasingly competitive health care environment, the most critical challenge facing decision makers is to stay abreast of technological advances that drive the delivery and cost of health care. Recent discoveries regarding the human genome, coupled with innovations in biotechnology and a virtual explosion in information technology, promise to transform medicine and health care in exciting new ways. These remarkable achievements, however, do not come cheaply, and their introduction into clinical practice and their ultimate impact on people's health will depend, at least in part, on their benefits and costs. Cost-effective delivery of evidence-based health care is becoming the sine qua non of American medicine at the dawn of the twenty-first century. Health care decision makers—providers, payers, policymakers, and consumers alike—all need vital information about the risks, benefits, and costs of new technologies to make informed decisions about which ones to adopt and how to use them. While the field of medical technology evaluation (MTE) has been evolving over the past twenty-five years to meet this burgeoning need, the discipline is plagued by continuing controversy about the evaluation and diffusion of medical technologies, ranging from the methods employed in their assessment to the myriad policies (public and private) that govern their adoption and use. In this three-part volume, individuals who are directly involved in MTE as well as those who are touched by it in their professional lives (policymakers, clinicians, managers, and researchers) will find a comprehensive, multidisciplinary guide to understanding the policy issues that shape the development and diffusion of new technologies and the methods for evaluating their effectiveness and cost-effectiveness. Students new to the field—especially those pursuing careers in medicine, public health, health care management, public policy, and other clinical professions—should find this book instructive. Experienced practitioners who are versed in the issues and methods should also find it useful as a practical guide to the evaluation and management of medical technologies in health care.

The Organization of the Book

The book is divided into three parts, plus an opening chapter that introduces basic definitions and recounts the history of technological change in American medicine and a second chapter that explores eight critical questions regarding medical technology in health care—from its diffusion and evaluation to its economic, ethical, organizational, and societal impacts. Part I (chapters 3–5) then discusses important concepts, theories, and strategies relating to biomedical innovation, the development of medical technology, patterns of diffusion, and the adoption and use of technology by hospitals, physicians, and other health care organizations and professions under changing health care market conditions. Part II (chapters 6–9) examines the methods of MTE—including randomized controlled trials, meta-analyses, economic evaluation methods (such as cost-benefit, cost-effectiveness, and cost-utility analyses), and clinical decision analysis—and describes MTE activities in the United States and selected other nations. Part III (chapters 10–15) focuses on key public policy issues and concerns that permeate the organization, financing, and delivery of health care and that relate importantly to medical technology, including safety, efficacy, quality, cost, access, equity, social, ethical, legal, and evaluation concerns. All three sections provide a historical perspective on the relevant issues, methods, and policy concerns and contain examples of technologies whose development, adoption, evaluation, and use have contributed to our understanding of the field.

To gain the broadest and most comprehensive grasp of these issues, readers are advised to peruse the entire volume. Knowledgeable readers, however, may selectively read only those chapters of special interest. Readers interested in learning more about specific evaluation methods and their application will find the lists of recommended readings at the ends of the methods chapters to be useful. The Web sites of key organizations involved in MTE are provided in chapter 9 and throughout the text where appropriate; resource information of this kind is indispensable in an electronic age.

Acknowledgments

The origins of this book may be traced to an early course in MTE taught by Alan B. Cohen at the Johns Hopkins School of Hygiene and Public Health between 1982 and 1984. At that time, no single text spanned the breadth of issues surrounding medical technology. In fact, each of the few texts that existed were directed toward only a small segment of the issues in the growing field. One had to rely instead on an eclectic combination of unpublished research monographs, federal government reports and case studies (mostly from the Congressional Office of Technology Assessment), and occasional journal articles in the medical and health policy literatures to cover the broad expanse of relevant topics, such as the biomedical innovation process, the diffusion of new technology into clinical practice, the methods for evaluating technology, the policies and practices governing the adoption and use of technology, and the impact of new technology on health care costs and spending growth in the United States.

At the urging of several Hopkins graduate students of that era (Joel Cantor, Frances Hanckel, James McAllister, Jeanette Rose, Liza Solomon, and Lu Zawistowich) as well as some Hopkins faculty members (the late Dr. Donald Cohodes, Dr. Carl Schramm, and Dr. Robert Rock), a draft outline for a comprehensive text was produced. However, because the vision for the book extended well beyond that of the course, additional specialized expertise was required in several areas, and the project evolved into a collaborative effort that eventually included a second principal author, Ruth S. Hanft, and important contributions from a multidisciplinary group of economists, policy analysts, health care managers, and legal scholars. Despite its long gestation, the book remains true to the original vision of a comprehensive text with a framework for exploring the complex policy issues that affect the strategic evaluation and management of medical technology in health care. To that end we remain firmly committed and wish to thank the University of Michigan Press and its editorial staff, especially Liz Suhay and Ellen McCarthy, for their belief in that vision and for their recognition of the book's inherent value as a unique work.

Over the years, the project benefited from the advice, input, and tireless efforts of numerous individuals. We could not have completed the text without the considerable intellectual contributions of our co-authors—Dr. William Encinosa (chapters 7 and 8), Shirley Stewart (chapters 10 and 11), Catherine White (chapter 6), and Dr. Stephanie

Spernak (chapter 14). In the early stages of the book's development, several individuals at the Robert Wood Johnson Foundation—Dr. Leighton Cluff, the late Dr. Robert Ebert, and the late Dr. David Rogers—graciously championed its cause, providing encouragement and insightful commentary on early drafts of some chapters. We are indebted to them as well as to Julie Jaquiss Collins, Dr. Miriam Orleans, Cecile Papirno, Dr. Seema Sonnad, Dr. Norman Weissman, and two anonymous reviewers for their thoughtful comments on later drafts of the full manuscript. We thank Nathan Andrew, Amy Chu, Julie Jaquiss Collins, Leslee Ikeda, and Michael Renfroe for their dedicated research assistance in reviewing the literature and helping to assemble the references. We also gratefully acknowledge the expert assistance of Janet Barden, Kim Lavan, and Deborah Malloy in the preparation of various drafts of the text as well as the design and layout of tables and figures. The Robert Wood Johnson Foundation generously provided partial support under grants 21335 and 26077, which proved instrumental in furthering the goals of this project. Finally, we wish to thank our spouses, Helaine and Herb, to whom this book is dedicated, for their steadfast love, support, and patience throughout the entirety of the effort.

1

Introduction
Alan B. Cohen

Nearly two centuries ago, in this room, on this floor, Thomas Jefferson and a trusted aide spread out a magnificent map, a map Jefferson had long prayed he would get to see in his lifetime. The aide was Meriwether Lewis, and the map was the product of his courageous expedition across the American frontier, all the way to the Pacific. It was a map that defined the contours and forever expanded the frontiers of our continent and our imagination.

Today the world is joining us here in the East Room to behold a map of even greater significance. We are here to celebrate the completion of the first survey of the entire human genome. Without a doubt this is the most important, most wondrous map ever produced by humankind. . . .

Today's announcement represents more than just an epoch-making triumph of science and reason. After all, when Galileo discovered he could use the tools of mathematics and mechanics to understand the motion of celestial bodies, he felt, in the words of one eminent researcher, that he had learned the language of the universe.

Today we are learning the language in which God created life.
—President William Jefferson Clinton, June 26, 2000

With those prophetic words, President Clinton announced a momentous achievement in human history—the completion of a genetic blueprint of humankind, the first product of the multibillion dollar Human Genome Project. The historic announcement marked the culmination of a ten-year effort by two rival research groups—a publicly funded consortium in the United States and Great Britain under the leadership of the National Institutes of Health and the Department of Energy, and a private biotechnology company, Celera Genomics, of Rockville, Maryland—to identify the DNA sequencing of every gene in the human body (Friend

2000; Saltus 2000; Wade 2000b). In calling the DNA code map "the most important, most wondrous map ever produced," the president drew a symbolic parallel between the cracking of the human genetic code and the charting of the American frontier two hundred years before: humanity now stands poised to conquer yet another frontier, one that is biological rather than physical. Others have likened the project both in terms of scope and significance to the wartime Manhattan Project that developed the first nuclear weapon and to the U.S. space program that produced the first moon landing in 1969 (Lander 2000; Saltus 2000).

The joint announcement by the president and British Prime Minister Tony Blair ushered in a new era of scientific discovery and technological innovation in the life sciences that is expected to revolutionize medicine and health care (Wade 2000b). The event also signaled the beginning of expansive efforts by biotechnology and pharmaceutical firms to identify specific genes and their proteins, to understand their functions and relationships to disease processes, and to search for new targeted drugs and gene therapies to cure or prevent a multiplicity of diseases, many of which were not previously known to have genetic components (Cowley and Underwood 2000; Rosenberg and Mishra 2000; Wade 2000a; Collins and McKusick 2001). And yet, despite the euphoria, some scientists have raised legitimate questions about the potential future impact of genetics on medicine, urging clinicians and policymakers not to lose sight of the fact that other factors—such as differences in social structure, lifestyle, and environment—account for larger proportions of disease than do genetic differences (Holtzman and Marteau 2000). Others have stressed the importance of the interplay between genes and the environment in determining an individual's health (Lewontin 2000). As one observer asserts, "the genome is a set of boundary conditions that limits the nature of the organism, not a blueprint that defines it" (Parham 2000, 667).

Nevertheless, the age of genomics, proteomics, and metabolomics is now upon us, and the explosive scientific and technological progress that began fifty years ago shows no signs of slowing. In fact, the rate of technological change in the twenty-first century appears to be accelerating. Improvements in silicon-chip technology, for example, continue to revolutionize the architecture of personal computers according to Moore's Law,* creating increasingly miniaturized microprocessors that

---

*Named for Gordon E. Moore, cofounder of Fairchild Semiconductor, who is credited with having articulated this concept in 1965 (Markoff 2002).

are so fast and powerful that the speed and storage capacity of random-access memory double roughly every eighteen months (Markoff 2002). Advances in global telecommunications and satellite technology enable us to gather and exchange complex multimedia information in real-time terms across vast distances. Space exploration, although not yet an integral part of our daily existence, demonstrates our ability to escape the physical bonds of Earth's gravity and serves to remind us of the almost limitless potential of the human spirit to overcome constraints. Further proof of our growing mastery over the physical world may be found in reports that Harvard University physicists have successfully harnessed the speed of light. This landmark feat of bringing light to a complete standstill and then sending it on its way was considered impossible only a few years ago, but its accomplishment now sets the stage for vast improvements in the speed of computers and the security of communications (Glanz 2001). As these examples illustrate, technological change is relentless and ubiquitous across all aspects of human endeavor. By constantly redefining what is possible, technology holds the power to transform our lives and our social institutions, altering how we think, learn, work, play, communicate, and interact with others in society.

Biomedical innovations, such as new drugs, biologics, devices, and surgical procedures, emerge today with ever-increasing speed, sophistication, and versatility, empowering modern physicians to prevent, cure, or otherwise ameliorate diseases that for centuries had eluded effective control. The decoding of the human genome and the identification of proteins for targeted drug development presage vast (but yet unknown) advances in the diagnosis, treatment, palliation, and cure of human diseases. If the growing trend in direct-to-consumer advertising of new pharmaceuticals is any guide, consumer demand will be a formidable force spurring the rapid adoption of biomedical innovations in coming years. However, mounting economic and social pressures to control health care spending and to reform the health care system cause policymakers and others to recognize that technological change may not be universally beneficial, that innovations must be assessed in timely ways using scientific methods of evaluation, and that new technologies often raise social and ethical concerns that must be addressed before such advances should be allowed to diffuse widely into use. Ultimately, it is in society's best interest to see that new technologies are evaluated carefully and that their use in medicine is channeled constructively in ways that temper their highly seductive appeal with clear knowledge of their effectiveness and potential negative consequences.

Widely hailed as the key to American dominance in medicine, medical technology figures prominently today in ongoing public debates over two highly contentious health policy issues—Medicare prescription drug coverage and the rights of patients under managed care. In the former case, Congress in 2003 approved prescription drug coverage for Medicare beneficiaries, but many questions remain about the adequacy of the coverage and the long-term impact on Medicare spending. Senior citizens are concerned about their out-of-pocket outlays for prescription drugs, whereas pharmaceutical firms are worried that the federal government might still interfere with their ability to set prescription drug prices, and managed care plans participating in the Medicare + Choice program fret about their ability to control rising pharmacy costs. In the second case, the issue centers on the accountability of health plans for decisions to deny their members access to certain services, most notably expensive lifesaving treatments, and the rights of patients to seek appropriate redress from their health plans (that is, through administrative and/or legal actions) when access to such services is denied and serious harm results. Patients' rights advocates favor legislation that would grant individuals the right to sue their health plans for damages, whereas managed care plans oppose such legislation on the grounds that it would unduly restrict their ability to make business decisions about health care. Questions regarding the appropriate evaluation, adoption, and use of medical technology are central to both of these public policy issues.

Medical technology historically has been regarded as a major cost "driver" of health care spending growth in the United States. According to the U.S. General Accounting Office, the swift adoption of medical technology was the "single most important" factor contributing to the rise of health care costs during the 1980s (GAO 1992b). Although several economic studies during the 1990s estimated that new technology may be responsible for as much as 50 to 75 percent of the annual growth in national expenditures for health care (Newhouse 1992, 1993; Peden and Freeland 1995), a recent analysis by P. E. Mohr et al. (2001) put the figure closer to 40 percent and forecasted a range of 25 to 33 percent for the period 2001–5. Even at this more modest level of growth, continued technology diffusion appears likely to overwhelm managed care's ability to temper future spending growth (Chernew et al. 1998; Cohen 1998; Neumann and Sandberg 1998). Yet despite these concerns, public enthusiasm for technological change in medicine remains generally unbridled, and other economic analyses suggest not only that the returns from technological change in health care are considerable (Cutler and McClellan 1996, 2001; McClellan 1996) but that the long-term economic benefits of medical research may dwarf even those of some highly touted innovations, such as information technology (Health Effect 2000; Murphy and Topel 2000).

Today, political support for increased public investment in biomedical research is unparalleled in history, with unusual bipartisan agreement between Congress and the president on the social value of biomedical research. In his federal budget for fiscal year 2002, President George W. Bush recommended a 14 percent increase in funding for the National Institutes of Health bringing the agency's budget to $23.1 billion (Shadid 2001). Federal funding for research in the life sciences has more than tripled in inflation-adjusted dollars since 1970 and now accounts for nearly half of all government dollars invested in science research (Shadid 2001). In addition to these social and political drivers, future government spending on medical research is likely to grow in response to public fear about the threat of bioterrorism, particularly in the wake of the tragic events of September 11, 2001, and the subsequent contamination of the U.S. mail with anthrax spores. As public investment in medical research continues to expand, demand will grow for accountability, improved evaluation, and effective management of how these research dollars are spent.

The tension—and seeming paradox—between the short-term objectives of managed care plans to contain health care costs and the long-term goals of public spending on medical research to improve health and longevity is a major economic and ethical dilemma facing American society. Solving this dilemma requires an understanding of the impact of medical technology on health care costs and spending as well as on the outcomes of care. Analyses of technological impact vary somewhat, depending on how medical technology is defined, how health care costs and outcomes are measured, and how estimates of costs and benefits are generated. Moreover, the potential use of some technologies—for example, in vitro fertilization, stem cell transplantation, human cloning, and fetal surgery—raise profound social, ethical, and cultural issues. Thus, any effort to understand the implications of continued technological growth in health care—whether under present-day market conditions or under future proposed system reforms—must begin with an understanding of the fundamental issues and definitions on which assessments of medical technology are based. In this introductory chapter, we define and classify medical technology and explore the history of technological change in American medicine.

Defining and Classifying Medical Technology

Technology, in rather simple terms, is knowledge applied for practical ends. Generally, it results in the performance of actions that either (1) were not previously possible or (2) were performed less efficiently by other means. Consider, for example, the case of photography. Before the invention of the camera, only an artist could capture the beauty of a landscape or the contours of a face, and the images portrayed were available mainly to the affluent. The breakthrough technology of the camera made photographic images reliable and accessible to the masses, with subsequent advances in the medium of film and in the camera itself (e.g., the Kodak Brownie) enabling photography to become more affordable and widespread. From these seminal events came motion pictures, followed by a line of imaging modalities based on diverse optical and electronic technologies—television; the video camera, videotape, and videocassette recorder; and the digital videodisc and player. In each case, the newer technology offered more powerful and convenient ways for recording and storing permanent images than its predecessors.

In medicine, one can trace a link from the breakthrough discovery of X rays and their application in medical diagnosis during the early twentieth century to the computer-assisted forms of diagnostic imaging today—X-ray computed tomography (CT), ultrasound, magnetic resonance imaging (MRI), and positron emission tomography (PET). Although the ultrasound, MRI, and PET rely on completely different technologies than do conventional X-ray and CT imaging—and each possesses different abilities to image internal anatomic structures and physiologic functions—they all draw their basic inspiration from a common source, the X ray. The combination of these diverse imaging modalities with telecommunications technology has led to the rise of teleradiology—the electronic delivery of radiologic information and services—which has potential for increasing access to effective care for patients living in underserved rural communities.

As one form of applied knowledge, *medical technology* has been defined as the ways in which resources are combined to produce medical care (Russell 1976; Iglehart 1977). In economic terms, *medical technology* is "the configuration of inputs to produce a specified medical output" (Warner 1979, 280). The now-defunct Congressional Office of Technology Assessment (OTA) defined *medical technology* in comprehensive terms as "drugs, devices, medical and surgical procedures used in patient care, and the organizational and supportive systems within which such care is provided" (U.S. Congress, OTA 1976, 1982). This broad definition includes the information systems that are vital to the management of health care delivery. Much of the current literature on the diffusion of medical technology is built around this inclusive definition and the major classes of technology embedded within it.

Numerous classification schemes for technology have been developed over the years. One typology, developed long ago by the OTA (1976), emphasizes the physical nature and medical purpose of technology; a second, devised by an Institute of Medicine (IOM) committee, stresses the importance of a technology's "function" in the health care delivery system and its "stage" in the medical care process (Committee on Technology and Health Care 1979); still another categorizes technology along the single dimension of "medical objectives" (Rosenthal 1979). All are useful in different ways and are shown in table 1.1.

In an early effort to address the relationship between medical technology and the cost of health care, Lewis Thomas (1977) differentiated between "halfway technologies" and "high technologies." He defined the former as technologies that intervene in the progression of an illness and may postpone death but do not really cure or eliminate the underlying problem—for example, renal dialysis, cardiac pacemakers, coronary angioplasty, and total hip replacement. Halfway technologies often are costly because they invariably depend on expensive equipment and personnel and usually are hospital based (L. Thomas 1977; Moxley and Roeder 1988). High technologies, on the other hand, provide definitive preventive or curative benefits aimed directly at the underlying illness—for example, vaccines and antibiotics that offer effective prevention and cure, respectively, for a host of infectious diseases. The future development of gene replacement therapy holds great promise for the effective prevention of such presently incurable genetic diseases as Huntington's chorea, sickle-cell anemia, and Duchenne's muscular dystrophy. High technologies may represent the least expensive approach to medical care because they avoid (1) the future health care costs associated with the

TABLE 1.1. Classification Schemes/Typologies for Medical Technology Data

Source	Major Dimension	Category/Class
OTA 1976	Physical nature	Technique—action of a provider without specialized equipment Drug—chemical or biological substance Equipment—large capital-embodied machines, as well as smaller devices and instruments Procedure—combination of technique with drugs and/or equipment
	Medical purpose	Diagnostic—identifies disease (e.g., CT scanner) Preventive—prevents disease (e.g., vaccine) Therapeutic/Rehabilitative—cures disease in some cases (e.g., antibiotics); offers only symptomatic relief in others (e.g., renal dialysis) Organizational—aids management of care (e.g., computerized information system) Supportive—provides need services in hospital (e.g., hospital bed, food services)
Committee on Technology and Health Care, National Academy of Sciences 1979[a]	Function	Clinical—used in provision of direct patient care (e.g., medical, surgical) Ancillary—used directly to support clinical services (e.g., laboratory, X ray) Coordinative—used to facilitate and support provision of services but not directly associated with patient care (e.g., communications systems, information systems)
	Stage in the medical care process	Preventive—e.g., genetic screening, multiphasic health testing, immunization, cardiac stress testing Diagnostic—e.g., CT scanning, fetal monitoring, cardiac catheterization and angiography, diagnostic ultrasound Therapeutic—e.g., coronary bypass surgery, renal dialysis, intensive care unit, radiation therapy Rehabilitative—e.g., kidney transplants, artificial organs, limb prosthetics, sensory aids
Rosenthal 1979	Medical objectives	Diagnostic—identifies disease (e.g., CT scanner, fetal monitor, automated clinical labs) Survival—maintains life until new or additional care becomes available (e.g., intensive care unit, iron lung) Illness management—ameliorates or offsets effects of a specific disease (e.g., pacemaker, renal dialysis) Cure—alleviates or eliminates virtually all of disability associated with disease (e.g., hip joint replacement, organ transplantation)

TABLE 1.1.—Continued

Source	Major Dimension	Category/Class
		Prevention—reduces mortality and morbidity (e.g., vaccines, diet control for phenylketonuria) System management—aids management of care (e.g., medical information systems, telemedicine)

Source: Data from OTA 1976; Committee on Technology and Health Care 1979; and Rosenthal 1979.
Note: All examples shown are those specifically cited by the authors of the given typology.
[a]Typology devised for equipment-embodied technologies only.

diseases that they prevent or cure and (2) many of the heavy costs (e.g., equipment, personnel, and so on) that are commonly associated with halfway technologies. High technology, by definition, requires a deep commitment to basic research, but the funding of such research should be offset by the savings realized through reduced reliance on halfway technology in medical care (L. Thomas 1977).

Another typology—which is a simplified variant of Rosenthal's (1979) scheme—divides technologies into four categories based on medical purpose: diagnosis, screening, therapy, and rehabilitation (IOM 1985; Thier 1988). In this typology, *diagnosis* is a process used to identify illness in a single, symptomatic patient, while *screening* is a process used broadly to identify a specific health problem in a large, asymptomatic population (Thier 1988). Thier argued that the nature of the benefits derived from medical technology should be used to set research priorities, with preventive innovations ranked higher than therapeutic interventions.

Some medical technologies—particularly equipment-embodied ones—have been classified according to the size of the initial capital investment needed to purchase them. "Big-ticket" items (e.g., MRI, X-ray CT, or renal lithotripsy) require high initial capital investments and thus have been the focus of government and private efforts to control the diffusion of technology. "Little-ticket" items (e.g., laboratory tests or conventional X rays), by contrast, have lower acquisition costs and lower service unit costs but ultimately may contribute more to the total cost of health care because of their high-volume use (Moloney and Rogers 1979; Scitovsky 1985; Shine 1997; P. E. Mohr et al. 2001), although at least one study (Showstack, Stone, and Schroeder 1985) disputed this finding.

Battista (1989) refined this concept, classifying technologies into

three groups—high, medium, and low—based on the intensity of the resources used. Under this scheme, a high technology would require not
only major investment in equipment but also significant expense associated with staff, administration, and other operations. This contrasted
sharply, however, with L. Thomas's (1977) vision of high technology
that is scientifically "elegant" in approach yet often the least resource intensive solution to a medical problem.

Still another means of classifying technologies was devised by I. L.
Bennett (1977), who defined *substitutive* innovations as those that dis-
place existing, less-effective approaches and *additive* innovations as
those that augment current practices. Substitutive technologies may
be cost increasing or cost saving, depending on the manner in which
they are used and the way that they alter the mix of medical inputs.
Additive technologies may be freestanding modalities, but many are
said to be complementary if they are designed explicitly for use in
combination with other technologies (PPRC 1992b). Some observers
contend that additive technologies, by nature, will always be cost
increasing (Garrison and Brown 1991); complementary technologies
may be particularly cost raising because they spur the added use of
their companions.

Some technologies, especially diagnostic tools, may possess both
substitutive and additive qualities. MRI, for example, may substitute
for X-ray CT in imaging the brain and central nervous system but may
complement CT in imaging other organs and anatomical structures.
The reality in medical practice is that physicians often do not employ
these technologies in substitutive fashion for some clinical applications
but instead utilize them as clinically duplicative—and costly—adjuncts
to each other.

Innovations also may be categorized by whether they represent
product technologies or process technologies (E. B. Roberts 1981; Garrison and Brown 1991; PPRC 1992b). Product technologies embody tangible items, such as major new equipment (MRI), instruments (surgical
lasers), and drugs. Process technologies refer to new methods for
achieving a given outcome. Laparoscopic cholecystectomy is an example of a new process technology brought about by applying an existing technique (laparoscopic surgery) in a novel way to a long-standing
medical problem (gallbladder disease). New product technologies are
somewhat easier than process technologies to identify because the introduction of products to medical practice often is heralded by the as-

signment of a current procedural terminology code for payment purposes that clearly denotes their contribution. New process technologies, conversely, generally are not assigned unique codes because they usually are variants of existing procedures and do not require separate identification for payment (PPRC 1992b). Since many medical technologies combine product and process innovations, this particular typology has limited utility.

Not surprisingly, there is a lack of consensus regarding the best way to classify technology, and none of these systems has been adopted universally. While some analysts have argued that terms such as *big-ticket* and *little-ticket* technologies as well as *high technology* are conceptually unclear and should be abandoned (Rettig 1994), others have criticized the term *low-cost technology* for being misleading, since widespread use of a *low-unit cost* technology may actually result in high aggregate costs (Shine 1997). However, as with many terms and concepts in health care—most notably *managed care* and *quality*—the adoption of uniform or standard definitions presents a major challenge and requires that the variations in the meaning and use of such terms be fully explicated and understood. The question of whether technologies can be classified in meaningful ways will be reexamined in chapter 5 in the context of a technology's effects on health outcomes (e.g., life extension or quality of life) as well as on costs.

More important than the terminology, however, is the need to understand the process of technological change, which many would agree is the key to the future of American medicine. Myriad factors affect the process of technological change in medicine. For example, political, economic, and social forces broadly shape the general direction of such change, determining the level of capital investment in research and development, the types of technologies that are developed, and the relative importance or priority assigned to special characteristics of new technologies, such as cost reduction or quality improvement. Other factors, such as the nature of specific medical problems and the intrinsic properties of technologies, are likely to play important roles in determining the rate of technological change, which, in turn, may be influenced by the management and regulation of the diffusion process as well as by public and professional perceptions of the benefits, risks, and costs of new technology. These forces are discussed in detail in chapters 3 and 4, but here follows a brief history of technological change in American medicine.

Technological Change in American Medicine

The notion of technological change or innovation as a positive, shaping force in society (I. L. Bennett 1977) is not foreign to Americans, having long been firmly rooted in their consciousness. In the late nineteenth century, many Americans believed that their nation's destiny was inexorably linked to the impending revolution in scientific thought and discovery. Events in the early twentieth century led to the popular view that science and technology were synonymous with progress, with developments in medicine contributing greatly to that notion (Ebert 1979; Howell 1996).

Biomedical advances in the first half of the twentieth century produced new therapies and drugs, particularly the antibiotics that profoundly improved the clinical management of infectious diseases (L. Thomas 1977; Warner 1978; Howell 1996). Expectations of potential benefits from medical technology ran high, overshadowing questions of possible risk and silencing concerns about cost. Public and private investment in the development of medical technology accelerated rapidly as medical researchers sought to control increasingly prevalent chronic diseases, especially coronary artery disease, stroke, end-stage renal disease, and various forms of cancer.

During the 1950s and 1960s, two parallel and somewhat paradoxical developments arose simultaneously. As medical technology experienced dramatic growth, drawing on advances in electronics, computer science, radioisotope chemistry, and nuclear physics, public support for technological development gradually waned (Iglehart 1977; Ebert 1979). Concerns over the environmental impact of unconstrained diffusion of technology began to replace the view that technology was inherently good. This change in attitude did not at first affect the medical community. As Ebert (1979) later noted in retrospect, "One could hardly be against the use of science and technology in the conquest of disease." The development of a poliomyelitis vaccine reinforced this sentiment, demonstrating that perseverance in scientific research ultimately had its rewards. American medicine dedicated itself to the pursuit of "quality" health care, which, in the eyes of many physicians, patients, and hospital managers, became equated with "high-intensity" care and the increased use of advanced technology.

Viewed universally as a core element of good health care, medical technology attained almost mystical status in the 1970s and threatened to usurp the physician's role as the central player in modern medicine

(Howell 1996, 1999). However, escalating health care costs began to raise public awareness about constrained medical resources and sparked new debate about the benefits and costs of expensive equipment-embodied technologies, most notably X-ray CT, that were being rapidly introduced into practice. While the American public's reverence for technological solutions to medical problems continued undiminished throughout the 1970s, growing concern over health care spending induced policymakers, purchasers, and managers to search for ways to contain costs and spending.

Throughout the 1980s and early 1990s, medical technologies became easy targets for cost-containment efforts aimed at controlling the adoption and use of technology in health care. Paradoxically, while these efforts were imposing new constraints on health care delivery, biomedical innovation and technology development in the United States were flourishing. Major advances in molecular biology, genetic engineering, and immunology enhanced the reproductive capacity of infertile couples, led to the synthesis of monoclonal antibodies for the detection and treatment of disease, and significantly reduced the threat of posttransplant tissue rejection. As previously discussed, the mapping of the human genome was a decade-long scientific undertaking of the 1990s that may soon be eclipsed by new federally funded research efforts. Launched in early 2002 as an offshoot of the genome mapping effort, the Proteome Project is aimed at compiling a complete inventory of the hundreds of thousands of proteins found in the human body and discovering new drugs to repair abnormal proteins that cause disease (Kranish 2002). Also launched in 2002 with NIH support, the International HapMap Project seeks to chart the location of haplotypes (large blocks of DNA that are inherited unchanged from generation to generation), which should help to identify the variant genes underlying common diseases, such as diabetes, asthma, and cancer (Wade 2002).

Yet despite the optimistic outlook for continued technological change in the twenty-first century, there is great concern in some quarters that health care spending today is still growing at an annual rate that outstrips the pace of the general economy (Aaron 1991; Weisbrod 1991; Fuchs 1993; Chernew et al. 1998; Levit et al. 2003). In the half century between 1950 and 2001, annual national expenditures for health care in the United States rose from $12.7 billion to $1.4 trillion (Levit et al. 2003). In terms of the gross domestic product, this represented a virtual tripling of the proportion attributable to health care spending— from 4.5 to 14.1 percent of the total (Levit et al. 2003). Although most of this growth may be explained by general economic inflation, by increases in wage rates and input prices paid by hospitals, and by changes in population size and age distribution, a substantial proportion also results from changes in the nature of medical care over time, most notably the increased use of medical technology (Newhouse 1992, 1993; Chernew et al. 1998; P. E. Mohr et al. 2001).

The increased use of medical technology has implications for health care and society, and the question of economic impact is but one of many that has been raised in policy discussions. If we are to chart new policy directions for the American health care system, it is imperative that we more effectively evaluate and manage medical technology. Doing so requires a comprehensive and broad understanding of the effects of medical technology. In chapter 2, we present a framework of eight critical questions that will aid our exploration of medical technology in health care.

2

Critical Questions Regarding Medical Technology and Its Effects
Alan B. Cohen

It is virtually impossible today to read a newspaper, watch television news, or browse the Internet without encountering a report of a medical advance or discovery, often culled from the pages of a leading medical journal, such as the *New England Journal of Medicine,* the *Journal of the American Medical Association,* the *British Medical Journal,* or the *Lancet.* Among the numerous medical breakthroughs reported in recent years are improved outcomes in organ transplantation, including pancreatic islet transplantation for patients with diabetes; various new potential cancer therapies, including angiogenesis-inhibiting drugs to arrest tumor growth and epidermal growth factor receptor blockers; the identification of specific genes for breast cancer, obesity, hypertension, and other conditions; fetal surgery for repair of various organs; enhanced tools for diagnostic imaging, including positron emission tomography (PET) and next-generation magnetic resonance imagers; the early development of a vaccine for HIV; devices for treating cardiac disease, including the Abiocor implantable artificial heart, various left-ventricular assist devices, intracoronary drug-eluting stents, and intravascular brachytherapy systems for delivering radiation to coronary arteries in cases of recurrent stenosis; new surgical therapies for treating Parkinson's disease, including pallidotomy and transplantation of embryonic stem cells; numerous applications of advanced robotics, ranging from artificial limbs to robotic drug dispensing systems and robotic (stereotactic) forms of surgery; bioengineered cornea replacement and skin grafts; nanotechnology involving microscopic cameras, sensors, and drug delivery systems for visualizing and treating disease deep inside the body; a multitude of new drugs and biologics for the treatment of such diseases and conditions as AIDS, Alzheimer's disease, stroke, heart disease, diabetes, mental illness, and spinal cord injuries; and the much publicized—and hotly debated—cloning of human cells.

Yet despite this impressive list of achievements, the adoption and use of medical technology raise a host of questions and concerns. Of the many concerns being voiced, eight broad questions are critical to any discussion of medical technology. Each is complex and consists of multiple subquestions. For the purposes of our discussion here, we summarize and label them as follows.

1. The *economic impact* question: How are medical technologies changing the practice of medicine and affecting health care spending, and are they cost-effective?
2. The *diffusion* question: Are technologies diffusing too swiftly— or too slowly—into medical practice?
3. The *evaluation* question: Are technologies being evaluated appropriately?
4. The *ethical choice* question: What ethical choices (or standards) should guide the evaluation, adoption, and use of technologies whose long-term as well as short-term effects may not be known or clearly understood?
5. The *organizational impact* question: In what ways are medical technologies influencing—and being influenced by—organizational changes in the health care marketplace?
6. The *access* question: Is access to certain technologies impeded for some population groups by financial, geographic, cultural, or other barriers?
7. The *societal impact* question: How are medical technologies affecting societal behavior and organization, including the basic demographic and institutional structures of society?
8. The *governmental role* question: What role (or roles) should federal and state governments play in attempting to deal with these issues?

To a large extent, these eight questions are interrelated. Treating them as individual, mutually exclusive items would vastly oversimplify the generic issue. For example, the "cascade effect" of some technologies in prompting the use of a second or third technology—such as with the triple screen for birth defects leading to ultrasound-guided amniocentesis, which is then followed by abortion or fetal surgery—often raises questions that cut across these broad issues. However, to understand these questions in the context of present market forces as well as future health care reform, we briefly examine each one here with regard to why it generates concern and defies feasible solution.

The Economic Impact Question

With cost containment an ongoing concern of health care purchasers, providers, and managers in the present market-driven system, there is great interest in understanding the economic effects of medical technologies, both individually and in the aggregate. For technology as a whole, the question is not whether or even how much it contributes to spending growth—there is broad consensus today among leading health economists and policy analysts that technology is responsible for a substantial share of annual real growth (Newhouse 1992, 1993; Rettig 1994, 1997; Chernew et al. 1998; P. E. Mohr et al. 2001)—but rather how and why technology is transforming clinical practice. For an individual technology, the question is whether it is cost-effective relative to existing alternatives. These questions are addressed in various chapters throughout the book, most notably chapter 5 (adoption), chapter 11 (quality concerns), and chapter 12 (cost concerns). What follows here is a summary of the evidence regarding the impact of medical technology on health care spending.

Quantifying medical technology's precise contribution to rising health care spending has been an elusive pursuit (Rettig 1994). The extensive literature on this subject dates back to the early 1970s. In a landmark paper, S. H. Altman and S. S. Wallack (1979) identified four principal methods for measuring the impact of technology on costs—residual, excess inflation, specific illness, and specific technology. Two of these—the residual and specific-technology methods—are the dominant ones in use today.

The residual and excess-inflation methods are related macroanalytic approaches that rely on multivariate econometric techniques to estimate the effects of numerous variables (e.g., population growth, demographic changes, medical service price increases, utilization changes, and so forth) on increases in health care costs. The residual method, which has been applied primarily to national expenditures for health care, accounts for the impact of various factors on annual spending increases and defines the remaining unexplained "residual" variance as attributable to "service intensity." Service intensity encompasses the quality as well as quantity of care, but both are presumed to be attributable, in large measure, to changes in technology.

The excess-inflation method is a similar macroanalytic tool that has been used mainly to analyze hospital expenditures. It measures the impact of various factors (e.g., wage increases, changes in input prices, and changes in utilization and service volume) on annual hospital spending and, as with the residual method, attributes the unexplained remainder (the "excess inflation") to service intensity (i.e., technology-related factors). However, because it focuses on hospital spending rather than total health care spending—and technology-intensive services are being shifted increasingly out of the hospital to other settings—this method has been used much less frequently than the residual method.

The specific-illness method and the specific-technology method are microanalytic techniques. As the name implies, the specific-illness method attempts to estimate the contribution of numerous factors, including technology, to the changing cost of treating a specific illness over time. In contrast, the specific-technology approach traces a single technology over time and attempts to quantify its impact on the cost of health care. Although these methods may seem to offer greater precision than the macroanalytic techniques, they are still hampered by an inability to (1) isolate costs and cost savings directly attributable to changes in technology and (2) disentangle the effects of a single technology from the influence of other technologies that may affect the same illness or population.

As stated earlier, estimates of the impact of technology on health care spending have been anything but consistent. Studies have varied according to the definition of technology, method of cost estimation, measurement time frame, and expenditure type analyzed. A search of the literature reveals more than two dozen analyses published in the three decades between 1972 and 2001: the majority of these works favored the use of the residual method, but only eight addressed total health care spending (see table 2.1). Most striking perhaps is the fact that even studies of reasonably similar design and time frame produced inconsistent estimates. The table summarizes the findings from the more notable recent studies according to the method used.

TABLE 2.1. Medical Technology and Health Care Cost Inflation

Study	Method	Expenditure Type	Time Frame	Percentage of Annual Rate of Increase
Fuchs 1972	R	TOT	1947–67	7.5
Davis 1974	R	HPD	1962–68	25.0
Cromwell et al. 1975	R	HPD	1965–73	9.0[a]
Gaus and Cooper 1976	R	HPD	1965–71	47.0
Russell 1976	T[b]	HPD	1974	10.0
Scitovsky and McCall 1976	I[c]	HPD	1951–71	net+[d]
Feldstein and Taylor 1977	R	HPD	1955–75	50.0
Mushkin, Paringer, and Chen 1977	R	TOT	1930–75	−6.5
Mushkin and Landefeld 1979	R	TOT	1900–30	0.04[e]
			1930–75	−0.5[e]
Warner 1979	R	HPD	1965–73	34.0[f]
Freeland and Schendler 1983	R	HPA	1971–81	20.8
Office of Technology Assessment 1984b	R	HPC	1977–82	24.0
Scitovsky 1985	I	HPD	1971–81	net+
Showstack, Stone, and Schroeder 1985	I	HPD	1972–82	net+
Schwartz 1987	R	HPD[g]	1977–83	33.3
Sullivan 1989	R	MPE	1976–86	45.0[e]
Garrison and Brown 1991[h]	T	MIE	1992	6.7[i]
Lee 1991	T	MPE	1985–87	0.8
				3.6[j]
				1.5[k]
Kolata/HCFA 1992[l]	R	TOT	1980–90	20.0
Newhouse 1992	R	TOT	1950–89	50.0–75.0[e]
ProPAC 1992	R	TIE	1985–90	41.0[e]
		TPE	1985–90	38.0[e]
Bradley and Kominski 1992	R	MIE	1984–87	35.0
HCTI 1993b[m]	R	ESP	1985–92	net−[n]
PPRC 1993[o]	T	MTE	1986–91	15.0
			1991–92	23.0
Peden and Freeland 1995	R	TOT	1960–93	70.0
Cutler and McClellan 1996	T	MTE	1984–91	net+[p]
Katz, Welch, and Verrilli 1997	R	MPE	1987–92	net+
Mohr et al. 2001	R	TOT	1960–98	4.0–64.0[e]
			2001–5[q]	25.0–33.0[e]
	T			net+[r]

Source: Adapted and updated from Cohen and Nichols 1993.

Note: The following abbreviations are used for method. R = residual; T = technology-specific; I = illness-specific.

Expenditure type abbreviations are as follows. ESP = equipment and supply prices; HPA = hospital (per admission); HPC = hospital (per capita); HPD = hospital (per diem); MIE = Medicare inpatient expenditures; MPE = Medicare physician expenditures; MTE = Medicare total expenditures; TIE = total inpatient expenditures; TOT = total health expenditures; TPE = total physician expenditures.

[a]Examined only capital costs of equipment-embodied technology.

[b]Examined intensive care units only.

[c]Analyzed eleven common conditions, including appendicitis, maternity care, pneumonia, forearm fracture, and myocardial infarction.

(continued)

TABLE 2.1.—*Continued*

---

^{d}Real costs decreased for five of eleven conditions, but the real cost increase for treating myocardial infarction far outweighed the combined cost savings of the five conditions.

^{e}Growth due to multiple residual factors, mostly technology.

^{f}Updated the estimate of Cromwell et al. (1975) by including operating costs to the hospital.

^{g}Used adjusted per diem expenditures (hospital outpatient service expenditures included).

^{h}Estimated the cost impact of sixteen new and emerging technologies on Medicare hospital costs, using 1992 projected expenditures.

^{i}Estimated $366 million in increased expenditures due to technologies; with $50 billion spent on hospital care by Medicare in 1991 and with projected annual spending growth of 11% in 1992, the portion attributable to technology is 6.7%.

^{j}Used a broad definition of related or complementary services.

^{k}Used a narrow definition of complementary services.

^{l}Cited HCFA estimates of the percentage of average annual increase for personal health care expenditures.

^{m}Examined price growth of medical equipment and supplies only—in relation to the PPI and CPI.

^{n}Found that medical equipment and supply price inflation was lower than the PPI and the CPI.

^{o}Examined new and emerging technologies in terms of their "direct" costs only.

^{p}Found that virtually all spending growth for treatment of heart attacks was attributable to expanded use of invasive procedures.

^{q}Employed a combination of the residual and technology-specific methods, intended to revise HCFA forecasts of health spending growth; projected annual growth of 6.0–7.0% for the period 2001–5 and estimated that the residual would account for 25.0–33.0% of that growth.

^{r}In the case studies of nine technologies, eight were found to be cost increasing in the short term (coronary stents being the sole exception), and two (colonoscopies and inhaled insulin) were thought to have cost-saving potential in the long term.

Residual Method

A study by the Prospective Payment Assessment Commission (ProPAC) employing the residual method estimated that in the period 1985–90, "intensity of service" accounted for 41 percent of the observed increase in the cost of inpatient services, 31 percent of the increase in outpatient services, 38 percent of the increase in physician services, and 33 percent of the increase in nursing home care (ProPAC 1992). Intensity of service was defined as the amount left unexplained after accounting for changes in population demographics, general economic inflation, medical price inflation, and patterns of utilization. Although technology was not the only factor that might account for the residual, it was assumed to be the dominant factor.

Newhouse (1992) reported a more dramatic finding. After accounting for the effects of general inflation, increases in service volume attributable to population aging, increased third-party payer coverage, and growth in real personal income over a forty-year period, Newhouse estimated the residual to be greater than 50 percent and argued that it could be largely accounted for by technological change. Peden and Freeland (1995) examined the period 1960–93 and concluded that 70 percent of the observed growth in real per capita medical spending resulted from cost-increasing advances in medical care induced by insurance coverage and by spending for noncommercial medical research. Yet only sixteen years earlier, a study by Mushkin and Landefeld (1979) using similar variables had concluded that technology had a net reducing effect on expenditures for health care between 1930 and 1975 (see table 2.1).

Using a unique blend of residual and technology-specific methods, P. E. Mohr and colleagues (2001) analyzed trends in the residual between 1960 and 1998, together with information from case studies of nine technologies, to revise HCFA health-spending forecasts in light of recent economic and health sector changes. The analysis revealed wide variation in the residual (the use of technology) as a percentage of total health spending over the thirty-eight-year period, ranging from 4 percent to 64 percent. During the 1990s, the percentage at first declined but then rose from 12 percent in 1994 to 39 percent in 1998, by which time the residual accounted for more of the spending growth than any other factor (e.g., economy-wide inflation, medical price inflation, or population changes), which had not been the case since 1987. For the period 2001–5, Mohr and colleagues projected annual growth of 6.0 to 7.0 percent in total personal health care expenditures and estimated that the residual would account for 25 to 33 percent of that growth. This projection may have been too optimistic; recent data indicate that total health spending grew 8.7 percent between 2000 and 2001 (Levit et al. 2003).

Excess-Inflation Method

Schwartz (1987) used the excess-inflation method to estimate that the intensity of services "resulting mainly from technologic change" increased the cost of hospital care alone by an average of 3.5 percent annually from 1977 through 1983, accounting for roughly one-third of the annual rate of increase. He suggested, however, that this figure might be too conservative because the increased skill level of hospital personnel associated with many new technologies tends to be counted under the wage factor in the medical price inflation category.

Specific-Illness Method

Scitovsky (1985) reported mixed results in three separate studies of the costs of medical technology using the specific-illness method. Each study examined the impact of technology on selected illnesses at two points in time: 1951 and 1964, 1964 and 1971, and 1971 and 1981. Little-ticket technologies, such as laboratory tests and X rays, were the primary culprits behind rising costs for the two earlier study periods, but big-ticket technologies had a greater impact among the seven illnesses studied in the third period. These big-ticket technologies included new treatments for breast cancer, the expanded use of coronary artery bypass graft surgery, and the increased use of cesarean deliveries. In all three studies, the most significant cost-reducing change was a shorter hospital stay.

Although these findings are not generalizable beyond the selected illnesses studied and the small patient populations observed in a single care setting (the Palo Alto Medical Foundation), the results are nevertheless informative because Scitovsky selected representative illnesses that were fairly common in the general population and for which the treatment patterns of physicians in her institution would not be expected to vary considerably from those of physicians at other institutions.

Another study using the specific-illness method was conducted at the University of California at San Francisco and compared ten diagnoses across 2,011 patients for the years 1972, 1977, and 1982 (Showstack, Stone, and Schroeder 1985). This analysis found that changes in clinical practice during the decade had relatively little impact overall on hospital costs for the ten diagnoses: cost-saving changes in practice for some diagnoses offset cost-increasing changes for others, with the net aggregate effect being slightly inflationary. Moreover, a comparison of big-ticket and little-ticket technologies showed that neither group accounted for a significant portion of the increase in total hospital costs, although big-ticket imaging procedures exhibited a slightly higher rise in utilization. Technology, however, did seem to be associated with an increased use of intensive care and an increased rate of several surgical procedures—coronary artery bypass graft surgery for myocardial infarction (heart attack), surgery for patent ductus arteriosus (a hole in the septum between chambers of the heart) in newborns, and cesarean deliveries.

Specific-Technology Method

Using data from the Medicare program and a specific technology approach, the Physician Payment Review Commission (PPRC) examined seven hundred new technologies identified by specialty societies and found that from 1986 to 1991 the average change in the volume of services resulting from the use of new technology was 15 percent (PPRC 1993). However, because outpatient drugs were not covered by the Medicare program, the PPRC analysis likely did not capture the full impact of these technologies on health care spending. Of greater interest, though, may be the differential contributions of various technologies. For example, service volumes for new surgical technologies increased 14 percent between 1986 and 1991 but grew only 10 percent in 1992, while volumes for new nonsurgical technologies rose 15 percent and 26 percent, respectively, during the same periods. Overall, nearly 52 percent of the growth attributable to technology in 1992 was accounted for by four medical specialties—diagnostic radiology, gastroenterology, orthopedic surgery, and urology (PPRC 1993). Cutler and McClellan (1996) analyzed hospital adoption of coronary revascularization treatments between 1984 and 1991 and found that virtually all of the growth in Medicare spending for heart attacks was attributable to expanded use of invasive procedures, including cardiac catheterization, bypass surgery, and coronary angioplasty. P. E. Mohr and colleagues (2001), in a combined approach with the residual method, studied nine technologies, including coronary stents for restenosis of the arteries; drug inhalation devices for delivery of insulin; electron beam CT to screen for coronary artery calcification; genetic testing for colorectal cancer; low-dose spiral CT for lung cancer screening; monoclonal antibodies for cancer; PET for the diagnosis and staging of cancer; thin-layer cytology for cervical cancer screening; and screening for colorectal cancer. They found that eight of the nine technologies increased costs in the short term (with coronary stents the only exception), that colonoscopies for colorectal cancer screening and inhaled insulin for diabetes had cost-saving potential in the long term, and that PET in the diagnosis of cancer could be cost saving if its use were restricted to targeted groups of patients.

In sum, the literature suggests that with few exceptions, medical technologies tend to inflate health care spending. One study—commissioned by the Health Care Technology Institute (HCTI), a short-lived (1992–95) think tank supported by technology manufacturers—disputed this viewpoint, arguing that the total sales of medical devices and diagnostic products accounted for less than 4 percent of national health expenditures in 1992 (HCTI 1993a) and that the annual average price changes for surgical, medical, and dental instruments and supplies were consistent with overall inflation (as reflected in the producer price index) between 1985 and 1992 (HCTI 1993c). The study's scope and methods, however, were limited, rendering its claims of a noninflationary effect unconvincing: the study examined prices rather than expenditures, failed to consider the effects of the use of technology on spending, and failed to include in the estimates technologies other than equipment and supplies (such as drugs). Furthermore, there was (and remains) disagreement among analysts about the use of producer price indexes to measure price inflation (GAO 1995).

The reasons why medical technologies often have inflationary effects relate to several factors intrinsic to the nature of technology. Some of these factors have already been mentioned: medical purpose (halfway versus definitive technology); use in clinical practice (substitutive versus additive); and price tag (big ticket versus little ticket). A fourth critical property is the labor-substitution effect. Whereas technological innovation in most industries tends to be labor saving, medical advances usually involve complex equipment or surgical procedures that require skilled personnel to operate or perform them. Such technologies, although not intrinsically labor increasing, may become so as new classes of specially trained technologists and technicians arise and become entrenched, adding to institutional operating expense. (See chapter 12 for an examination of cost concerns and payment policies and chapter 7 for a discussion of cost-effectiveness analysis.) In the end, however, what matters most is whether the inflationary effects of technology are worth it to society in terms of the benefits conferred (Cutler and McClellan 2001).

The Diffusion Question

Laypersons and health professionals alike commonly perceive that some medical technologies may be diffusing into clinical practice more quickly than they should. This impression is based not so much on the abrupt speed with which some technologies seem to find their way into the physician's medical arsenal as on the belief that many emerging technologies become an accepted part of clinical practice well before their risks and benefits have been satisfactorily evaluated. In a few cases, broad adoption of new technology has preceded clear development and documentation of the underlying clinical theory on which the technology is based.

A well-documented example of a technology that gained widespread use before its risks and benefits were assessed in rigorous fashion is electronic fetal monitoring (EFM), an obstetric diagnostic technology intended to evaluate fetal condition during labor and delivery. As a much-heralded innovation of the late 1960s, EFM promised to alter clinical management of obstetric patients to produce dramatic improvement in perinatal mortality and morbidity. Although the clinical theory behind EFM was still in the developmental stage when the technology first became commercially available in 1969, obstetricians and hospitals quickly embraced it, purchasing thousands of units long before the first scientifically sound studies could be mounted (1973) and published (1976) in the obstetric literature (Banta and Thacker 1979; Cohen 1983). One reason EFM diffused so rapidly was that its capital cost of between $8,000 and $12,000 (depending on the options and features selected) was not prohibitively expensive, thereby encouraging hospitals to invest in the equipment and at the same time enabling them to escape the scrutiny of regulatory mechanisms, such as certificate-of-need (CON) programs, which reviewed equipment purchases exceeding thresholds of $100,000 (Cohen and Cohodes 1982).

By contrast, the introduction of X-ray CT scanning in 1973 raised a hue and cry among health planners, politicians, consumers, and others concerned about the technology's high purchase price and undemonstrated medical benefit. As a truly revolutionary diagnostic imaging device, X-ray CT appeared to offer virtually unlimited promise, but it was questionable at that time whether every hospital in the United States needed to have it. Undaunted by the heavy price tag associated with acquiring and operating the equipment, many hospitals nonetheless decided to invest in CT. Consequently, a frenzied rush ensued to obtain necessary CON approval before blanket regulatory action might be taken to limit the diffusion of this new technology. The net effect of the competition for CT in many local markets was to create an inequitable pattern of CT diffusion among hospitals, conferring favored status on some, especially major teaching institutions, while effectively disenfranchising others, most notably public hospitals serving relatively poor populations (Banta 1980a).

These two examples illustrate how multiple, complex forces interact to determine the rate and pattern by which a technology may diffuse into medical practice. The most commonly cited forces influencing diffusion are consumer demand and public expectations; promotional efforts of technology manufacturers, including direct-to-consumer advertising strategies; influence of medical education, specialization, and the "technological imperative" of physicians; availability of capital financing for technology research and development; effects of health insurance and payment systems; competition in the marketplace; severity and urgency of medical problems; intrinsic properties of the technology; prestige and visibility of advocates and opinion leaders; technology adoption practices of hospitals and other providers; and governmental regulatory policies regarding the adoption and use of medical technology, such as federal Food and Drug Administration (FDA) legislation and regulations and state CON statutes (Whitted 1981; Goddeeris 1987; Halm and Gelijns 1991; GAO 1992a; Banta and Luce 1993).

In most instances, these forces combine to facilitate or accelerate diffusion; however, in some cases they may act to inhibit or slow the adoption of technology. Therefore, while the general perception may be that medical technology is diffusing too rapidly, the opposite impression of unduly slow or impeded diffusion may hold for some technologies (e.g., RU-486 for medical abortion or various new drugs for HIV), given the available evidence regarding benefits, risks, and costs. Finding an appropriate balance among the forces governing the diffusion of technology is neither easy nor imminently likely, but it clearly remains an important goal if society is to employ and manage its technology wisely. (See chapters 3–5 for more complete discussions of these issues.)

The Evaluation Question

As suggested earlier, many medical technologies follow a similar diffusion process in which, once they are developed, they are quickly tried by physicians, informally assessed, and—barring any serious drawbacks—usually accepted into clinical practice. On occasion, initial optimism may fade, hard questions may arise, and a technology may fall into disfavor among practitioners. In such instances, more rigorous evaluation (generally in the form of clinical trials) often follows, leading sometimes to a vindication of the technology but more commonly to either significant modification or eventual abandonment. Two frequently cited examples of abandoned technologies are gastric freezing for the treatment of duodenal ulcer (Miao 1977; Fineberg 1979) and internal mammary artery ligation for the treatment of angina pectoris (Barsamian 1977). Both technologies were evaluated via randomized controlled trials relatively soon after their introduction, and both were discredited on the grounds that they were ineffective and unsafe. More recently, a well-designed clinical trial found that high-dose chemotherapy plus autologous bone marrow transplantation does not improve survival (compared with conventional-dose chemotherapy) in women with metastatic breast cancer (Stadtmauer et al. 2000). Although this evidence has led some members of the medical community to call for the abandonment of this form of treatment (Mello and Brennan 2001), patient advocacy groups contend that even though the treatment is unproven, it still should be allowed outside of clinical trials as long as some potential benefit exists (Lippman 2000). It remains to be seen how the available evidence will affect the use of this treatment.

Timely evaluation of most medical technologies unfortunately tends to be the exception rather than the rule. At present, only pharmaceuticals and devices undergo rigorous premarket clinical testing in the United States, and even these evaluations have some limitations. For example, in the case of pharmaceuticals, a new drug is evaluated in terms of its individual safety and effectiveness, according to FDA regulatory policy. Some analysts believe that this approach is inadequate because it does not call for the joint evaluation of commonly clustered drugs that physicians often prescribe in tandem. Criticism also has been leveled at short-term studies of drugs or devices with biologically plausible long-term effects. With surgical procedures, several years commonly elapse before rigorously designed studies are initiated to assess these newly emerging technologies (see chapter 10). In all cases of technology, though, there has been concern over the prevalence of young, white, male subjects in many clinical trials, with underrepresentation of women, minorities, and the elderly in study populations. Conversely, in some clinical trials involving pediatric technologies, ethical concerns related to informed consent have been raised, thereby limiting the use of children in such trials.

An extreme case of technology diffusion unsupported by evaluation was the Wassermann diagnostic test for syphilis, which enjoyed widespread use for nearly fifty years before physicians realized that its high false-positive error rate had unnecessarily stigmatized many people and subjected them to other dangers posed by the era's antisyphilitic treatment (McDermott 1977). Although the medical community is far more vigilant and sensitive to these concerns today than in the past, there still remains the chance that unexpected or untoward side effects of technology may go unrecognized for long periods of time. Technology-induced iatrogenic illness (Illich 1976; I. L. Bennett 1977) remains of concern, especially the appearance of second- or third-order consequences of medical technology, years removed from the initial use or contact. In some instances, long-term consequences may include serious risk to the offspring of affected individuals, as in the case of diethylstilbestrol producing second-generation carcinogenic effects. Both the federal government and physicians unwittingly contributed to this problem by encouraging the manufacture of the drug and its prescribed use for the prevention of spontaneous abortion, even though evidence from controlled studies had shown it to be ineffective for such use (Fineberg and Hiatt 1979). In fact, as late as fifteen years after findings from these studies had been published, diethylstilbestrol was still being given to approximately fifty thousand pregnant women annually in the United States (T. C. Chalmers 1974).

As these examples illustrate, our ability to evaluate the clinical safety and efficacy of medical technology often has been hampered by several factors, including imperfect knowledge of the natural history of many diseases, inconsistent definitions and terminology regarding safety and efficacy, inherent limitations in assessment methods, and ethical considerations posed by research involving human subjects. The design of a study to determine whether a given technology is safe and effective for routine clinical use is a difficult task in itself. The desire to conduct the most scientifically sound trial (one involving the random assignment of patients to experimental and control groups) frequently must be tempered by logistical constraints, ethical considerations, and budgetary realities. The search for a suitable alternative methodology then becomes a trade-off of scientific rigor at the margin for what is both workable and financially feasible given the available resources.

Complicating the matter further are the hard questions of when to perform the evaluation and under whose sponsorship. The question of evaluative timing is particularly troublesome because although early evaluation of emerging technology would be socially ideal, we often lack the data and the means by which such early assessment could be reasonably accomplished. Instead, we frequently face the dilemma of having the evaluation of technology lag well behind its diffusion. The question of sponsorship is equally worrisome, not only because the locus of responsibility between the public and private sectors for carrying out technology evaluation is unclear but also because the sponsorship of individual assessments, particularly by private groups with vested interests, may render the evaluation process more vulnerable to bias.

Despite these limitations, medical technology evaluation (MTE)—or health technology assessment (HTA), as it is known in international circles—is an important activity in the health care system. Indeed, in many other countries where national governments play leading roles in evaluating medical technology, HTA is a highly visible national priority. Because medical technology often produces wide-ranging economic, social, ethical, and legal implications for society, MTE/HTA has come to be a broad policy research approach that engenders far more than simple evaluation of clinical safety and efficacy. Instead, it strives to examine all short-term and long-term consequences of the use of technology (U.S. Congress, OTA 1976, 1982). (Chapters 6–8 discuss various evaluation methods; chapter 9 describes MTE efforts in the United States and in other nations; chapter 10 addresses safety and efficacy concerns; and chapter 11 examines quality concerns.)

The Ethical Choice Question

The ethical choice question in the debate over medical technology actually consists of multiple questions bound together by a common thread—that of deciding when and how to evaluate and use technology. Prominent issues involve (1) experimentation, evaluation, and the ethics of MTE; (2) patient involvement in clinical decision making, (3) managed care practices and consumer sovereignty, and (4) distributive justice and the rationing of health care resources. Two related issues are the legal implications of "defensive medicine" in clinical practice and the increasing conflicts among social, cultural, and religious values in health care.

As with any scientific advance, a medical technology makes its way into clinical practice after some period of development and testing. To some individuals, this process appears to be too short and unstructured, leading to premature diffusion of technology. To others, the same process seems lengthy, restrictive, and unduly rigorous, almost to the point of stifling creativity and innovation. From either perspective, the real issue has to do with the ethics of evaluating new technology. Is it ethical for physicians to use emerging technologies before they have been thoroughly tested? Conversely, is it ethical to withhold promising but untested technologies from terminally ill patients? Neither question prompts an easy answer, and both propagate new questions: How rigorous must an evaluation be before a technology may be declared safe and effective for routine clinical use? Does evaluative rigor imply that randomized trials should be attempted in all cases? Is it ethical to conduct such experiments? Who should be the subjects in these trials? Is it ethical to draw subjects from "captive" populations (those whose health care is delivered or financed through governmental agencies or programs, such as the military, veterans, prisoners, and the poor)? What safeguards exist to ensure that "informed consent" in these trials is truly informed? These are but some of the difficult questions that have generated debate.

An equally perplexing ethical dilemma confronts physicians when employing technologies whose clinical value may be reasonably well established. The issue in this case hinges not on whether a technology should be used at all but on how routinely it should be used in clinical practice. A prime example is the use of cesarean delivery in obstetrics. Although the advantages and disadvantages of this procedure are well known, factors external to medicine have forced many physicians to practice "defensively"—that is, to use cesarean section more frequently than they otherwise would, largely to avoid the threat of malpractice litigation in instances where unfavorable neonatal outcomes seem possible. Some would assert, however, that financial incentives in the form of higher payment rates for cesarean as opposed to vaginal delivery also have contributed to the rising cesarean rate. In both cases, it would seem that physicians are faced with having to weigh their personal or financial interests against the interests of their patients. For some, the choice is obvious, but for others, the threat of litigation, coupled with a payment system that still rewards the physician more generously for providing technology-based services than for using cognitive skills, poses an ethical quandary that would try even the most conscientious and dedicated physician.

The patient's role in clinical decision making adds to the difficulty of the physician's choice in such matters. Historically, patients have played relatively minor roles in clinical decisions, preferring in most instances to delegate responsibility to physicians as "agents"—or decision makers. Physicians generally are comfortable in this role and, not surprisingly, impose their own values on the decision-making process. In recent years, increasingly educated consumers have become more vocal in their desire to retain—or, in some cases, regain—sovereignty over their health care, more often asking physicians to explain the problem, the available medical options, and the likelihood of various outcomes. In addition, patients and their families are demanding that their personal values and preferences be factored into medical decisions. Consequently, conflicts have arisen between professionals and laypersons—and in some cases the courts—over such issues as when to withhold lifesaving technologies, when to undertake heroic measures, and by whom these matters should be decided.

Fueling these ethical controversies—and complicating the physician-patient relationship in the process—are two opposing forces: technology manufacturers' vigorous multimedia advertising campaigns, which are intended to create demand for new products; and the aggressive managed care practices of health maintenance organizations (HMOs) and health plans, aimed at reducing service use and costs (e.g., limits on hospital stays for vaginal deliveries). Pharmaceutical firms, for example, have succeeded in generating consumer demand for many prescription drugs, posing new challenges for physicians in their clinical decision making and their drug-prescribing behavior. Managed care plans' restrictive policies, conversely, have angered so many consumers and physicians that the two groups have coalesced in many states to influence lawmakers in passing "bills of rights" for patients, an issue that also has garnered the U.S. Congress's attention.

Perhaps the most fundamental ethical issue among those listed earlier is the allocation of resources, which revolves around the question of who receives the latest in medical technology and who does not. To some, this is a philosophical issue with an economic base—is health care a right or a privilege? If the former, is everyone entitled to the best that medicine can offer, regardless of cost? If the latter, what criteria should be used to determine the nature and quantity of services that may be provided to various individuals? While it seems clear that the present U.S. system rations care by price (Merrill and Cohen 1987), some economists (Fuchs 1984; Thurow 1984) have argued that medical resource allocation in the United States is governed by ethical choices rather than by economic forces. Medical technology is at the heart of this issue because of its high visibility in the media. Not every hospital will obtain a magnetic resonance imager, nor will every person who needs a liver transplant receive it. But in acknowledging that health care resources are indeed constrained, thereby making difficult trade-offs inevitable (Aaron and Schwartz 1984), society must seek an equitable and ethically sound solution to the allocation question. It will be important, therefore, for physicians, patients, policymakers, and payers to agree on a mutually satisfactory course for making these determinations. The ethical dilemma lies in how those determinations will be made—that is, by whom and with what criteria. (See chapter 14 for further exploration of these and other issues.)

The Organizational Impact Question

The interrelatedness of the eight major questions involving medical technology should be readily apparent from our discussion thus far. Perhaps nowhere is the confluence of these concerns more evident than in the case of organizational impact. Just as the organizational setting can be instrumental in shaping the diffusion, evaluation, and cost impact of a given technology, so too can these factors in turn influence the organization and delivery of health care. For example, the high cost of providing certain specialized services—such as burn care, injury/trauma care, and neonatal intensive care—has led to the regionalization of these services in major tertiary care centers. In a similar vein, the promise of cost savings resulting from economies of scale has induced some hospitals to engage in shared service arrangements and joint ventures for selected ancillary services, such as clinical laboratory and radiology. In recent years, technological advances have led some devices and procedures increasingly to move out of hospitals into outpatient clinics, physicians' offices, and even patients' homes. For example, chemotherapy and radiation therapy for cancer may be provided safely in physicians' offices, and many monitoring devices, such as uterine activity monitoring, are finding their way into the home setting.

The 1980s witnessed the emergence of entirely new organizational forms of health care delivery. While some evolved in response to changing conditions in the health care marketplace, such as the movement toward HMOs and preferred provider organizations, many were free-standing facilities designed to deliver specialized services, such as emergicenters, ambulatory surgicenters, and cancer treatment centers (Russell and Sisk 1988). In all of these cases, economic considerations appeared to drive organizational development more than did technological factors, although time and convenience likely played some role. Emergicenters and ambulatory surgicenters, for example, have grown in popularity because of lower operating costs, greater capacity to handle large patient volumes, and, in some areas, more favorable payment levels. Diagnostic imaging centers, specializing in state-of-the-art MRI, CT, and ultrasound, have appeared for similar reasons but also represent in some locales deliberate attempts to circumvent state CON policies governing hospital acquisition of new technology. The Medicare Prospective Payment System is thought to have stimulated the spread of these technology-centered facilities, since it encourages hospitals to "unbundle" (shift) cost-raising technologies out of the hospital setting (S. Altman and Young 1993).

In the present environment—marked by the rapid rise of managed care and intense competition among private health plans—various hospitals, physician groups, and other health care providers are forming large, integrated service-delivery systems or networks. In some cases, formal merger or consolidation of organizational structures is occurring, while in others, strategic alliances are being created among independent groups. Whatever the particular arrangements, these systems or networks are intended to increase market share by capitalizing on the complementary strengths of individual providers to deliver a comprehensive array of services. The effect of such integration on technology adoption decisions is already becoming evident, as integrated delivery systems are shifting the locus of strategic decision making for some technologies from the institutional level to the system level. (See chapter 5 for a discussion of the implications of these trends.)

Medical technology also is believed to be responsible for subtle changes in the content of medical practice itself. Traditional methods of physician payment, such as fee for service, and the fear of malpractice suits are factors that might cause some physicians to overuse or ineffectively use technology. In some instances, the presence of technology may induce physicians to alter their modes of practice, causing them to utilize technology more intensively and to become more reliant on purely technical solutions to many medical problems (Reiser 1978). By constantly seeking technological fixes to these problems, some physicians risk becoming servants rather than masters of technology, substituting sophisticated diagnostic tests and equipment-embodied procedures for the basic cognitive and interpersonal skills that are the hallmarks of the physician healer—perception, reasoning, clinical judgment, and above all patience, understanding, and compassion. In a world dominated by technology, it is not surprising that technology dominates health care as well, but as Howell (1999) contends, the physician's role must remain central to patient care if the promise of better health care for all is to be fulfilled. Thus, physicians must use technology wisely and responsibly in the care of their patients while preserving the balance between the science and the art of medicine. (See chapter 11 for a discussion of quality concerns.)

The Access Question

Although the broader issue of access to health care, especially primary care, has been and remains a dominant theme in the national health care debate, access to medical technology is gaining recognition as a major concern. Despite having made great strides since 1965 toward improved access to care for much of the population, the United States still faces the challenge of extending health insurance coverage to more than 43 million uninsured Americans. In addition, it will be necessary to expand primary care residency training, to encourage a broader geographic distribution of personnel and health centers in medically underserved areas, and to establish regionalized networks of specialty and tertiary care. Although many Americans have benefited from having access to the latest technological advances through the Medicare and Medicaid programs (a prime example being the Medicare end-stage renal disease benefit), there is growing evidence that African-Americans and Latinos have substantially lower rates of various surgical procedures, including organ transplants, than do Caucasians, even though the minority groups may have higher incidence rates of some diseases. Therefore, significant financial, geographic, and in some cases demographic barriers to medical technology still remain for substantial segments of the U.S. population.

Another access problem related to the diffusion of technology arises from some states' inconsistently applied and difficult-to-enforce CON policies. By choosing in most cases to regulate the adoption of technology only in hospital-based settings and by failing in some instances to develop explicit review criteria that address both access and cost concerns, many states have inadvertently created geographic and institutional inequities. In some areas, this has amounted to the disenfranchisement of whole populations served by "unlucky" institutions that did not receive CON approval for specific technologies. In addition, third-party payers' decisions not to reimburse for the use of certain costly but safe and effective technologies have also adversely affected some hospitals' and their patients' access to technology. Conversely, strong public demand for technology in some locales may effectively thwart CON goals by creating oases of excess in which small community hospitals obtain access to advanced technologies even though they lack the necessary services to support their use—for example, obtaining a linear accelerator when no oncology services are available. This results in the maintenance of inefficient hospitals stocked with under-used technologies.

Still another aspect of the access problem generating concern is the issue of "orphan" technologies, whose high production costs and limited markets effectively preclude their widespread manufacture and sale despite well-documented evidence of their benefit. The problem of orphan drugs, for example, led to a reexamination of FDA policy and to the passage of legislation for premarket approval of these products. However, the same basic problem exists for other technologies, especially medical devices. The problem of orphan devices is most acute for disabled and handicapped members of society, whose special physical needs might benefit from either existing or new technology were it not for financial barriers to the availability and/or affordability of a device. Federal legislation that would remove some barriers for medical devices has been proposed, and several private-sector initiatives to encourage special R&D efforts are under way, but disabled persons' access to specialized technologies will likely remain a problem for some time to come. (Access concerns are addressed in chapter 13; the issue of orphan technologies is discussed in chapter 10.)

The Societal Impact Question

As scientific advances enrich our understanding of the most basic biologic processes and facilitate our ability to intervene in those processes, issues regarding the societal impact of technology grow in importance. The use of a technology may have far-reaching and unintended consequences for the fundamental demographic composition of a society and its cultural institutions. Not surprisingly, concerns about societal impact are influenced to some extent by religious values and cultural mores, much in the same way that some ethical issues—such as euthanasia and physician-assisted suicide—are influenced. (See chapter 14 for a discussion of religious values and ethical concerns.) For example, recent innovations in reproductive biology, in stem cell and other embryonic research, and in the potential for gene replacement therapy raise concerns about how the use of such technologies may affect the demographic composition of a population. The ability to determine the gender of a fetus in vitro not only affects private decisions about pregnancy and abortion but also may have profound effects on the gender distribution of a population (e.g., China), which in turn may affect cultural institutions such as marriage and future population growth or decline. Changes in demographic composition also ultimately affect economic productivity and migration patterns within a society.

The decoding of the human genome and the potential ability to intervene in the genetic structure of an individual have unknown consequences, raising numerous questions and concerns about societal effects (Kitcher 1996). Will life expectancy be further extended, thereby changing the population age structure so that increased numbers of retirees will have need for different kinds of housing stock, for Social Security benefits, and for various social services? Will society allow the use of such technologies to develop populations based on specific characteristics or genetic traits, such as intellect, physical appearance, muscular strength, or some other attribute whose propagation would profoundly change the social structure of society? Will new technologies be available only to the economic and intellectual elite, creating inequities in access and further dividing society by socioeconomic status and possibly by race and ethnicity?

New technologies may affect society in other ways, such as by altering the face of the health care workforce though the creation of new occupations and the simultaneous abandonment of others. At the level of service delivery, the adoption of certain technologies, such as devices and surgical procedures, often leads to the emergence of new classes of technologists needed to operate complex equipment or to perform specialized functions—for example, ultrasound technologists or perfusionists in open-heart surgery. At the societal level, shifts in public or private investment in scientific research can have profound implications for educational policy, for the financial fortunes of universities and academic research institutions, and for individuals' career decisions. For example, the phenomenal growth of biotechnology over the past decade produced employment opportunities that attracted many talented researchers to the field at the expense of other fields of endeavor. The continuing trend in favor of higher federal support for medical research over research in engineering, the environment, and the physical sciences appears to be having vast repercussions across the country—universities with prominent medical schools and hospital affiliations are prospering in the grant-rich funding environment, and top graduate students are choosing doctoral programs and careers in life sciences over those in physical sciences (Shadid 2001). This shift could adversely affect the physical sciences by determining "everything from the strength of future faculties to the pace and breadth of advances in individual fields of study" (Shadid 2001, A4). Thus, the future of higher education in America could well hang in the balance as a result of government policies toward research funding that threaten to tilt the entire science landscape.

The Governmental Role Question

The federal government historically has adopted multiple, diverse, and sometimes conflicting roles regarding medical technology, including promoter of technology development, regulator of technology diffusion, evaluator of technological impact and effectiveness, and purchaser of technological products and services. For the most part, these roles developed in parallel and have been conducted by organizationally separate agencies in generally uncoordinated and at times contradictory fashion. A brief historical overview of each role is presented here; an overview of the evaluation activities currently undertaken by federal and state agencies may be found in chapter 9.

Promoter of Technology Development

Of the four roles, the promotion of technology development is the oldest, spanning seventy years and rooted in the creation of the National Institutes of Health (NIH) in 1931 and the National Cancer Institute in 1937. Over time, the federal government has maintained a steady involvement in development activities, including massive funding for biomedical research through the expanding NIH, financial support for both basic scientific research and limited applied research through the National Science Foundation, and sponsorship of initiatives aimed at "technology transfer" from the laboratory to clinical practice. The regional medical programs, established in 1965 to focus the diffusion of research and training on the conquest of heart disease, cancer, and stroke, exemplify technology-transfer activity. Research funded by the Veterans Administration (now the Department of Veterans Affairs), the Department of Defense, the Department of Energy, and the National Aeronautics and Space Administration also contributes in important ways. Strong bipartisan congressional sentiment in favor of increased investment in biomedical research led to a five-year commitment to double the NIH's budget between 1998 and 2003 (Kennedy 1997), and this trend is continuing with the support of President George W. Bush's administration (Shadid 2001).

Regulator of Technology Diffusion

With the exception of the FDA, whose activities to ensure drug safety were initially authorized by the Food, Drug, and Cosmetic Act of 1938, federal efforts to regulate the diffusion of medical technology were not instituted in great measure until the 1970s. Stemming largely from cost-containment concerns, some of these regulatory activities were not specifically intended to address medical technology, but all have none-theless had some impact, particularly on equipment-embodied tech-nology. The principal federal activities included section 1122 capital expenditure review (authorized in 1972), which required health plan-ning agency review of all major purchases of medical equipment by hospitals and other institutions serving Medicare and Medicaid pa-tients; CON requirements (established under the national health plan-ning legislation in 1974) that enjoined all states to adopt such regula-tion by 1980 to continue receiving certain federal monies; and the enactment of the Medical Devices Amendments of 1976, which essen-tially gave the FDA authority over the premarket approval of new medical devices. Subsequent legislation in the 1980s and 1990s strengthened the FDA's role in regulating new drugs and devices both before and after market entry. (These FDA policy changes, including the FDA Modernization Act of 1997, are described in chapter 10; CON regulation is discussed in chapter 13.)

Evaluator of Technological Impact and Effectiveness

Federal evaluation activities, by contrast, have been fragmented and transitory. In fact, until 1978 no federal agency even possessed a leg-islative mandate to evaluate medical technologies (Banta and Thacker 1979). The FDA had been performing important regulatory functions for drugs and devices, but these responsibilities did not include sys-tematic evaluation of medical technologies. The NIH and the Veterans Administration each had been conducting clinical trials as part of their general missions, but these efforts were limited in number and scope (Behney and Banta 1979). Likewise, the National Center for Health Ser-vices Research and Development had been funding a limited number of HTA studies, but its extramural resources each year were devoted largely to general health services research. Only the U.S. Congress's Office of Technology Assessment (OTA) had been clearly involved in systematic analysis of medical technologies, but its studies were oriented more toward policy research than toward clinical assessment, and its activities dated back only as far as 1972.

The year 1978 saw the establishment of two federal programs aimed at evaluating health care technologies: the NIH-sponsored series of consensus-development conferences through the Office of Medical Applications of Research, and the National Center for Health Care Technology. The NIH consensus-development conferences continue to the present day, but the ill-fated national center, which had a statutory mandate to assess the safety and efficacy of medical technology, was abolished in 1981, after suffering the effects of funding cutbacks and political isolation under an unsupportive Reagan administration as well as powerful opposition from the American Medical Association and the Health Industry Manufacturers Association (Perry 1982; Perry and Pillar 1990).

In the years immediately following the national center's demise, responsibility for advising the HCFA on the safety and effectiveness of new technologies rested with the Office of Health Technology Assessment within the National Center for Health Services Research. These assessments, however, were largely literature reviews and syntheses of information gleaned from secondary sources, including the FDA and the NIH.

Federal legislation in 1984 and 1985 created a public-private partnership between an expanded National Center for Health Services Research and Health Care Technology Assessment and a newly created Council on Health Care Technology within the Institute of Medicine (IOM). Although the national center's domain was broadened by these acts, federal funding to support evaluation activities actually was earmarked for the Council on Health Care Technology, whose mandate was "to promote the development and application of technology assessment in health care and to review health care technologies for their appropriate use." All council members were drawn from the private sector and appointed by the IOM. Because federal funding was inadequate to carry out the council's responsibilities, the IOM also aggressively sought private funding.

Aside from its publications on methods for technology assessment (IOM 1985) and on organizations engaged in HTA activities (IOM

1988), the Council on Health Care Technology performed few assessments. In 1989, growing disappointment among congressional leaders regarding the council's inability to attract adequate private funding led to a one-year phaseout of federal support for the council.

In late 1989, the newly established Agency for Health Care Policy and Research (AHCPR) became the federal agency principally responsible for the evaluation of medical technologies, although the Department of Veterans Affairs and the Department of Defense conducted their own independent evaluation efforts. The AHCPR was created through the Omnibus Budget Reconciliation Act of 1989 to succeed both the National Center for Health Services Research and Health Care Technology Assessment and the IOM's Council on Health Care Technology. The AHCPR initially received a broader scope than its predecessors as well as a higher organizational and political profile within the Department of Health and Human Services so that its administrator reported to the assistant secretary for health and operated at the same organizational level as other Public Health Service agency administrators. From the beginning, the agency solicited input from academic researchers and from the health care technology industry through its seventeen-member National Advisory Council for Health Care Policy, Research, and Evaluation (Ginsburg, LeRoy, and Hammons 1990; Gray 1992). The council's primary focus in the early 1990s was to support outcomes research and medical treatment effectiveness research, including analyses of large clinical databases (such as those generated by Medicare claims) and the development of clinical practice guidelines. By 1999, however, the agency had been reauthorized by Congress with a new name, the Agency for Healthcare Research and Quality (AHRQ), that emphasized its expanded mission as the lead federal agency on research to improve the quality of health services (Eisenberg 2000).

Even so, the 1990s were turbulent times for the agency. In 1995, congressional efforts to reduce the federal budget led some members of the House of Representatives to seek the dismantling of both the AHCPR and the OTA. The OTA lost its funding and closed its doors in September 1995, after twenty-three years of nonpartisan service to Congress and the public (U.S. Congress, OTA 1995). The AHCPR survived the turmoil but endured a severe reduction in its budget and a shift in its role from that of an active developer of clinical practice guidelines to that of a "convener" and "science partner" with private professional organizations, managed care companies, and purchasers that validated the "impartiality and thoroughness of guidelines" developed by such groups (Cotton 1996; C. N. Kahn 1998). Two years later, in 1997, the political winds shifted, and Congress restored funding for the agency to a level that enabled it to establish its Evidence-Based Practice Centers Program, charged with reviewing and analyzing the scientific literature on health care effectiveness (AHCPR Names Evidence-Based Practice Centers 1997). In addition, with the passage of the FDA Modernization Act of 1997, Congress expanded the agency's authority in the area of outcomes research to include new uses or combinations of drugs, biologics, and therapeutics (C. N. Kahn 1998). Today, the AHRQ enjoys bipartisan congressional support and is undertaking major new initiatives in quality improvement and patient safety. Its role in MTE continues through its Center for Practice and Technology Assessment, the successor to the Office of Health Technology Assessment. (See chapters 9 and 11 for further information.)

Purchaser of Technological Products and Services

The federal government's role as a purchaser of technology should not be underestimated. Both the Department of Veterans Affairs and the Department of Defense purchase large quantities of medical equipment and supplies. Owing to its administration of the Medicare program and its partnership role in state Medicaid programs, the Centers for Medicare and Medicaid Services (CMS) is by far the single largest purchaser of health care. Formerly known as the HCFA, the CMS relies on the AHRQ's Center for Practice and Technology Assessment for advice on decisions regarding the coverage of medical technologies under the Medicare program. The criteria and the review process employed in making coverage decisions are discussed in chapter 12. Surprisingly, cost-effectiveness has never been a criterion. In fact, a rule first proposed in 1989 that would have included cost-effectiveness explicitly in the process was debated for a decade before being withdrawn.

During the 1980s, ProPAC and the PPRC were created to advise Congress and the HCFA in matters relating to the Medicare Prospective Payment System, including the effects of technology on spending growth and the effects of payment policies on technology use. These two commissions were disbanded and superseded in 1997 by the Medicare Payment Advisory Commission (MedPAC), whose mandate under the Balanced Budget Act of 1997 is to advise Congress on Medicare payment policy. The CMS and other federal agencies need to be prudent buyers of technological goods and services. (See chapter 12 for a discussion of Medicare payment policies and chapter 5 for a description of the changing incentives affecting technology adoption and use in a managed care environment.)

Susan Bartlett Foote (1991) characterized the panoply of federal government policies toward medical technology as "polyintervention," a multivalent environment in which diverse and complex policies are imposed by multiple institutions, with potentially adverse consequences for medical innovation. The question remains whether the multiple uncoordinated roles of the federal government should persist unchanged or whether an integrated federal policy should be developed and adopted to mediate the inherent conflicts between some roles. Either way, much will depend on whether new or expanded federal coordination can prove fruitful in addressing the many concerns that have been voiced about medical technology. Part III of this book addresses in detail those policy concerns.

State agencies also historically have played multiple roles regarding medical technology, primarily as purchasers of health care (through the Medicaid program) and as regulators of capital expenditures in hospitals and nursing homes (through statutory CON programs). During the 1990s, some states (e.g., Oregon, Minnesota, and Washington) developed more focused programs for evaluating new medical technologies, including collaborative ventures with other states, the federal government, and private industry (Mendelson, Abramson, and Rubin 1994). (Oregon's unique Medicaid program is described in chapter 12; CON programs and their effects are discussed in chapter 13.)

In the chapters that follow, these eight interrelated questions will serve as a useful framework for exploring the many complex issues and policy concerns that influence the effective evaluation and management of medical technology.

The Development, Diffusion, and Adoption of Medical Technology

In this first part of the book (chapters 3–5), we build on the foundation of chapter 2 and its eight critical questions by examining the process through which medical technology comes to be conceived, developed, and adopted into health care in the United States. Specifically, we look at

- biomedical innovation, including the processes and factors that encourage new ideas to take form, the strategies employed by manufacturers for research and development of medical technologies, and the structure and behavior of the industries that produce innovations in pharmaceuticals, biotechnology, and medical devices;
- diffusion of new technology, including the major theories, models, and patterns by which new technologies diffuse into practice as well as the economic, social, organizational, environmental, and professional drivers that either facilitate or inhibit this spread; and
- adoption and use of new technology, including the decision-making processes and strategies utilized by hospitals, physicians, and other health care providers in acquiring new technologies, particularly under health care market conditions that increasingly reflect incentives, choices, and trade-offs dictated by managed care.

3

Biomedical Innovation and the Development of Medical Technology
Alan B. Cohen

Any attempt by society to strike an appropriate balance among the myriad forces that govern the adoption and use of medical technology requires an understanding of the process by which medical technology undergoes invention and development—the genesis of an idea through the various stages of science-based research and development (R&D) to the dual endpoints of industrial production and initial adoption into clinical practice. In this chapter, we examine the process of biomedical innovation, including the interdependence between scientific research and technology development, and the ways in which new medical technologies are conceptualized, nurtured, and introduced into health care. We also explore the pharmaceutical, biotechnology, and medical devices industries, taking a look at how they are structured and how they operate.

Biomedical Innovation

The literature on biomedical innovation is relatively sparse. Prior to 1980, few studies had examined the development of medical technologies. Several studies had focused on the diffusion of specific technologies into clinical practice (e.g., Coleman, Katz, and Menzel 1966; Russell 1976, 1979; Comroe and Dripps 1977; Greer 1977), but none offered insight into the nature of the innovation process itself. (For a discussion of these and other works on diffusion of medical technology, see chapter 4.) Thus, much of our early understanding of innovation came primarily from the pioneering work of Everett Rogers (1962) on the diffusion of new ideas and practices and from multiple fields and disciplines outside medicine, including management science and industrial organization (Myers and Marquis 1969; Zaltman, Duncan, and Holbek 1973), economics (Mowery and Rosenberg 1979), social psychology (D. Katz and Kahn 1966), sociology (Hage and Aiken 1970), and political science (L. Mohr 1969). As interest in the biomedical innovation process grew during the 1980s and 1990s, several new conceptual models came forth to provide fresh insights (Moskowitz et al. 1981; Gelijns 1990; Halm and Gelijns 1991; Weisbrod 1991, 1994; Geisler 1999; Christensen, Bohmer, and Kenagy 2000).

In the following sections, we define and classify innovation, examine key characteristics and factors that influence the nature and rate of innovation adoption, and explore different models of the biomedical innovation process.

Defining and Classifying Innovation

From the seminal work of Everett Rogers (1962) comes a definition of *innovation* that has been frequently used in the literature: "an idea, practice, or object perceived as new by an individual" (as qtd. in Rogers 1981, 76). In this definition, the "objectively" measured newness of an idea holds relatively less importance than the subjective perception of its novelty (Rogers and Shoemaker 1971). In other words, if an idea or practice seems new to an individual, it is indeed an innovation, even if the individual had been aware of it for some time and had neither formed an opinion nor acted on it. Over time, this definition has been modified to include units of adoption larger than an individual, such as groups and organizations (Zaltman, Duncan, and Holbek 1973; Rogers 1981, 1995). Under this expanded definition, not all members of a group or organization must share in the perception of the item as new for it to be innovative.

Innovation is highly uncertain. It is commonly the culmination of basic research that produces new knowledge drawn from multidisciplinary themes, but sometimes it may be the result of a serendipitous breakthrough, such as in the discoveries of penicillin or the first X rays (Howell 1996). More often, it is the outcome of a long incremental and iterative process of inquiry and analysis. Gelijns (1990) stressed the interdependence between science and technology in producing innovation and pointed to the shift during the twentieth century from the sole innovator to the group or firm model of development. The firm model of technology development presently dominates the pharmaceutical, biotechnology, and medical devices industries, with technological advances coming from small, start-up firms as well as from large, established companies (as discussed later in this chapter). However, to achieve innovation on the order of magnitude exemplified by the Human Genome Project requires a carefully planned major investment of resources by a congeries of public and private organizations. The Human Genome Project thus illustrates not only the critical interdependence between scientific discovery and technology development but also the multiorganizational collaboration that increasingly may be needed to produce breakthrough advances in the life sciences.

Innovations may be classified in different ways. Three dimensions of importance relate to how innovations are viewed by adopters.

- *Instrumental* or *ultimate.* Whereas ultimate innovations are ends in themselves, instrumental innovations achieve intermediate steps that later make possible the introduction of ultimate innovations (Zaltman, Duncan, and Holbek 1973). This distinction somewhat resembles Lewis Thomas's notion of high versus halfway technologies (see chapter 1).
- *Radical* or *incremental.* Radical innovations represent entirely new approaches to problems, while incremental innovations can be novel changes of smaller scale or simply the modification and upgrading of old items (E. B. Roberts 1981). Most innovations in nonbiomedical as well as biomedical areas are incremental changes that dominate research and development.
- *Industrial goods, consumer goods,* or *services.* Goods are tangible products, and services are either practices or processes (E. B. Roberts 1981). Industrial goods are those sold to professionals (e.g., physicians or hospitals) rather than directly to consumers. In the case of pharmaceuticals, the line between industrial and consumer goods has been obscured in recent years by the advent of aggressive direct-to-consumer advertising, intended to leverage the prescribing habits of physicians through heightened consumer demand.

To demonstrate how these dimensions relate to biomedical advances, consider the following examples. Magnetic resonance imaging (MRI), for instance, is an industrial good reflecting a radical development in diagnostic imaging. Heart-lung transplantation also is an industrial good, but it differs from MRI in that it is a practice based on incremental change (modification) of existing surgical procedures. Both, however, are instrumental rather than ultimate innovations because neither is an end in itself—MRI is a diagnostic tool that might be supplanted in the future by an even more powerful and accurate diagnostic technology, and heart-lung transplantation eventually could be replaced by yet undiscovered gene replacement therapies arising from the Human Genome Project. Pharmaceuticals, by contrast, are more varied; although they are essentially consumer goods (obtained with a physician's prescription), their approach to disease management can be either radical or incremental and their effects on disease outcomes may represent either instrumental or ultimate innovations. For example, the drug Viagra, which is used to treat male erectile dysfunction, may be considered an ultimate innovation that is radical in approach, whereas the drugs known as statins (e.g., Lipitor, Pravachol, or Zocor), which are intended to reduce the risk of heart attack by lowering blood cholesterol levels, may be viewed as instrumental innovations reflecting incremental changes in the treatment of heart disease.

Key Characteristics and Factors Influencing the Adoption of Innovation

In a landmark book, Rogers and Shoemaker (1971) identified five characteristics of innovations that are key to the rate of adoption by users:

- *Relative advantage*—the degree to which an innovation is perceived to be better than the product or practice that it supersedes. Advantage may be viewed in terms of economics, social prestige, convenience, and/or satisfaction.
- *Compatibility*—the degree to which an innovation is perceived as being consistent with the existing values, experiences, and needs of potential adopters.
- *Complexity*—the degree to which an innovation is perceived as difficult to understand and to use.
- *Trialability*—the degree to which an innovation lends itself to experimentation by adopters on a limited basis.
- *Observability*—the degree to which the results of an innovation are visible to others.

An innovation that is perceived as advantageous, compatible with the adopter's values and needs, comparatively easy to use, amenable to experimentation, and able to produce clearly visible results is likely to be adopted rapidly. These characteristics are universally applicable to innovations today, including advances in medicine and health care. One example that has been well studied and documented in medicine is X-ray computed tomography (CT), which diffused swiftly during the 1970s precisely because the medical community perceived it as highly advantageous, highly compatible with values and clinical needs, only slightly more complex than conventional X-ray equipment, very amenable to experimentation, and clearly superior in terms of its imaging capabilities. Physicians' perceptions of an innovation's characteristics, however, do not always coincide with the real properties of the technology. Some medical innovations, such as electronic fetal monitoring, were adopted more rapidly than their true relative advantage and complexity should have dictated (Cohen 1983; Banta and Thacker 1990, 2002).

Other key influences on the adoption of an innovation or on the innovation process itself include organizational factors, the stage of the innovation, and patents. Organizational factors play important roles in three ways—first, by helping to foster innovative activities (e.g., through corporate perceptions of market demand or of government regulation); second, by offering effective technical solutions for problems that often arise in the innovation process; and third, by providing channels for successful exploitation, such as research laboratories and academic centers, through which technology transfer may occur as a precursor to broader external diffusion (E. B. Roberts 1981, 1982). The importance of industry-university ties will become more apparent later in our examination of the various medical technology industries.

The stage of an innovation usually has strong bearing on the focus or orientation of a firm's R&D activities. For example, firms involved in early "stage 1" or intermediate "stage 2" development of a technology likely will concentrate their activities on product innovation, whereas firms engaged in advanced or mature "stage 3" development may instead orient their innovation activities toward improving the manufacturing process. Early work by E. B. Roberts (1981) indicated that small firms often play important roles in stage 1 development but that larger companies tend to become dominant in stages 2 and 3. He also found that successful innovations were marked by major invention during stage 1, with later-stage innovation involving mostly incremental change as the industry matured. In today's fast-growing biotechnology and medical device industries, small start-up firms are common, but their success in bringing their products to market often depends on their ability to secure venture capital for their early stage R&D activities.

Patents are critical to many technologically innovative industries, but their importance in biomedical innovation varies by individual industry. For example, patent royalties contribute significantly to product revenues in the pharmaceutical and biotechnology industries but have less effect in medical device industries (A. Kahn 1991; Littell 1994; PhRMA 2000). In similar fashion, the intellectual property protection afforded by patents appears to have greater importance for the R&D strategies of pharmaceutical and biotechnology firms than for those of medical device companies (Boston Consulting Group 1996). In one survey of U.S. firms in different industries, pharmaceutical companies indicated that 65 percent of their products would not have been developed or commercially introduced had patent protection not been available (Barfield and Beltz 1995). In contrast, patents neither impeded technological development nor effectively barred market entry for enterprising firms during the early years of the MRI device industry (Steinberg and Cohen 1984). With U.S. companies legally able to hold patents on genetically engineered tissues and products, including specific human genes, patents likely will play important roles in the future development of gene replacement therapies and tissue-based technologies but also likely will raise serious ethical issues (see chapter 14).

The Biomedical Innovation Process

Figure 3.1 shows an early conceptual model of the biomedical innovation process. The model by Moskowitz and colleagues (1981) contains three parallel progressions—the top arrow depicts the flow of innovation from idea genesis to idea dissemination; the middle arrow shows the continuum of biomedical research from its most basic exploratory phase through applied development to its ultimate application in health practice; and the bottom arrow specifies the objectives to which each research activity is directed.

In this model, ideas first are generated through basic and clinical research in an effort to acquire new knowledge. These ideas are then communicated among researchers to integrate the essential pieces of knowledge for targeted technology development. In the next step, applied research is used to validate acquired knowledge and to refine ideas for practical clinical applications of the technology. Knowledge

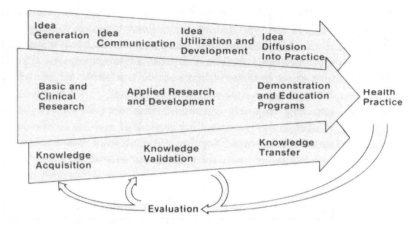

Fig. 3.1. The biomedical innovation process. (From Moscowitz et al. 1981.)

validation may include clinical trials and peer review of research as further means of idea communication and development. In the final step, the technological product or medical practice moves out of the research community toward adoption in the health care field. Demonstration and education programs foster the transfer of knowledge, making idea diffusion complete. Evaluation forms a continuous feedback loop, linking the various stages in the process, and thus can have profound effect on the result (i.e., whether technology diffusion is stimulated or inhibited) as well as on the interactions among people that bring the ideas to fruition. However, scientific studies alone often do not change opinions or behavior, and even Rogers (1995) later noted that the diffusion of ideas is a social process comprising five stages—knowledge acquisition, persuasion, decision, implementation, and confirmation.

Recent contributions to the literature have challenged the conventional wisdom in novel ways. For example, Geisler (1999) has proposed a multiperspective model of medical technology in which six different perspectives of its definition—physical, information, knowledge, process, change, and enabling resource—are integrated to form an organizational dimension (see figure 3.2). The first three of these perspectives refer to what medical technology is, whereas the last three describe either what technology does or what it generates. When medical technology is viewed as an organizational construct, many of its attributes (e.g., its rate of change and its complexity) can be characterized in ways

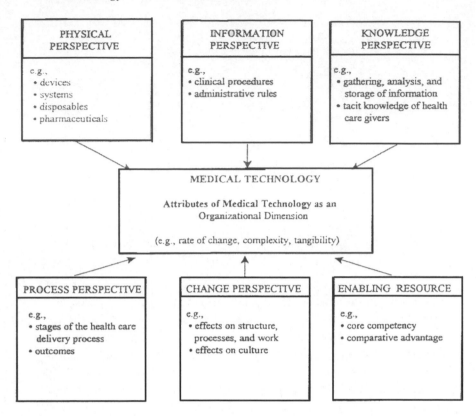

Fig. 3.2. A multiperspective model of medical technology. (From Geisler 1999.)

that may be used to design health care organizations in terms of their formalization, centralization, coordination, and control.

In another paradigm that challenges the status quo (see figure 3.3), Christensen, Bohmer, and Kenagy (2000) differentiate between sustaining innovations (the improvements created by an industry as it introduces new and more advanced products to serve its most sophisticated customers) and disruptive innovations (the cheaper, simpler, and more convenient products and services that are aimed at meeting the needs of less demanding customers). In almost any industry, the dominant firms tend to concentrate on improving their products or services to a point that exceeds the needs of most consumers. This allows upstart companies to enter the market with simpler, less costly, and more convenient technologies designed to satisfy the needs of low-end users. Eventually, these disruptive innovations improve so much that they capture the market by meeting the needs of a majority of mainstream

Dominant players in most markets focus on sustaining innovations – on improving their products and services to meet the needs of the profitable high-end customers. Soon, those improvements overshoot the needs of the vast majority of customers. That makes a market ripe for upstart companies seeking to introduce disruptive innovations – cheaper, simpler, more convenient products or services aimed at the lower end of the market. Over time, those products improve to meet the needs of most of the market, a phenomenon that has caused many of history's best companies to plunge into crisis.

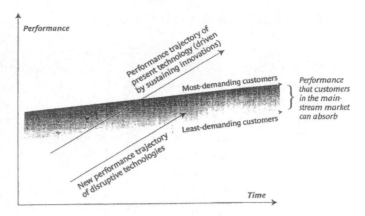

Fig. 3.3. The progress of disruptive innovation. (From Christensen, Bohmer, and Kenagy 2000.)

users, imperiling the fortunes of the dominant players in the process. Christensen and colleagues cite the following examples of disruptive technologies—the telephone (which replaced the telegraph), the Eastman camera (which expanded amateur photography), photocopying (which supplanted carbon paper and typesetting), minicomputers and personal computers (which disrupted mainframes), and most recently on-line brokerage services (which have challenged professional brokerage houses).

Christensen, Bohmer, and Kenagy (2000, 102, 104) argue that "health care may be the most entrenched, change-averse industry in the United States" because its institutions (hospitals, medical schools, and research organizations) and its professions (specialist physicians, primary care physicians, and nurse practitioners) have collectively "overshot the level of care actually needed or used by the vast majority of patients" and are resistant to the opportunities offered by disruptive innovations. The authors contend that the health care system needs to be transformed by innovations that enable less highly skilled professionals to perform progressively more sophisticated tasks in less costly settings—for example, nurse practitioners doing the work of physicians and primary care physicians treating conditions in their offices that used to require the care of specialists in hospitals. The authors recommend, therefore, greater investment in technologies that simplify complex problems, the easing of restrictive government regulation, and the creation of new institutions that can effectively deliver the disruptive products or services.

Technology Research and Development

An early classic model of technology R&D, first formulated in 1976 by the U.S. Congress's Office of Technology Assessment (OTA), contained four principal steps: (1) basic research, (2) applied research, (3) targeted development, and (4) clinical testing. Figure 3.4 illustrates these four steps within the larger context of technology development and diffusion (U.S. Congress, OTA 1976). The model assumes a generally linear progression of technology R&D in which steps are followed in sequential fashion (Banta, Behney, and Willems 1981). A brief description of each step follows.

Basic Research

The genesis of many biomedical innovations may be found in basic scientific research in the fields of biology, chemistry, and physics. Basic research may be characterized as original investigation that is theory driven but non–mission oriented (Battelle 1976). Its primary objective is to acquire new knowledge or understanding of scientific phenomena and observable facts without specific applications in mind (U.S. Congress, OTA 1984b). As described earlier, basic research can be unpredictable, even serendipitous in its outcome—for example, Wilhelm Roentgen's "accidental" discovery of X rays while studying the physics of rays emitted from a Crookes's tube led to unanticipated benefits in medical diagnosis (Comroe and Dripps 1981; Howell 1996). In addition, because basic research leads to subsequent discovery and invention as new knowledge is added to the base, many biomedical innovations today can trace their roots to discoveries made long ago. For example, the mapping of the human genome is a direct product of Francis Crick, James Watson, and Maurice Wilkins's pathbreaking 1953 work to construct a model of the double-helical molecule of DNA, but this work could not have been accomplished without the benefit of Gregor Mendel's 1865 genetic research involving plants (Wade 2000b). The importance of such basic, undirected, nonclinical research to advances in medicine cannot be overstated. Thus, basic research is often regarded as the cornerstone of the development of new medical technology.

Applied Research

Whereas basic research may be viewed as an attempt to understand nature, applied research may be seen as an effort to control or manipulate

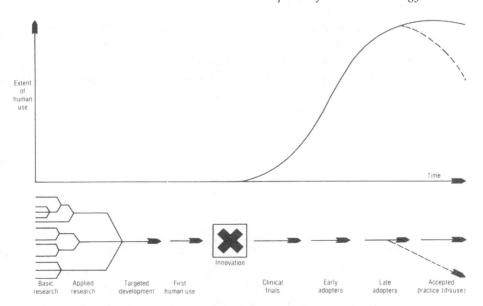

Fig. 3.4. The development and diffusion of medical technology. (From OTA 1976.)

natural phenomena (U.S. Congress, OTA 1976). It is generally goal oriented, but its immediate goal may not necessarily be the development of a specific technological product (Banta, Behney, and Willems 1981). Rather, applied research seeks new knowledge or understanding necessary for determining the means by which specific needs may be met or particular problems solved (U.S. Congress, OTA 1984b). In the pharmaceutical industry, this takes the form of translational research that enables the transition from basic research to the targeted development of drugs (PhRMA 2000). The products of applied research in other medical technology industries tend to be new materials, tools, or processes that may serve a variety of applications. Applied research thus draws on various subfields within biology (e.g., molecular biology and genetics) as well as on numerous fields outside biology, including electronics, nuclear physics, quantum mechanics, and radioisotope chemistry. Computer science increasingly plays an integral role in all areas of scientific research, especially in applied research, where new fields—such as computational chemistry, computational genetics, computational molecular biology, and computational immunology—have quickly emerged (G. Johnson 2001). The Human Genome Project, for example, would not have been possible without the use of powerful computers to determine gene sequencing. In fact, the traditional forms of preclinical testing of new products—that is, in vitro studies (performed in the laboratory) and in vivo studies (performed with living animals)—are being replaced in some cases by what researchers call "in silica" studies (simulations performed on the silicon chips of computers) that are now possible with advanced computer modeling software (G. Johnson 2001; Rosenberg 2001a). Computer modeling of the absorption, distribution, metabolism, excretion, and toxicity of compounds is likely to revolutionize applied pharmaceutical research (Rosenberg 2001a).

Targeted Development

Targeted development, as the name implies, is distinguished by its emphasis on activities that systematically use the knowledge gained from research to design and to develop prototypical products and processes (U.S. Congress, OTA 1984b). It is fundamentally an extension of applied research but is more narrow in its focus on a single technology and is clearly mission oriented in purpose (Battelle 1976). As with applied research, the use of computer simulation and modeling techniques in the design and development of new molecular entities such as drugs, vaccines, and biotechnology products is becoming commonplace (G. Johnson 2001). In the case of medical devices, targeted development usually involves the construction of a working industrial model or prototype. Product evaluation in this step relies on experimental testing procedures similar to those used in applied research. Because of the potential commercial value of new products, targeted development has long been the domain of private firms and business ventures. However, partnerships between industry and academia have grown in number in recent years as pharmaceutical firms, biotechnology companies, and medical device manufacturers have pursued joint ventures with universities and their academic medical centers to develop and test new technologies. (See also this chapter's case example of the MRI industry, which describes how companies have used such partnerships to commercial advantage.)

Clinical Testing

The initiation of clinical testing in humans often (but not always) signals the completion of targeted development of a technology. Clinical testing thus may be conducted concurrently with the previous step, generally to evaluate the technology on a pilot or trial basis (see the case example of the MRI industry). Rigorous assessment of technological safety and efficacy—in the form of well-designed clinical trials—usually takes place during this phase, especially in the cases of new drugs and devices, which must undergo regulatory scrutiny by the federal Food and Drug Administration (FDA). Most clinical trials occur in major medical centers and hospitals and are conducted by academic researchers and private research organizations under contract to technology firms (see chapter 9). Trials increasingly are being designed to include economic evaluation components (e.g., cost-effectiveness analyses), especially in the case of pharmaceuticals, where an entire field known as pharmacoeconomics has emerged over the past decade. In the case of surgical procedures, however, rigorous evaluation often does not occur until after the technology has already begun to diffuse into clinical practice. Clinical testing of a new technology while in an "experimental" or "investigational" phase of its development, therefore, should be distinguished from clinical evaluation of the technology following its adoption in medical practice (U.S. Congress, OTA 1976).

It is important to recognize that this linear model of innovation and technology development is limited in several important ways: (1) it overstates the role that research advances play in stimulating technology development and understates the growing influence of market demand and government regulation on R&D decisions (Halm and Gelijns 1991); (2) it does not capture the iterative nature of the R&D process, in which a technology is continuously evaluated and refined (Gelijns 1990; Weisbrod 1991), especially in an uncertain environment (Nelson and Winter 1977; Gelijns and Rosenberg 1994); (3) it fails to reflect the close interaction that often exists between industry-based developers of technology and the prime users of technology (e.g., hospitals and physicians); and (4) it ignores an increasingly important fifth step that frequently occurs in concert with clinical testing—the performance of cost-effectiveness analyses and market research to determine the financial viability of and potential demand for new products, especially pharmaceuticals.

Because of these limitations in the classic model, new dynamic models of technological innovation arose during the 1990s that more accurately represented the influence of consumers, payers, and regulators (the FDA) on the demand for new technology (Halm and Gelijns 1991; Gelijns and Rosenberg 1994). In one model (see figure 3.5), technology

Fig. 3.5. A dynamic model of technology development. (From Halm and Gelijns 1991.)

R&D is portrayed as an iterative process linked to the adoption and use of technology through a feedback loop that reflects the interaction of market demand considerations with the emerging scientific and engineering knowledge base (Halm and Gelijns 1991).

In another model (see figure 3.6), the health insurance system, technological change, and health care expenditures are depicted as interdependent forces—technological change affects the demand for health care and the demand for insurance, while the form and level of insurance coverage affect the nature of technology development and diffusion over time (Weisbrod 1994). In this model, incentives are of paramount importance because they drive decision making and behavior. The changing incentives for R&D investment created by these interactive forces—and their implications for manufacturers, providers, purchasers, and consumers—are discussed more fully in chapter 5 within the context of decisions to adopt and use medical technology.

Patterns of Technology R&D

Patterns of R&D activity vary depending on the type of medical technology in question.

Pharmaceuticals

Traditionally, drug development has drawn heavily from basic research in organic chemistry, biochemistry, bacteriology, pharmacology, and human pathophysiology (U.S. Congress, OTA 1993). Today, molecular biology and computational genetics are playing increasing roles in drug development, and with advances in genomics, pharmaceutical firms are expected to focus a great deal of future R&D activity on the development of targeted drugs for specific genetic defects. One industry source estimates that about five hundred genes currently are being targeted for drug interventions and that an additional three thousand

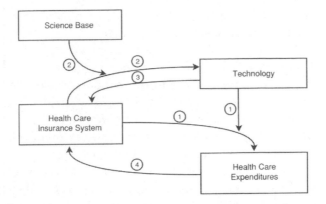

Fig. 3.6. An incentive-based interactive model of technological change. (From Weisbrod 1994.)

to ten thousand targets for innovation may be generated by findings from the Human Genome Project (PhRMA 2000). Drug development is also likely to draw more heavily from the plant sciences, where natural botanic materials with pharmaceutical properties may have promising therapeutic effects (e.g., tamoxifen, which is derived from the yew plant and is used in the treatment of breast cancer).

Vaccines and Biotechnology Products
In addition to drawing on research from the fields cited earlier, vaccine development draws on advances from virology, serology, immunology, and genetic engineering. The development of biotechnology products, which include biologics and bioengineered tissues, draws most heavily on advances from molecular and cellular biology, immunology, and plant, animal, and human genetics (Biotechnology Industry Organization 2001). Advances in genomics are also expected to influence future vaccine and biotechnology R&D activities.

Medical Devices
The development of medical devices and equipment differs in that much of the basic research is performed outside the biomedical sector in such fields as physics, chemistry, and electronics (A. Kahn 1991). In the area of applied research, device manufacturers today draw on bioengineering, biomaterials, genomics, computing, and telecommunications to develop innovative technologies (Lewin Group 2000). In some cases, devices are being combined with drugs (e.g., drug-eluting stents

for coronary artery disease) to produce new combination products that draw on multiple fields of scientific research.

Surgical Procedures

Patterns of R&D for surgical procedures are more complex. Because surgical procedures involve the combination of surgical techniques with drugs, devices, or both, the development of new procedures draws on advances from multiple fields. For example, successful development of cardiac pacemaker implantation required knowledge and research in solid-state physics, electrical engineering, anatomy, cardiac physiology, surgical techniques, and the manufacture of biocompatible materials (U.S. Congress, OTA 1976). Other examples include organ transplantation procedures, which depend on advances in immunosuppressive drugs that quell tissue rejection, and various laparoscopic, arthroscopic, and other minimally invasive procedures, whose use would not be possible without advances in flexible fiber-optic imaging tools and surgical instrumentation (Lewin Group 2000). Surgical procedures also have benefited over the years from general improvements in infection control, anesthesia, and an increased understanding of disease processes (Gelijns 1990).

Investment in Biomedical Research and Development

Over the past two decades, there has been astonishing growth in investment in biomedical R&D in both the public and private sectors. In 1980, total investment in health R&D was estimated at $7.9 billion—31 percent of this amount provided by industry, 52 percent by the federal government, and 17 percent by state and local governments, nonprofit institutions, and foreign sources (NIH 1992; U.S. Congress, OTA 1984b). By 1993, total health R&D expenditures had climbed to $16.1 billion, but the federal government's share had dwindled to 43 percent of the funds, while industry's share had risen to 51 percent, with universities, nonprofit institutions, state and local governments, and foreign sources supplying the rest (National Science Board 1993; Read and Lee 1994). By 1998, the budget for the National Institutes of Health (NIH) alone had reached $13.6 billion (more than doubling since 1986), and Congress embarked on an ambitious bipartisan plan to double the agency's funding over the next five years (Kennedy 1997). President Bush's proposed NIH budget of $23.1 billion for fiscal year 2002 was clearly on target to meet Congress's goal of approximately $27 billion by 2003. However, despite the huge increases in its budget, the NIH's share of total health R&D spending in the United States continues to decline as the funding balance shifts toward the private sector (Neumann and Sandberg 1998; Shadid 2001).

Whereas basic biomedical research is funded largely by federal agencies, particularly the NIH, applied research and targeted development of new drugs, biologics, and medical devices are supported primarily by the pharmaceutical, biotechnology, and device industries, respectively (Romeo 1988; Gelijns 1990; A. Kahn 1991; U.S. Congress, OTA 1993; Neumann and Sandberg 1998; PhRMA 2002; Advanced Medical Technology Association 2001; Biotechnology Industry Organization 2001). Significant support for vaccine research still comes from the federal government, but the pharmaceutical and biotechnology industries have been assuming a larger share over time (Gelijns 1990; PhRMA 2000). Investment in surgical R&D, by contrast, is less costly and less dependent on funding from external sources (Gelijns 1990; Halm and Gelijns 1991; Advanced Medical Technology Association 2001). Because surgical procedures cannot be patented, profit considerations play somewhat less of a role in R&D decisions unless the procedures in question involve the use of drugs and/or devices (Chang and Luft 1991, Halm and Gelijns 1991). In some cases, prestige enhancement may be more important as a motivating factor for surgical innovations, which tend to be developed by specialists in major academic centers (Chang and Luft 1991).

Private industry's strong commitment to applied biomedical R&D may be measured not only by its increasing share of the total financial burden but also by the relative percentage of industry sales devoted to R&D. For example, in 1992, the average R&D expenditure across all American industries was 3.7 percent of sales, compared with figures for the U.S. medical devices, pharmaceutical, and biotechnology industries of 6.7 percent, 10 percent, and 81 percent, respectively (Littell 1994; Read and Lee 1994). By 2001, the average for all industries had risen to 4.1 percent of sales, while the corresponding figure for research-based pharmaceutical companies had grown to 18.2 percent, more than double the percentage of any other industry, including such high-tech industries as electronics, aerospace, computer software and services, and telecommunications (PhRMA 2002). Total spending for pharmaceutical R&D in 2002 was estimated at $30.3 billion (PhRMA 2002). Such high levels of investment in R&D are hardly surprising, given the enormous worldwide sales and potential profits involved and the huge costs associated with bringing new products to market (Read and Lee 1994; Boston Consulting Group 1996; Moore 1996; Aoki 2001a). For example, PhRMA members' 2002 worldwide sales totaled $171 billion (PhRMA 2002), and the pharmaceutical industry outranked all other industries in profitability as measured by median return on revenue, assets, and equity, according to Fortune magazine (Aoki 2001a). During the 1980s and 1990s, the average cost of developing a new drug was estimated to range from $194 million after taxes to as much as $500 million before taxes (both figures in 1990 dollars), with only three of ten marketed drugs producing revenues that matched or exceeded average R&D costs (Anders 1993; U.S. Congress, OTA 1993; Boston Consulting Group 1996; PhRMA 2000). The cost of demonstrating the bioequivalence of a generic drug was estimated in the mid-1990s at $1 million (Barfield and Beltz 1995). Recently, a Tufts University study estimated the average cost of drug development at $802 million (DiMasi, Hansen, and Grabowski 2003), a figure hotly disputed by the group Public Citizen, which analyzed the Tufts methodology and placed the figure closer to $110 million (Bayot 2001; G. Harris 2001).

As this discussion illustrates, biomedical innovation and technology development emanate from multiple sources in the United States—academia, government, industry, and combinations thereof. Turning now to the industrial side of technology development, we present an overview of three such industries—the pharmaceutical, biotechnology, and medical devices industries.

The Pharmaceutical Industry

The U.S. pharmaceutical industry has undergone remarkable growth and restructuring during the past decade. In 2002, domestic sales alone were $166 billion, and the industry employed more than 223,000 workers (PhRMA 2002). Since the mid-1980s, the industry also has witnessed much consolidation among its leading firms, although it is not as highly concentrated as other industries such as airlines, automobiles, and telecommunications. Nevertheless, the constant merger and acquisition activity within the industry has created new corporate giants (e.g., GlaxoSmithKline, Bristol-Myers Squibb, AstraZeneca, Pfizer, Roche, Aventis, Novartis, Boehringer-Ingelheim, Pharmacia, and TAP) to challenge longtime industry leaders such as Merck, Johnson and

Johnson, Abbott Laboratories, Eli Lilly, American Home Products, Schering-Plough, Searle, and Bayer, to name just a few. In addition, the number of strategic alliances (partnerships and licensing arrangements) among firms increased almost sixfold from 121 in 1986 to 712 in 1998. Such alliances were formed for diverse purposes, ranging from collaborative research arrangements to joint ventures in product development, marketing, and distribution (PhRMA 2000). Further consolidation is expected in the near future as merger mania abounds even among the giants (e.g., Pfizer and Pharmacia have announced plans to merge).

According to the Pharmaceutical Research and Manufacturers of America (PhRMA), the trade association that represents the industry, 402 different medicines were in development in 2003 for the treatment of various forms of cancer. Other major targets of drug development in 2003 included AIDS/HIV (83 drugs and vaccines in development), coronary heart disease (109), neurological diseases (76), arthritis (28), diabetes (26), Alzheimer's disease (24), osteoporosis (19), asthma (17), depression (17), congestive heart failure (17), cystic fibrosis (17), stroke (14), schizophrenia (12), and hypertension (10). In addition, pharmaceutical development was targeted to new preparations for the digestive and genito urinary systems, the skin, and various infective and parasitic diseases (PhRMA 2003).

The mapping of the human genome, with its promise of identifying genes that could become new targets for drug development, has blurred the boundary between pharmaceuticals and biotechnology products. Fearing that small biotechnology firms would rush to patent their gene discoveries, thereby either keeping such information private or charging huge fees for access to it, the leading drug firms in 1999 began to discuss plans for forming a unique nonprofit consortium that would produce its own map of chemical landmarks found throughout human DNA (Langreth, Waldholz, and Moore 1999). However, no such consortium has developed to date, and drug firms appear to be seeking alternative ways of protecting their interests by entering into cooperative agreements for joint discovery of genetic markers called single-nucleotide polymorphisms (Langreth, Waldholz, and Moore 1999), by acquiring biotechnology companies involved in drug discovery (Rosenberg 2001a), and by joining the ranks of the Biotechnology Industry Organization. Conversely, several leading biotechnology firms have become members of PhRMA in recent years.

The Biotechnology Industry

According to the Biotechnology Industry Organization (2003), the U.S. biotechnology industry today boasts 1,457 companies employing more than 191,000 people. Some sources have placed the number of companies above 1,500, and many start-up firms are expected to fail during the current economic downturn (Rosenberg 2001b). The majority of biotechnology firms are small—one-third employ fewer than 50 employees and more than two-thirds employ fewer than 135 people. Composed of several broad segments—most notably, health care products, agricultural products, and chemical and environmental products—the industry in 2001 spent $15.6 billion on R&D and had product sales of $20.7 billion. The top five biotechnology companies spent an average of $89,400 per employee on R&D, compared with an average of $31,200 per employee for the top drug firms. Although market capitalization (the amount of money invested in the industry) was $97 billion in 1998, only 20 percent of biotechnology firms had approved products and revenue streams that year, and only 30 percent had a stock market value exceeding $1 billion (Matherlee 1999). Nevertheless, the future of the industry looks bright, especially in the area of health care.

Biotechnology is used in four main areas in health care: medicines, vaccines, diagnostics, and gene therapy. The Biotechnology Industry Organization (2003) estimates that more than 350 biotechnology drug products and vaccines currently are in clinical trials, and hundreds more are in early development, with such major targets as AIDS/HIV (151 different companies working on therapies/cures), various vaccines (98 firms), infectious diseases (70), breast cancer (68), prostate cancer (56), diabetes (54), gene therapy (53), lung cancer (45), osteoporosis (44), leukemia (35), ovarian cancer (27), and colon cancer (25).

Unlike the well-established pharmaceutical industry, which saw fairly steady growth throughout the 1980s and 1990s, the biotechnology industry experienced periods of boom and bust during the same twenty-year period (Aoki 2000). With each cycle, however, the industry grew stronger, as new companies emerged and others disappeared. The five leading firms of today—Amgen, Biogen, Chiron, Genzyme, and Genentech—successfully weathered the pendulum swings of the investment cycle, but others, including Alpha-Beta Technology and ImmuLogic Pharmaceuticals, were not as fortunate (Aoki 2000). As the industry matures, subsectors are beginning to appear, with large firms resembling small drug companies and behaving quite differently from the smaller genomics firms, drug discovery firms, and "tools" firms that supply and service other biotechnology companies (Aoki 2000).

Over time, many biotechnology firms have been able to go beyond the traditional venture capital markets to raise funds through public investment (Aoki 2000). In 1994, for example, the industry raised $1 billion from public offerings, split almost evenly between initial offerings and secondary, follow-on offerings; by 1999, secondary offerings accounted for more than 80 percent of the $6.4 billion in public investment (Aoki 2000). The pattern continued in 2001, with industry-wide financing totaling $15.1 billion (BIO 2003). Even so, biotechnology firms have had to seek other ways to raise capital—partnerships, joint ventures, and licensing arrangements with large pharmaceutical firms (Langreth, Waldholz, and Moore 1999; Aoki 2000; BIO 2003). With the recent growth of genomics and proteomics, future investment in the industry is expected to rise, but industry insiders and observers also expect the volatility to continue (Aoki 2000).

The Medical Devices Industry

According to the Advanced Medical Technology Association (2003), the trade association that represents more than 1,100 companies, the medical devices industry is quite varied. It includes firms that manufacture surgical and medical instruments, surgical appliances and supplies, dental equipment and supplies, ophthalmic devices, electromedical devices, laboratory apparatus, intravenous devices, X-ray and diagnostic imaging devices, and medical information systems. In the early 1990s, the industry ranked among the fastest-growing U.S. manufacturing industries, with an annual growth rate of 8 percent (exceeded only by the semiconductor industry, which had a 12 percent annual growth rate) (HCTI 1993a). In 2002, industry sales totaled $71 billion in the United States alone and $169 billion worldwide (Advanced Medical Technology Association 2003). Although the growth rate in the U.S. industry has slowed since the early 1990s, it remains the global leader in medical device innovation (Matherlee 1999; Lewin Group 2000).

Two earlier studies of the medical devices industry during the 1980s (Arthur Young 1981; U.S. Congress, OTA 1984b) found an industry that (1) was fairly concentrated but allowed easy entry for small firms; (2) conferred economies of scale on larger firms; (3) had heavier investment in R&D activities and greater patent activity than did many other industries; (4) was characterized by aggressive advertising and sales campaigns; (5) had considerable merger and acquisition activity aimed more at product extension (gaining access to new product lines) than at market extension (gaining market share in the same product line) but with growing emphasis on vertical integration (acquiring firms whose activities are important to the processing, manufacture, sale, or distribution of existing products); and (6) had high overall profitability that compared favorably with other industries. In a more recent study commissioned by the Advanced Medical Technology Association (formerly known as the Health Industry Manufacturers Association), the Lewin Group (2000) found a U.S. medical devices industry in which (1) nearly 300,000 persons were employed in 1997; (2) the largest 2 percent of companies dominated the market, accounting for 45 percent of total sales; (3) 80 percent of all companies were small, stage 1 firms with fewer than 50 employees and were responsible for 28 percent of R&D expenditures but only 10 percent of total sales; and (4) R&D spending as a percentage of sales had grown from 8.4 percent in 1995 to 12.9 percent in 1998. Together, these studies paint a portrait of a dynamic, innovative, profitable, and highly competitive industry.

For the purposes of further exploration, we present a case examination of a medical device industry that blossomed during the late twentieth century, MRI.

A Case Example: The MRI Device Industry

During the 1980s, MRI emerged as *the* growth technology in the diagnostic imaging field. The possibility of unrivaled image quality, coupled with perceived demand for a less risky alternative to X-ray CT and radionuclide scanning, led numerous firms to invest heavily in MRI research and development. Between 1976 and 1986, twenty-seven companies worldwide entered the intensely competitive MRI marketplace (Steinberg and Cohen 1984; Health Industry Manufacturers Association 1992). However, by 1991, only fifteen firms remained (Health Industry Manufacturers Association 1992). Sales of MRI devices have been in the billions of dollars.

The capsule profile of the industry presented here is a snapshot in time, based on a 1984 case study prepared for the OTA (Steinberg and Cohen 1984). The profile's presence is not intended to reflect current industry conditions but rather to illustrate how industrial analysis methods may be applied to an emerging technological industry. Changes in market conditions, corporate strategies, regulatory policies, and other factors are likely to modify the industry profile over time.

Employing a framework devised by Caves (1972) in his classic exploration of American industry, the case study assessed the MRI industry in terms of its structure (number, concentration, and size distribution of its firms and their ability to enter the marketplace); conduct (behavior of firms as they engage in competition, including their policies for setting prices and their strategies for differentiating their products from those of their rivals); and performance (how well firms achieve recognized goals of efficiency, profitability, and innovativeness). These dimensions are important because industry structure influences market conduct, which in turn affects performance.

Industry Structure

Seller Concentration

Of the twenty firms analyzed in the 1984 OTA report, eight had reached an advanced stage in which they had conducted extensive preproduction technical testing and had placed numerous MRI units in clinical sites outside their factories. Each also had developed a commercial prototype system that was available for clinical placement (table 3.1). By May 1984, three companies (Diasonics, Technicare, and Picker International) had received FDA premarket approval for the sale of their devices.

Three other firms had progressed by late 1983 to an intermediate stage of R&D in which engineering and experimental models had been completed but commercial prototype systems had either not yet been developed or not yet been installed in clinical sites. The extent of clinical study also varied widely among these manufacturers. The remaining nine companies were engaged in early R&D work, with only one (CGR Medical) having completed an experimental prototype on which clinical testing was expected to begin in 1984.

The industry had a remarkably multinational character, with firms based in the United States, Japan, West Germany, Great Britain, France, Israel, and the Netherlands (table 3.2). All but four of the firms had multiple product lines. Thirteen manufacturers were public corporations, some of them recognized giants in other fields (General Electric, Hitachi, Philips, Sanyo Electric, Siemens, and Toshiba). In terms of organizational structure, eleven manufacturers were independent firms, seven were wholly owned subsidiaries, and one was the medical systems division of a major public corporation (General Electric).

Because in 1983 the FDA considered MRI units to be investigational devices and they thus could not be sold at a profit in the United States,

---

TABLE 3.1.   The MRI Device Industry, October 1983

Companies in advanced stage of development
 Engineering model(s) complete; multiple clinical placements outside factory; ongoing clinical studies since 1982 or earlier; commercial prototype system(s) available for placement
  Bruker Instruments
  Diasonics, Inc.[a]
  Fonar Corp.
  Philips Medical Systems
  Picker International[a]
  Siemens Medical Systems
  Technicare Corp.[a]
  Elscint, Ltd.[b]

Companies in intermediate stage of development
 Engineering model(s) complete; limited clinical placements outside factory; generally limited clinical study thus far; commercial prototype system(s) generally not yet available for placement
  General Electric Co.
  M&D Technology, Ltd.[c]
  Toshiba Corp.

Companies in early stage of development[d]
 Engineering model(s) under development; no clinical placements outside factory; commercial prototype system(s) still to be defined
  ADAC Laboratories
  CGR Medical Corp.[e]
  Fischer Imaging Corp.[f]
  Hitachi, Ltd.
  JEOL USA
  Nalorac Cryogenics[g]
  OMR Technology[h]
  Sanyo Electric
  Shimadzu Corp.

Source: Steinberg and Cohen 1984.

[a]FDA granted premarket approval in spring 1984.

[b]In the advanced stage by August 1984.

[c]Had extensive clinical experience before the formation of the company.

[d]Other firms that announced plans to develop MR imaging systems are Ansoldo SPA, of Genoa, Italy, and Instrumentarium Oy, of Helsinki, Finland.

[e]Engineering model complete but clinical placement not expected until 1984.

[f]Had been developing its own MR imaging systems until acquired by Diasonics, Inc., in May 1983.

[g]Nalorac Cryogenics had two clinical placements by August 1984. However, these are small-bore, high-field-strength systems currently being used for research purposes only.

[h]Acquired by Xonics, Inc., in late 1983.

information on U.S. sales was unavailable. However, using the number of clinical placements as a proxy for sales, the industry appeared to be concentrated among four firms (Technicare, Picker International, Diasonics, and Siemens), which accounted for 79 percent of worldwide placements and 83 percent of U.S. placements (table 3.3).

Buyer Concentration

Unlike the high seller concentration in the industry, the number and diversity of potential buyers in the market was (and remains) extraordinarily large, covering research laboratories and various types of clinical facilities. Likely buyers in the clinical segment of the market

TABLE 3.2. The MRI Device Industry: Company Profile as of October 1983

Company	Ownership	Product Line (single or multi)	Organizational Structure	Country
ADAC Laboratories	Public	Multi	Independent	United States
Bruker Instruments	Private	Multi	Subsidiary of Bruker Physik R.A.G.	West Germany
CGR Medical Corp.	Private	Multi	Subsidiary of Thompson-Brandt	France
Diasonics, Inc.	Public	Multi	Independent	United States
Elscint, Ltd.	Public	Multi	Independent	Israel
Fonar Corp.	Public	Single	Independent	United States
General Electric Co.	Public	Multi	Independent[a]	United States
Hitachi, Ltd.	Public	Multi	Independent	Japan
JEOL USA	Public	Multi	Subsidiary of JEOL	Japan
M&D Technology, Ltd.	Private	Single	Independent	United Kingdom
Nalorac Cryogenics	Private	Single	Independent	United States
OMR Technology[b]	Private	Single	Independent	United States
Philips Medical Systems	Public	Multi	Subsidiary of North American Philips[c]	Netherlands
Picker International	Private	Multi	Subsidiary of GEC	United Kingdom
Sanyo Electric	Public	Multi	Independent	Japan
Shimadzu Corp.	Public	Multi	Independent	Japan
Siemens Medical Systems	Public	Multi	Subsidiary of Siemens A.G.	West Germany
Technicare Corp.	Public	Multi	Subsidiary of Johnson & Johnson	United States
Toshiba Corp.	Public	Multi	Independent	Japan

Source: Steinberg and Cohen 1984.

Note: Other firms that announced plans to develop MR imaging systems are Ansoldo SPA, of Genoa, Italy, and Instrumentation Oy, of Helsinki, Finland.

[a]Medical Systems Division is responsible for MR imaging R&D.

[b]Acquired by Xonics, Inc., in late 1983. Information on the merger not available.

[c]North American Philips is a trust associated with N. V. Philips of the Netherlands.

included hospitals, private radiology groups, and health maintenance organizations. The initial prime buyers were leading teaching hospitals and medical centers, followed by large urban and moderate-sized community hospitals with bed capacities of at least 200. The medical research community was also regarded as an important market segment. At least two firms (Nalorac Cryogenics and JEOL) were committed in 1983 to developing MRI systems specially intended for research applications.

Barriers to Market Entry

Despite industry dominance by a few large companies, small firms entered the market, but their entry depended heavily on their ability to attract capital, to develop collaborative research arrangements with academic centers, and to market their products aggressively. As of October 1983, three small, single-product firms constituted 16 percent of the industry. Among them, one (Fonar) had attained advanced R&D status and a second (M&D Technology) stood on the threshold of commercial production. To appreciate the importance of these achievements, it is necessary to examine the industry's early chronological development.

TABLE 3.3. The MRI Device Industry: Market Share as Reflected in Clinical Placements[a]

Company	Current Placement (as of August 1984)		Current Market Share (%)[b]	
	Worldwide	U.S. Only	Worldwide	U.S. Only
Technicare Corp.	44	36	30	39
Picker International	28	12	19	13
Diasonics, Inc.	23	19	16	20
Siemens Medical Systems	19	10	13	11
Fonar Corp.	9	6	6	6
Philips Medical Systems	5	1	3	1
Bruker Instruments	4	2	3	2
Elscint, Ltd.	4	2	3	2
General Electric Co.	4	3	3	3
M&D Technology, Ltd.[c]	2	0	1	0
Nalorac Cryogenics	2	2	1	2
Toshiba Corp.[c]	1	0	1	0
N	145	93	100	100

Source: Steinberg and Cohen 1984.

[a]MR imaging systems placed in clinical sites outside factory; human systems only (whole body and head).

[b]Expressed as a percentage of the total current placements. Detail may not sum to 100% because of rounding.

[c]As of October 1983.

The Origin and Development of the Industry

The birth of the MRI industry may be traced to 1976, when EMI began work on its prototype machine. In 1977, two other companies (Bruker Instruments and Philips Medical Systems) embarked on parallel courses of MRI research and development (figure 3.7). Between 1978 and 1980, five more firms entered the industry, followed by four new entries in 1981 and another four in 1982.

The pattern of MRI development generally followed four major steps:

1. A *corporate decision* was made in which the firm committed to investing in R&D and marshaling its resources to assemble a program whose objective was to produce an experimental prototype or engineering model.
2. An *experimental prototype* was produced, allowing the firm to initiate in-house testing that proceeded through successive stages (from inanimate objects to animals to human subjects) for the purpose of refining both system hardware and imaging techniques.
3. An *outside clinical placement* was achieved, in which the firm gathered critical data for improving the product and for defining the optimal configuration of a commercial system to be produced.
4. A *commercial prototype* was manufactured, based on thorough clinical testing of the engineering model, that aided the firm in specifying the best design for commercial production of its MRI device.

The time span required for the completion of these four steps decreased over the years. Whereas early entrants (e.g., EMI, Bruker, Philips, Siemens, and Fonar) each took two to four years to produce their first experimental systems, firms entering in 1981–83 either attained this goal or planned to attain it in significantly less time (see figure 3.7). The actual or projected time frames of later entrants were compressed by strong competitive pressures and by an expanding knowledge base conferred on them by the pioneering efforts of their predecessors.

Pathways to market entry varied widely, with essentially four routes being followed, sometimes simultaneously:

Company[a]	1974	1975	1976	1977	1978	1979	1980	1981	1982	1983	1984	1985
EMI[b]			D		E			C,W				
Bruker Instruments				D		E			C	M		
Philips Medical Systems				D				E,C		M		
Siemens Medical Systems					D		E		C	M		
Fonar Corp[c]					D		E,C			M		
Technicare Corp[d]							D	E	C	M		
CGR Medical Corp.							D		E		(C,M)	
General Electric Co.[e]								D		E,C	(M)	
Diasonics Inc.[f]									D,E,C	M		
Picker International[g]									D,E,C	M		
Elscint Ltd.									D	E	C,M	
Nalorac Cryogenics[h]	D		A						D		(E,C)	(M)
M&D Technology Ltd.[i]									D,E	C	(M)	
ADAC Laboratories									D		(E)	(M)
Fischer Imaging Corp.[j]									D	A		
JEOL USA									D		(E)	

Note: Information on chronology of events not available for Ansoldo SPA, Hitachi Ltd., Instrumentation Oy, OMR Technology (now Xonics), Sanyo Electric, Shimadzu Corp., and Toshiba Corp. D = corporate decision to invest in R&D efforts for MR imaging; E = first experimental prototype/engineering model available; C = first clinical placement of an MR imaging unit outside the company's plant; M = first commercial/marketing prototype system available for placement; A = acquisition of company by other firm; W = withdrawal of company from the industry. Letter symbols in parentheses ( ) indicate projected events in the future. Dotted lines to the left of decision (D) points reflect R&D work that preceded formal company involvement or formation.

[a] In order of market entry based on corporate decision to invest in MR imaging.

[b] Began MRI R&D in 1976; produced first engineering model in 1978; sold its MR imaging technology to Picker International in October 1981.

[c] Founded in 1978 as RAANEX Corp.; became Fonar Corp. in 1980.

[d] Parent company, Johnson & Johnson, made initial commitment as early as 1977, but major R&D effort did not begin until the acquisition of Technicare in 1979.

[e] Early R&D work in phosphorus spectroscopy began in 1978, but firm corporate commitment to MR imaging was not made until 1980.

[f] Initial R&D began as a University of California, San Francisco (UCSF), project with outside funding. In 1976, the Pfizer Corp. began funding the work. In 1981, Diasonics, Inc., purchased the rights to all patentable MRI technology developed under the UCSF-Pfizer agreement.

[g] Formed in April 1981 after GEC of England acquired Picker Corp. and merged it with GEC Medical and Cambridge Medical Instruments. GEC of England had begun MR imaging R&D in 1977. In October 1981, Picker International purchased all MR imaging technology that had been developed independently by EMI of England since 1976.

[h] Began early R&D on superconducting MRI systems in 1976. In 1977, the company was acquired by Nicolet Instruments Corp. In 1981, the original founder of Nalorac Cryogenics purchased the company back from Nicolet and reaffirmed its commitment to developing MR imaging systems.

[i] Formed in 1982 to commercially develop the MR imaging system that had evolved from the work of Professor Mallard at Aberdeen, Scotland, since 1974.

[j] Made decision to pursue MRI technology in 1982; acquired by Diasonics Inc. in 1983.

Fig. 3.7. Chronological development of the MRI device industry. (From Steinberg and Cohen 1984.)

- *Government-supported R&D.* EMI entered the MRI market in 1976 with grant support from the British government. British government support of university-based R&D at Nottingham and Aberdeen also later benefited Picker International and M&D Technology, respectively, when they decided to enter the MRI market. Three firms (Bruker, Philips, and Siemens) received grants from the West German government but did so only after having initiated MRI program development with company resources.
- *University-based R&D.* All of the small, single-product firms emerged as a result of university-based R&D. Several larger firms also looked to this pathway for assistance in designing their devices, but it was not the primary route for market entry.
- *Acquired technology.* Two firms successfully employed this strategy to accelerate their market entry and their progress toward advanced R&D. Picker International in 1981 purchased all MRI technology developed by EMI since 1976. That same year, Diasonics purchased the rights to all patentable MRI technology developed by Pfizer, thus enabling Diasonics to produce a commercial prototype system within two years of entry.
- *Internally based R&D.* The remaining firms relied on internal R&D operations to develop their prototypes, without benefit of government funding or off-the-shelf technology.

Diversification of Firms

Firms in the industry displayed remarkable diversity in their product lines and operations. Of the fifteen multiproduct firms, all but two (Bruker and JEOL) manufactured diagnostic imaging equipment other than MRI. Twelve companies (63 percent) manufactured non–health care–related products, ranging from assorted electrical equipment and household appliances to electron microscopes and instruments for testing. In many cases, sales of these products far exceeded those of health care–related products. Such diversity offered several benefits, including technical expertise gained from other R&D activities, accelerated MRI product development based on corporate experience in related fields, and an enlarged R&D resource base resulting from sales in non–health care fields.

Acquisition and Merger Activity

Most acquisitions and mergers in the industry were oriented toward product extension involving other diagnostic imaging modalities. Two of these explicitly involved MRI. In one instance, Diasonics acquired the rights to MRI technology developed under an agreement between Pfizer and the University of California at San Francisco (UCSF) Radiological Imaging Laboratory. In the other, Fischer Imaging was acquired by Diasonics in a product extension merger whose prime target was Fischer's line of X-ray equipment.

Market extension mergers occurred less frequently, but one case stood out—Picker International's acquisition of the MRI technology developed by EMI of Great Britain. As with Diasonics' purchase of the Pfizer-UCSF technology, Picker used its EMI technology to accelerate market entry and to catapult to the industry forefront.

Three other mergers involved vertical integration. In one case, integration was backward (Technicare purchased Magnet Corporation of America to build superconducting magnet systems). The remaining two mergers involved forward integration, in which Diasonics acquired companies to expand its sales and distributorship networks to specific geographic areas.

Industry Conduct

Product Pricing Policies

Because manufacturers in 1983 had not yet received FDA premarket approval to sell MRI devices, the companies had little experience with product pricing, and this experience was only outside the United States. Interviews with MRI manufacturers at the time suggested that the sales price of a resistive magnet system would likely range between $800,000 and $1.2 million. Superconducting magnet systems, depending on size and field strength, were expected to command prices between $1 million and $3 million, with the median expectation closer to $2 million.

When queried about sales price, most manufacturers felt that the future company market share would be determined instead by nonprice factors that would differentiate a company's products from those of its competitors. Only four firms viewed the sales price as key to competition for market share. Two planned to segment the market by offering less expensive, lower-magnet-strength MRI systems to community hospitals and private radiology groups lacking the resources of larger organizations. Two other firms believed that larger companies would eventually use predatory pricing policies to weaken and drive out smaller competitors. Such policies, in the long run, would likely lead to greater industry concentration after a shakeout period.

Nonprice Competition

Interviews with manufacturers identified nine nonprice factors considered important to MRI product differentiation. These elements, in descending order of importance, were

1. *Image quality.* High-resolution images of soft tissue in the head and body were considered essential to product sales.
2. *Product features and capabilities.* Product features (e.g., magnet type and field strength, bore size, computer system) and product capabilities (e.g., imaging and spectral analysis capabilities) were also considered important to sales.
3. *Product reliability.* Product reliability was thought to be valued by buyers, so any perceived lack of it could have serious adverse effect on sales.
4. *Product service.* Timely, responsive maintenance and repair service was considered important both for ensuring client satisfaction and for preserving company image.
5. *Delivery time.* Delivery time was very important to some buyers but was expected to decrease in importance.
6. *Long-term viability of the manufacturer.* The larger, well-established firms believed that size and tradition were valuable to sales; the smaller, newer firms argued that product characteristics (e.g., features, capabilities, image quality, and reliability) would take precedence over company characteristics in determining future sales.
7. *Guarantee against technological obsolescence.* With an evolving technology, such as MRI, guarantees against obsolescence in the short run were difficult to make, but some manufacturers felt a need to reassure clients that equipment could be upgraded to accommodate changing needs or future advances in technology.
8. *Collaborative research.* For firms in premarket stages of R&D, collaborative research arrangements were vital to outside clinical placements, but this was less likely to be important to future sales.
9. *Training and education.* A few firms believed that training for buyers would be an important feature of future marketing and sales strategies, but this factor would not rank high overall.

In general, product differentiation was viewed as an important component of each manufacturer's nonprice competition strategy. Vertical integration, however, had implications for production costs and hence for product-pricing policies. It also represented a weapon that firms could use to coerce rivals and to influence market entry of other firms. For example, forward integration of distributorship networks could impede other firms' efforts to sell their products in the same locales; similarly, backward integration of magnet suppliers could bar entry to potential competitors not capable of producing their own magnets. Over the long run, vertical integration was more likely to influence industry conduct (i.e., pricing and product differentiation) than industry structure (i.e., market entry).

Industry Performance

Data on advertising and sales in the MRI industry were virtually nonexistent in 1983 as a result of FDA prohibition of sales promotion and profit making and because of the proprietary nature of such information. Thus, the relative efficiency with which various firms allocated their resources to the building of MRI devices could not be determined. However, as soon as firms obtained FDA approval, promotional activities abounded. Lack of information on sales also precluded an assessment of industry profitability, even though MRI sales were projected to become an important source of company revenues for many manufacturers (Emmitt and Lasersohn 1983).

In conclusion, the rapidly changing character of the MRI industry made the prediction of industry performance—and, to a lesser degree, industry structure and conduct—exceedingly difficult. The dynamism of this industry and its constituent firms nevertheless stands as an interesting example of emerging technological industries in general.

Epilogue: 1984 to the Present

Since 1984, the use of MRI has diffused widely in the United States despite efforts in the name of cost containment to limit its spread. Over time, advances in MRI technology led to new clinical applications and to new functional forms of the imagers that were not even contemplated when the devices first began to diffuse—perfusion MRI, diffusion-weighted MRI, and echo planar imaging for imaging blood flow and evaluating ischemic stroke (Norkin 1993); magnetic resonance elastography (MRI in combination with sound waves) for differentiating between hard cancerous lesions and softer normal tissues (Skolnick

1996); MRI-guided biopsy using a specially designed interventional MRI system with an open configuration in the magnet, allowing the physician to enter the area surrounding the patient (Evens 1996); and magnetic resonance angiography as a clinical alternative to conventional X-ray contrast angiography in many regions of the body (AHCPR 1994; Goldsmith 1994; Evens 1996). In the case of magnetic resonance angiography, for example, a recent meta-analysis concluded that it is highly accurate for the assessment of lower extremity arterial disease (Koelemay et al. 2001), and a study of three-dimensional coronary magnetic resonance angiography found it to be accurate in detecting coronary stenoses in the proximal and middle segments while reliably ruling out left main coronary artery or three-vessel disease (Kim et al. 2001).

During the 1980s, the perceived value of MRI compared with alternative imaging modalities was so great that professional pressure acted as a countervailing force against certificate-of-need policies and payment systems that sought to control its adoption. By 1991, approximately 2,000 units were in operation, and Medicare Part B (outpatient) payments had grown from $37 million in 1986 to almost $237 million in 1990 (GAO 1992a). By 1993, 19 percent of all general short-term acute-care hospitals were providing MRI with fixed equipment, according to American Hospital Association survey data (Baker 1997). By 1995, 3,705 (fixed and mobile) sites nationwide provided MRI (Baker 1997; Baker and Wheeler 1998). By early 1998, the total number of MRI units in the United States had risen to an estimated 4,000 (Schrader 1998).

By late 1990, the industry shakeout foreshadowed in 1984 had left only fifteen survivors, with General Electric the dominant force in the MRI market, having acquired the MRI technologies of three competitors (most notably, Technicare and CGR Medical) and having installed 849 units in the United States alone (Diemunsch 1990; Health Industry Manufacturers Association 1992). Other firms in the U.S. market ranked as follows: Siemens was second, with 323 placements; Toshiba was third, with 265, including products from its 1989 purchase of Diasonics MRI Division; Picker International was fourth, with 205; Fonar was fifth, with 130; and Philips was sixth, with 106 (Diemunsch 1990). No other company had more than 40 placements, and few early entrants remained—Elscint, for example, had 30 installations, and Bruker had only 6 (Diemunsch 1990).

Over the next decade, the top firms solidified their market positions through aggressive acquisition strategies that enabled them to broaden their imaging technology offerings beyond MRI and CT, especially in the areas of nuclear medicine and positron emission tomography (PET). In a two-year period (1999–2000), General Electric acquired SMV (a nuclear medicine company); Siemens acquired Shared Medical Systems (a medical information systems company) and Acuson (an ultrasound company); and Philips acquired or announced plans to acquire ATL Ultrasound, ADAC Laboratories (for its nuclear medicine and PET), and Agilent Technologies' Healthcare Solutions Group (C. Becker 2000b). Today, General Electric is the acknowledged global leader in imaging technology and medical information systems, with $7 billion in annual sales of conventional and digital X ray, CT, MRI, ultrasound, PET, nuclear medicine, health care information systems, and patient monitoring systems (GE Medical Systems 2000). General Electric, Siemens, and Philips represent the core firms that dominate the industry.

The future potential of MRI seems virtually unlimited, with extremely powerful magnet systems (4.0 Tesla field strength) now being used to investigate brain activity in such disorders as depression, schizophrenia, and substance abuse (Tye 2001). General Electric also has unveiled its newest model of MRI (called Excite) which produces higher quality images four times faster than current models (Winslow 2002). MRI technology undoubtedly will undergo further refinement as the industry looks for new ways to capitalize on this and other imaging modalities, such as the newest generation of imagers (including GE's Millennium Hawkeye, SMV's POSiTRACE, and Siemens/CTI's Biograph) that combine CT with PET to produce more precise images than either technology alone and at double the speed of PET (C. Becker 2000a).

4

The Diffusion of New Medical Technology
Alan B. Cohen

To address the diffusion question posed in chapter 2—whether medical technologies are diffusing too swiftly or too slowly into medical practice—we must trace the path of new technology as it emerges from the laboratory and the factory to become part of the health care delivery system. In this chapter, we explore the theories and patterns of technology diffusion, with attention to examples of specific technologies. In addition, we examine the key factors that influence technology diffusion, stimulating it in some instances while impeding it in others.

What Is Diffusion?

In the broadest sense, *diffusion* is "the dispersion of ideas, techniques, practices, knowledge, information and products to adopters at various distances from an innovation's point of origin" (Gordon, MacEachron, and Fisher 1975, 201). In the context of medicine, diffusion is "the process by which a technology enters and becomes a part of the health care system" (Banta, Behney, and Willems 1981, 53). Taken together, these definitions imply that the diffusion process in medicine encompasses the sequence of events occurring between two points in time—the point of dispersion (when a new medical technology stands on the threshold of being introduced into clinical practice) and the point of termination (when the technology reaches its greatest penetration of the medical marketplace and either attains widespread acceptance by practitioners or falls into disuse). In the narrower context of certificate-of-need (CON) programs, *diffusion* also is used to describe the physical distribution or allocation of medical technology among individual health care providers, such as hospitals (Cohen and Cohodes 1982). However, we employ here a broad definition in which *diffusion* includes decisions to adopt and to use new technology (Banta, Behney, and Willems 1981).

The interaction between the adoption and the use of technology is illustrated in figure 4.1. In this paradigm, originally proposed by Fineberg (1979), technology diffusion leads to four possible consequences. Positive outcomes are achieved either when a beneficial technology is adopted, resulting in "appropriate use," or when a nonbeneficial or harmful technology is ignored, resulting in "appropriate nonuse." The remaining two outcomes pose negative implications for the quality of medical care, resulting either in inappropriate use of a nonbeneficial technology or inappropriate nonuse of a valuable one. Fineberg termed these complementary situations errors of overdiffusion and underdiffusion, respectively. To minimize such errors, one must consider not only the rate and extent of a technology's adoption but also its mode of use by potential adopters.

Theories of the Diffusion of Technology

In chapter 3, we acknowledged our debt to the fields of management science and industrial organization, economics, social psychology, sociology, and political science for their contributions to our understanding of innovation and, by extension, of biomedical innovation. Although we focus here on the process by which new medical technologies are communicated and disseminated, the diffusion literature not surprisingly draws heavily from the same disciplines and fields. But it also contains studies targeted specifically at medical technology. Among the earliest works were those of Coleman, Katz, and Menzel (1966), who analyzed the role of interphysician communication in facilitating the adoption of a drug (gammanym) into practice; Comroe and Dripps (1977), who studied the diffusion patterns of the ten leading advances in cardiovascular and pulmonary medicine occurring between 1945 and 1975; and Gordon and Fisher (1975), who synthesized findings from the literature to produce an agenda for policy and planning. In two of the most often cited studies in the area, Russell (1976, 1979) traced the diffusion of several major medical advances among American hospitals after World War II and analyzed the factors responsible for the adoption of these advances.

ADOPTION DECISION

	Technology Adopted	Technology *Not* Adopted
"Good"	Appropriate Use	Error of *Underdiffusion*
"Bad"	Error of *Overdiffusion*	Appropriate Nonuse

NET VALUE
OF TECHNOLOGY

Fig. 4.1. Consequences of technology diffusion. (From Fineberg 1979.)

Since 1980, however, the literature has expanded only modestly, with new case studies of individual medical innovations modeled mostly after Russell's work. However, as these new reports come to light, it is increasingly clear that classical theories of technology diffusion may not be as relevant to health care as to other fields. Consequently, new theories are needed to explain the dynamics of the diffusion process in a changing health care environment.

Classical Diffusion Theory

Classical diffusion theory holds that innovations are adopted by individuals who become the first in their community to use them and then pass along the information to others (Rogers 1962, 1995; Rogers and Shoemaker 1971). Research has focused on the characteristics of the innovation and the adopter, the role of communication networks among adopters, and the nature of the information passed. But, as some scholars have noted, classical theory contains several limitations, including its proinnovation bias, which treats new ideas as intrinsically good (Banta, Behney, and Willems 1981), its inability to explain adoption by units larger than single individuals (Greer 1977), and its linear view of one-way knowledge transfer from a source to a receiver (Rogers 1995). These weaknesses are especially troublesome in the case of health care, where not all technology diffusion is desirable, where organizations— not individuals—often are the primary adopters, and where two-way learning between the innovator and the adopter often is the norm.

Classical theorists have attempted to deal with the first two of these issues by assuming either that individuals in positions of authority act on behalf of their organizations or that organizations themselves behave as individuals (Greer 1977). However, neither assumption adequately explains observed experience with the adoption of medical technology. To explain two-way learning, classical theorists have moved toward the use of convergence models of diffusion (Rogers 1995), but such models still fail to capture the full experience with medical technology. Health care organizations are complex and comprise multiple constituencies (see the discussion of political theories of diffusion later in this chapter). Health care organizations do not behave like unitary decision makers, and their decisions to adopt and use new technology are subject to both environmental forces and internal influences that are not easily ex-plained by classical theory. Consequently, diffusion research has turned increasingly toward organizational, economic, and political theories of decision making.

Organizational and Economic Theories of Diffusion

Organizational models of technology diffusion are based on the work of organization theorists (e.g., Simon 1957; March and Simon 1958; Cyert and March 1963; J. D. Thompson 1967; Perrow 1972; Zaltman, Duncan, and Holbek 1973; E. B. Roberts 1981, 1982). Early research con-centrated on organizations' decision-making processes, with particular emphasis on structural factors that influence technology adoption. For example, E. B. Roberts (1981, 1982) stressed the importance of strategic variables in organizational decisions to adopt new technologies (see chapter 3), while Zaltman, Duncan, and Holbek (1973) argued that cen-tralized decision-making processes and formalized rule systems play key roles in technology diffusion. Economic theories of technology dif-fusion, conversely, emphasize such variables as hospital size, owner-ship, teaching status, consumer demand, capital and operating costs, and relative profit advantage gained by the adopter through increased efficiency and/or productivity (Utterback 1974; Warner 1974, 1975; Russell 1976, 1977, 1979).

The early literature on technology diffusion was filled with contradictory findings regarding the significance of organizational or economic variables, and because most health care organizations at that time behaved differently from profit-seeking firms in other industries, theorists were left to ponder the explanatory power of these models in helping us to understand medical technology diffusion (Warner 1974; Greer 1977). In fact, one early empirical study of Boston-area hospitals (Cromwell et al. 1975) found that economic factors (e.g., estimated demand for services, and the capital and operating costs of technology) were less important to decisions regarding capital equipment purchases than were a technology's prestige-enhancing qualities for attracting both patients and physicians to the hospital. (See chapter 5 for a detailed discussion of technology adoption in hospitals and the role of prestige enhancement in such decisions.)

However, in today's highly competitive health care environment, marked by managed care and integrated service-delivery systems, economic and organizational models of technology diffusion are again growing in relevance and importance. The renewed interest in studying the effects of market competition, regulation, and strategic forces on technology diffusion is evident in the expanding number of published reports on such technologies as open-heart surgery (Chernew Hayward, and Scanlon 1996), laparoscopic cholecystectomy (Fendrick et al. 1994; Chernew, Fendrick, and Hirth 1997), MRI (Teplensky 1990; Teplensky et al. 1993, 1995; Baker 1997; Baker and Wheeler 1998), lithotripsy (Bryce and Cline 1998), and renal dialysis (Hirth, Chernew, and Orzol 2000). In addition, new studies examining the economic effects of medical technology—for example, productivity gains and returns on investment—suggest that the long-term benefits of innovation and diffusion are considerable for a range of conditions, including cardiovascular disease, depression, childbirth, and cataract surgery (Cutler and McClellan 1996, 2001; McClellan 1996; Murphy and Topel 2000; Cutler and Berndt 2001; McClellan and Kessler 2002).

Political Theories of Technology Diffusion

Another promising area of theoretical work centers on political elements of decision making in health care organizations. Politically based theories explicitly recognize such organizations as complex entities composed of diverse groups of actors (managers, trustees, physicians, nurses, and other personnel), each of which brings different interests and priorities to bear on decisions to adopt technology. Research in this area has been directed toward analyzing the political resources (power and influence) and relationships of these actors in institutional decision-making processes and the influence on decisions of external environmental forces, such as consumer and community groups, third-party payers, governmental agencies, other providers, technology manufacturers, and private philanthropies (Greer 1977; Banta, Behney, and Willems 1981).

Although its contributions to diffusion research have been limited thus far, political theory seems well suited to the task of deciphering the pluralistic decision-making behavior of health care organizations. For example, in an early study of technology adoption in Milwaukee-area hospitals, Greer and Zakhar (1977, 1979) examined decisions affecting three medical technologies—open-heart surgery, phacoemulsification (an ophthalmic procedure), and X-ray CT. The authors identified three groups of physicians—community practitioners, hospital-based physicians, and referral specialists—who differed in their attitudes toward new technology, their affiliations with hospitals, and their relationships with one another. Finding that community physicians tended to be more skeptical of new technology than did hospital-based physicians and that community physicians were less likely to use their patients to "leverage" technology adoption decisions in hospitals than was originally thought, Greer and Zakhar (1979) theorized that hospital managers—acting alone or in concert with selected physicians—made decisions regarding technology adoption in anticipation of their medical staff's desires rather than in response to them.

In a later expansion of this work involving twelve technologies in twenty-five community hospitals, Greer (1985) observed that these institutions differed markedly from teaching hospitals in their adoption dynamics. The study also produced a new tripartite typology of hospital decision-making systems that considered all relevant internal actors with respect to goals and objectives, bases of influence, methods of structuring decisions, and decision processes employed (see chapter 5).

With organizational restructuring rampant in American hospitals today, the dynamics of decision making in these institutions and in large integrated service-delivery networks also are changing, particularly in ways that may lend themselves as much to political theories as to organizational and economic theories of technology adoption (see chapter 5). Moreover, political theories may help to compare diffusion policies across nations, as in the case of a recent cross-national study by

R. Klein and H. Sturm (2002) that analyzed the rationing strategies adopted in four countries (United States, Britain, Germany, and Sweden) to control the use of Viagra (a lifestyle drug prescribed for erectile dysfunction). Therefore, political models are likely to become more valuable in the future. We turn now to the basic patterns and determinants of technology diffusion.

Patterns of Technology Diffusion

Medical technologies diffuse into clinical practice at different rates of speed and to different degrees. It is common practice to depict the diffusion process graphically as the extent of adoption over time. The graph produced is called a diffusion curve. Time is usually shown in years on the horizontal axis. On the vertical axis, the extent of adoption may be portrayed as the number of technological units dispersed (e.g., devices sold, equipment placed, or procedures performed), as the number or percentage of patients treated, or as the percentage of adopters reached (e.g., potential hospitals or physicians adopting the technology). In each case, either annual figures or cumulative figures over time may be used.

The Classic Diffusion Curve

The classic diffusion curve typically takes the form of an S-shaped curve that traces a technology's absorption into the health care community. As illustrated in figure 4.2, the classic diffusion curve contains four parts, or phases. The initiation phase begins with a technology's emergence from development and its introduction into clinical practice. The curve starts out flat and gradually slopes upward. Adopters of an emerging technology are considered pioneers—usually a few selected medical centers that test the new technology to learn about its capabilities and limitations. Because a principal goal of this phase is to gain clinical experience with the technology, Whitted (1981) referred to it as the experiential phase.

The acceleration phase (what Whitted [1981] called the contagion phase) marks the period in which technology adoption takes off. The curve steepens sharply as the pace of diffusion quickens. In this stage, the technology is considered new, and health care providers who adopt it during its ascendancy are recognized as early adopters and tend to be large academic institutions noted for their innovative qualities.

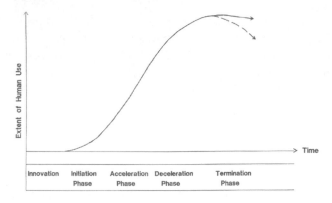

Fig. 4.2. Diffusion of medical technology: The classic model. (Adapted from OTA 1976.)

The deceleration phase begins when the technology reaches the midpoint of its ascendancy. Although still rising, the curve shows signs of a slackening pace. This corresponds generally to the adoption of an established technology by secondary institutions, or so-called late adopters. Toward the end of this phase, the curve begins to flatten out once again, indicating that the technology is approaching an asymptotic limit.

The termination phase represents the period in which the technology reaches its diffusion apex. The curve now has the appearance of a steady-state plateau and marks the maximal extent of technology adoption. If the technology has become widely accepted in medical practice, the curve remains flat and stable. If, conversely, the technology has fallen into disfavor or has been superseded by some other technology, the curve instead slopes downward as a sign of the eventual partial or complete abandonment of an obsolete technology.

Few medical technologies ever attain this perfect, idealized diffusion curve, although many follow the general pattern with varying speeds and degrees of acceptance. Early adopters of technology frequently have been academic medical centers and major teaching hospitals interested in enhancing their prestige and providing their medical staffs with the latest opportunities for clinical research, teaching, and patient care. Late adopters, by contrast, typically have been smaller community hospitals, whose needs and motivations for adopting new technology differ from those of the large institutions, and urban public hospitals, whose ability to adopt innovations often is hindered by constrained resources and by the politics of CON decisions in some locales (Banta 1980a).

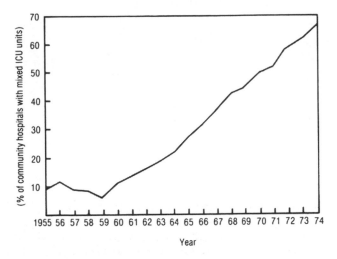

Fig. 4.3. The diffusion of intensive care units in the United States. (From Banta, Behney, and Willems 1981.)

Examples of Technology Diffusion

Several examples of classic technology diffusion in hospitals may be found in the pathbreaking work of Louise Russell (1976, 1977, 1979). As shown in figure 4.3, intensive care units in the United States diffused slowly at first, reaching 10 percent of all community hospitals in the late 1950s. Beginning in 1959, the rate of diffusion accelerated rapidly, so that by 1974 nearly 70 percent of hospitals had adopted intensive care units, and the curve continued to climb steadily.

Differences in the diffusion rates among hospitals of varying bed size may be seen in figure 4.4. Institutions with 200–299 beds adopted intensive care units and postoperative recovery rooms at faster paces than institutions with 100–199 beds. Figure 4.5 graphically displays these institutional differences over time for several other technologies, including cobalt therapy, open-heart surgery, and inpatient and outpatient renal dialysis (Russell 1979). In each case, larger hospitals were likely to adopt the technology sooner.

Diversity in diffusion patterns may be seen in figure 4.6, which derives from work by Greer (1985). Of twelve technologies studied, only five (fiber-optic endoscope, automated batch analyzer, radioimmunoassay, ultrasonic imaging, and radionuclide scanner) approximated the classic diffusion curve. Four others (fetal monitor, CT scanner, coronary artery bypass surgery, and neonatal intensive care) demonstrated

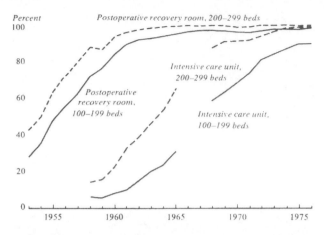

Fig. 4.4. The diffusion of intensive care units and postoperative recovery rooms. Percentages of voluntary nonprofit hospitals in the United States with postoperative recovery rooms and intensive care units are shown by size of hospital, 1953–76. Gaps in the lines reflect years in which the facility was omitted from the survey. (From Russell 1976.)

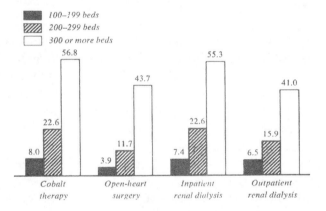

Fig. 4.5. Percentage of nonfederal short-term hospitals with cobalt therapy, open-heart surgery, and renal dialysis, by size of hospital, 1976. (From Russell 1979.)

faster-than-average rates of adoption but also showed attenuated levels of adoption. In the cases of CT, bypass surgery, and neonatal intensive care, limited adoption was likely the result of governmental policies that constrained diffusion and encouraged regionalization of specialized services, but in the case of fetal monitors, nonadoption by some hospitals probably reflected their lack of obstetric services. As for the remaining three technologies, laser surgery at that time was an

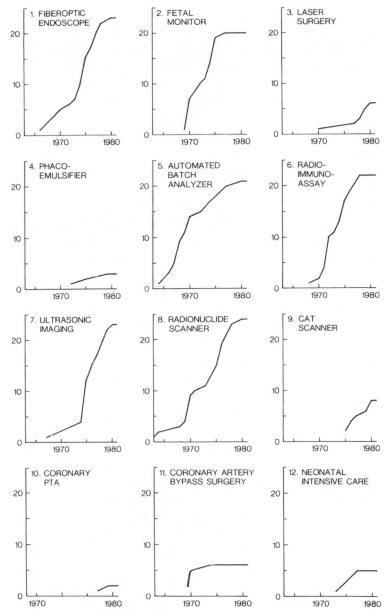

Fig. 4.6. Technology diffusion in twenty-five southeastern Wisconsin hospitals. (From Greer 1985.)

experimental procedure awaiting technical refinement, phacoemulsification appeared to have a bleak future, and coronary percutaneous transluminal angioplasty had not yet realized its potential.

A completely different pattern of diffusion occasionally emerges, such as when a technology is quickly adopted after its initial introduction. A prime example was the rapid adoption of chemotherapy for the treatment of childhood leukemia (U.S. Congress, OTA 1976). As shown in figure 4.7, chemotherapy experienced a brief initiation phase and an exceedingly sharp acceleration phase in the span of five years after its introduction in 1946. During this period, it was used to treat almost 80 percent of patients with leukemia.

Warner (1975) termed this unusually rapid diffusion pattern the desperation-reaction model because it represented a reflexive response by the medical community to problems for which no other therapeutic solutions existed. In this case, chemotherapy, although not yet proven to be safe and effective, was adopted swiftly in the hope that it might save lives. The lack of alternative treatments, coupled with the lethal nature of leukemia at that time, spurred physicians to use the drug more frequently than they otherwise might have in the presence of evaluative information or in the face of less dire circumstances. The sudden fall in its use between 1951 and 1953 suggests that physicians likely reevaluated its merits in the light of evidence on its side effects. However, its expanded use over the next decade reflected its ultimate acceptance into established cancer therapy.

Other examples of desperation-reaction patterns of diffusion include protease inhibitors and various drugs for treating AIDS/HIV and autologous bone marrow transplantation in conjunction with high-dose chemotherapy for treating metastatic breast cancer. In each case, the lethality of the disease, the absence of an effective cure, and strong political pressure from patient advocacy groups drove the diffusion process; however, in the case of breast cancer, evidence from a recent clinical trial has seriously questioned the value of bone marrow transplantation for treating breast cancer and may have ended a decade-long debate between clinicians and cancer patient advocates (Stadtmauer et al. 2000; Mello and Brennan 2001). Also fitting the pattern is the rapid diffusion of Viagra for the treatment of a nonlethal condition, male erectile dysfunction. In this instance, consumer demand has driven diffusion of this lifestyle drug in the absence of alternative therapies (Klein and Sturm 2002). Such swift diffusion of new drugs, though, points out a troubling dilemma faced by potential adopters—whether to adopt the

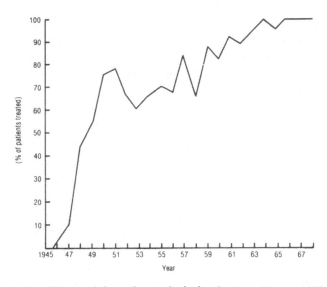

Fig. 4.7. The diffusion of chemotherapy for leukemia. (From Warner 1975. Redrawn in Banta, Behney, and Willems 1981.)

drug when evaluative information on clinical safety and efficacy is either limited or nonexistent. Although this problem is generic to virtually all technologies that are emerging or new, it is especially harsh in situations demanding desperate remedies, such as in the case of new drug therapies for AIDS/HIV and for drug-resistant forms of tuberculosis. As Banta, Behney, and Willems (1981, 55) noted years ago, "the aggregate behavior of many desperate physicians may result in the extensive and premature diffusion of technologies that are incompletely developed, inefficacious, or possibly even dangerous." The value of linking the evaluation of new technologies directly to the diffusion process is discussed in chapters 6–8 as well as in chapter 15. For now, it is important to recognize not only that the rational adoption of technology cannot be accomplished without the benefit of good information on efficacy, safety, and cost-effectiveness but also that ethical considerations on humanitarian grounds may sometimes influence the rapid diffusion of a new technology before full information is available, as in the case of AZT, where clinical trials were suspended so that compassionate use of the drug in treating AIDS and HIV could occur swiftly.

The literature also contains notable examples of the abandonment of technologies once randomized clinical trials revealed them to be inefficacious (Barsamian 1977; Finkelstein et al. 1981), but most medical technologies never undergo such rigorous or timely evaluation. Perhaps the most celebrated case of failed technology was gastric freezing, a procedure developed as an alternative to surgical intervention for duodenal ulcer (Miao 1977; Fineberg 1979). Introduced in 1962 by Dr. Owen Wangensteen, a prominent surgeon and former president of the American College of Surgeons, gastric freezing was intended to reduce the secretory activity of stomach cells that produce gastric acid, thereby alleviating irritation and promoting the healing of the stomach wall. The technology was quickly adopted and, over the next seven years, approximately 2,500 units were sold and at least 25,000 patients were treated in the United States (Fineberg 1979). The diffusion of gastric freezing machines sold by one manufacturer (Swenko) is depicted in figure 4.8. Factors contributing to the rise of this technology included Wangensteen's professional stature and outspoken advocacy for the procedure, the risks associated with alternative surgical treatments, heightened public expectations of its benefits, the relative ease with which it could be performed, and the economic benefits to physicians performing it (Fineberg 1979).

Beginning in 1963, however, expressions of doubt about the clinical value of gastric freezing appeared in the literature, including an editorial in the *New England Journal of Medicine* (Miao 1977). Several well-designed clinical studies were mounted, and by 1964 the first of these concluded not only that gastric freezing was ineffective but also that the risks associated with it were substantial (Fineberg 1979). Medical interest began to wane, and by 1966 the clinical use of gastric freezing in the United States effectively ended. Studies of various designs continued to appear, many of them unfavorable in their assessments of the technology. By 1969, at least thirty-three studies had been published, including six randomized, double-blind trials. Although the abandonment of gastric freezing could be attributed in part to the dissuasive influence of published reports, the findings of the most convincing studies (the randomized trials, including a multicenter collaborative study) were not published until after many physicians had already decided the technology's fate.

While this example illustrates a lack of coordination between proper clinical evaluation and the diffusion process (McKinlay 1981), it also calls to mind the fact that many physicians persist in using treatments that well-controlled studies have proven inefficacious or even harmful (T. C. Chalmers 1974). The lamentable facts are, as Fineberg (1979, 189)

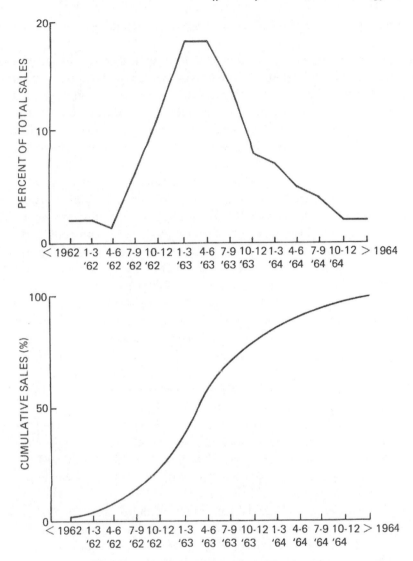

Fig. 4.8. The diffusion of gastric freezing. Sales of gastric freezing machines by leading manufacturer, Swenko of Minneapolis, Minnesota. (From Fineberg 1979.)

suggested, that "when finally published, an elegant study may be too late, and, even if timely, it may have little effect on medical practice." The appropriate relationship between diffusion and technology evaluation is examined later in this book and particularly in chapter 15.

Factors Influencing the Diffusion of Medical Technology

As the preceding examples suggest, a variety of factors may shape the character, rate, and extent of diffusion of medical technology. The same incentives and disincentives that govern systemwide behavior of hospitals, physicians, and patients essentially also influence the spread of new technology. Using a general framework developed by Whitted (1981), the various forces may be arrayed in four discrete categories:

- *Environment*-specific factors, which include third-party payment policies; governmental regulatory policies; the availability of capital for technological R&D; competitive pressures in the medical marketplace; perceived consumer demand and public expectations; the severity and urgency of specific medical problems; promotional efforts by technology manufacturers; influences of medical education and specialization; and the threat (whether implied or real) of malpractice litigation.
- *Organization*-specific variables, which include compatibility with organizational goals and objectives; decision makers' attitudes toward risk, uncertainty, and innovation; ease of implementation within the organizational framework; practitioners' and others' perceived need for the technology; and organizational experience and expertise with similar technologies.
- *Personnel*-specific factors, which include types of skills required for operation of the technology; degree of staff training (or retraining) required for implementation; staff attitudes toward the technology; and expectations for improved staff productivity, efficiency, and accuracy.
- *Technology*-specific variables, which refer to properties or attributes of the technology, including relative advantage (as defined by Rogers; see chapter 3); ease of use; versatility as a multipurpose agent; operating expense; potential for enhancement and updating; and prestige-conferring qualities.

All of these factors are important, but the most salient ones have been the environmental variables, most notably consumer demand, manufacturers' promotional efforts, medical education and specialization, availability of financing for R&D, health insurance and payment, competition in the marketplace, and governmental regulatory policies. The following sections describe these factors. (For a discussion of technology-specific variables, such as relative advantage, see chapter 3; organizational and personnel-related variables are discussed more fully in chapter 5.)

Consumer Demand and Public Expectations

In most industries, technological change is both a product of and a trigger for consumer demand in the marketplace. Until very recently, the market for health care generally did not operate in a price-competitive fashion, primarily because physicians rather than patients historically determined the nature and quantity of services to be provided and decided the nature and quantity of inputs to be used in the provision of services. As agents for their patients, physicians functioned as the real consumers of medical technologies, deciding which ones to adopt and use. Nonetheless, unrealistic public expectations of modern medicine's capabilities clearly have fueled the diffusion process over time (Iglehart 1979; Banta, Behney, and Willems 1981; Weisbrod 1991, 1994).

Today, consumer demand exerts ever stronger influence on technology adoption decisions as a result of the confluence of several forces—the explosion of Internet-based information services regarding health and medicine; the role of the electronic and print media (television, radio, and newspapers) in disseminating information regarding clinical advances reported in the leading medical journals (some of which are also publishing on-line); and the intensive efforts of medical technology manufacturers to promote their products to consumers and health care providers alike (see the discussion in the following section). While these forces arguably empower consumers, such factors also threaten to inundate laypersons with massive amounts of complex and conflicting information from varied—and in some cases biased—sources. Because most consumers are unqualified to judge the scientific validity of the information at hand, they often will uncritically accept reported "findings," with the net effect being the promotion of technology diffusion in the aggregate. In addition, the impact of patient advocacy groups on consumer demand for specific technologies should not be underestimated. As mentioned earlier in this chapter, breast cancer patient advocates lobbied Congress, the FDA, the Medicare program, and managed care plans during the 1990s for approval and coverage of autologous bone marrow transplants with high-dose chemotherapy despite a lack of scientific evidence regarding its efficacy in treating breast cancer (Mello and Brennan 2001).

Promotional Efforts of Technology Manufacturers

The rate of technology diffusion in many cases may be accelerated by the aggressive promotional efforts of technology manufacturers, who always have engaged in marketing and advertising their products to practicing physicians and hospitals. Pharmaceutical firms, for example, traditionally utilized "detail men" (sales representatives) to visit physicians' offices and to provide free samples of prescription drugs in the hope of changing doctors' prescribing habits. Medical residents recently have become prime targets of drugmakers' promotional efforts and are being treated to perks that include gifts, free meals, and drug samples. Between 1996 and 2000, drug companies doubled their sales force from 41,000 to 83,000 representatives, expanded the distribution of free samples from $4.9 billion to $7.9 billion annually, and increased their total annual spending on promotion to physicians from $9.3 billion to $15.1 billion (Dembner 2001).

Of perhaps even greater significance, pharmaceutical firms during the 1990s embarked on intensive direct-to-consumer advertising campaigns that utilized electronic and print media very effectively to create demand among consumers, who in turn influenced the drug-prescribing behavior of their physicians. Campaigns for such drugs as Lipitor (a cholesterol-lowering agent), Prevacid (an ulcer drug), Claritin (a non-drowsy-formula antihistamine), Vioxx and Celebrex (pain relievers for arthritis), Singulair (an asthma drug), and Viagra (described earlier in this chapter) have resulted in significant sales growth and market share increases for their producers (Pear 2001). Spending by the pharmaceutical industry on direct-to-consumer advertising mushroomed from $156 million in 1992 to $2.7 billion in 2001 (Cowan et al. 2001; PhRMA 2003), and between 1998 and 1999, prescription drug costs grew 18 percent and accounted for 44 percent of the increase in private insurance premiums (Center for Studying Health System Change 2000). Although MCOs have tried such measures as three-tiered copayment mechanisms (see chapter 12) to counter increased consumer demand for drugs, the influence of manufacturers' promotional efforts on technology diffusion is likely to increase in the future.

Medical Education, Specialization, and the Technological Imperative of Physicians

Medical schools and their affiliated teaching hospitals always have been repositories of medical technology, traditionally serving as loci of activity during the initiation and acceleration phases of technology diffusion. In addition to having a direct facilitating effect on technology adoption, medical schools and residency training programs exert indirect influence by shaping medical trainees' attitudes toward innovation. Broad exposure to technology early in training affects not only clinical preferences but also ultimately future professional behavior and practice patterns. Consequently, many practicing physicians feel compelled to follow a "technological imperative" that asserts the rights of patients to all that medicine has to offer (Fuchs 1968, 1986). Too often, this dictum has equated high-quality care with high-intensity care, leading to expanded diffusion of new technology. Physicians play highly influential roles in hospitals' decisions to adopt new technology, as evinced by a study of MRI diffusion in southern California, Oregon, and Washington hospitals that found physicians to be key players in hospital decision-making processes (L. H. Friedman and Jorgensen 1994). Once physicians accept a new technology into practice, the technological imperative reinforces its use, possibly leading to suboptimal clinical decisions (Fuchs 1986).

Medical specialization, which increasingly has revolved around technology, also encourages the adoption of innovations by medical residents (Iglehart 1979; Schroeder and Sandy 1993). In some cases, the development of new technologies has led to the establishment of new specialties—for example, radiology, nuclear medicine, and cardiovascular surgery trace their origins to specific devices or procedures (Banta, Behney, and Willems 1981). Because most specialty groups have vested interests in acquiring and employing specific technologies, specialization likely will continue to promote the diffusion of new technology.

Several countervailing forces, however, have arisen in recent years to contest the power and influence of medical specialty groups. Within the medical profession, there has been a movement to train more generalist physicians and to reform medical school curricula to place greater value and emphasis on family practice (Schroeder and Sandy 1993). The rise of managed care and of payment systems that reward physicians more for their cognitive skills than for their use of technology in treating patients also provide a potential counterbalance to practicing physicians' technological imperative. And more than ever before, consumers are seeking alternatives to traditional medical care, resurrecting some old "folk" remedies and giving rise to new ones. These disparate forces, however formidable, are not likely to offset the influence of medical specialization and the many other factors that foster technology diffusion. Moreover, growing consumer acceptance of nontraditional treatments has led to widespread diffusion of various alternative and complementary remedies such as acupuncture, homeopathy, naturopathy, dietary supplements, and herbal remedies. Dietary supplements and herbs, for example, often are advertised with claims of improving memory, slowing the aging process, and delaying the onset of numerous diseases, but unlike prescription drugs, which are highly regulated by the FDA, these remedies and the claims about their effects generally have not been subjected to rigorous evaluation—that is, clinical trials—until very recently. Although the number of trials involving alternative and complementary medicines has increased in the medical literature, the unchecked diffusion of inadequately evaluated alternative medicines continues to pose stern challenges for consumers, physicians, and policymakers.

The Availability of Financing for Technology Research and Development

As described in chapter 3, funding for the development of medical technology generally has been widely available from various public and private sources. Through the NIH, the federal government finances the lion's share of basic biomedical research, while private industry investment is targeted more toward applied R&D, with decisions to develop specific technologies based largely on potential marketability and return on investment. Without question, the availability of capital for R&D has been and remains a strong motivator for the diffusion of medical technology, although this motivator has at times sparked debate over its relative social merits, as was the case with cardiac care units, which diffused rapidly during the 1960s and 1970s (Bloom 1979; Waitzkin 1979).

The continued availability of capital for investment in medical technology development seems reasonably assured, as annual investment in the U.S. pharmaceutical, biotechnology, and medical devices industries continues to soar (see chapter 3). However, there also is concern that managed health care could retard future growth in these technology industries, especially if stringent cost-containment efforts were to cause technology manufacturers to avoid investing in costly but marginally beneficial technologies (Weisbrod 1991, 1994; Chernew et al. 1998). Some observers might argue that this would be a socially desirable outcome, since capital investment could instead be channeled toward R&D of relatively cost-effective technologies (Neumann and Weinstein 1991).

Health Insurance and Payment Systems

The traditional, dominant forms of private health insurance and payment to providers in the United States—broad coverage with minimal cost sharing, cost-based payment to hospitals, and fee-for-service payment to physicians—have long provided inappropriate incentives for the diffusion of technology (J. L. Wagner 1979; G. F. Anderson and Steinberg 1984; S. H. Altman 1988; Neumann and Weinstein 1991; Weisbrod 1994). By insulating patients from most of the cost burden associated with their care and by buffering providers against the cost consequences of their clinical and service-delivery decisions, these incentives historically have encouraged the adoption and use of technology (G. F. Anderson and Steinberg 1984; Weisbrod 1991), leading to the rapid diffusion of costly technologies (GAO 1992a), which, in turn, have driven health care cost growth (Goddeeris 1987; U.S. Congress, Congressional Budget Office 1991; GAO 1992b; Banta and Luce 1993).

With the 1983 introduction of the Medicare Prospective Payment System (PPS) for hospital inpatient care, based on payment rates adjusted by diagnosis-related group, some analysts (G. F. Anderson and Steinberg 1984) predicted that hospitals and physicians would engage in more prudent acquisition of new technology. By not paying for the full cost of using expensive technologies, the inpatient PPS was thought to encourage the adoption of lower-cost alternatives. In reality, though, hospitals during the 1980s and early 1990s faced little incentive to distinguish between cost-saving and cost-raising technologies in their purchasing decisions because they could recover their investments by shifting costs to other payers, particularly private insurers (S. Altman and Young 1993). Physicians likewise had little incentive to use technology parsimoniously, since they too were reasonably assured of receiving payment for their services and were not required to share in hospitals' operating costs.

There is consensus today that the Medicare inpatient PPS over time had little constraining effect on the diffusion of technology in hospitals and that it did not effectively direct the technology industry to develop more cost-reducing technologies (Neumann and Weinstein 1991). In fact, many hospitals' continuing ability to shift costs among payers likely stimulated the growth in medical and surgical service volumes that was observed in the early 1990s (S. [H.] Altman and Young 1993; PPRC 1993) and may have signaled technology manufacturers that cost-increasing technologies were still likely to be covered. Moreover, there was evidence that the use of expensive new technologies actually grew during this period (S. H. Altman 1988; Bradley and Kominski 1992; Peden and Freeland 1995; Cutler and McClellan 1996) despite the seeming incentives to use lower-cost technologies. S. H. Altman (1988) postulated that higher-than-expected operating margins generated by inpatient PPS payments during the 1980s created perverse incentives for hospitals to adopt more expensive procedures (e.g., higher-cost pacemakers) in some cases, even when lower-cost alternatives existed.

Before 1992, physicians were not paid prospectively by Medicare and faced incentives in many parts of the country that encouraged the shifting of technology-based services out of the hospital and into doctor's offices, where physicians could acquire the technology (often without CON review) and be paid for its use not only by Medicare but also by other payers. The 1992 introduction of a prospective Medicare physician fee schedule based on a relative-value scale that corrected for existing biases favoring surgical and technological services was thought to offer technology-neutral incentives for rational adoption and use of technology, but some experts criticized the implementation of the payment system, arguing that specialists still were paid too generously for performing invasive procedures (Hsiao, Dunn, and Verrilli 1993).

During the 1990s, multiple factors—the growing influence of purchasers (employers and insurers), intense competition among health care plans, the rise of integrated service-delivery systems, and the use of aggressive managed care practices (capitated payment methods, selective contracting, utilization management, and gatekeeper mechanisms)—combined to reduce the opportunities for hospital cost shifting and fostered new incentives for adopting and using cost-saving technology (Weisbrod 1991, 1994; Cohen 1996, 1998). Although these incentives appeared to be strong, it was—and remains—unclear from the available evidence whether managed care in the long run could successfully contain health care cost growth driven by the diffusion of new technology (Neumann and Sandberg 1998; Chernew et al. 1998). (For further discussion of health care payment policies, see chapter 12; for an in-depth look at how these incentives have changed and are likely to influence the behavior of technology manufacturers and of users [e.g., health care providers and consumers], see chapter 5.)

Competition in the Marketplace

Competition in one form or another has existed in health care for many years. Until recently, the most prevalent form was product differentiation, in which hospitals competed for patients and medical staff by distinguishing their products and services from those of their rivals. As mentioned earlier in this chapter, an early empirical study of hospital behavior regarding technology adoption suggested that prestige enhancement was a motivating force driving some hospitals' decisions to purchase capital equipment, especially if payment conditions were favorable (Cromwell et al. 1975). Another study found that competition encouraged the proliferation of coronary angioplasty and bypass surgery services—that is, hospitals situated in competitive market areas were more likely to offer these two services than were hospitals without competitors in their local markets, regardless of patient case mix and teaching status (Robinson, Garnick, and McPhee 1987).

Competition among health plans and service-delivery organizations intensified dramatically in many market areas during the 1990s, inducing various organizations to merge, consolidate, or form strategic alliances with one another (Miller and Luft 1994; Miller 1996). The creation of these large integrated service-delivery systems and networks poses severe challenges for organizational managers, not the least of which involves decision making regarding the adoption of new technology (see chapter 5). Moreover, as competitive pressures mount and managers seek new ways to lower service costs, the relative cost-effectiveness of new technologies likely will take on greater importance and urgency than in the past.

Governmental Regulatory Policies

The principal federal and state governmental regulatory policies aimed at controlling the diffusion of medical technology (mentioned briefly in chapter 2) include FDA premarket approval of new drugs and devices and state CON review of capital expenditures. Increasingly, as information and communications technologies play a greater role in the delivery of health care, new laws and regulations are being generated to govern their diffusion. For example, federal telecommunications law and state medical and pharmacy licensure laws are likely to significantly affect the diffusion of such technologies as telemedicine and on-line pharmacies. In general, though, governmental policies such as FDA and CON regulation have inhibited both the rate and the extent of technology adoption by hospitals and other health care providers (Bucci, Reiss, and Hall 1985; Robinson, Garnick, and McPhee 1987). However, the success of these two primary regulatory efforts in meeting their intended objectives has been the subject of great debate over time (U.S. Congress, OTA 1984b). (Chapter 10 discusses the FDA's role and processes, while chapter 13 addresses CON review.)

The repeal of federal health planning laws in 1986 (and the later repeal of capital-expenditure-review provisions under section 1122 of the Social Security Amendments) greatly weakened states' capacity to perform CON reviews of new medical technologies, and in those states where CON statutes were also repealed, a sharp rise in new construction was subsequently observed (Jee 1993). Although the conventional wisdom holds that CON during the 1970s and 1980s had negligible aggregate impact on both hospital costs and technology diffusion because of serious structural weaknesses and political obstacles (J. B. Brown and Saltman 1985; Simpson 1985; Diller 1993; U.S. Congress, Congressional Budget Office 1991), CON briefly enjoyed a mild resurgence during the national reform debate of 1992–94, as some states contemplated reforms that would link CON with other controls as part of a broad cost-containment strategy (Diller 1993; Jee 1993; C. Thomas 1993). Evidence from an analysis of MRI diffusion between 1983 and 1993 found that CON had little if any constraining effect (Baker 1997; Baker and Wheeler 1998). By the late 1990s, more than thirty states retained functioning statutory CON programs, and the most commonly reviewed technologies were (in descending order) cardiac catheterization, MRI, renal lithotripsy, organ transplantation, PET, CT, and the gamma knife (AHA 1997).

In addition to these seven primary forces operating in the health care environment, several other factors are noteworthy, and table 4.1 summarizes the generic effect of each on technology diffusion. For example, the severity and urgency of specific medical problems may provide strong impetus for technology adoption, as was the case with chemotherapy for leukemia and various drug therapies for AIDS/HIV. The prestige and visibility of advocates and opinion leaders also may promote the acceptance of new technology, as with gastric freezing. The intrinsic properties of a technology also may facilitate diffusion in some cases (as with the performance-enhancing effects of Viagra) yet may slow or deter diffusion in others (e.g., the high cost and complexity of early PET scanner design initially impeded the technology's diffusion in the 1990s). Finally, providers' technology adoption practices likely will affect the rate and extent of technology diffusion, with formalized programs of medical technology evaluation being the most constraining. (More will be said about such practices in chapter 5.)

Dealing with the Diffusion Question

Having examined general theories of medical technology diffusion along with commonly observed diffusion patterns and factors responsible for producing those patterns, we must now address the fundamental question of whether medical technologies are diffusing too swiftly or too slowly into medical practice. The answer, not surprisingly, depends on the particular circumstances surrounding a given technology. If the technology is well developed and evaluation evidence exists to support its safety and efficacy, the next step is to determine its cost-effectiveness relative to existing clinical alternatives (see chapter 7). If demonstrated to be cost-effective, then diffusion of the technology is desirable and should be encouraged (see chapter 5). Even so, unconstrained diffusion of essentially beneficial technology may not be entirely desirable or appropriate. In fact, such extensive diffusion may have serious implications for the cost of medical care. Thus, we first must weigh the technology's putative clinical value against its potential risks and costs before deciding whether to adopt it and then must consider the extent to which it should diffuse into medical practice. In doing so, we also must recognize that (1) a given technology found to be cost-effective in one clinical situation may not be so in others (Neumann and Weinstein 1991; M. Gold et al. 1996) and (2) the subsequent appearance of negative long-term effects may alter our assessment of the technology's net benefit.

TABLE 4.1. Factors Affecting the Diffusion of Medical Technology

Factor	Likely Effect on Adoption
Consumer demand and public expectations	+
Promotional efforts of technology manufacturers	+
Medical education, specialization, and the "technological imperative" of physicians	+
Availability of financing for technology research and development	+
Health insurance and payment systems	+/−[a]
Competition in the marketplace	+/−[b]
Severity and urgency of medical problems	+
Intrinsic properties of technology	+/−[c]
Prestige and visibility of advocates and opinion leaders	+
Technology adoption practices of providers	+/−[d]
Governmental regulatory policies	−

Note: + = factor is likely to stimulate or promote the diffusion of technology; − = factor is likely to deter or constrain the diffusion of technology.

[a]Cost-based, fee-for-service payment strongly encourages diffusion of technology, whereas prospective payment and capitation methods provide incentives that foster more judicious diffusion of technology.

[b]Evidence is mixed; competitive pressures in some cases may motivate diffusion of technology but in other cases may have an inhibitory effect.

[c]Cost-saving properties and relative advantages offered by technology are likely to stimulate diffusion, whereas less favorable properties may serve to deter or decrease diffusion.

[d]These practices vary in terms of evidence-based decision making (see chap. 5), with providers that employ formalized programs of medical technology evaluation (MTE) being the most likely to demonstrate evidence-based technology adoption strategies.

The balance between too rapid and too slow diffusion is delicate and requires ongoing assessment of a technology as it diffuses. It also raises a host of ethical and social questions that cannot be easily resolved (see chapter 14). For example, should the diffusion of a potentially lifesaving or life-enhancing technology be withheld until there is sufficient evidence of its long-term effects, even if a life could be saved in the short-term? Who should pay for the cost of long-term evaluation of the technology? These questions are constantly being debated by all stakeholders in the health care system—researchers, providers, payers, policymakers, and consumers. The majority of emerging technologies, however, probably diffuse too rapidly relative to (1) their state of development and (2) their state of clinical evaluation. The widespread diffusion of an incompletely developed technology may lead to ineffective clinical use, since the underlying clinical theory and indications for use are often neither well articulated nor communicated in timely fashion to clinicians. Likewise, the diffusion of an inadequately evaluated technology may pose serious and possibly hazardous consequences for patient care. Considerable effort, therefore, is needed to revise current medical technology evaluation practices so that the assessment of a technology may begin as early as possible in its development and continue through its diffusion into practice (see chapters 6–8 and 15). This change will require improved methods of evaluation as well as more timely and effective means of communicating evaluative findings and other relevant information to potential adopters.

The failure to adopt potentially beneficial, cost-effective technology has equally worrisome implications for medical care, especially with regard to the quality of and access to care. Although well intentioned, policies that are aimed at constraining technology diffusion suffer if they are not based on scientific grounds, since the resulting delay in diffusion often leads to suboptimal use of the technology for some individuals and to effective denial of access for others. (See chapter 10 for a discussion of FDA regulatory policy and chapter 13 for CON policy.) As in the case of rapid, uncontrolled diffusion, the required remedy here is to improve the timeliness and rigor of technology evaluation methods and to develop new mechanisms for disseminating evaluation findings at appropriate points in the diffusion process. The methods chapters in part II of this book, as well as chapter 15 in part III, address these issues in further detail.

5

The Adoption and Use of Medical Technology in Health Care Organizations
Alan B. Cohen

Having dealt with the general process of technology diffusion in chapter 4, we now focus on the decision-making dynamics behind the adoption and use of technology by health care providers. Hospitals traditionally have been the primary adopters of new medical technology, but with the increasing movement toward managed care and prospective payment methods during the 1990s, many technologies (e.g., diagnostic imaging and ambulatory surgery) began to move out of the hospital setting into physicians' offices and freestanding centers. In addition, managed care organizations and other purchasers of health care increasingly began to weigh in on some providers' decisions to adopt and use new technology.

In this chapter, we first examine the decision-making structures and processes employed by health care organizations—most notably, hospitals, physician group practices, and managed care organizations—for the adoption of new technology, whether medical and surgical supplies, information systems, drugs and biologics, or major devices and specialized services. Next, we look at the strategic considerations that go into these decisions and the choices that adopters must make in selecting an appropriate adoption strategy (e.g., whether to adopt a technology early or late in its diffusion pattern, whether to purchase it in discrete stages or in a continuous series). Two medical devices—electronic fetal monitoring (EFM) and magnetic resonance imaging (MRI)—are used as case examples to illustrate these strategic options. Finally, we consider how the incentives for the adoption and use of medical technology have changed dramatically under managed care and discuss the implications for manufacturers, providers, purchasers, and consumers.

Decision-Making Structures and Processes

Among health care providers, virtually all hospitals have formal decision-making structures for the adoption of new technological products
and services, but the nature and form of the structures vary depending
on the class or type of technology in question. To a lesser degree, large
physician group practices—whether single-specialty or multispecialty—also employ formal structures (e.g., committees), while smaller
practices rely on less formal means of decision making. Among purchasers of care, health plans and private insurers use formal decision-
making structures to make coverage and payment decisions—that is,
whether to cover a specific technological service in the benefit package
and how much to pay providers for its use in patient care. This chapter describes the decision-making structures and processes of health
plans, especially managed care organizations. (For a discussion of the
technology coverage and payment methods used by the Medicare and
Medicaid programs, see chapter 12.)

In the following sections, we explore the means by which hospitals,
physician group practices, and health plans make decisions about four
broad categories of technologies: medical and surgical supplies, information systems and technologies, pharmacy and therapeutics, and
major equipment-embodied technologies (e.g., X-ray CT, MRI, PET,
and lithotripsy) and specialized services (e.g., cardiac surgery, organ
transplantation, burn units, trauma care, oncology services, and specialized intensive care units).

Medical and Surgical Supplies

In most hospitals, an organizational unit or department of materials
management plays a vital role in purchasing the goods and supplies
needed to deliver care. Many of these items are medical technologies,
ranging from patient beds and durable medical equipment to surgical
instruments and biomaterials to assorted consumable medical and surgical supplies. The materials management unit analyzes the costs and
benefits of alternative products, negotiates with manufacturers and
suppliers, and purchases the necessary items at reasonable cost. However, clinicians, technologists, and other staff members provide valuable input into the decision-making process. Smaller hospitals may join
together in purchasing cooperatives to leverage their pooled buying
power with technology vendors.

In large physician group practices, responsibility for decisions regarding materials management (e.g., consumable supplies) usually rests with the practice manager, although physicians—either individually or through a committee structure—test products and provide clinical input to purchase decisions. Managed care organizations and other purchasers of care tend not to focus on hospitals' and physician groups' materials management decisions unless the materials involved have serious implications for service costs and payment.

Information Systems and Technologies

In a manner similar to that for materials management, most hospitals have an information systems (IS) department that plays a critical role in decisions to adopt new information systems and technologies for the improvement of health care delivery, including medical records systems (for collecting, transcribing, and storing clinical data); radiology and clinical laboratory reporting systems (for gathering, archiving, and reporting test results); pharmacy data systems (for monitoring medication use and for avoiding errors, adverse reactions, and drug interactions); scheduling systems for clinic visits, diagnostic tests, and surgical cases; and financial reporting systems (for collecting, processing, and storing claims and billing data for patient care). While the principal responsibility for purchasing and installing these systems and technologies rests with the IS department staff, crucial analytic input about information needs and data flows must be obtained from all affected users, including clinicians, technologists, operations managers, financial managers, and support staff.

In physician group practices, the practice manager is responsible for information technology (IT) purchases, especially for medical records, scheduling, and financial reporting systems, but as with medical supplies, physicians have an important voice in purchase decisions. Health plans and managed care organizations do not at present get involved in the IT decisions of individual hospitals or physician group practices, except in areas of mutual interest where coordinated information exchange is needed for payment purposes, such as with medical records and financial reporting systems. These purchasers, however, maintain extensive information systems regarding service use and expenditures, especially services involving the use of pharmaceuticals, devices, and surgical procedures. In the future, even greater coordination between purchasers and providers will be needed in the IS/IT area—particularly in the standardization of procedures for electronic data exchange and for data confidentiality and security—as required under the federal Health Insurance Portability and Accountability Act of 1996.

Pharmacy and Therapeutics

Most hospitals have an in-house formulary that contains a range of therapeutic agents, including drugs, biologics, vaccines, and blood products. Decisions regarding the adoption of these agents are usually made by a Pharmacy and Therapeutics (P&T) Committee, whose role is to identify, review, and analyze all new products entering the market for patient use and to make recommendations for their inclusion in the hospital's formulary. In large teaching hospitals, the P&T Committee typically consists mainly of physicians drawn from a cross-section of clinical departments as well as pharmacists, other clinicians, and managers (Mannebach et al. 1999). The committee oversees the evaluation of new therapeutic agents in terms of safety, effectiveness, and cost-effectiveness based on information gathered from the medical literature, from medical specialty societies, and from government agencies such as the FDA, the AHRQ, and the CMS. As part of the institution's quality assurance program aimed at minimizing medication errors, adverse drug reactions, and drug-drug interactions, the committee often is responsible for monitoring the use of these products once they have been added to the hospital's formulary.

Formularies also are common to health plans and insurers, especially managed care organizations, all of which maintain lists of approved drugs and therapeutics for which they are willing to pay on behalf of their members or subscribers. These health plans maintain standing Formulary (or P&T) Committees to evaluate new pharmaceuticals and biologics, to monitor prescription drug use and patient compliance with recommended treatment regimens, and to guide health plan policies regarding pharmacy benefits management, most notably the use of generic equivalents and the design of multi-tiered copayment systems. Although physician group practices are less likely to employ formal committees for such purposes, some large ones do so, while smaller practices tend to make decisions about prescription drugs based largely on the consensus of physicians in the practice.

Major Equipment-Embodied Technologies and
Specialized Services

Before 1970, American hospitals often acquired new medical devices or
introduced new specialized services simply by using existing operating
funds or by relying on the munificence of private philanthropy. Retrospective, cost-based reimbursement reinforced this behavior by paying
incurred costs and by failing to question the need for acquisition of expensive new technology. Over time, however, as hospital cost inflation
outstripped available operating funds and philanthropic sources of capital and as government programs were established for the review of
capital expenditures, hospitals were forced to analyze and make more
prudent capital investment decisions (Berman, Kukla, and Weeks 1994).
Capital budgeting thus became the principal means by which hospitals
acquired new equipment-embodied technologies and established new
specialized services.

In many hospitals today, the responsibility for making such decisions
rests primarily with a core group of individuals that includes trustees,
top managers, and key medical staff. However, with technologies becoming increasingly specialized and complex, with costs continuing
their upward spiral, and with hospital consolidation growing, the decision-making structures and processes for equipment purchases and
service expansions also are becoming more complex. For example, most
hospitals now have special technology review committees to oversee
the capital budgeting process and to allocate resources among departments and operating units, many employ caps on annual spending for
new equipment-embodied technology and specialized services, and
many have capital equipment budgets that are entirely separate from
capital funds intended to support major construction and renovation
projects. The capital budgeting process has become a multistep process
for identifying, evaluating, and choosing among alternative programs
and technologies to be established or acquired on an annual basis. The
general procedure outlined in table 5.1 is a synthesis of several capital
budgeting approaches described in the financial management literature
(Griffith 1972; Esmond 1982; Silvers, Zelman, and Kahn 1983; Berman,
Kukla, and Weeks 1994; Cleverley 1997; Nowicki 1999). As such, the
table provides a simplified illustration of the capital budgeting process
and thus may not reflect the intricacies of committee structure in some
hospitals or the complexities of the decision feedback process employed

in others. Moreover, some financial managers argue that two decisions are required—a capital investment decision that weighs the intrinsic merits of each proposed investment opportunity in absolute terms and a capital budgeting decision that weighs each opportunity in relative terms and indicates the subset that can and should be funded under the budget constraints (Berman, Kukla, and Weeks 1994). Other analysts stress the value of capital budgeting as a tool rather than an end in itself (McLean 1997), while still others view it as a less comprehensive, short-term (annual) component of a broader, ongoing management control process known as capital project analysis (Cleverley 1997). In general, while most hospitals follow the basic budgeting approach outlined in table 5-1, they also may vary in several important ways, including the degree of decentralized decision making afforded individual departments, the degree of negotiation permitted in steps 5 and 6, the criteria and methods used for setting priorities and budget cap limits (see the discussion of Prince 1998 later in this chapter), the decision rules governing the selection of funded projects, and the relative decision-making influence exerted by managers, trustees, and physicians.

TABLE 5.1. The Capital Budgeting Process in Hospitals

Step	Responsible Group
1. Determine institutional priorities and create a capital budget "cap"[a]	Top managers and trustees
2. Generate departmental "wish list" for new equipment purchases and major projects over the coming year	Individual departments—medical staff, clinical chiefs, and managers
3. Submit departmental request (with supporting documentation) to top managers	Individual departments—managers
4. Compile, review, and analyze departmental lists (including financial analysis[b])	Top managers and/or special committee
5. Rank departmental requests by priority, based on criteria such as urgency, contribution to patient care, cost-benefit ratio, and hospital-wide implications	Top managers and/or special committee
6. Review recommended purchases and projects with each department	Top managers and/or special committee (with individual department managers and clinical chiefs)
7. Approve total capital budget for the hospital for the coming year	Top managers and trustees

[a]Reflects how much a hospital is willing or able to invest in new technology and service programs.
[b]Includes net present value analysis, cash flow projections, and cost-benefit analysis.

Hospital Decision-Making Systems for Technology Adoption

The sophistication of hospital decision-making systems for technology adoption has evolved from early rudimentary approaches to formal appraisal methods. In the 1970s, hospital decision making was largely decentralized, with responsibility for technical review resting with department clinical chiefs and technical engineers, who were better able to judge the clinical attributes and technical properties of new technologies (Cromwell et al. 1975). Beginning in the 1980s, hospitals increasingly incorporated formalized systems of technology adoption into their long-range strategic planning (Whitted 1981; Sanders 1982; Greer 1985; Wheeler, Porter-O'Grady, and Barrell 1985). Ann Greer's research in this area (1985, 1988) is illustrative and remains relevant to hospital decision making today.

In a study of twenty-five southeastern Wisconsin hospitals, Greer (1985) identified three discrete systems of decision making. In the medical-individualistic system, physicians were dominant actors who sought to acquire new technologies that would enable them to treat private patients. Technology review usually occurred in medical committees in which clinical effects were assessed consensually based on professional training, clinical experience, and collegial respect. Technologies considered and adopted in this manner included laser surgery, fiber-optic endoscopy, and EFM.

In the fiscal-managerial system, prominent actors were hospital chief executive officers, financial officers, department chiefs, key hospital-based specialists, and technical staff. Review was more structured, placing organizational concerns before the interests of individual patients or physicians and emphasizing quantitative assessment of benefits, risks, and costs. Technologies scrutinized in this way included X-ray CT, automated blood analyzers, and radionuclide scanning.

In the strategic-institutional system, trustees and chief executives assumed dominant roles in decisions regarding technologies that posed substantive changes in the hospital's nature or future. With their formal authority over long-range planning and policy-making and their legal responsibility for monitoring changes within the institution, hospital trustees and managers oversaw a review process that involved the construction of alternative scenarios for assessing a technology's potential opportunities for and threats to the hospital's mission. Technologies reviewed through such a process included coronary artery bypass surgery and neonatal intensive care units.

These decision-making systems are germane to the present health care environment in two ways. First, they are not mutually exclusive but instead coexist in virtually all hospitals. They usually operate in parallel but sometimes work in concert with one another. Second, when taken together, they underscore the view of the modern hospital as a complex organization with multiple internal decision makers. The question of which system should apply in a given circumstance will depend on factors that include the intrinsic nature of the technology at issue, the potential impacts on the hospital of the technology's adoption and use, and the organizational and political relationships among key actors within the institution. Thus, complex equipment-embodied technologies and specialized services, which may be costly to acquire, establish, and operate but which also present significant opportunities for (or departures from) the hospital's stated mission, are more likely to be judged via a strategic-institutional decision-making system than by any other. The addition of new pharmaceuticals to the hospital formulary is more likely to be evaluated through a fiscal-managerial process, and technologies that lend themselves to easy incorporation within physicians' private practices—with potentially low impact on the hospital (e.g., some small devices and instruments)—are more likely to be assessed from a medical-individualistic perspective.

Whether a technology is dynamic or formed also may have bearing on which decision making system is employed (Greer 1988). For example, fully "formed" technologies are more likely to be evaluated by strategic-institutional or fiscal-managerial systems. However, many technologies today tend to be dynamic—that is, they develop and evolve as they diffuse. This poses uncertainty for adopters and may even stir controversy in the community. Regardless of the decision-making system employed, the adoption of dynamic technologies likely will be aided in the community by local innovators, who help to introduce a technology to the community, and by idea champions, who provide the enthusiasm and support necessary to help a technology take hold (Greer 1988).

In an interesting case analysis of an academic health center's decision to adopt biliary lithotripsy for the treatment of gallstones, Weingart (1995) examined seven key decision-making criteria: (1) efficacy and effectiveness, (2) safety, (3) profitability, (4) social responsibility, (5) institutional strategy, (6) feasibility, and (7) risk. Despite the hospital staff's conscientious effort to weigh these factors, adoption of the technology was disappointing. Weingart attributed the unsatisfactory outcome to the ad hoc nature of the committee structure and to the decision-making process employed. The hospital would have been better served (1) had managers thought strategically about the decision, particularly in the context of the hospital's long-range plans; (2) had managers paid greater attention to competing alternatives that were about to emerge from the R&D pipeline in the short run; and (3) had a standing review committee existed to deal with the medical technology evaluation (MTE) issues and questions that were central to the adoption decision.

A potential aid to managers of community hospitals in the future is a medical technology index constructed and tested empirically by Prince (1998). The index contains six weighted components: (1) case-mix index for Medicare inpatients, (2) facility and medical services in house at the hospital, (3) facility and medical services at competing institutions, (4) average age of physical plant and equipment, (5) medical school affiliation, and (6) membership in the Council of Teaching Hospitals. Prince found the index to be a meaningful benchmark for strategic assessment of a hospital's current technological capabilities relative to those of other hospitals in a competitive marketplace. Information obtained from the index regarding an institution's clinical services—taking into account the complexity of its patient population, the condition of its physical plant, and the strength of its teaching program—could be used for multiple purposes, including strategic and financial planning, capital budgeting, and operations management.

Strategic Considerations and Choices

As mentioned earlier in this chapter and in chapter 2, many technologies either have moved or increasingly are moving out of the traditional hospital inpatient setting into physicians' offices and freestanding diagnostic or therapeutic centers. Prime examples include outpatient renal dialysis, ambulatory (or same-day) surgery, diagnostic imaging (e.g., ultrasound, CT, MRI), and minimally invasive procedures. Hospitals, physician group practices, and freestanding centers all face formidable challenges when making decisions regarding the adoption of new medical technology. Regardless of the particular decision-making structure and process employed, the underlying strategic considerations that go into such decisions—and the choices that must be made—are remarkably similar across different organizations. Table 5.2 lists key strategic considerations, which are discussed in the following section.

Strategic Considerations

The practical issues and factors that must be considered by any health care organization in deciding whether to adopt new technology and in choosing a particular adoption strategy include the following.

State of Technology Formation
The state of a technology's formation—that is, the extent to which it is fully formed or still evolving in structure and function—may play an important part in an organization's decision to adopt it (Greer 1988). Although well-formed technologies tend to be more attractive to adopters for various reasons (e.g., the clinical applications are known), some organizations may prefer the flexibility of adopting a technology that is in flux, such as in the case of a device when the optimal design configuration has not yet been determined.

Stage of Technology Diffusion
The timing of a decision to acquire a technology relative to its stage of diffusion is often critical. For example, as described in chapter 4, adoption in the initiation stage of diffusion is likely to confer "pioneer" or "first mover" status on the adopter, along with tangible economic and noneconomic benefits. Conversely, it may be wise in other cases to defer technology adoption until the acceleration or even deceleration phases of diffusion. Much depends on the information available concerning a technology's safety, efficacy, and cost-effectiveness; its relationship to the hospital's clinical needs; and the relative ease and affordability of acquisition (see this chapter's discussion of early versus late adoption strategies).

TABLE 5.2.   **Strategic Considerations in the Adoption of Medical Technology**

State of technology formation
Stage of technology diffusion
Availability of information about the technology
Relationship to clinical needs
Site needs
Staffing needs
Estimation of costs and benefits
Financing
Vendor selection
Regulatory constraints

Availability of Information about the Technology

An important determinant in any adoption decision is the quantity and quality of existing information regarding a technology's known capabilities and limitations, not only from a clinical perspective but also from technical, financial, social, ethical, legal, organizational, and regulatory standpoints. For example, the knowledge that a technology has not yet received FDA premarket approval or is not likely to receive third-party payer coverage may deter some organizations from acquiring the technology at that point in time. Conversely, preliminary evidence of a technology's potential clinical benefit, coupled with favorable financial terms and collaborative research opportunities from a technology manufacturer (who may offer it at no cost to early adopters), may persuade groups to adopt the technology. Unfortunately, evidence concerning safety and efficacy is usually difficult to obtain for emerging technologies. Lack of data on competing technologies (those used for the same purpose and for which there is no clear evidence establishing the superiority of one over another) also tends to hamper adoption decisions (Petitti 1986). Hospitals, physician group practices, and health plans typically must make their decisions armed only with imperfect information.

Relationship to Clinical Needs

The introduction of a new technology should be consonant with the organizational mission of the hospital or group practice, fitting within its clinical services and contributing meaningfully to patient care. There may be instances, however, in which decisions to adopt technology may be used strategically to spearhead entry into new areas of service delivery, such as specialized surgery or intensive care. Even in such cases, the decision should be predicated on projected as well as current clinical needs of the organization's service population. Careful consideration, therefore, must be given to present and future clinical applications and uses of the technology.

Site Needs

Site considerations are especially important for equipment-embodied technologies (such as MRI) and for others requiring major construction or reconfiguration of physical plant (such as ambulatory surgery suites). Consideration must be given to proper physical placement (proximity to related clinical services) and to careful installation to avoid potentially dangerous environmental hazards. In the case of multihospital systems, site decisions are more complex and are likely to include such factors as number of beds in each hospital, projected patient volume, patient case mix, existing space (land and physical plant), architectural requirements, availability of related clinical and support services, and an institution's position within its surrounding community and market area.

Staffing Needs

Some new technologies, particularly complex devices or surgical procedures, often require the creation of entirely new classes of personnel. Careful attention must be paid to the organization's staffing needs for delivering the new service and for maintaining the technology. Hence, the availability of qualified personnel to operate and service the technology will influence the adoption decision. In addition, the training needs of all staff—including physicians—must be ascertained and addressed through appropriate education. This is especially the case with new surgical procedures where the slope of the clinical learning curve may appear to be gentle but in fact may be fraught with the risk of complications (Hatlie 1993). For example, in a study of laparoscopic surgery after formal training, See, Cooper, and Fisher (1993) found that surgeons who performed these procedures without additional training following initial formal education were three times more likely to experience at least one serious complication than were surgeons who had sought additional training. Adopters of an emerging technology thus are obliged to assure that staff are properly trained to use the technology safely and effectively (Hatlie 1993).

Estimation of Costs and Benefits

Cost-benefit estimation is essential to any adoption decision. The organization must consider (1) all capital expenses involved in acquisition of the technology, including the purchase price, relevant facility modification costs, and the cost of financing debt; (2) all operating expenses associated with implementation, including costs of supplies, personnel, and maintenance of equipment; and (3) indirect costs, or overhead expenses, including those related to administration, insurance, and training. In estimating benefits, consideration must be given to (1) cost savings relative to existing clinical alternatives and (2) the averted costs of future treatment. Estimation of costs and benefits on an annualized basis, taking into account the net present value of all relevant cash flows, allows managers to gauge the financial impact of the acquisition on the hospital (Berman, Kukla, and Weeks 1994) and to compare the expected marginal costs of the new technological service with the projected marginal benefits (M. Gold et al. 1996). (See chapter 7 for a more extensive discussion of cost-benefit analysis and other economic evaluation methods.)

Financing

For major equipment-embodied technologies and specialized services, the question of whether to purchase or to lease new equipment often looms large in the individual hospital or group practice. Whereas many organizations prefer to purchase new equipment, especially low-capital-cost items, leasing may confer other advantages, such as greater flexibility in choosing a vendor and assuring technological currency, particularly when a device's design is in flux. Information about the technology's capabilities and estimated costs is vital to the selection of an appropriate financing arrangement. For high-capital-cost items, such as MRI devices, PET scanners, or renal lithotripters, the organization may decide to enter into joint ventures or shared service arrangements with other hospitals or physician group practices. Such arrangements permit access to new technology while allowing organizations to pool financial risk. In some states, CON regulatory policies may provide explicit incentives for hospitals or group practices to pursue shared arrangements.

Vendor Selection

The selection of a reliable vendor (device manufacturer, drug distributor, or materials supplier) is important to any technology adoption decision. For devices, the choice of a manufacturer usually depends on such factors as price, product features and options, product performance and reliability, services (e.g., product maintenance, training), guarantees against technological obsolescence, the long-term viability of the manufacturer, and opportunities for collaborative research (especially for emerging dynamic technologies). For various IS hardware and software products, the selection of a vendor depends on factors similar to those for devices, but in the case of pharmaceuticals or medical supplies, the choice of an appropriate distributor or supplier often will depend more on price and volume discounts.

Regulatory Constraints

Regulatory controls, such as FDA premarket approval, state CON review, and third-party payer coverage decisions, are key to any adoption decision and can greatly influence the choice of a strategy. Depending on the circumstances surrounding a given technology, regulatory influences might induce some organizations to invest early in the diffusion process while giving others pause. Similarly, regulatory factors at a given point in time might encourage some hospitals or group practices to pursue phased acquisition of a technology while persuading others to acquire it in serial fashion (see the following discussion of strategic options). (Chapters 10–13 discuss the specific influences of various regulatory policies on such decisions.)

The following discussion of common adoption strategies, plus subsequent examples of actual hospital decisions in the cases of EFM and MRI, should illustrate how these strategic considerations interact to shape the adoption of new medical technology.

Early versus Late Adoption: A First-Order Strategic Question

As described in chapter 4, early adopters of medical technology—whether devices, surgical procedures, or drugs—tend to be academic health centers and major teaching hospitals. Early adoption is appealing for several reasons (see table 5.3). First, it confers prestige-enhancing status on the adopter by placing it on the cutting edge of innovation. A hospital or physician group practice may use the powerful image of being a first mover to great advantage in recruiting physicians and staff and in attracting patients. In a study of hospital adoption of MRI, Teplensky et al. (1995, 457) found that the likelihood of adoption by a hospital "was strongly related to its strategic positioning as a technological leader."

Second, early adoption may offer financial benefit, even though third-party coverage for the technology may be uncertain for some time. For example, a device manufacturer eager to establish clinical evidence required for FDA premarket approval may be willing to install the device at decreased cost (or even no cost) in exchange for clinical data. FDA prohibitions against the sale of unapproved devices encourage such collaborative ventures. In addition, acquisition costs may be defrayed in some cases by collaboration with universities interested in joint research. Such ventures may generate revenue for the hospital in the form of research grants either from the manufacturer or from governmental sources.

A third advantage of early adoption is the ability of the hospital or physician group to perform in-house evaluation of the technology. In the case of a new device, this allows physicians and managers to judge for themselves the technology's merit, the reliability and services of the selected vendor, and the improvements in technological design considered desirable for the near term. In the case of a new surgical procedure or drug, clinical experience of this type can help to familiarize physicians and staff with the technology's strengths and limitations and can inform the development of clinical policies regarding its use.

A fourth advantage is the potential franchising effect that early adoption may yield in places where state CON policies are stringently enforced. For example, a hospital or health care provider that adopts an emerging device or specialized service ahead of its competitors not only reaps the benefits of being a clinical leader in its market area but also may achieve virtual monopoly status by effectively preempting other organizations and groups from obtaining the same technology (should local CON policies call for limits on the technology's diffusion). In areas where "investigational" devices (those not yet generally accepted in practice) are exempt from CON review, hospitals may use this strategy to acquire devices well in advance of widespread clinical acceptance on

TABLE 5.3.   Alternative Strategies for Technology Adoption: Early versus Late Adoption and Phased versus Serial Acquisition

Early adoption	Late adoption
Enhancement of prestige	Uncertain environment
Recruit/retain physicians	Technology in flux
Attract patients	Inadequate information on clinical
Financial benefits	applications
Decreased acquisition costs	Inadequate information on operat-
Potential revenues from research	ing costs and third-party pay-
grants	ment coverage
In-house technology evaluation	Buffer against obsolescence
Clinical experience/policies	Insufficient patient volume and/or in-
Service experience with vendor	appropriate case mix
"Franchising effect"	Better coordinate adoption with
Competitive edge in market area	hospital's clinical needs
Investigational device exemption	Reduce exposure to financial risk
from CON review	
Phased acquisition	Serial acquisition
Guard against technological	Flexibility in upgrading technology
obsolescence	on regular basis
Preferred vendor arrangements	Attain target level of service
Volume discounts	availability
Enhanced service	Replace outmoded or aging units
Attainment of strategic goal	Cash flow considerations
Reorganize department	
Enhance provider status	
Enter new service market	
Expand existing service	

the theory that once installed, an expensive equipment-embodied device is difficult if not impossible to remove. Therefore, whenever a hospital successfully acquires such a technology (e.g., MRI, PET, or lithotripsy), it essentially becomes enfranchised to provide that service.

Despite these inducements for early adoption of technology, there are several reasons for employing a late adoption strategy in specific circumstances (see table 5.3). One is the need for caution in an uncertain environment, especially when a technology is in flux, its acquisition costs are high, and available information is inadequate concerning its capabilities, clinical uses, operating costs, and prospects for third-party payment coverage. In such circumstances, hospitals and physician group practices may be wise to wait and see before risking an investment.

A second advantage of late adoption—particularly with major devices—is the ability to guard against possible technological obsolescence by purchasing the technology after it appears to have reached its optimal configuration. Late adoption ensures that the device has been thoroughly refined and increases the likelihood that further changes or improvements in design will be only marginal.

Finally, an organization's clinical needs—as reflected in the service volume and case mix of its patient population—might argue in favor of late adoption under certain conditions. For example, insufficient volume and/or inappropriate case mix to support a new device or surgical service might dissuade or at least postpone adoption of the technology. Without convincing evidence of clinical need for a given technology, early adoption may be unwise, and a more prudent strategy would be to wait until patient demand for the service reaches an appropriate and sustainable level.

As mentioned previously, smaller hospitals—particularly community hospitals—and some physician group practices employ late adoption strategies for these reasons. By waiting for more complete information about a technology and its clinical applications, they avoid the pitfalls of rapid technological change. Also, by deferring adoption in some cases, they are better able to coordinate these decisions with their clinical needs and to minimize their financial risk.

Phased versus Serial Acquisition: A Second-Order
Strategic Question

In instances where hospitals, physician group practices, and freestanding centers face the adoption of multiple units of a technology (e.g., monitoring devices, surgical instruments) or must contend with new generations of a rapidly changing technology (e.g., information systems hardware and software), a second-order strategic question involves the manner of acquisition—whether to make purchases in phased or serial fashion.

In a phased acquisition strategy, a technology is purchased in discrete phases or stages at periodic intervals over time. The initial acquisition may involve the purchase of one or more units. High-capital-cost technologies, such as MRI or PET, usually are acquired singly by individual hospitals, whereas multihospital systems and integrated delivery systems are more likely to acquire multiple units. Subsequent purchases of additional units of the same technology, however, usually occur several years later and are guided by (1) changes in technological capability (e.g., first generation, second generation); (2) economic factors (e.g., discounted prices for upgrades); and (3) strategic factors within the organization (e.g., new service development).

Phased acquisition has several commendable attributes (see table 5.3). First, it may help to guard against technological obsolescence by enabling careful evaluation of the initial unit before additional investments are made. Hospitals and physician group practices, for example, may assess the initial unit under varying conditions and with different patient populations. They also may be able to compare its relative advantages with those of competing models of the same technology when acquisition costs are low. This may be difficult to do, however, with high-capital-cost devices.

Second, phased acquisition may permit the hospital or group to capitalize on preferred vendor arrangements, in which it contracts with a technology manufacturer to purchase a specified number of units over time at discounted prices. The adopter also usually receives favored status from the vendor—for product maintenance, training, and other support services—and thus minimizes acquisition costs, while the vendor obtains a guaranteed revenue source for its products. Large hospitals and multihospital systems are best able to negotiate these types of arrangements because of their formidable buying power.

Third, phased acquisition may be employed for strategic goal-attainment purposes, such as (1) departmental reorganization (e.g., upgrading staff skills and gaining familiarity with the latest medical advances); (2) provider status enhancement for high-level care (e.g., a change in institutional designation from Level II to Level I emergency medical services center); (3) new service entry (e.g., ambulatory surgery, organ transplantation); or (4) service expansion into a new geographic area (e.g., regional referral center for cancer care). For each of these goals, technological requirements are considerable, and acquisition in a serial or piecemeal fashion may not be a logical strategy.

In a serial acquisition strategy, by contrast, a technology is purchased in successive installments over time in almost continuous fashion. As with phased acquisition, the initial purchase may involve one or more units, but additional units are serially acquired within a much shorter time interval than in phased acquisition (usually annually or biennially). Serial acquisition may be the superior strategy (see table 5.3) in cases where a hospital or group practice seeks to (1) upgrade its technology flexibly on an annual basis; (2) meet a specified target level of service availability (a specific ratio of technology units to patients); (3) replace outmoded or aging units with more modern or advanced models of the technology; or (4) avoid cash flow problems that often accompany large capital purchases. In each case, successive purchases in consecutive years permit the hospital or physician group practice to augment or replace its existing technological stock without unduly taxing its financial resources. Serial acquisition also enables the organization to take advantage of incremental improvements in a technology's capability or sophistication on a timely basis. Many low-capital-cost technologies lend themselves to acquisition in this manner.

In the end, the choice of first-order and second-order adoption strategies depends on specific circumstances surrounding the decision at hand, especially the nature and properties of the technology, the adopting organization's decision-making process, financial and strategic considerations, and various environmental and regulatory forces.

Two Case Examples: Electronic Fetal Monitoring and Magnetic Resonance Imaging

To illustrate the adoption strategies described earlier in this chapter, we present two case examples of equipment-embodied diagnostic technologies, EFM and MRI. As described in chapter 2, EFM is an obstetric technology that emerged in the late 1960s as a promising means of detecting potential fetal distress during labor and thereby to reduce perinatal mortality and morbidity. Early optimistic reports of uncontrolled trials and low capital costs (approximately $8,000–$12,000 per unit) caused it to diffuse widely across the United States during the 1970s.

The capsule summary presented here is based on a case study of EFM adoption in six Massachusetts hospitals for the period 1969–78 (Cohen and Cohodes 1979, 1982).

As described in chapter 3, MRI is a versatile device capable of producing clear images of internal structures and soft tissue, thus promising improved diagnosis of various conditions. During the 1980s, MRI emerged as the dominant growth technology in the diagnostic imaging field and spawned a major multibillion-dollar industry. Its noninvasive properties and superior imaging capabilities led to its adoption by many hospitals despite high acquisition costs (approximately $1–3 million). As with the case example in chapter 3, the MRI adoption strategies presented here are drawn from a 1984 report prepared for the Congressional Office of Technology Assessment (Steinberg and Cohen 1984).

EFM

Table 5.4 displays the institutional characteristics of the six Massachusetts hospitals studied. All had bed capacities exceeding the 1978 norm for American hospitals, and all provided some degree of specialized perinatal care (either Level II or Level III regionalized care). Three hospitals had active obstetric residency training programs, with one (Hospital F) being an obstetric specialty hospital. Annual deliveries ranged from just under 700 (Hospital A) to nearly 7,000 (Hospital F).

The number of EFM units ranged from two operable units in Hospital A to seventeen in Hospital F (table 5.5). The teaching hospitals (B, E, and F) generally possessed more monitors than did the nonteaching institutions. Hospital preferences for specific EFM methods varied considerably. Hospital B, for example, had no monitors with abdominal electrocardiography capabilities because its obstetrical staff lacked confidence in this method. Hospital C's staff had a negative view of the intrauterine pressure catheter, so the hospital refrained from acquiring that equipment. Individual physician preferences influenced these decisions and the institutions' patterns of EFM acquisition.

The general pattern of EFM diffusion in the study hospitals resembled those of other hospital technologies (Russell 1979). As with other innovations, the teaching hospitals were early adopters, acquiring their initial monitors soon after the equipment became commercially available in 1969 (table 5.6). Hospital E, in fact, was among the first in the nation to employ EFM. The nonteaching institutions adopted EFM somewhat later, including two that did not acquire their

TABLE 5.4. Characteristics of Sample Hospitals

Characteristic	Hospital					
	A	B	C	D	E	F
Geographic setting	Suburban	Urban	Community	Suburban	Urban	Urban
Service orientation	Short-term acute care	Short-term acute care	Short-term acute care	Short-term acute care	Short-term acute care	Obstetrics and gynecology
Level of perinatal care[a]	II	III	II	II	II	III
Teaching orientation Obstetrics/Gynecology residency program	No	Yes	No	No	Yes	Yes
Total beds	300	371	221	335	452	162
Maternity beds (number/% of total)	20/6.7%	26/7.0%	27/12.2%	33/9.9%	46/10.2%	108/66.7%
Labor room beds	4	6	7	6	10	16
Total licensed bassinets	30	40	28	37	54	135
Special care bassinets (number/% of total)	10/33.3%	22/55.0%	4/14.3%	9/24.3%	12/22.2%	35/25.9%
Number of deliveries in past year	692[b]	2,000[b]	1,150[b]	1,360[c]	2,200[c]	6,858[b]

Source: Cohen and Cohodes 1979.
[a]Level of perinatal care based on classification scheme of Committee on Perinatal Care: Level I (community hospital), Level II (perinatal unit), Level III (regional perinatal center).
[b]Figures for calendar year 1978.
[c]Figures for fiscal year 1978.

first monitors until five or six years after the technology's introduction. Four hospitals also adopted fetal scalp pH sampling, a complementary technology, within two years of adopting EFM. Hospital D, however, decided to avoid this technology on the grounds that insufficient evidence of clinical benefit existed to warrant its adoption.

After the initial EFM acquisition, each hospital made at least one subsequent purchase of equipment, with several institutions making multiple purchases. Three hospitals (A, B, and F) pursued strategies of phased acquisition, whereas the others acquired monitors serially in roughly consecutive years (see table 5.6). These divergent patterns suggested different motivating factors underlying the purchases. For example, Hospital A obtained its monitors in stages because it wished to "rejuvenate" its obstetrics department between 1975 and 1978. Hospital B purchased equipment in discrete phases because its designation for regionalized perinatal care changed from Level II to Level III and its labor room bed capacity increased sharply. Hospitals C and D, in contrast, acquired their units serially as EFM gained greater acceptance among skeptical staff members and as the demand for the units increased steadily over time.

Decisions to acquire subsequent units were influenced by one or more of the following factors: (1) the need or desire to increase the availability of EFM; (2) the desire to upgrade existing EFM inventory with technologically advanced equipment; and (3) the need to replace older, mechanically troublesome units. All of the teaching hospitals

TABLE 5.5. Fetal Monitoring Equipment in Sample Hospitals

Characteristic	Hospital					
	A	B	C	D	E	F
Number of operable monitors	2[a]	7[b]	5	3	8	17
Capabilites of monitors						
Fetal heart rate						
Fetal scalp ECG	2	7	3	3	8	17
Abdominal ECG	2	0	3	1	3	17
Ultrasound	1	6	2	3	5	15
Uterine activity						
Intrauterine pressure catheter with strain gauge	2	7	0	3	8	17
Tocodynamometer	2	6	3	3	6	17

Source: Cohen and Cohodes 1979.
[a]One monitor (the older of the two) is used only for backup service.
[b]One monitor (the oldest model) is used only for backup service.

attempted to attain a one-to-one or better ratio of monitors to labor beds: Hospitals B and F had ratios greater than one to one, while Hospital E planned to add two monitors in the near future (see table 5.6).

Financing strategies varied considerably among hospitals. Hospitals B and E, for example, purchased their monitors with capital expendi-

TABLE 5.6. The Acquisition of Fetal Monitors by Sample Hospitals

Characteristic	Hospital					
	A	B	C	D	E	F
Year first monitor acquired (number acquired)	1975 (1)[a]	1970 (1)[a]	1974 (1)	1972 (1)	1969 (2)[a]	1972 (3)
Year scalp sampling introduced	1975	1974	1974	Not used	1971	1972
Year of additional acquisitions (number acquired)	1978 (1)	1974 (4) 1977 (2)	1975 (1) 1976 (1) 1978 (2)	1974 (1) 1975 (1)	1970 (1) 1972 (1) 1973 (1) 1976 (2) 1978 (1)	1973 (2) 1974 (10)[b] 1977 (2) 1978 (13)[b]
Total number of monitors acquired	2	7	5	3	8	30
Method of financing acquisition						
Operating funds	1	0	5	3	0	23
Capital expenditure funds	1	7	0	0	8	5
Special gift funds	0	0	0	0	0	2
Present number of operable monitors	2	7	5	3	8	7
Number of present monitors that are replacement units (%)	1 (50%)	1 (14%)	0 (0%)	0 (0%)	0 (0%)	13 (76%)
Number of present monitors acquired since 1976 (%)	1 (50%)	2 (29%)	3 (60%)	0 (0%)	3 (38%)	15 (88%)
Ratio of monitors to deliveries, 1978	1:346	1:286	1:230	1:453	1:275	1:403
Ratio of monitors to labor room beds, 1978	1:2	1:0.9	1:1.4	1:2	1:1.3[c]	1:0.9

Source: Cohen and Cohodes 1979.

[a]These monitors were not items contained in the budgets of their respective institutions. Hospital A purchased its first monitor with contingency funds from its operating budget. Hospital B did likewise with contingency funds from its capital expenditure budget. Hospital E received its first two monitors at no charge from a manufacturer that was eager to test its equipment in a clinical setting.

[b]These monitors were leased, rather than purchased.

[c]Hospital E anticipated the purchase of two additional monitors in 1979 in order to attain a 1:1 ratio between monitors and labor room beds.

ture funds, whereas Hospitals C and D used operating funds. Hospital A, which normally preferred to purchase equipment with capital expenditure funds, used operating budget monies in 1975 because the purchase was unexpected and required immediate action. Hospital F relied instead on leasing arrangements with selected EFM manufacturers, offering flexibility to replace units as they aged and as EFM technology changed. Of its seventeen units in 1978, fifteen (88 percent) reflected current technology obtained within the previous two years.

Finally, the purchase prices of basic EFM units varied widely across hospitals (see table 5.7). Even so, capital costs were relatively low, especially when two facts were considered: (1) most hospitals amortized each investment (average cost of about $9,000) on a four-year useful life basis, yielding an annual cost per unit of approximately $2,250; and (2) hospitals expected to obtain full return on investment within a few months of EFM operation. Depending on its annual volume of deliveries, its EFM use rate, its operating expenses, and its EFM patient charge per delivery, a hospital was easily able to develop EFM services into a profitable revenue center. The case study also suggested that this could be accomplished without substantial changes in nursing staff or maintenance staff (see table 5.7). EFM changed the role of obstetric nurses in labor and delivery, making them more active participants, but appeared to have minimal effect on nurse staffing patterns.

MRI

In the case of MRI, the general diffusion pattern mirrored those of other technologies, but different segments of the hospital industry employed different adoption strategies (Steinberg and Cohen 1984). As with most advanced devices, early adopters of MRI were major academic health centers, given their penchant for being at the cutting edge of technology development, the need for MRI manufacturers to conduct clinical research to obtain FDA premarket approval, and the simple fact that such hospitals have large and clinically complex patient populations.

Several other benefits influenced the decisions of early MRI adopters. First, they were able to obtain MRI units at virtually no cost because manufacturers valued the institutions' vast research talents, unique laboratory settings for the collection of clinical data, and academic prestige. Second, early adopters were able to protect themselves from technological obsolescence because of their relationships with manufacturers. Third, operating costs of experimental MRI systems often were partly

TABLE 5.7. Costs and Patient Charges Associated with Electronic Fetal Monitoring in Sample Hospitals

	Hospital					
Characteristic	A	B	C	D	E	F
Capital cost of equipment (year/ number of units/ unit price)	75/1/$7,885 78/1/$8,685	70/1/$6,000 74/4/$6,000 77/2/$6,000	74/1/$ 6,820 75/1/$ 7,890 76/1/$10,810 78/2/$12,795	72/1/$6,500 74/1/$7,000 75/1/$7,000	69/1/N.C.[a] 70/1/$2,500[a] 72/1/N.A. 73/1/N.A. 76/1/$6,884 76/1/$8,256 78/1/$9,200	72/ 3/$6,500 73/ 2/$8,000 74/10/$7,500[b] 77/ 1/$6,900 77/ 1/$6,245 78/13/$5,363[b]
Changes in nursing staff due to EFM	None	None	None	None	+2 Specialists	None
Changes in maintenance staff due to EFM	None	None	None	None	None	+1
Charge to patients for EFM (separate or included in delivery)	Included in delivery charge; supplies extra[c]	Included in delivery charge; supplies extra	Separate standard charge	Included in delivery charge; supplies extra	Separate standard charge	Separate standard charge
Amount per delivery	—	—	$50[d]	—	$51[d]	$65[e]

Source: Cohen and Cohodes 1979.

[a]Hospital E obtained its first two monitors free of charge and its third monitor at nominal cost from a manufacturer who was eager to have its equipment tested.

[b]These monitors were leased, rather than purchased.

[c]Hospital A is investigating the possibility of adopting a separate charge of $35–$40 per delivery.

[d]Includes cost of electronic monitoring only.

[e]Includes cost of electronic monitoring and cost of scalp sampling, regardless of whether or not latter procedure is performed.

subsidized by research grants from manufacturers. Fourth, these academic centers were able to capitalize on special research opportunities, such as the National Cancer Institute's Comparative MRI Studies Program, initiated in 1984.

For institutions that delayed adoption of MRI beyond the initiation phase of diffusion, there were indications in 1984 that patience would pay off in other ways as some manufacturers geared up for the acceleration phase by offering selected hospitals two-for-one packages of MRI systems at prices close to those of the lowest-priced systems (those with lower magnet field strengths). These offers also carried strong inducements to accept collaborative research arrangements with manufacturers.

Factors governing the choice of a MRI vendor have already been described in chapter 3, but for university hospitals, it was difficult to say who courted whom. In a few instances (such as with Siemens and Washington University in St. Louis), MRI installations were outgrowths of long-standing relationships.

In contrast to many university hospitals, the Department of Veterans Affairs took a more cautious approach to MRI, electing in 1981 to defer acquisition until more information came to light and then to adopt the technology only through a program of phased acquisition in which the first phase would be a single MRI demonstration project. This decision was motivated by concern that the technology was changing rapidly and that multiple purchases of soon-to-be obsolete units would be unwise. In early 1983, the Department of Veterans Affairs solicited bids from several vendors for a single system and used three factors to guide its choice of a system and vendor: (1) "corporate durability" of the vendor; (2) the vendor's proven record of reliability in its existing MRI installations; and (3) the price of the system. Selection of the first installation site was also directed by three factors: (1) the availability of all other major diagnostic imaging modalities; (2) proven ability in high technology; and (3) a good working relationship with an affiliated university. CON policies were not a consideration because they did not apply to veterans' hospitals.

The MRI acquisition strategies employed by large systems of investor-owned hospitals were markedly diverse. Humana, for example, collaborated with Vanderbilt University in a joint venture stressing shared clinical data and technical advice. Humana planned to undertake a three- to five-year phased approach in which its initial purchase would allow it to assess MRI before making future acquisition decisions. Its decision to adopt MRI in an early diffusion stage was based more on strategic considerations than on a belief that MRI's clinical value had been established.

National Medical Enterprises and Lifemark each decided to defer the acquisition of MRI but did so for different reasons. National Medical elected to wait because of perceived technological uncertainty, whereas Lifemark cited uncertainty over third-party payment coverage as the reason behind its decision. Unlike National Medical, which had not yet formulated its future strategy, Lifemark indicated plans for phased acquisition over a three- to four-year time frame.

Finally, the approach undertaken by Hospital Corporation of America represented a departure from its own historical corporate policies, which traditionally had caused it to lag behind others in technology adoption by as much as eighteen months. In the case of MRI, Hospital Corporation's internal diagnostic imaging technology advisory board decided in favor of early adoption to generate information about MRI more relevant to the company's special needs than that emanating from university hospital studies. Hospital Corporation also planned to purchase five differently configured MRI systems from four manufacturers, thus enabling comparative evaluation of various magnets and vendors. Site selection for initial acquisition favored acute-care hospitals with 250 to 400 beds, a sophisticated diagnostic imaging department, and a large nearby clinical referral base with a patient case mix emphasizing neurology, oncology, cardiology, and orthopedics. After this phase, the company planned to select two or three vendors for favored status in future stages of MRI acquisition.

Incentives and Trade-Offs under Managed Care

Financial and professional incentives always have figured in hospitals' and physicians' decisions to adopt and use medical technology (Weisbrod 1991, 1994). However, the direction and strength of these incentives have shifted over time, depending largely on the type of payment method employed by private insurers and by the Medicare program (see table 5.8).

Changing Incentives over Time

Prior to 1984, hospitals as well as physicians were paid retrospectively by the Medicare program and by private insurers (Blue Cross plans and commercial insurance companies). Hospital payment generally was based on per diem (daily) costs, with some plans and companies paying charges in excess of cost, while physician payment was predominantly fee for service. As stated earlier, these retrospective, cost- or charge-based payment methods produced powerful incentives for hospitals and physicians to adopt and use virtually any new technology regardless of its cost or the magnitude of its potential benefit. The net result was unconstrained diffusion of new technology, especially major equipment and specialized services, despite the existence of cost-containment mechanisms such as capital expenditure review (the federal section 1122 program and CON programs in many states) and hospital rate setting in a few states (see chapters 12 and 13).

TABLE 5.8. Payment Methods and Incentives for Technology Adoption and Use Over Time

		Time Period	
	Pre-1984	1984–94	1994–present
Principal payment methods (by provider and payer)			
Hospitals			
Medicare	Retrospective (cost based)	Prospective (DRG based)	Prospective (DRG based)
Private	Retrospective (cost based)	Mostly retrospective (cost based), with some prospective (DRG based or discounted)	Increasingly prospective under managed care (DRG based or discounted)
Physicians			
Medicare	Retrospective (fee for service)	Retrospective (fee for service) until 1992; prospective (RBRVS) fees thereafter	Prospective (RBRVS) fees
Private	Retrospective (fee for service)	Mostly retrospective (fee for service), with some prospective (discounted or capitated fees)	Increasingly prospective under managed care (discounted or capitated fees)
Incentives for technology adoption and use			
All providers	Adopt and use virtually any technology—regardless of cost or magnitude of benefit	Adopt and use net-beneficial technology—with preference for cost-saving technology	Adopt and use net-beneficial technology—with preference for cost-saving, quality-enhancing technology

Beginning in 1984 with the introduction of the Medicare Prospective Payment System for hospital inpatient care, which paid hospitals prospectively set amounts per patient stay on a diagnosis-related group (DRG) basis, the incentives for technology adoption and use began to change. Prospective payment encouraged hospitals to become more prudent buyers and users of new technologies that demonstrated net benefits, especially those possessing cost-saving properties (G. F. Anderson and Steinberg 1984; U.S. Congress, OTA 1984a). Private insurers slowly followed the Medicare program's lead during the 1980s by moving away from traditional cost-based payment for hospitals toward either DRG-based prospective payment or some form of discounted payment. However, because many hospitals were able to shift costs among payers and thereby recover technology-related costs, these incentives were not especially strong and the desired systemwide constraining effects on hospital adoption and use of technology were not achieved (see chapter 12).

In 1992, the Medicare program introduced a prospective fee schedule for physicians. Using a resource-based relative value scale, coupled with volume performance standards, the new fee schedule attempted to constrain both the price and volume of physician services by dampening physicians' technological imperative through a technology-neutral payment method (see chapter 12). Also during the early 1990s, the rise of managed care led many private health plans to undertake aggressive cost reduction strategies, including the increased use of prospective payment methods for hospitals and physicians. This confluence of private and Medicare payment policies toward cost containment had two principal effects: (1) hospitals and physicians could not shift costs among payers as easily as in the past to recover investments in new technology, forcing the reassessment of strategies for adopting and using technology; and (2) the incentives engendered by these payment methods encouraged providers to adopt and use cost-saving technologies and to eschew, where feasible, the adoption and use of cost-raising ones (Neumann and Weinstein 1991; Weisbrod 1991, 1994).

Following the 1994 defeat of the Clinton administration's proposed Health Security Act, market forces intensified within the health care system. Further expansion of managed care efforts among public and private payers during the 1990s led to increased use of prospective payment methods—including capitated fees for physicians—and to stronger incentives for hospitals and physicians to adopt and use cost-saving technologies (see chapter 12). However, the cost impact of new medical technology alone is not sufficient to drive provider decision making. In an environment that is increasingly dominated by managed care, the potential quality impact of new technology on health care outcomes also must be considered, as must other variables.

Cost/Quality Trade-Offs: A Framework for Analysis

The potential cost and quality impacts of new technology arguably are the two most influential factors in provider decision making under managed care. In some cases, the cost and quality impacts of a new technology may be synergistic and mutually enforcing, but in most instances, trade-offs between cost and quality are impossible to avoid.

Raisa Deber (1992) articulated such trade-offs in terms of "adoption zones," in which the cost of a new technology is weighed against the expected clinical impact relative to an existing alternative. For example, a technology that promises greater benefits for no additional cost, or the same benefits for less cost, should be adopted while a technology that sacrifices benefits without an advantage in cost should not be adopted (Deber 1992).

Figure 5.1 builds on these concepts and presents a framework for analyzing potential cost/quality trade-offs in decisions to adopt and use new technology under managed care (Cohen 1996, 1998). The framework recognizes the importance of consumer preferences in these decisions, as technology manufacturers tend to base their R&D and marketing strategies on the likely preferences and behavior of both consumers and providers.

Three assumptions are essential to the conceptual framework presented: (1) providers employ a comprehensive decision-making process, involving assessment of all relevant technical, clinical, financial, organizational, legal, ethical, and logistical considerations when making technology adoption decisions; (2) cost-effectiveness analysis (CEA) contributes importantly to the evaluation of technology; and (3) potential cost and quality impacts of new technology are assessed relative to existing clinical alternatives (Cohen 1996, 1998). An important caveat, however, is that CEA determinations of a technology's worth early in the R&D process will be difficult to obtain, hindering the ability to acquire adequate advance knowledge about the cost/quality trade-off characteristics of the technology.

Potential cost impact may be defined in terms of cost-saving, cost-neutral, or cost-increasing properties, and potential quality impact may

Impact on Cost of Care

		Cost-Saving	Cost-Neutral	Cost-Increasing
	Quality-Enhancing	ADOPT (Big Winner)	ADOPT (Winner)	CLOSE CALL (Marginal CE Is Key)
Impact on Quality of Care	Quality-Neutral	ADOPT (Winner)	NO COMPARATIVE ADVANTAGE (Other Factors May Decide)	DO NOT ADOPT (Loser)
	Quality-Decreasing	CLOSE CALL (Marginal CE) Is Key	DO NOT ADOPT (Loser)	DO NOT ADOPT (Big Loser)

Fig. 5.1. Cost/quality trade-offs in decisions regarding the adoption and use of medical technology. (From Cohen 1998.)

be classified in quality-enhancing, quality-neutral, or quality-decreasing terms. Figure 5.1 shows nine possible scenarios.

Whether a new technology is adopted and used often depends on the extent to which the individual interests of four key stakeholder groups—providers, purchasers/payers, consumers, and manufacturers—are aligned with one another. When stakeholder interests and microincentives are generally aligned in favor of adoption, technological winners are likely to result (the three scenarios in the upper left corner of figure 5.1). When interests and microincentives are generally aligned against adoption, technological losers will occur (the three scenarios in the lower right corner of the figure). When interests and microincentives are not aligned or appear uncertain, marginal cost-effectiveness criteria may be used to inform these close calls (the two scenarios in the upper right and lower left corners). Finally, when a technology offers no comparative advantage based on cost or quality, other factors likely will determine its fate (the scenario in the center box). Each individual scenario is briefly discussed here.

Technological Winners

Under managed care, a technology that shows promise for saving dollars (e.g., by lowering expenses, by increasing efficient use of resources, or by averting future treatment costs) undoubtedly will be sought by providers, purchasers, and manufacturers alike. But a technology with both cost-saving and quality-enhancing properties will be the most highly prized (see table 5.8). Thus, technological winners are likely to arise in three scenarios—a cost-saving technology with either quality-enhancing or quality-neutral properties and a cost-neutral technology with quality-enhancing properties.

Cost-Saving, Quality-Enhancing Technology
The decision in this scenario appears to be unequivocal. Barring adverse ethical or legal concerns, the technology should be adopted since it is likely to be a big winner for all parties because the individual interests of diverse stakeholders are strongly aligned with one another (see figure 5.2). An example of a potential big winner technology would be a minimally invasive surgical procedure, such as laparoscopy or arthroscopy, in which patient outcomes are improved, provider costs are reduced, purchaser/payer outlays are lowered, and manufacturers reap profits from the sales of fiber-optic scopes and related devices.

Cost-Saving, Quality-Neutral Technology
The decision in this scenario also seems clear—the technology should be adopted if it reduces costs without sacrificing quality. Examples might include: (1) generic equivalents of brand-name drugs (similar chemical composition and therapeutic action but at lower cost); (2) telemedicine, teleradiology, and other communications-based technologies that permit delivery of care in remote places at reduced cost; and (3) various information technologies that improve health care productivity and efficiency but may not necessarily affect the quality of health care outcomes. Stakeholder interests and microincentives are not as fully aligned as in the previous case—providers and purchasers are more likely than consumers to be interested in such innovations because the cost savings will be more visible to those parties. Manufacturers, nonetheless, will be drawn to such potential winners (see figure 5.2).

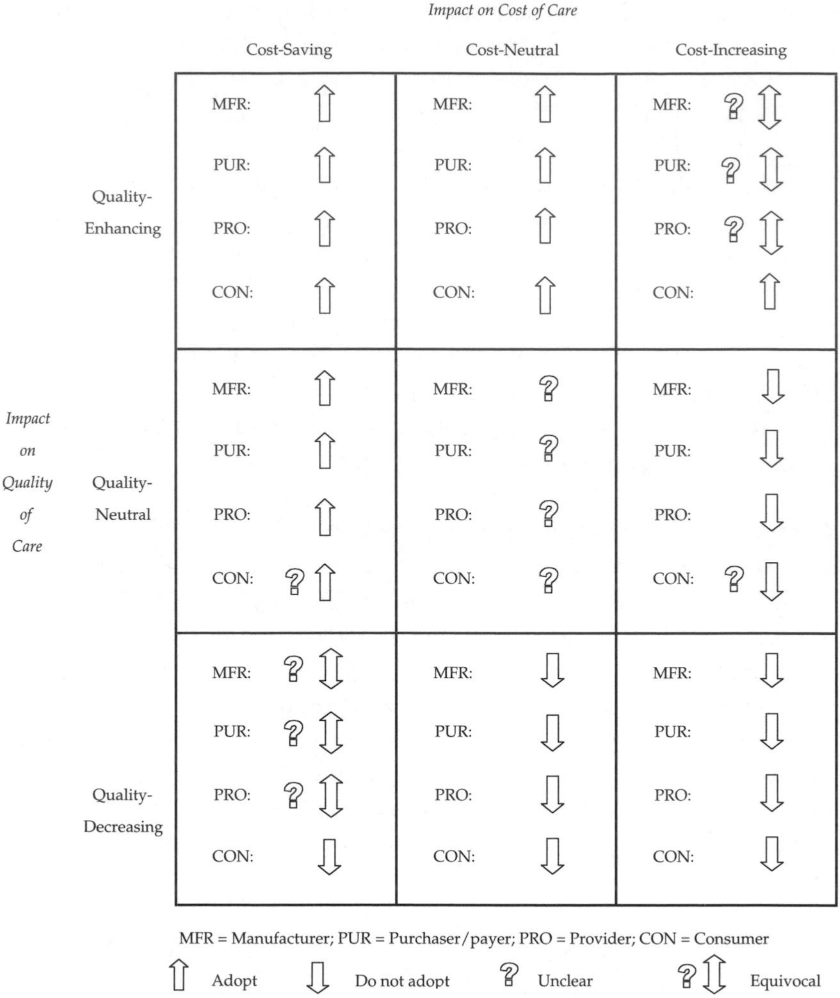

Fig. 5.2. Individual stakeholder interests and microincentives in cost/quality trade-off scenarios

Cost-Neutral, Quality-Enhancing Technology

The decision here is again clear—the technology should be adopted because it appears to be a winner that confers improved outcomes while costing no more than existing alternatives. Although the technology may be more attractive to consumers than to providers, the microincentives are fairly well aligned, and manufacturers likely will see value in tailoring their marketing and advertising efforts for such a product more toward consumers than toward providers.

Technological Losers

Under managed care, a technology that increases health care costs while either failing to improve health care outcomes or producing an actual decline in quality probably will be unattractive to stakeholders. Technological losers, therefore, are likely to appear in three scenarios—a cost-increasing technology with either quality-decreasing or quality-neutral properties and a cost-neutral technology with quality-decreasing properties.

Cost-Increasing, Quality-Decreasing Technology

The decision in this scenario is unambiguous—the technology should not be adopted because it confers neither cost nor quality advantages over existing alternatives. With the interests of all stakeholders strongly aligned against adoption (see figure 5.2), manufacturers will usually abandon a big loser technology early in the R&D process, long before marketing of the product receives serious consideration.

Cost-Increasing, Quality-Neutral Technology

The decision in this scenario also is clear—the technology should not be adopted since it is likely to be a loser in the eyes of consumers, providers, and purchasers, all of whom see only increased costs without gains in quality. In rare instances, a quality-neutral technology may offer greater convenience or some other comparative advantage, causing some consumers to prefer it to the existing alternative, thus weakening the alignment of the microincentives. Nevertheless, manufacturers will not want to invest in these technologies, and they likely will languish in the R&D pipeline.

Cost-Neutral, Quality-Decreasing Technology

The decision here is fairly clear as well—a technology that produces poorer outcomes of care while conferring no cost advantage over current alternatives should not be adopted. The microincentives are well aligned, but perhaps not as strongly as in the case of a cost-increasing, quality-decreasing technology. Consumers clearly will reject such a loser, and providers and purchasers, who are sensitive to consumer concerns, will follow suit, inducing manufacturers to avoid this type of innovation.

Technological Close Calls

Two scenarios that epitomize perplexing cost/quality trade-offs are virtual mirror images of each other—a technology that enhances health care outcomes at higher cost and a technology that achieves cost savings at the expense of quality. Under managed care, each represents a close call in which stakeholder interests and microincentives are either unaligned or uncertain. In such cases, analysis of the marginal cost-effectiveness of the new technology versus existing alternatives may be critical to determining whether to adopt the technology, but the decision ultimately will be a value judgment.

Cost-Increasing, Quality-Enhancing Technology

While consumers may be attracted to the quality-enhancing properties of such a technology, providers will have to determine whether the marginal gain in quality improvement justifies the marginal cost and whether purchasers are willing to pay this incremental expense (see figure 5.2). Manufacturers also will be reluctant to invest heavily in R&D for such a technology unless there is substantial evidence that a sizable market exists for it. Most new technologies probably fit this scenario, forcing physicians to make decisions based on available evidence regarding comparative efficacy and cost-effectiveness of the new technology versus established treatments. A well-documented example was the adoption of tissue plasminogen activator (TPA), a thrombolytic drug, in place of a lower-cost alternative, streptokinase, for the treatment of acute myocardial infarction. Although TPA today is widely regarded as the intravenous thrombolytic treatment of choice in the hours immediately following a heart attack, early assessments found it to be only marginally cost-effective compared to streptokinase (Mark et al. 1995). This information was interpreted in different ways as TPA diffused into medical practice, convincing some purchasers (e.g., private health plans) early on to pay for TPA use while persuading others with severe budgetary constraints (e.g., some state Medicaid programs) to opt instead for the less expensive streptokinase. The recent emergence of new therapeutic agents, such as beta-blockers, low-molecular-weight heparin, and glycoprotein IIb/IIIa inhibitors, is once again challenging clinicians and purchasers to make close calls in the treatment and management of myocardial infarction based on comparative cost-effectiveness (Boden and McKay 2001; Throckmorton 2001).

Yet another example of a close call involves the management of heartburn and gastroesophageal reflux disease. There is currently debate over the choice of a therapeutic agent—proton pump inhibitor or histamine$_2$-receptor antagonist. The proton pump inhibitor is marginally more effective in treating patients with mild to moderate forms of the disease but is also more expensive than the histamine$_2$-receptor antagonist. A recent cost-utility analysis by Heudebert et al. (2000) recommended that physicians first gauge the impact of heartburn on the patient's quality of life before deciding which agent to prescribe. Thus, the use of the more expensive proton pump inhibitor for patients with severe symptoms that affect daily living would be justified, but the use of the histamine$_2$-receptor antagonist in patients with less severe symptoms could result in significant cost savings. Heudebert and colleagues also suggested that organizations that are high-volume purchasers of gastroesophageal reflux disease agents might find the histamine$_2$-receptor antagonist economically attractive, given the present price differential between the two alternatives.

Cost-Saving, Quality-Decreasing Technology

While it may seem incongruous to imagine the adoption of a new cost-saving technology that adversely affects quality, some providers may find such innovations tempting, especially if the cost savings are substantial and the decrement in quality is minimal (see figure 5.2). Thus, the decision in this scenario essentially is the flip side of the previous one and is also a close call, with CEA potentially playing an instrumental role in guiding the decision. Even with careful analysis of the marginal cost-effectiveness of the new technology relative to existing alternatives, a value judgment ultimately may be necessary to determine whether the marginal cost savings justifies the corresponding marginal quality loss. Adoption of such a technology likely will pose difficult ethical questions for providers keenly interested in cost reductions.

Lack of a Comparative Advantage

Of all nine possible trade-off states, the most difficult one to assess is that of a cost-neutral, quality-neutral technology. Without some comparative cost and/or quality advantage, other factors such as ease of use, physicians' preferences, and convenience to consumers likely will guide the decision to adopt and use the technology, but only if stakeholder interests and microincentives are reasonably aligned to support its adoption. Even so, manufacturers may not be compelled to invest unless potential profits are sufficiently attractive.

As Weisbrod (1994) notes, incentives matter greatly in technology adoption decisions. The framework presented in this discussion suggests that the incentives generated by aggressive managed care may indeed influence stakeholder groups in different ways. The key, then, is alignment of incentives and stakeholder interests. Figure 5.3 summarizes the extent to which alignment is likely to occur among stakeholders in the nine trade-off scenarios. The future implications for these different groups are discussed in the remainder of this chapter.

Implications for Technology Manufacturers

With aggressive forms of managed care dominating the health care marketplace since the mid-1990s, and with Medicare and Medicaid payments to hospitals and physicians still constrained by federal legislation dating back to the Balanced Budget Act of 1997, the signal to technology manufacturers today is quite clear—the cost-effectiveness of new technologies is an important issue, and those innovations that have cost-saving and quality-enhancing properties will be most favored for coverage by purchasers of care. Not surprisingly, the search for lucrative technological winners has induced many manufacturers to focus their R&D efforts on technologies that yield tangible savings through either (1) improved technique (e.g., minimally invasive surgery that reduces the risk of complications and shortens hospital stays) or (2) shifts in care from inpatient settings to less costly ones, such as physicians' offices or even patients' homes (Arno, Bonuck, and Padgug 1994; Hirsch 1995).

Among technology industries, though, the pharmaceutical industry may be a notable exception. As discussed in chapter 3, pharmaceutical R&D costs continue to rise, but so does consumer demand for new drugs, driving up prescription drug spending and generating huge profits for industry firms from domestic sales. Direct-to-consumer advertising has been very effective in creating this demand and in insulating the drug companies from the full cost-constraining effects of managed care and the Balanced Budget Act (Iglehart 2001). The managed care industry is attempting to restrain spending growth by redesigning pharmacy benefit plans to include financial incentives for patients to choose lower-cost drugs (including generic equivalents) over expensive brand-name drugs whenever possible.

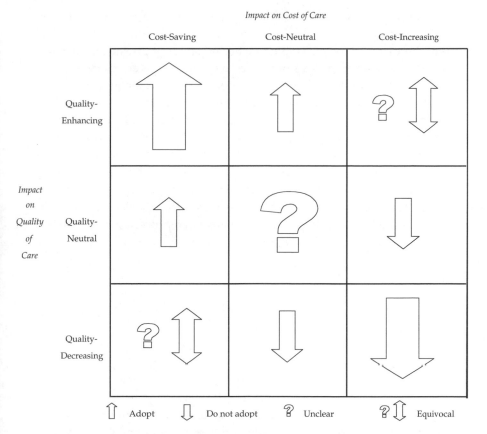

Fig. 5.3. Alignment of incentives in cost/quality trade-off scenarios regarding the adoption and use of medical technology

Other technology manufacturers—most notably device firms, medical and surgical supply companies, and IT software vendors—are positioning themselves to develop technologies that will yield demonstrable cost savings. These manufacturers, as well as pharmaceutical and biotechnology firms, are looking increasingly toward research networks and collaborative ventures with universities and hospitals for the development of clinical databases, information systems, and methods for evaluating the potential cost-effectiveness of new products. In some cases, this has given rise to new professional fields, such as pharmacoeconomics for the evaluation of the cost-effectiveness of new drugs and biological agents (Grabowski 1991; A. K. M. Marshall 1994).

Pharmaceutical firms are not the only ones adopting aggressive marketing tactics: various other manufacturers are beginning to embark on campaigns to advertise directly to consumers in the hope that they, in turn, will influence the practice behavior of physicians. In some markets, key hospital staff members are being targeted for direct marketing. For example, U.S. Surgical Corporation, a major supplier of surgical staples and a leading manufacturer of laparoscopic surgical instruments, changed its marketing strategy in the mid-1990s to focus more heavily on hospital materials managers, who have become the principal decision makers regarding the purchase of surgical supplies. U.S. Surgical also offers to train any surgeon interested in performing laparoscopic procedures, a clever way of promoting the company's products, while working closely with hospital medical staffs to assure that potential savings from minimally invasive procedures are realized in those institutions (Hirsch 1995).

Implications for Providers

Managed care has had somewhat different effects on academic health centers, community hospitals, and physicians.

Academic Health Centers

Academic health centers have felt and continue to feel enormous pressure under managed care and reduced federal payments, largely as a result of their history as high-cost institutions and of their need to fulfill a teaching mission that requires the presence of high technology (Griner 1992; Soper and Ferriss 1992; G. F. Anderson and Steinberg 1994; Epstein 1995). In fact, a recent report (Blumenthal, Reuter, and Thier 2001) paints a rather bleak picture of the financial status of U.S. teaching hospitals. Throughout the 1990s, academic health centers in a number of cities responded to growing financial and competitive pressures by merging, consolidating, or forming strategic alliances with one another as well as with community hospitals, physician groups, and other providers (Shortell, Gillies, and Devers 1995; Brennan 1996; Lutz 1996; Meredith and Steever 1996; Much Ado 1996). Over time, some of these mergers have dissolved, but in many such integrated delivery systems and networks, it is evident that decisions to adopt and use new technologies are no longer the sole province of each institution's managers and physicians. Rather, these decisions now come under the control of managers in the parent organization, who must evaluate whether the decisions are consonant with the entire system's mission and goals (Crater 1995; Cohen 1996). In other words, a decision by one hospital to acquire new technology has direct implications for other institutions within the network.

In general, while managed care is forcing academic health centers to make tougher business decisions than in the past, these institutions traditionally have been early adopters of new technology and are unlikely to forgo the latest and most advanced technologies (Gelijns 1990; Banta and Luce 1993; Epstein 1995). Moreover, the increasing trend toward industry-academic research partnerships is likely to keep academic health centers in the forefront of technology development and ultimately technology adoption and use. In fact, some academic health centers, such as Massachusetts General Hospital and the Partners HealthCare System in Boston, are aggressively pursuing partnerships with biotechnology and genomics firms (Crowley 2003).

Community Hospitals

As a result of the aforementioned competitive pressures, many community hospitals have experienced identity crises about whether they should remain independent organizations serving their local populations or join networks of other hospitals and physician groups (Cohen 1996). They basically have struggled with the question of whether to remain a full-service provider to their communities or to become a niche player in a system, offering a few specialized services to managed care organizations at discounted prices (Cole 1995).

These questions are not easily answered, and the implications for technology adoption and use vary by the strategy selected. It seems clear, though, that community hospitals face an enormous challenge in the current managed care environment, as financial pressures bear down on operating margins, causing some institutions to downsize and others to close. Hospitals most likely will choose to adopt new technology only when it is in their strategic interest, and constrained resources may impede their ability to become centers of excellence for specialized services, such as cardiac surgery.

Physician Groups

Physicians traditionally have played instrumental roles in hospitals' decisions to adopt and use medical technologies. In fact, most of the factors identified in chapter 4 as driving forces behind technology diffusion—consumer demand, promotional efforts by manufacturers, medical education, specialization and the technological imperative, health insurance and payment systems, marketplace competition, and highly visible "opinion leaders"—have directly influenced physician behavior. In the unconstrained financing environment of the past, these forces combined to promote physicians' technology adoption and use. The 1980s was a period of tremendous growth in office-based technology, ranging from clinical laboratories to MRI. As long as physicians could raise the necessary capital and state CON laws did not apply to their offices (as was the case in most states), physicians had unparalleled access to many new technologies (Cohen and Nichols 1993; M. Gold et al. 1993).

Managed care, however, changed the situation. While the incentives for physicians are essentially the same as those for hospitals (i.e., cost-saving, quality-enhancing technologies are favored over others), the payment environment has become decidedly less hospitable for physicians in many areas (B. J. Hillman 1992; Cohen 1996). Reduced payment rates, payment denials, and stringent utilization management practices by managed care organizations have caused many physicians to experience a loss of professional autonomy (Hadley et al. 1992; Blendon et al. 1993) and, for the first time, curtailment of their net incomes (Burda 1996). With industry movement toward managed care, physicians' feelings of autonomy loss are likely to intensify rather than wane in the future. Moreover, the ability of independent group practices to obtain capital for technology purchases is more constrained than in past years.

As physicians look toward an uncertain future, they are confronted by dual dilemmas: (1) how to position themselves organizationally for survival in a more competitive environment and (2) how to respond behaviorally to new and unfamiliar incentives under managed care. Some physicians are responding to this challenge by forming joint ventures or alliances with hospitals and health plans to maintain practice bases, expand existing referral networks, and reduce costs. These new organizational arrangements also afford collaborating partners greater financial security, enhanced prestige, and, in many cases, improved access to new technology.

However, because some joint ventures involve only providers and not insurers or purchasers, physicians find themselves having to play multiple, conflicting roles as (1) principal agent for the patient, (2) gatekeeper to health care resources, (3) neutral information source, (4) surrogate decision maker for the patient, and (5) patient advocate. In the agent role, physicians help patients negotiate a complex and sometimes forbidding health care system. As gatekeepers, physicians must guard against overuse of the system's resources and at times may have to deny patients access to some services—usually costly, technology-embodied ones (Eisenberg 1986). Patient advocacy carries an equally heavy burden, especially when it opposes the gatekeeper role. Patient advocacy can also contradict the surrogate-decision-maker role when physicians find their value systems conflicting with those of patients and their families.

Physicians routinely are thrust into these roles when making clinical decisions regarding technology use for their patients (Eisenberg 1986). How doctors mediate among the competing pressures of these roles varies by individual and likely varies by patient and circumstance.

Implications for Purchasers

Under managed care, purchasers of care—especially employers—gained broader influence over the management of health care during the 1990s (Soper and Ferriss 1992; Cohen 1996). As physicians experienced loss of autonomy and power within the health care system, purchasers increasingly were able to pursue their cost-reduction agendas. However, recent signs have indicated that the power equilibrium between purchasers and providers may be shifting once again, as some integrated delivery systems (e.g., Partners HealthCare System in Boston) have demanded and obtained concessions from managed care companies (e.g., Tufts Health Plan and Harvard Pilgrim Health Care in Boston) in the form of higher payment levels for hospitals and physicians in their networks. Even so, the adoption of new technology that offers greater efficiency will always hold central importance for purchasers and payers. Private-sector purchasers are skilled at employing cost-containment methods (see chapters 11 and 12), with HMOs particularly well versed in MTE (Borzo 1996). For example, Kaiser Permanente has maintained since the 1980s a new technologies committee that reviews emerging technologies and makes recommendations regarding their adoption and use (see chapters 9 and 11). A 1997 national survey of private health plans found that HMOs were two to three times more likely than were indemnity plans to recommend coverage of new laser technologies that had potential for reducing cost (Steiner et al. 1997).

Conversely, public-sector organizations have had relatively limited experience with managed care to date, but this is changing as states increasingly look to managed care to control Medicaid program expenditures and as the Medicare program seeks to implement managed care options under the Medicare + Choice provisions contained in the Balanced Budget Act of 1997. Technology coverage and payment decisions by the CMS (formerly the Health Care Financing Administration) and by state Medicaid agencies are likely to become more complicated in the future, although the AHRQ and its Center for Practice and Technology Assessment continue to assist the CMS in making coverage determinations (see chapter 12).

Implications for Consumers

The shifting incentives for technology adoption and use have broad implications for consumers that involve not only the nature of available information about medical technologies but also the role of consumers in decision making regarding the use of technology in their care.

For many consumers, managed care is an enigma, offering a bewildering array of choices while constraining access to certain therapies. In addition, consumers face a constant barrage of television and print advertising that promotes new drugs and health products, and people are turning in increasing numbers to alternative and complementary therapies. Their need for independent sources of information about the safety, effectiveness, and value of both conventional and alternative therapies is both great and growing. But many individuals may not be able to obtain the information that they need.

The Internet provides a wealth of health and medical information from varied sources, including such popular general health Web sites as Allhealth.com, CBS Health Watch, Intelihealth, Onhealth, and Web-MD as well as a growing number of condition-specific sites sponsored by private organizations or government agencies (Berland et al. 2001). However, there are no standards governing the accuracy and completeness of information in these and many other domains, often leaving consumers confused or misinformed. Moreover, there are few objective sources of information on medical technology and its effects. For many years, the U.S. Congress's Office of Technology Assessment routinely disseminated information on medical technology that was written at a high school reading level, but the office's demise in 1995 left a major void (U.S. Congress, OTA 1995). The AHRQ currently attempts to fill this information vacuum through its Evidence-Based Practice Centers Program, its National Guideline Clearinghouse, and its Centers for Education and Research on Therapeutics (see chapter 11). For both the AHRQ and other information sources, it will be critical in the future to provide information on medical technology in both easily readable English-language form and in other languages.

Because employers are expected to exert ever-increasing power over consumers' choice of health plans, consumers stand to lose control over the direction of their care. Whereas employers—and some providers— may care most about cost reduction, consumers almost universally are concerned more with quality enhancement. Therefore, when it comes to cost/quality trade-offs in technology adoption and use decisions, consumers and employers will often—and almost unavoidably—find themselves on opposing sides of an issue or question.

Medical Technology Evaluation

In part I of this book, we explored the development, diffusion, and adoption of new technology. In this second part (chapters 6–9), we turn to the methods of medical technology evaluation (MTE) and to the organizations in the United States and selected other nations that engage in MTE activities. The methods of MTE include techniques for evaluating

- the clinical safety and efficacy of a technology, using various empirical methods (e.g., randomized controlled trials) as well as synthetic methods (e.g., meta-analyses) of assessment;
- the economic value of a technology, using methods that relate the health benefits of the technology to its costs in ways that measure and value such benefits either in monetary terms (e.g., cost-benefit analysis) or nonmonetarily (e.g., cost-effectiveness analysis, cost-utility analysis); and
- the optimal clinical means for using a technology, based on methods (e.g., clinical decision analysis) that take into account the risks, costs, and benefits of alternative clinical strategies in which the technology is used under uncertain conditions.

Organizations that perform MTE activities in the United States are diverse, ranging from governmental agencies to private payers and research organizations. By contrast, efforts in other nations are conducted almost exclusively by governmental agencies, with considerable international collaboration.

6

The Evaluation of Clinical Safety and Efficacy
Ruth S. Hanft, Alan B. Cohen, and Catherine C. White

In this chapter, we explore basic approaches to evaluating clinical safety and efficacy, including empirical forms of study (e.g., randomized controlled trials, epidemiologic studies, analyses of large databases) and synthetic methods (e.g., meta-analyses, cross-design syntheses, and consensus-development conferences). We also examine two obstetric technologies, electronic fetal monitoring and diagnostic ultrasound, to illustrate how meta-analysis may be applied to their evaluation.

The Definition and Role of Medical Technology Evaluation

Given the speed and complexity of medical advances and the need to determine the value of their contribution to health care, the field of medical technology evaluation (MTE) has grown substantially around the globe over the past thirty years. (See chapter 9 for a discussion of MTE in other nations.) In the United States, the U.S. Congress's Office of Technology Assessment (OTA) was established in 1972 to address technological issues of importance to the nation. The OTA instituted a health program in 1974, and the phrase *health technology assessment* (HTA) was coined to describe the activities involved in evaluating the diverse effects of medical technology. The term *HTA* is still used widely today in international circles, but in the United States many people have come to view *HTA* as referring primarily to government-directed evaluation efforts. Because most U.S. technology evaluation efforts are conducted by private organizations rather than public agencies, the term *MTE* has gained prominence in recent years, and although the literature is filled with references to *HTA*, this chapter uses *MTE*.

From the early literature comes a commonly accepted definition of MTE as "any process of examining and reporting properties of a medical technology used in health care, such as safety, efficacy, feasibility, and indications for use, cost, cost-effectiveness, as well as social, economic, and ethical consequences, whether intended or unintended" (IOM 1985, 25). This broad definition covers a wide spectrum of properties and effects of medical technology that deserve careful evaluation. It also recognizes the need to consider the unintended as well as the intended effects of technology in evaluation efforts.

A major objective of MTE is the need to assure economically valid resource allocation and cost containment (Evans 1983; Aaron and Schwartz 1984; McGregor 1989; Fuchs and Garber 1990; Grimes 1993). As Banta and Thacker (1990) pointed out, in a society with a fixed budget ceiling for health care, such as in the United Kingdom, choices must be and are made at the national level. Technology evaluation, particularly from a societal perspective, can and does inform those choices. But what about the pluralistic U.S. health care system, where funding sources are numerous and direct control of all budgetary resources currently is not possible? Even so, the decentralized technology adoption decisions of private decision makers must be informed, and the health and safety of the public must be monitored and protected through regulation. Thus, MTE plays a critical role in aiding private decision makers, such as managed care organizations, health insurers, and health care providers (hospitals and physicians), in making better informed choices about which technologies to adopt and cover (pay for) and about how to use them. MTE also can assist government regulators in ensuring that the public health is not compromised by adverse effects of new technology and that economic, health, and research resources are not squandered on ineffective or marginally useful technologies (Durenberger 1993; Durenberger and Foote 1993).

MTE may be classified as follows based on a scheme devised by the Institute of Medicine (IOM 1985). Safety evaluations assess the risks associated with the application of a technology. Evaluations of efficacy address the ability of a given technology to yield benefits when applied to a specified population for a particular medical purpose under ideal (i.e., controlled) conditions. Evaluations of effectiveness, in contrast, recognize that ideal conditions do not exist in practice and thus assess a technology's ability to yield medical benefit under average real-life conditions. Cost evaluations examine the benefits derived from a technology relative to its costs; such evaluations not only look at the technology's costs under different applications but also attempt to differentiate between benefits accruing to individuals and those accruing to society (Eddy 1989). Evaluations of the ethical, legal, and social implications of medical technology generally are less quantitative than the preceding categories of evaluation but are critical to understanding the impact of technology on societal norms and institutions and on individual rights and values.

In addition, MTE may vary according to a technology's stage of development—that is, whether it is an emerging innovation not yet accepted into general practice, a new technology that has diffused to some extent but is not yet in widespread use, an established technology that is broadly available and considered a standard of care for particular conditions, or an obsolete technology that has been superseded by a superior technology or has been shown through practice to be ineffective or harmful (IOM 1985).

As a complement to these approaches, Littenberg (1992) proposed a five-level hierarchy in which a technology's biologic plausibility first would be compared with current biologic theory. Next, its technical feasibility for delivery to a target population would be assessed, followed by an evaluation of its short-term intermediate outcomes, its long-term impact on patient outcomes (including unintended effects), and its societal outcomes (in terms of resource use, ethical issues, and social and political hazards). Littenberg cautioned, however, that this evaluation sequence may not always be justified and that a technology's success at one level does not necessarily guarantee its success at another level.

Given the range of issues to be addressed, MTE is a formidable task, and no single approach or method can capture the complete picture of the benefits, risks, and costs associated with a specific technology. However, several analytic methods, in the aggregate, can produce a body of knowledge from which reasonable inferences may be drawn to guide both clinical practice and public policy decisions. The principal methods for evaluating the clinical safety, efficacy, and effectiveness of technologies include the most rigorous form of scientific inquiry (randomized controlled trials, or RCTs), other empirical approaches (e.g., analyses of large patient databases and epidemiologic studies), synthetic analyses (e.g., meta-analyses and cross-design syntheses), techniques based on expert opinion (e.g., consensus-development conferences), and less formal assessments (e.g., case studies). Economic evaluation methods (e.g., cost-effectiveness analysis) and clinical decision analysis are synthetic methods of assessment that combine safety and efficacy/effectiveness information with cost and other information to aid decision makers in choosing among clinical alternatives (Petitti 1994). Table 6.1 presents an overview of each method in terms of its usefulness for assessing technologies of varying types and stages of development. By contrast, analyses of ethical and social considerations employ mainly qualitative methods and focus either on issues affecting individuals (e.g., patient autonomy and distributive justice) or on issues affecting society and its institutions (e.g., technological impact).

Clinical Safety and Risk

Although most debate about medical technology until recently tended to focus on cost containment, MTE's major purpose is to ensure that the benefits of any technology outweigh its risks. The present interest in MTE may be traced to Archie Cochrane's 1972 treatise on the value of various health care practices under the British National Health Service,

TABLE 6.1. Methods of Evaluating Medical Technology

Method	Stage(s)	Concern(s)	Technology Type(s)
Case study	New, established, and obsolete	Effectiveness, cost, and social/ethical/ legal	Drugs, devices, proce- dures, and systems
Consensus develop- ment	New, established, and obsolete	Safety, effectiveness, cost, and social/ ethical/legal	Drugs, devices, proce- dures, and systems
Randomized con- trolled trial (RCT)	Emerging, new, and established	Safety and efficacy	Drugs, devices, and procedures
Meta-analysis	New and established	Safety and effective- ness	Drugs, devices, and procedures
Epidemiologic study	New and established	Safety and effective- ness	Drugs and procedures
Database analysis	Emerging, new, estab- lished, and obsolete	Safety, effectiveness, and cost	Drugs, devices, and procedures
Cross-design synthesis	New and established	Safety and effective- ness	Drugs, devices, and procedures
Economic evaluation (CBA/CEA/CUA)	Emerging, new, and established	Effectiveness and cost	Drugs, devices, proce- dures, and systems
Clinical decision analysis	Emerging, new, and established	Effectiveness, cost, and uncertainty	Drugs, devices, and procedures

Source: Adapted from Cohen and Nichols 1993.

in which he found that many medical practices then in use were not based on any formal measures of effectiveness (A. L. Cochrane 1972; Banta and Thacker 1990).

In the United States during the 1970s, concerns about escalating health care costs led to a search for ways to evaluate emerging and new technologies before they came into widespread use. Evaluation of the ongoing use of established procedures and devices initially generated less interest, even though some studies had shown that a large proportion of the rise in hospital costs could be attributed to the unquestioned, automatic use of "little-ticket" technologies, such as routine chest X rays on admission to the hospital in the absence of symptoms or other indications for the procedure (Scitovsky and McCall 1976; Moloney and Rogers 1979; Angell 1985). This pattern changed in the mid-1970s, and subsequent increases in costs have been associated with the introduction of "new procedures and high-technology care" (Schwartz 1987, 221).

Technology evaluation seeks to weigh clinical safety and efficacy in terms of the risks and benefits associated with a new technology. Safety and efficacy are both relative concepts. *Safety* has been defined as "a judgment of the acceptability of risk in a specified situation" (U.S. Congress, OTA 1982, 33). *Risk* may be defined as "the probability of an adverse or untoward outcome occurring and the severity of the resultant harm to health of individuals in a defined population, associated with the use of a medical technology applied for a given medical problem under specified conditions of use" (U.S. Congress, OTA 1982, 33).

The clinical risks of untested and unproven technologies can be considerable (Grimes 1993). The tragic history of the drug thalidomide and the contentious debate over silicone breast implants are but two examples of the challenges facing the medical community in assessing technological risk, especially when long periods of time might pass before deleterious side effects become manifest. This problem is particularly acute for technologies that pose toxic environmental threats. In addition, new emphasis on the societal impact of technological advances has been brought to the fore recently by the controversy over the potential risk to the public posed by xenotransplantation of genetically altered pig organs (Hanson 1999). In the case of new drugs, the FDA's protocols and procedures have been intended in part to minimize such risks; however, once a drug receives approval for a particular clinical application, its use for other unapproved ("off-label") indications generally is not restricted.

Efficacy and Effectiveness

Efficacy has been defined as "the probability of benefit to individuals in a defined population from a medical technology applied for a given medical problem under ideal conditions of use" (U.S. Congress, OTA 1982, 33). *Effectiveness*, by contrast, establishes the probability of benefit as measured under "average or actual conditions of use" (U.S. Congress, OTA 1982, 33). In other words, this represents the difference between the ideal and the real-world situation.

In a study of efficacy, patients are selected very carefully according to preset criteria for inclusion, a clinical protocol for the use of the technology is established beforehand, the study employs the latest version of the technology and the most skilled clinicians, and both patients and clinicians usually are blinded to the assignment of subjects to groups (IOM 1989). Studies of efficacy generally take place in academic health centers under strict research controls.

A study of effectiveness, in contrast, enrolls all patients who would receive the technology based on broad indications for use. Participants are not subject to any special preparation. Clinicians use and interpret the technology in the ordinary confines of their average practice environments. Many studies of effectiveness include community-based practice. Table 6.2 compares the characteristics of these types of studies.

The IOM (1989) listed five criteria by which the clinical efficacy of diagnostic technologies should be judged.

TABLE 6.2. Characteristics of Efficacy and Effectiveness Studies

Characteristic	Efficacy Study	Effectiveness Study
Patient population	Homogeneous—based on preset criteria for inclusion and exclusion	Heterogeneous—indications for patient use are more relaxed than in efficacy trial
Use of technology	Standardized protocol	Flexible use
Study conditions	Ideal (experimental)	Average (everyday practice)
Masking of assignment to study groups	Usually double blinded (to patients and physicians); sometimes triple blinded (to investigators as well)	Single blinded (to patients only) or double blinded, wherever possible
Outcomes measured	Mostly clinical outcomes (e.g., death, illness, disability) but with increasing focus on other outcomes (e.g., economic and quality of life)	Clinical outcomes, as well as other outcomes

- *Technical capability.* Does the technology do what it is intended to do or what the manufacturer claims it does? Does it perform reliably and produce accurate information?
- *Diagnostic accuracy.* Does the technology lead to accurate diagnoses, as measured in terms of sensitivity (the percentage of diseased individuals who are accurately detected, or the true positive rate) and specificity (the percentage of nondiseased individuals who are accurately diagnosed, or the true negative rate)?
- *Diagnostic impact.* Does the use of the technology alter the pattern of diagnostic testing (does it replace other tests, including some that are more invasive, hazardous, or costly)?
- *Therapeutic impact.* Does the use of the technology alter the choice of a treatment plan for the patient?
- *Impact on patient outcomes.* Does the technology lead to improvements in patient outcomes (e.g., prolonged life or enhanced quality of life)?

Basic Approaches to Evaluating Clinical Efficacy

As outlined in table 6.1, several approaches may be used to evaluate the efficacy and safety of a drug, device, or procedure. Each approach has its strengths and limitations. Because case study methods are used primarily as descriptive tools for profiling the adoption and use of technology, they will not be considered here. Economic evaluation methods are discussed in chapter 7, and clinical decision analysis is addressed in chapter 8. Thus, our exploration of approaches for evaluating efficacy will be confined to randomized controlled trials, meta-analyses, epidemiologic studies, database analyses, cross-design syntheses, and consensus-development methods.

Randomized Controlled Trials

RCTs arguably represent the best method for evaluating the safety and efficacy of medical technologies, particularly emerging ones (L. M. Friedman, Furberg, and DeMets 1981; IOM 1985; Schersten 1986). An RCT is "a planned experiment to assess the effectiveness of treatments by comparing the outcomes in subjects drawn from the same population and allocated to two or more treatment groups by a random method" (McPeek, Mosteller, and McKneally 1989, 319). By definition, RCTs are designed to minimize potential sources of selection and observer bias. Subjects in these trials are randomly assigned to one of several mutually exclusive groups in which they either receive or do not receive the medical intervention in question (IOM 1985). Assignment to the intervention group or to one of the control or comparison groups is usually blinded, so that participants are not aware of which treatment they receive, although the physician or other caregiver may know which patients are receiving which treatments. If neither the physician nor the patient knows which treatment is being given, the trial is double-blind (Brook et al. 1986). In a growing number of trials, the investigators are being blinded to patient group assignments and to study results while the trial is ongoing, resulting in a triple-blind study design. In the past, the control "treatment" often was a placebo (an inert substance with no therapeutic value), but increasingly the comparison treatment is an alternative therapy with proven effectiveness because many scientists believe that the use of placebos in situations where effective therapies already exist is unethical and should be discontinued (Rothman and Michels 1994). Outcome measures of controlled trials may be physiological (e.g., blood pressure) or functional (e.g., ability to walk), although death (mortality) and disease complications (morbidity) are the most common endpoints (IOM 1985).

Although RCTs are universally regarded as the gold standard for evaluating the safety and efficacy of a technology, they are costly, time-consuming, and difficult undertakings that are fraught with methodological pitfalls and ethical quandaries (Foote 1987).

Methodological Issues
The many ongoing methodological issues raised regarding the design and conduct of RCTs include (1) potential lapses in the randomization process (Schulz et al. 1994); (2) inadequate sample sizes and inconsistent reporting of findings (Moher, Dulberg, and Wells 1994); (3) a lack of design flexibility once trials have been mounted, making it difficult to evaluate the long-term impact of dynamic technologies whose optimal configurations and clinical applications evolve over time (Guyatt et al. 1986); (4) an overemphasis on measuring clinical outcomes, coupled with the failure to measure other effects, such as improved social function, psychological status, and ability to return to work (IOM 1989); (5) a paucity of economic analyses (M. E. Adams et al. 1992); and

(6) inadequate representation of women, minorities, and the elderly (Gurwitz, Col, and Avorn 1992; Healy 1992; Wenger 1992).

The problem of small sample size may be mitigated somewhat by performing a multicenter trial in which data are pooled. However, a multi-institutional study design requires strict adherence to study organization, design and protocol development, patient-recruitment procedures, and quality control and monitoring—with all the administrative difficulties and analytic complexity that such requirements entail (IOM 1989; McPeek, Mosteller, and McKneally 1989). Synthetic methods (e.g., meta-analysis and cross-design synthesis) were developed specifically for the purpose of combining the results of multiple trials to achieve greater statistical power and are discussed later in this chapter. Of the 50,000 RCTs published between January 1966 and June 1988, only 121 (0.2 percent) included economic analyses, and many of those suffered from methodological deficiencies (M. E. Adams et al. 1992). Pharmaceutical firms recently have been building cost-effectiveness analyses into the designs of clinical trials for new drugs and biologics, but trials of devices and surgical procedures still lag behind.

In the mid-1990s, efforts to improve the quality of reporting from RCTs led to the development and publication of the Consolidated Standards of Reporting Trials (CONSORT) statement, which comprised a checklist and flow diagram for reporting a randomized trial (Moher, Schulz, et al. 2001). The statement was supported by a number of medical and health care journals and editorial groups. In a comparative before-and-after evaluation of reports of RCTs that were published in 1994 and 1998, Moher and colleagues found a statistically significant improvement in the quality of the reports in the post-CONSORT period (Moher, Jones, et al. 2001). In an analysis of 270 RCTs published in 1998, Egger and colleagues (2001) found that approximately half of the studies contained flow diagrams, which were associated with improved quality and completeness of reporting. Based on these analyses and on other evidence, a revised CONSORT statement recently was published (Moher, Schulz, et al. 2001). The revised statement contains a twenty-two-item checklist (see table 6.3) and a flow diagram (see figure 6.1). The checklist includes items that are essential to judging the reliability or relevance of reported findings, while the flow diagram depicts vital information from four stages of a trial—enrollment, patient allocation to interventions, follow-up, and analysis.

TABLE 6.3.   CONSORT Statement Checklist of Items to be Included in Reports of Randomized Trials

Section and Topic	Item	Descriptor
Title and abstract	1	How participants were allocated to interventions (e.g., "random allocation," "randomized," or "randomly assigned")
Introduction Background	2	Scientific background and explanation of rationale
Methods Participants	3	Eligibility criteria for participants and the settings and locations where the data were collected
Interventions	4	Precise details of the interventions intended for each group and how and when they were actually administered
Objectives	5	Specific objectives and hypotheses
Outcomes	6	Clearly defined primary and secondary outcome measures and, when applicable, any methods used to enhance the quality of measurements (e.g., multiple observations, training of assessors)
Sample size	7	How sample size was determined and, when applicable, explanation of any interim analyses and stopping rules
Randomization Sequence generation	8	Method used to generate the random allocation sequence, including details of any restriction (e.g., blocking, stratification)
Allocation concealment	9	Method used to implement the random allocation sequence (e.g., numbered containers or central telephone), clarifying whether the sequence was concealed until interventions were assigned
Implementation	10	Who generated the allocation sequence, who enrolled participants, and who assigned participants to their groups
Blinding (masking)	11	Whether or not participants, those administering the interventions, and those assessing the outcomes were blinded to group assignment. If done, how the success of blinding was evaluated.
Statistical methods	12	Statistical methods used to compare groups for primary outcome(s); methods for additional analyses, such as subgroup analyses and adjusted analyses
Results Participant flow	13	Flow of participants through each stage (a diagram is strongly recommended). Specifically, for each group report the numbers of participants randomly assigned, receiving intended

TABLE 6.3.—*Continued*

Section and Topic	Item	Descriptor
		treatment, completing the study protocol, and analyzed for the primary outcome. Describe protocol deviations from study as planned, together with reasons.
Recruitment	14	Dates defining the periods of recruitment and follow-up
Baseline data	15	Baseline demographic and clinical characteristics of each group
Numbers analyzed	16	Number of participants (denominator) in each group included in each analysis and whether the analysis was by "intention to treat." State the results in absolute numbers when feasible (e.g., 10/20, not 50%)
Outcomes and estimation	17	For each primary and secondary outcome, a summary of results for each group, and the estimated effect size and its precision (e.g., 95% confidence interval)
Ancillary analyses	18	Address multiplicity by reporting any other analyses performed, including subgroup analyses and adjusted analyses, indicating those prespecified and those exploratory
Adverse events	19	All important adverse events or side effects in each intervention group
Comment		
Interpretation	20	Interpretation of the results, taking into account study hypotheses, sources of potential bias or imprecision, and the dangers associated with multiplicity of analyses and outcomes
Generalizability	21	Generalizability (external validity) of the trial findings
Overall evidence	22	General interpretation of the results in the context of current evidence

Source: Data from Moher et al. 2001.

For many years, randomized trials discriminated against the participation of women, minorities, and elderly persons, thus limiting the potential generalizability of these studies to broader populations and to average practice conditions (Brook et al. 1986; Eddy 1989). Under pressure from women's health groups and from Congress (which passed the NIH Revitalization Act of 1993), the NIH and the FDA in the mid-1990s began to correct these biases by revising their policies and guidelines regarding the design and conduct of clinical trials (J. C. Bennett and Board 1993; Merkatz et al. 1993). While the NIH specifically required that women and minorities be included in clinical trials and that

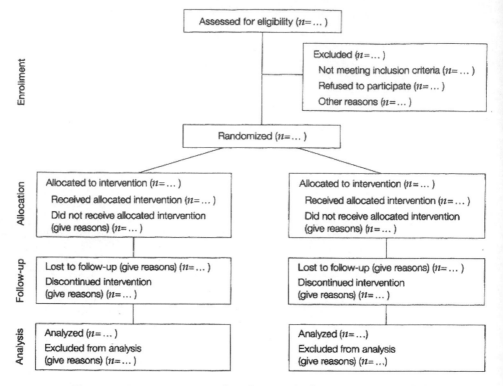

Fig. 6.1. CONSORT statement flow diagram of subject progress through the phases of a randomized trial to be included in reports of randomized trials. (From Moher et al. 2001.)

an analysis of gender and racial differences in treatment effects be performed, the FDA took less aggressive steps, stating that women should be included in clinical trials if they would receive the drug when marketed and that the agency would expect (but not require) a gender analysis to be performed (Baird 1999). Recent analyses of the NIH's efforts have suggested general success in increasing the participation rates of women in clinical trials (GAO 2000, 2001; Harris and Douglas 2000). However, Buring (2000, 506) argued that increased representation of women, minorities, and vulnerable populations is not enough and that the selection of the best research design "must always be driven by good science, and the inclusion of relevant populations must be addressed in developing the research design that is most appropriate to the scientific objectives of the study." Thus, if gender-specific differences are to be evaluated in a trial, then careful consideration must be given to the choice of study design (e.g., single-sex trial versus mixed-sex trial) and to issues of sample size.

Ethical Issues

Ethical concerns have been raised over (1) whether physicians' participation in trials violates the sacred covenant with their patients (Hellman and Hellman 1991), (2) whether to discontinue a trial when early evidence shows clear lifesaving effect, (3) whether informed consent of patients is truly necessary and how to best obtain it, (4) whether potential bias is introduced by commercial sponsorship and how to deal with conflicts of interest (Bero and Rennie 1996), and (5) whether RCTs represent a cost-effective investment of constrained research resources.

Regarding the participation of physicians in trials, Passamani (1991, 1589) argued convincingly that properly designed trials—carried out with informed consent and clinical equipoise—protect both physicians and patients from ineffective or toxic therapies and thus "are in fact the most scientifically sound and ethically correct means of evaluating new therapies." As for the discontinuation of trials, there is growing consensus that trials should be discontinued when there is clear evidence of clinical benefit for a life-threatening disease for which no therapeutic alternatives presently exist. For example, during the 1980s, clinical trials of AZT (the first effective drug for the treatment of AIDS) may have been prolonged unnecessarily despite early indications that the drug was efficacious.

In the case of informed consent, there have been numerous calls for improved protection for human subjects in clinical trials (Shalala 2000) as well as serious discussion about whether informed consent is truly necessary (Ellenberg 1997). For example, a physician may experiment with a new treatment within the context of clinical care provided that patients give general consent for the treatment. However, if that same physician were to conduct a rigorous RCT to compare the effectiveness of two alternative therapies, approval must be obtained from the institutional review board and written consent must be secured from potential subjects (Truog et al. 1999). Thus, small-scale, early-stage experiments paradoxically may evade external scrutiny, while RCTs must overcome substantial hurdles.

In defining what constitutes ethical clinical research, Emanuel, Wendler, and Grady (2000) contended that informed consent alone is insufficient and that seven requirements must be fulfilled: (1) the research must have social or scientific value for improving health or enhancing knowledge; (2) the study must be scientifically valid and methodologically rigorous; (3) the selection of subjects must be fair and just; (4) the research must offer a favorable risk-benefit ratio (the potential benefits to individuals and the knowledge gained for society must outweigh the risks); (5) independent review of the research design, methods, and findings must be conducted by unaffiliated individuals; (6) informed, voluntary consent must be obtained from subjects; and (7) researchers must demonstrate respect for potential and enrolled subjects by protecting their privacy, offering them opportunities to withdraw, and monitoring and maintaining their well-being throughout the trial. Even so, the roles of research scientists and clinical practitioners differ, and potential conflicts of interest may arise when clinicians stand to gain from enrolling their own patients as subjects in clinical trials that they conduct (Morin et al. 2002). In such cases, it is recommended that someone other than the treating physician obtain the participant's informed consent and that, in general, physicians should be trained in the ethics of clinical trials so as "to preserve the integrity of research and to protect the welfare of human subjects who enroll in trials" (Morin et al. 2002, 78).

The question of whether RCTs represent a cost-effective investment of constrained research resources was examined by Detsky (1989), who analyzed seven selected trials in terms of the costs of performing them and the benefits to the health status of their target populations. He found that even though clinical trials may require substantial expenditures (e.g., $150 million for the Lipid Research Clinics Trial), these costs paled in comparison with the costs of applying the interventions in practice and—when viewed in the context of potential benefits to the target populations (e.g., in the form of lives saved)—the return on investment in such research was high. Fletcher (1989) warned, however, that not every trial is a good investment and that decisions about the value of randomized trials depend not only on cost-effectiveness but also on judgments about how to allocate resources. Two recent comparative analyses of RCTs and observational studies (Benson and Hartz 2000; Concato, Shah, and Horwitz 2000) rekindled debate over the value of observational studies in the evaluation of therapies. Both studies reported that observational studies yielded results similar to those of RCTs performed for evaluation of the same treatment. However, Pocock and Elbourne (2000, 1909) criticized the methods of these two studies, arguing that observational databases may be useful adjuncts to RCTs but that society expects new medical interventions to be evaluated "by the most scientifically sound and rigorous methods available."

Policymakers responsible for making decisions about the adoption and use of new medical technology must also weigh the evidence regarding RCTs' ability to influence medical practice patterns. Lamas and colleagues (1992), for example, found that well-executed trials of cardiovascular drugs published in highly visible clinical journals had a measurable and prompt effect on practice patterns. However, the literature contains many more reports of failure to influence physician behavior (T. C. Chalmers 1974; Gutzwiller and Chrzanowski 1986), including examples that involve the continued use of diethylstilbestrol in pregnant women years after trials showed a lack of benefit (see chapter 2) and the use of various drugs such as beta-blockers, long-acting nitrates, clofibrate, and platelet antiaggregants. Reports of hazards associated with tolbutamide for adult-onset diabetes did not produce a decrease in drug-prescribing behavior by physicians for almost six years.

Yet despite these concerns and shortcomings, well-constructed randomized studies form the cornerstone of efficacy evaluation. In the future, the challenge for those who design and conduct clinical trials will be to design studies that include economic outcomes, such as cost-effectiveness measures, as well as the traditional clinical outcomes.

Meta-Analysis

Meta-analysis is a synthetic method for combining the results of multiple studies to obtain summary conclusions regarding a body of scientific research (Petitti 1994). The term itself was coined by Gene Glass (1976) as "the statistical analysis of a large collection of results from individual literature, for the purpose of integrating the findings" (Thacker 1988, 90). Meta-analysis was developed initially in the 1930s, gained popularity in the social sciences during the 1970s as a tool for improving the quality of literature reviews, and subsequently was introduced into medicine in the early 1980s (Thacker 1988; Petitti 1994). By 1992, 435 meta-analyses of RCTs had been published in the medical literature, with an additional 527 articles appearing between 1992 and 1995 (Moher and Olkin 1995). Today, the literature is increasingly filled with meta-analyses: some recent examples include reviews of the relation of silicone breast implants and connective-tissue diseases (Janowsky, Kupper, and Hulka 2000), reviews of prehospital thrombolysis for acute myocardial infarction (L. J. Morrison et al. 2000), reviews of magnetic resonance angiography for evaluating lower extremity arterial disease (Koelemay et al. 2001), and comparison of coronary artery bypass surgery and stenting for treatment of multivessel disease (Serruys et al. 2001).

Meta-analysis is not a single methodology but actually a set of methods. Thacker (1988) describes three basic approaches that have been employed.

- *Vote counting.* In this simplest of approaches, results of studies are classified as statistically significant in one direction, significant in the opposite direction, or not significant. The category garnering the most votes is accepted as the "truth." This approach, however, fails to consider issues of sample size, effect size, study design quality, or data quality that vary across studies.
- *Natural aggregations or clusters.* This approach examines problems as they occur in natural clusters within a population and analyzes the observed differences across clusters. If the differences can be explained, then the data are combined and adjusted statistically.
- *Data pooling.* This approach has become the favored method of meta-analysts. Most applications in medicine involve the pooling of results from studies with similar designs (Droitcour, Silberman, and Chelimsky 1993). Advantages include the greater statistical power afforded by the combined samples and the ability to adjust for differences in individual study designs, measurement methods, and study populations. This approach may be particularly useful when multiple studies have produced conflicting results (see the case example of electronic fetal monitoring in this chapter). Critics of the approach, however, contend that some of the statistical techniques used to manipulate and adjust the data are not methodologically sound, calling into question the value of the synthetic findings (L. K. Altman 1990).

Most meta-analyses that use data-pooling methods employ the following general process (Thacker 1988; Petitti 1994):

1. *Problem formulation*—defining explicitly the outcomes and possible confounding variables to be examined.

2. *Selection criteria formulation*—establishing rules for inclusion or exclusion of studies from the analysis.
3. *Literature search*—identifying and locating relevant studies for inclusion in the analysis.
4. *Data abstraction*—obtaining from relevant studies all data (i.e., outcomes, patient characteristics, and study design characteristics) that will be needed for the analysis.
5. *Statistical analysis*—aggregating study findings to obtain a summary estimate of effect size, measuring its variance and confidence interval, adjusting for sampling and measurement error, and testing for homogeneity of effect size across studies.
6. *Interpretation and reporting*—performing sensitivity analyses of variations in key parameters and assumptions and interpreting the meta-analytic findings for application to clinical practice.

As the number of meta-analyses published in medical journals increased during the 1980s and 1990s, concerns arose regarding their quality (Sacks et al. 1987; Kassirer 1992; Moher and Olkin 1995). In one review, Sacks et al. (1987) evaluated eighty-six meta-analyses in terms of six areas (study design, ability to be combined, control of bias, statistical analysis, sensitivity analysis, and application of results) and found inadequacies in a majority of studies, prompting the authors to call for greater uniformity and for the same rigor that would be demanded of a RCT. In another review, Moher and Olkin (1995) also identified methodological deficiencies and called for the establishment of standards for reporting meta-analytic findings. More recently, Ioannidis and Lau (1999) concluded that meta-analysis—as a tool for the systematic and quantitative synthesis of evidence—offers benefits and limitations that must be addressed in its application. In addition to improving statistical power, meta-analysis helps to reveal how heterogeneity among populations affects the effectiveness of medical interventions in different settings and in different patients and helps to detect biases in the research literature, such as publication bias ("positive trials" are more likely to be published than are "negative trials") and Tower of Babel bias (studies generated in non-English-speaking countries tend to appear in the English-language literature only if they have statistically significant findings). Limitations of meta-analysis include the inability to improve the quality of data or reporting in the original studies and the ecological fallacy of extrapolating from group data to the individual patient when the specific individual may not be representative of the group.

One promising effort aimed at helping people to make well-informed decisions about health care is the Cochrane Collaboration (2001). Founded in 1993 and named in honor of Archie Cochrane, an eminent British physician and epidemiologist who challenged the medical profession to base clinical decision making on sound evidence, the collaboration is an international, not-for-profit organization that prepares, maintains, and disseminates systematic, up-to-date reviews of all relevant RCTs (Bero and Rennie 1995; Cochrane Collaboration 2001). Cochrane reviews are prepared by collaborative review groups and are published electronically in the *Cochrane Database of Systematic Reviews*. The collaboration also maintains the *Cochrane Controlled Trials Register*, a bibliographic database of RCTs. The number of Cochrane reviews is now approaching 1,000, with 472 available in the form of consumer synopses (Cochrane Collaboration 2001). All reviews are continuously updated as new evidence dictates.

Epidemiologic Studies

Although not generally used as technology evaluation methods per se, epidemiologic studies provide important support for evaluating medical technologies. Epidemiologic methods include cross-sectional studies, case-control studies, and cohort studies (Moses 1986). Cross-sectional studies focus on a single point in time and may be used to assess the prevalence of a particular technology or a particular disease, but they do not lend themselves to longitudinal analysis of a technology's effects. A major advantage of cross-sectional studies is that they may be used to address multiple questions at one point in time.

Case-control and cohort studies, conversely, are legitimate longitudinal analyses whose value lies in their ability to look at the outcomes of certain behaviors or interventions over time (IOM 1985; Hennekens and Buring 1987). Case-control studies permit the comparison of two populations defined by a common outcome variable (e.g., comparing a group of lung cancer patients with a disease-free group with regard to history of exposure to cigarette smoke), whereas cohort studies permit the comparison of two populations defined by a common risk or exposure variable (e.g., comparing a newly vaccinated at-risk group with an unvaccinated at-risk group to determine how many individuals in each will contract the disease over time).

These methods demonstrate only associations among variables under study: cause and effect cannot be firmly resolved. Additionally, in drawing comparison groups, researchers have difficulty ensuring that all confounding variables are controlled, though Moses (1986) suggested that the use of several different comparison groups might solve this problem if similar findings emerge for all groups.

Epidemiologic studies are most useful for assessing the prevalence of technology use and health outcomes and for tracing the availability and rate of diffusion of a technology (IOM 1985). Increasingly, epidemiologic and statistical methods are being used to analyze the effectiveness of technology in large medical practice databases for defined populations.

Database Analyses

With the 1989 establishment of patient outcomes research teams by the federal Agency for Health Care Policy and Research (now the Agency for Healthcare Research and Quality) to analyze large clinical databases generated by Medicare claims, database analysis ushered in a new era of research on effectiveness. Intended primarily to develop clinical practice guidelines for physicians providing care to Medicare beneficiaries, research team studies were structured around a common medical problem (e.g., coronary artery disease) or a specific intervention (e.g., cataract surgery) and were used for comparative evaluations of alternative technologies (AHCPR 1991). These database analyses offered valuable information on the use of technology in the Medicare population, including data on costs, patient outcomes, and risk factors. Critics argued, however, that such analyses were inherently limited by the nature and content of the databases themselves (Cross Design Synthesis 1992) and suffered from treatment-assignment bias, which undermined the studies' ability to provide convincing evidence of unbiased comparison (Droitcour, Silberman, and Chelimsky 1993). The AHRQ's new Evidence-Based Practice Centers program is the successor to the patient outcomes research team studies and is described in chapters 9 and 11.

Cross-Design Synthesis Methods

The U.S. General Accounting Office issued a report in 1992 advocating a new meta-analytic method, cross-design synthesis, that was intended to overcome the shortcomings of RCTs and database analyses (GAO 1992c). Unlike conventional meta-analysis, which attempts to deal with the limitations of small sample size by combining the results of several studies with similar designs, cross-design synthesis combines results from studies with different but complementary designs. The technique involves three steps (Droitcour, Silberman, and Chelimsky 1993): (1) a focused assessment of the biases in each study that may derive from design weaknesses (e.g., selection of patients or methods employed), (2) an adjustment of each study's results to correct for identified biases, and (3) the development of an appropriate synthesis framework for combining results within and across designs.

Applied to MTE, cross-design synthesis promises to combine the complementary strengths of RCTs and database analyses to answer important questions about the effectiveness of treatment in medical practice (Droitcour, Silberman, and Chelimsky 1993). Its potential advantages include the ability to deal statistically with differences in estimates from disparate sources and to project results to patients not covered by RCTs, thus simultaneously enhancing the scientific rigor of database analyses and the generalizability of relevant randomized trials. Its main drawbacks are that it relies on judgment for many decisions and may overvalue some studies that contain inappropriate data. The *Lancet* (Cross Design Synthesis 1992, 946) cautioned that "formal methods of combining results from different study techniques can confuse rather than clarify the issues and should not substitute for informed interpretation of all the evidence."

Consensus-Development Methods

An approach that has been useful for evaluating new, established, or potentially obsolete technologies is the consensus-development conference, which was first used in the United States by the NIH in a 1977 report on breast cancer (Jacoby 1985; Perry 1987). The main objective of consensus-development conferences has been to inform the health care community of the "status of emerging biomedical technologies and the need for change in the use of existing health-related technologies" (Jacoby and Rose 1986, 107).

Topics for these conferences have had to meet three major conditions: (1) they must be subjects of controversy in clinical care or must be medical practices that have remained unchanged despite research evidence of a need for change, (2) they must be "medically important issues" that are of "considerable interest to practicing physicians," and (3) there must be research evidence available that makes them amenable to resolution. Other considerations used in selecting topics for conferences have included timing, importance to public health, cost impact, preventive potential, and public interest (Jacoby and Rose 1986, 108).

In each conference, an interdisciplinary panel of experts meets for two and a half days to synthesize and review evidence from available research on five or six key questions related to the selected condition or technology. The product of each conference is a consensus statement summarizing conclusions regarding the safety, effectiveness, and appropriate use of the technology. Open discussion of the draft consensus statement by the panelists, speakers, and audience members is encouraged (Kanouse 1989), and final consensus statements are published and disseminated widely (Jacoby and Rose 1986).

In the first ten years of the NIH program (1977–86), sixty consensus statements were issued on subjects as diverse as cesarean childbirth, total hip-joint replacement, CT scanning of the brain, and health implications of obesity (Perry 1987). Since 1987, the annual number of conferences has ranged between 4 and 9 (IOM 1990), with the total number of conferences passing 120 in 2001 (NIH 2001).

Criticisms of this approach have centered on such issues as the appropriateness of technologies/topics selected for conferences, the appropriateness of experts convened for the panels, the extent to which the conferences incorporate all pertinent information on the technology under review, and the effectiveness with which conference recommendations have been disseminated to practicing providers (Perry 1987; Wortman, Vinokur, and Sechrest 1988; Kanouse 1989; IOM 1990).

Three major evaluations of the NIH program have been published. In one study, Wortman, Vinokur, and Sechrest (1988) concluded that the consensus-development process was ideally suited to uncomplicated, noncontroversial technologies but that these were likely to be the least interesting to both practitioners and the public. Recommendations for improvement included more thorough search processes for questions, panelists, and research evidence; greater use of meta-analyses; use of multiple formats reflecting the circumstances; more time for drafting consensus statements; and more clearly written statements suitable for broad dissemination.

In a content analysis and survey of practitioners, Kanouse (1989) found that consensus recommendations were far more likely to reach specialists than generalists. To remedy this situation, Kanouse recommended broader and more aggressive dissemination of consensus statements through general medical journals as well as specialty journals, continuing medical education programs, direct mailings, and various health care delivery organizations. Kanouse also proposed improvements in the planning and management of the conferences and in the monitoring of the program.

In a third evaluation, the IOM (1990) recommended expanding the scope of inquiry to include relevant economic, social, and ethical aspects of technology assessment; stating more explicitly the program's ultimate goal of changing behavior toward the appropriate use of health practices and technologies; and adding more structure to the program, especially with regard to topic selection, analytic method, and standardized conference format.

Other suggestions for improving the process have included using decision analysis to assist panelists in synthesizing relevant research data (Pauker 1986), more systematic selection of panelists (McGlynn, Kosecoff, and Brook 1990), and formal inclusion of minority views (Perry 1987). Ultimately, the value of the consensus statements can be estimated only in terms of their effects on medical practice. Although some of the earlier conferences (e.g., those on breast cancer screening and liver transplants) appear to have had some impact on practice, others (e.g., those on cesarean delivery and screening for cervical cancer) appear not to have led to significant changes in modes of practice (Wortman, Vinokur, and Sechrest 1988; Kanouse 1989; IOM 1990).

Despite their flaws and limitations, consensus-development methods have been employed extensively throughout Europe (Vang 1986). A comparison of consensus-development efforts in the United States, Canada, and several European countries found that while they all began with the U.S. model, several introduced important variations (McGlynn, Kosecoff, and Brook 1990). In Denmark, for example, consensus conferences have been organized to examine biotechnology in industry and agriculture (Andreasen 1988). In Canada, the conferences have been used both to generate practice guidelines and to rate indications for the use of a technology in different patient groups (McGlynn, Kosecoff, and Brook 1990).

Case Examples of Meta-Analysis: Electronic Fetal Monitoring and Diagnostic Ultrasound

To illustrate how meta-analysis may be used to examine the safety and effectiveness of a medical technology, we present case examples of two obstetric technologies—electronic fetal monitoring (EFM) and ultrasound scanning in prenatal diagnosis, both of which diffused rapidly despite evidence of limited clinical benefit (Banta and Thacker 1990; Stauning 1994).

EFM

On October 29, 1991, the *Washington Post* carried a front-page story on the continuing controversy over the use of EFM (Booth 1991). The article quoted Dr. Benjamin Sachs, chief of obstetrics at Beth Israel Hospital in Boston, as attributing the high rate of cesarean delivery in the United States to the use of EFM. An unnamed physician in the article stated that unless an expectant mother under his care was prepared to sign a release, "she would be monitored." This article merely highlighted a debate that had raged for more than twenty years while EFM had been adopted and used widely despite RCTs suggesting that it increased the number of cesarean births yet offered only marginal benefit for low-risk pregnancies (Banta and Thacker 1990).

A meta-analysis conducted by Thacker (1987) assessed the quality of three RCTs conducted in Denver as well as four others conducted in Dublin, Ireland; Melbourne, Australia; Sheffield, England; and Copenhagen, Denmark. The analysis had a twofold objective: (1) to judge the quality of these studies against general criteria for applying tests of statistical significance and for drawing conclusions and (2) to reexamine the studies' findings regarding the routine use of EFM.

Using a standardized method for evaluating the quality and comparability of reports from clinical trials, Thacker (1987) found that except for the Melbourne study, the reports met most of the criteria. By pooling data, he was able to apply tests of significance to the findings from six of the smaller studies (the Dublin trial was excluded), and he found that the EFM group experienced a statistically higher rate of cesarean section than did the control group. Otherwise, there were no discernible statistical differences between the EFM and control groups.

In the Dublin trial, which included more than 13,000 women, the EFM group experienced a higher but nonsignificant rate of cesarean delivery, a significantly higher rate of operative deliveries (those using mid- or high forceps), and a lower rate of neonatal seizures than the control group, which received manual auscultation instead of EFM. Further stratification of the data revealed the lower rate of neonatal seizures to be associated with the use of oxytocin, a drug used to stimulate labor.

As a result of these findings, the Dublin study recommended that EFM be used on a selective rather than universal basis (Thacker 1987).

Thacker's (1987) meta-analysis confirmed the findings of the Dublin study and reinforced the conclusions of a 1979 NIH consensus-development conference devoted to methods of antenatal diagnosis, which had asserted that auscultation was an acceptable alternative to EFM (Banta and Thacker 1990). In 1989, the American College of Obstetricians and Gynecologists stated that monitoring with intermittent auscultation in both low- and high-risk pregnancies is an acceptable policy (Banta and Thacker 1990). Other meta-analyses failed to find benefit from EFM in high-risk pregnancies (I. Chalmers, Enkin, and Keirse 1989). In addition, a large population-based study of cerebral palsy in children questioned the "uncertain" value of EFM and its high false positive error rate, citing concerns that if widely used, "many cesarean sections would be performed without benefit and with the potential for harm" (K. B. Nelson et al. 1996, 613).

Yet despite the lack of evidence demonstrating efficacy, EFM persists in U.S. obstetric practice, and in recent years a form of uterine monitoring has been introduced for home use to detect premature labor and to permit early intervention. Grimes and Schulz (1992) reviewed RCTs of home uterine monitoring and found no significant difference in the rate of premature births. Grimes (1993, 3031) further noted that "in the most sophisticated study to date, this expensive monitoring telemetry was not significantly more effective . . . than was sham monitoring with similar nursing care."

Among the reasons cited for the continued use of EFM are a shortage of nurses to perform frequent auscultation, the fact that EFM services may be billed at a higher rate, and the fear of malpractice litigation in the event of an adverse neonatal outcome (Shearer 1991). Grimes (1993, 3031) also suggested that the "inertia that drives medical practice" may be a reason, but more likely the misplaced technological imperative of obstetricians may be at work. The FDA recently approved the first pulse oximeter for continuous monitoring of intrapartum fetal oxygen saturation, which is indicated as an adjunct to EFM in the presence of a nonreassuring fetal heart rate pattern (Henney 2000). The pivotal evidence supporting FDA approval was a RCT that found fewer cesarean deliveries performed for nonreassuring fetal status in the pulse oximeter group than in the control group. However, although it is not clear that use of the oximeter resulted in better neonatal outcomes, the presence of this new adjunct technology is likely to reinforce obstetricians' technological imperative to use EFM.

Ultrasound Scanning in Prenatal Diagnosis

The earliest descriptive studies of the use of ultrasound in pregnancy appeared during the early 1970s. These studies emphasized ultrasound's superior diagnostic capabilities (Ewigman 1989), leading to widespread adoption by physicians and great demand among patients. In response to questions regarding the technology's routine use in pregnancy, the NIH (1984) issued a consensus statement that listed twenty-eight possible indications for its use, including evaluating fetal growth, estimating gestational age in certain circumstances, determining fetal presentation, and evaluating suspected ectopic pregnancy. Ultrasound's popularity as a routine diagnostic tool in pregnancy has continued despite the NIH panel's finding that routine use of the technology could not be recommended without conclusive evidence regarding its safety and efficacy (Ewigman 1989).

Iain Chalmers and associates at the National Perinatal Epidemiology Unit in Oxford, England, spent fifteen years researching the effectiveness of perinatal care (I. Chalmers 1991). Through descriptive analysis of observational data and meta-analysis of RCTs, they were able to classify interventions into four categories, according to known effects and effectiveness (I. Chalmers, Enkin, and Keirse 1989): (1) effective; (2) promising but requires further evaluation; (3) unknown effects, requires further evaluation; and (4) ineffective and should be abandoned.

Selective use of ultrasonography fell into the first category, with known effects including confirmation of life, estimation of fetal size, and detection of fetal malformation. Routine use of ultrasonography, however, fell into the third group, having unknown effects and requiring further evaluation (I. Chalmers, Enkin, and Keirse 1989; I. Chalmers 1991).

Only one small study (Youngblood 1989) supported routine use of ultrasound, contending that in twenty years of use, there had been no demonstrable evidence of untoward clinical effects on the fetus. Youngblood cited among the advantages of routine scanning the reassurance and intangible emotional benefits to the patient of a normal sonogram. He also noted that while the NIH recommended a conservative approach to the use of ultrasound, physicians responded instead to patient demand and routinely performed the procedure.

Ewigman (1989), conversely, held ultrasound up to the criteria used to evaluate any screening test: sensitivity and specificity; ease of performance and acceptance by the patient; lack of adverse effects; availability of therapy for detected problems; and cost-benefit ratio. With regard to diagnostic accuracy, Ewigman examined three clinical studies of intrauterine growth retardation and found the predictive value of a positive ultrasound diagnosis to be 36.6 percent. Out of 2,631 infants, he estimated that 263 (10 percent) would have been falsely diagnosed with intrauterine growth retardation, leading to increased anxiety for mothers and to possible induction of labor or cesarean delivery.

As for the ease of use and patient acceptance, ultrasound was judged to be relatively easy to perform, and the imaging of a healthy fetus was viewed with enjoyment by patients and physicians alike (Ewigman 1989). While no adverse effects of ultrasound were identified, Ewigman likened the knowledge of ultrasound to that of X rays in the 1950s, where an association with increased risk of leukemia was not discovered until years later. He believed that long-term follow-up to detect conditions with long latency periods, such as cancer, was needed (Ewigman 1989).

Using data from nine clinical trials of ultrasound in pregnancy, Ewigman conducted a meta-analysis and found no consistent evidence of significant improvement in perinatal morbidity and mortality attributable to ultrasound screening (Ewigman 1989). He also pointed out that the largest reported trial included only 4,997 patients, whereas a sample of approximately 15,500 persons would be needed to detect a significant improvement in perinatal morbidity and mortality. On the question of benefits relative to costs, Ewigman noted that no economic studies had been undertaken at that point but that it was virtually axiomatic that routine use of ultrasound would increase costs.

Subsequently, between 1987 and 1991, Ewigman and colleagues (1993) conducted a large RCT—the Routine Antenatal Diagnostic Imaging with Ultrasound Study—that involved 15,121 pregnant women at low risk for perinatal problems. The study found that compared with selective use of ultrasound, routine use did not reduce perinatal morbidity or mortality and that routine screening added an average of 1.6 scans per pregnancy. At roughly $200 per scan, this contributed more than $1 billion a year to national health care expenditures, without added benefit.

Finally, a survey by the American College of Obstetricians and Gynecologists reported that few obstetricians possessed the requisite skills to perform and interpret ultrasound scans (Shearer 1991). The survey also indicated that almost 75 percent of these scans were conducted by an employee of the physician.

MTE is not an end in itself. Its purpose is twofold—to evaluate the safety and effectiveness of technology and to change medical practice to conform with evaluation findings. However, as these case examples indicate, early positive findings for a new technology can accelerate its adoption, often before it can be rigorously evaluated. Once a technology is in use, factors other than safety and efficacy—patients' expectations, physicians' experiences, the health care environment, and payment policies—come into play and make it difficult to alter medical practice, even when the technology is later shown to be ineffective.

7

Economic Evaluation Methods
William E. Encinosa* and Alan B. Cohen

As competition in the health care marketplace has intensified in recent years, attention has focused increasingly on evaluating the economic effects of medical technologies. Efforts to quantify the aggregate contribution of technology to rising health care costs have already been described in chapter 2. Efforts to assess the cost-effectiveness of individual technologies are of equal or greater importance; thus, economic evaluation methods form an integral part of technology assessment today.

There are three main methods of assessing the economic value of medical technology. The first method, cost-benefit analysis (CBA), attempts to find out how much society is willing to pay for a new technology. That is, CBA ascertains the dollar value that society is willing to place on all of the technology's benefits and outcomes. There are two drawbacks to CBA. First, it is exceedingly difficult to place a monetary value on human life and on less tangible health conditions such as pain. Second, since wealthy individuals are more willing to pay for technology, the measurement of benefits under CBA inherently favors the wealthy over the poor.

Cost-effectiveness analysis (CEA) was developed to address the limitations of CBA. In CEA, costs are still measured monetarily, but the health benefits of the technology are measured in their natural units, such as number of lives saved, days of disability saved, or cases of disease prevented. No dollar value is placed on health outcomes, and the measurement of health outcomes is independent of wealth and income.

---

*The views herein do not necessarily reflect the views or policies of the AHRQ or the U.S. Department of Health and Human Services.

The problem with CEA is that it measures health outcomes in a single unit—for example, life years saved. In reality, health outcomes often have multiple dimensions, such as mortality and morbidity. That is, the life years saved should also include a quality measure of those life years saved. Cost-utility analysis (CUA) was designed specifically to solve this problem with CEA. By using societal preference ratings of the quality of various health states, CUA collapses all dimensions of a health outcome into a single index that allows any medical technology to be compared with another. As a result, CUA has become the standard method for assessing the economic value of medical technology.

This chapter offers a detailed outline of the methodology of CUA, emphasizing the recommendations made in 1996 by the Panel on Cost-Effectiveness in Health and Medicine to standardize the methodology of CUA. The panel's full report, which was commissioned by the U.S. Public Health Service, may be found in several documents, including M. Gold et al. 1996, Siegel et al. 1996, and Weinstein et al. 1996. As a matter of terminology, it is important to note that the panel employed the less common convention of including CUA under the rubric of CEA (M. Gold et al. 1996). However, in this chapter, we keep the two terms distinct. The chapter also discusses CUA's principal weakness—its inability to elicit society's willingness to pay for technology—and illustrates how CBA may be used to solve this problem.

The Methodology of CUA

The basic methodology of CUA is straightforward. The seven-step sequence presented here (and summarized in table 7.1) is a synthesis of several major approaches that have appeared in the literature (Warner and Luce 1982; Drummond, Stoddart, and Torrance 1987; Freund and Dittus 1992; Petitti 1994; M. Gold et al. 1996).

TABLE 7.1. The Methodology of Cost-Utility Analysis

Major Steps
1. Framing the question and the decision-making perspective
2. Measuring and valuing health effects
3. Estimating and evaluating costs
4. Discounting and time preferences
5. Comparing the cost-effectiveness of technologies
6. Analyzing uncertainties
7. Addressing noneconomic issues

1. Framing the Question and the Decision-Making Perspective

As in any evaluative effort, the initial step in CUA is to formulate the study question. In technology assessment, the question historically has been: Are the benefits produced by a new technology sufficiently greater than its costs to warrant its adoption? However, in considering the opportunity cost of resource use, especially in cases where clinical alternatives exist, the question becomes: Are the technology's benefits sufficiently greater than its costs, compared with those of existing alternatives, to warrant its adoption? Both questions imply a need to achieve net benefit, but the second demands demonstration of net marginal improvement in existing medical practice. In CUA, the latter question would specifically be stated as: Are the technology's health effects per unit of cost, compared with those of existing alternatives, sufficiently greater to warrant its adoption? This form of the question demands direct comparison of the new technology with alternatives in incremental or marginal cost-effectiveness terms. The value of this approach will become apparent as our discussion progresses (see step 5).

Once we have defined the question to be studied in the CUA, we need to ascertain the decision-making perspective that the study will take to answer the study question. In choosing an appropriate perspective, one usually adopts either a private perspective (that of an individual patient or HMO) or a societal perspective that asks whether the technology's effects are good for society as a whole. For example, in evaluating a new technology, Medicare may consider only costs to the Medicare program, while an HMO may consider only costs incurred while an individual remains covered by the HMO. Similarly, the patient's costs may reflect only her insurance copayments and deductible, while the patient's employer may consider costs reflecting lost days of work. In contrast, the societal perspective would consider all costs to society: the costs of all resources used in the technology as well as the cost of lost days of work. The Panel on Cost-Effectiveness in Health and Medicine recommends that CUA studies always take the societal perspective.

2. Measuring and Valuing Health Effects

Medical technology essentially affects health status along two dimensions: length of life (or longevity) and quality of life (e.g., side effects). Since death is a readily identifiable event, early CEA studies found it easy just to estimate the number of life years gained with a new technology. The quality of the life years gained, however, generally was not measured. One of the earliest studies that included quality-of-life measurement was a study of kidney dialysis in which a weight of 1.25 was placed on the life years saved through kidney transplantation to indicate that the quality of life under dialysis was comparatively worse (Klarman, Francis, and Rosenthal 1968).

Shepard and Zeckhauser (1976) were the first to develop a formal method of weighting quality. Their method allows one to compute a quality-adjusted life year (QALY, pronounced "kwa-lee"). QALYs have become popular and easy to use, owing to the work of George Torrance (1986) in Canada and Alan Williams (1985) in the United Kingdom. The Panel on Cost-Effectiveness in Health and Medicine recommends that any reference case study should use the QALY approach. Thus, we present a detailed overview of how to compute a QALY.

Computing a QALY
First, suppose that a patient receives treatment involving a technology at time period $t = 0$. For simplicity, at each time period (year) $t > 0$ for which the patient is still alive after treatment, assume that there are three possible health outcomes besides death, H_a, H_b, and H_c, occurring with probabilities $p_a(t)$, $p_b(t)$, and $p_c(t)$, respectively. Next, let q_j be the probability that a person alive in the preceding period $(j - 1)$ will be alive during period j. The survival function

$$F_t = \prod_{j=1}^{t} q_j$$

is the cumulative probability that a person is alive at period t (Garber and Phelps 1997). Then, the (undiscounted) expected number of QALYs attained through the use of the technology is

$$QALY = \sum_{t=1}^{T} F_t\{p_a(t)w_a + p_b(t)w_b + p_c(t)w_c\}, \tag{7.1}$$

where T is the time horizon of the study (e.g., maximum life span) and where w_a, w_b, and w_c are the quality weights placed on the health outcomes H_a, H_b, and H_c, respectively.

These quality weights are key to the analysis. A weight of 1 indicates perfect health, and a weight of 0 indicates death. Suppose that we did not adjust all three health outcomes for quality so that all three states were weighted the same as perfect health ($w_a = w_b = w_c = 1$). Then, equation (7.1) reduces to an expected life years equation of

$$LY = \sum_{t=1}^{T} F_t. \tag{7.2}$$

This is the standard expression for (undiscounted) expected life year, which is often used in CEA but not CUA studies. That is, LY gives the number of years that the patient is expected to live after undergoing treatment with the technology.

The problem with life years is clearly that, in reality, all health outcomes are not weighted the same as perfect health. To improve on this, the QALY in equation (7.1) attempts to weight health outcomes according to their quality of life, scoring them a weight between 0 (death) and 1 (perfect health). This scoring system for health states can be derived using three methods—standard gamble, time trade-off, or rating scale. The simplest method is the rating scale method. Here the respondent is simply asked to rate his or her health state on a scale of 0 to 100, with 0 being death and 100 being perfect health. The score is then divided by 100 to obtain the QALY weight.

The time trade-off method presents the respondent with a choice between the given health state with a fixed survival time s and perfect health for a shorter survival time t. There is a value for t for which the respondent would be indifferent to the choice. The QALY weight would then be t/s, where t is the point of indifference. A problem with the time trade-off method is that it confounds preferences for the health states with time preferences. This is because the years of life that are sacrificed in the time trade-off come at the end of the life span and therefore may be valued less because they would be in the future. Consequently, the time trade-off method may yield results that are biased upward. Johannesson, Pliskin, and Weinstein (1994) developed a method to correct for this time preference bias.

The standard gamble method presents the respondent with a hypothetical choice between the given health state and a gamble (or lottery). The gamble involves two possible outcomes: perfect health with probability p, and death with probability $1 - p$. The QALY weight for the given health state will be equal to the value of p for which the respondent is indifferent between the given health state and the gamble.

Unfortunately, all three methods yield different results. The Panel on Cost-Effectiveness in Health and Medicine did not reach consensus on this issue and advised that all three methods are acceptable. Here we provide a brief example of the use of the time trade-off method to derive the quality weights.

Deriving Quality Weights: The Time Trade-off Method
The time trade-off method involves asking a respondent a series of questions in an interview. For example, if we were trying to weight the health state H_b, the first survey question could be of the form: "Would you prefer ten years in perfect health before death or twenty years in the less than perfect health state H_b?" If the respondent prefers the twenty years in less than perfect health, then the second question would be reformulated so that the option now is between ten years of perfect health and nineteen years in state H_b. Suppose that this line of questioning continues until the respondent reveals that she is indifferent between the two options when the length of time in state H_b is fifteen years. The respondent essentially has valued health state H_b at two-thirds (10/15) of perfect health. Thus, health state H_b is weighted as 0.67. So if the individual were in state H_b for ten years, the number of (undiscounted) QALYs experienced would be 6.7.

Most CUA studies do not have to go through this long process of time trade-off interviews. Instead, they can use preference weights collected previously in health-state classification systems. There are two types of health classification systems, preference based and non–preference based. Preference-based systems assign weights to health states by collecting information regarding individual preferences for various health states. These weights can then be used to compute QALYs. Examples of preference-based systems that collect weights for generic health states include the Health Utilities Index, the Rosser Disability/Distress Index, the EuroQol, the 15D Measure, the Quality of Well-Being Scale, the Quality of Life Health Questionnaire, and the Years of Healthy Life Measure. A nice overview of these generic indexes may be found in M. Gold et al. (1996) and in Patrick and Erickson (1996).

Sometimes, generic health classification systems do not capture particular disease-specific health states. Therefore, preference-based disease-specific measures have been developed in some cases, such as the Arthritis Impact Measurement Scale (Meenan 1982) and the Q-tility Index for cancer (Weeks et al. 1994). Non-preference-based systems, such as the Medical Outcomes Study SF-36, the Sickness Impact Profile, and the Nottingham Health Profile, are not suitable for computing QALYs, which require preference-based measures.

So far, we have discussed how to obtain the quality weights w_a, w_b, and w_c required for the computation of the QALYs in equation (7.1). Next, we consider three other pieces of information that are needed: (1) all possible health outcomes (H_a, H_b, and H_c); (2) the probabilities of each health state—$p_a(t)$, $p_b(t)$, and $p_c(t)$—occurring in each period t; and (3) the survival function F_t.

Obtaining Probabilities of Outcomes

Before collecting data on probabilities, we need first to examine the probability structure of the QALY model in greater detail. So far, the QALYs in equation (7.1) have been presented as a Markov process (see chapter 8) in which the probabilities at each period t have been independent of events occurring in past periods. That is, we expressed the probability $p_a(t)$ as a function of only t. The process would not have been Markov if we had written $p_a(t, t-1, t-2)$, for example. Assuming that QALYs follow a Markov process is very common in CUA studies. If we further assume that the probabilities are stationary (independent of time—e.g., $p_a(t) = p_a$ for all periods t), then the formula for QALYs in equation (7.1) reduces to

$$QALY = \sum_{t=1}^{T} F_t \{p_a(t)w_a + p_b(t)w_b + p_c(t)w_c\} = \{p_aw_a + p_bw_b + p_cw_c\} \cdot LY, \quad (7.3)$$

where LY was given in equation (7.2). We can reduce equation (7.3) further by using the declining exponential approximation of life expectancy (DEALE) method (see Beck, Kassirer, and Pauker 1982). DEALE allows one to approximate the life expectancy ($LY = \sum_{t=1}^{T} F_t$) as the reciprocal of the mortality rate induced by the technology:

$$\sum_{t=1}^{T} F_t = 1/m,$$

where the technology's mortality rate m reflects the average percent ($100 \times m$) of patients that die after being treated with the technology. Using DEALE, equation (7.3) reduces to

$$QALY = \frac{\{p_aw_a + p_bw_b + p_cw_c\}}{m}. \quad (7.4)$$

The beauty of the DEALE method is that it results in a very simple formula for QALYs. However, the DEALE method underestimates life expectancy for mild diseases with very low morbidity rates. Keeler and Bell (1992) and Kuntz and Weinstein (1995) analyze more accurate life expectancy approximation methods that solve this problem as well as other problems with DEALE.

The estimates of the morbidity rate m and the probabilities p_a, p_b, and p_c can come from a number of sources. The hierarchy for obtaining evidence suggested by the U.S. Preventive Services Task Force (1995) is, in decreasing order, randomized controlled trials (RCTs); observational data, including data from cohort, case-control, and cross-sectional studies; uncontrolled experiments; descriptive series; and expert opinion. These methods were discussed in chapter 6.

These studies, particularly RCTs, often are terminated too soon, so that morbidity rates and disease probabilities are not readily available. In such cases, the Panel on Cost-Effectiveness in Health and Medicine (M. Gold et al. 1996) encourages the use of modeling techniques to extrapolate the required probabilities from the incomplete data. Several of these models—decision tree models, influence diagrams, Markov models, and logical networks—are discussed in chapter 8.

3. Estimating and Evaluating Costs

There are three substeps to estimating and evaluating the total cost of the resources consumed by society in the use of a medical technology: identifying the resources, measuring the resources, and valuing the resources.

Identifying Resources
Three broad types of costs are generally considered in economic evaluations of medical technology: direct costs; indirect costs; and intangible costs. Direct costs include the value of all goods, services, and resources consumed in using the technology or in dealing with the side effects and future consequences of the technology's use. Direct health care costs may stem from changes in resource use or from changes in health state. Examples of each are presented here.

Changes in resource use are effects involving the basic inputs to health care delivery, such as land, facilities, personnel, and equipment. Technology use always consumes one or more of these inputs. For example, in the case of electronic fetal monitoring (EFM), identifiable service costs include the amortized capital cost of purchasing the device plus direct operating expenses for personnel, consumable supplies, and maintenance (see table 7.2). For larger devices, such as magnetic resonance imagers or shock-wave lithotripters, service costs also include expenses associated with facility construction or possibly land acquisition.

Changes in health state are effects involving disease prevalence, mortality, and functioning of individuals. Technology-induced reductions in mortality, morbidity, and disability sometimes lead to cost savings, whereas deleterious side effects almost always result in additional service costs. EFM provides illustrations of both (table 7.2): reducing the incidence of neonatal neurologic disorders offers potential averted treatment costs, but EFM's negative influence on the primary cesarean rate also may produce increased subsequent cesarean deliveries, with their attendant service costs.

In addition to direct costs of care, there are direct non-health-care costs. These include such expenses as child care costs for parents un-

TABLE 7.2. Costs and Benefits of Electronic Fetal Monitoring

Costs	Benefits (Cost Savings)
Direct service costs	Direct health benefits
Capital equipment costs (amortized)	Changes in the incidence of mental re-
Operating costs—supplies, personnel,	tardation, cerebral palsy, and other
maintenance	neurologic disorders
Other direct health care costs	Averted treatment and institutionaliza-
Neonatal morbidity—scalp infection	tion costs for severely retarded indi-
Maternal morbidity—postpartum	viduals
infection	Averted training and therapy costs for
Changes in the cesarean delivery rate	mildly retarded individuals
Service costs (net of vaginal delivery	Averted treatment costs for individuals
costs)	with cerebral palsy
Costs of treating complications—	
postoperative infection, neonatal	
respiratory distress syndrome	
Costs of subsequent cesareans result-	
ing from primary cesarean (net of	
vaginal delivery costs)	
Indirect costs	Indirect benefits
Lost productivity due to changes in ma-	Gain in productivity due to changes in
ternal mortality secondary to cesar-	the incidence of perinatal mortality
ean delivery associated with EFM	Gain in productivity due to changes in
Lost productivity due to changes in	the incidence of mental retardation
neonatal mortality secondary to res-	and brain damage
piratory distress syndrome associ-	
ated with cesarean delivery and EFM	

Source: Cohen 1983.

dergoing medical treatment, the cost of special diets, the costs of transportation to and from the clinic, and the time costs that family members or volunteers incur in providing home care to the recovering or chronically disabled individual after treatment.

The second broad category includes indirect costs, which generally involve four types: productivity costs; friction costs; transfer costs; and future unrelated costs. Productivity costs are (1) the costs associated with lost or impaired ability to work or to engage in leisure activities because of morbidity and (2) lost economic productivity as a result of death. Improvements in life expectancy or in physical and social functioning often yield indirect benefits in the form of productivity gains for the general economy. However, declines in health state, conversely, are likely to result in productivity losses for affected individuals. Table 7.2 shows that with EFM, reductions in the incidences of perinatal mortality and of neonatal neurologic disorders may offer productivity gains, while increases in maternal mortality and in neonatal mortality secondary to cesarean section and respiratory distress syndrome, respectively, may adversely affect productive output.

It is important to recall that in CUA, QALYs capture the net benefits of the productivity effects of the technology. That is, QALYs account for both the productivity benefits and the costs of the technology. Thus, to avoid double counting—taking the same cost into the calculation twice—the Panel on Cost-Effectiveness in Health and Medicine recommends that a productivity cost, such as lost income of affected individuals, should not be considered as a cost in the numerator of a CUA ratio, since it is really counted as a negative benefit in the QALYs of the denominator of a CUA ratio.

However, QALYs do not capture friction costs associated with productivity changes. These are economic costs associated with employee absenteeism and with the replacement of a worker. Thus, these expenses do indeed need to be considered as costs in the CUA ratio.

Income transfers, such workers' compensation, are redistribution payments from the government to the worker. These payments do not involve the consumption of any resources. Thus, they should not be considered as costs in CUA. However, transfer costs—the costs of administering these transfer payments—should be considered as costs to society in CUA studies, particularly if the amounts are substantial.

Future unrelated costs are the future health care costs of unrelated medical problems arising during the years of life extended by the current medical intervention. These are the health costs incurred as a result of living longer. For example, if heart disease incidence is reduced, morbidity for various cancers likely will increase, with attendant costs for treatment. Because these future costs are hard to predict, there is much debate over whether such costs should be included in CUA studies. The Panel on Cost-Effectiveness in Health and Medicine recommends that analysts exercise discretion—if such future unrelated costs are high compared to all other costs, they probably should be included in the CUA study.

Finally, intangible costs include the costs of pain and suffering. Before the advent of QALYs in CUA, there was great interest in quantifying separately the costs (or savings) associated with reducing pain and suffering through the use of a technology. However, now that the degree of pain and suffering is automatically measured in the QALY, intangible costs no longer need to be considered in the numerator of the CUA ratio.

Measuring Resources

There are two basic methods for measuring cost: microcosting and gross-cost estimation. Microcosting methods inventory the cost of every resource input used in treating the patient with the technology. Gross-cost-estimation techniques, in contrast, use the national average total cost of performing the treatment with the technology.

In microcosting, one usually obtains input costs from RCTs and observational studies or from large, computerized patient-based data systems in managed care organizations. RCTs often are terminated before all of the economic consequences of an intervention can be realized and measured. However, Fenn et al. (1996) developed a technique for calculating within-trial mean costs when data from RCTs are incomplete or "censored."

The gross-cost-estimation method often uses the national average Medicare DRG payments as proxies for acute care hospitalization costs. A physician's cost per visit can be obtained from the new Medicare fee schedule. Future costs of unrelated health problems due to living longer may be predicted using age- and/or sex-specific medical spending rates from the general population, obtained from the Agency for Healthcare Research and Quality's (AHRQ) Medical Expenditure Panel Survey.

Valuing Resources

Prices for medical services often do not reflect costs as a result of monopolistic pricing practices, such as when service charges are much higher than actual costs so that hospitals can maximize their operating margins (or make profits). One solution to this problem with hospital prices has been to deflate the charges by a cost-to-charge ratio. This is the method used by the AHRQ's patient outcomes research teams. The details of this method may be found in Lave et al. 1994.

When data on medical prices are being used from different years, the prices need to be adjusted for inflation. Past medical prices may be converted to current terms by employing the medical component of the consumer price index. Using an example from M. Gold et al. (1996), if nominal medical prices have risen by 10 percent (as indicated in the medical consumer price index) but the productivity of the medical technology has risen by 8 percent, then the true price correction is 2 percent. To know the rise in medical productivity requires knowledge of the specific technology.

Finally, a common problem with valuing the cost of technology is the cross-subsidization problem. Some technologies, such as MRI and lasers, are now being used to treat many diverse diseases. Thus, the fixed capital costs of the technologies are hard to itemize and to allocate to a specific disease treatment. A greater share of these fixed costs may be allocated to one procedure than to another, inflating the price of one procedure to cross-subsidize a less common, less profitable procedure. As a result, the prices, or charges, for many different procedures that use the same technology may be distorted. To solve this problem, Drummond, Stoddart, and Torrance (1987) developed an elaborate simultaneous allocation accounting method for allocating the capital costs and overhead costs of technology to competing uses.

4. Discounting and Time Preferences

Both costs and health outcomes measured by QALYs may accrue over a number of years and often may occur at different points in time. For example, the costs of preventive technologies (e.g., vaccines) are usually incurred all at once, with the expectation that positive health effects will accrue continuously over time in the form of averted treatment costs (Drummond 1980). In contrast, the costs of many halfway technologies (e.g., renal dialysis) often persist throughout a patient's lifetime. Owing to time differences in the value of money, it is necessary in CUA studies to employ a method known as discounting to make all costs and benefits of a technology commensurable with respect to time—that is, expressed in net present value terms (what a future dollar would be worth if it were spent today). Discounting of future events is necessary for three reasons: (1) to account for the time preference of money (people prefer present consumption to future consumption, all other things being equal), (2) to reflect the value of money invested in alternative ventures yielding more dollars in the future, and (3) to adjust for the effects of economic inflation (Warner and Luce 1982). These forces generally tend to make future dollars worth less than current dollars.

For the discounting of costs of technology in CUA studies, the Panel on Cost-Effectiveness in Health and Medicine recommends that the discount rate be derived with the shadow-price-of-capital method used in CBA studies. In this method, one first converts the stream of all technology costs over time into a stream of consumption losses that would be induced by the forgone investment and consumption opportunities. Next, recalling that in CBA studies all benefits of the technology are in monetary terms, the stream of all technological benefits is converted into a stream of consumption gains. Ultimately, one discounts these consumption streams to present value using the social rate of time preference—the interest rate at which the social planner is willing to trade off present consumption for future consumption. Recent economic studies indicate that the social rate can be approximated by market interest rates reflecting the cost of capital. These interest rates are indexed by the rate of return on government bonds whose time to maturity is roughly equal to the duration of the technology being evaluated. In recent years, this has meant a real annual discount rate ranging from 2.5 to 5 percent.

This discount factor obtained with the shadow-price-of-capital method in CBA studies should also be used to discount the costs measured in CUA studies. There is little disagreement on this point. However, there is some controversy over which discount rate should be used to discount the health outcomes measured with QALYs in CUA studies. For example, should a life year gained ten years from now be valued differently than a life year gained one year from now? The Panel on Cost-Effectiveness in Health and Medicine recommends that the discount rate used for QALYs should be the same one used for costs—the rate derived with the shadow-price method. The panel based its recommendation on the observation that people have opportunities to exchange money for health, and vice versa, throughout their lives, so the same discount rate should apply at both times.

Moreover, failure to discount QALYs at the same rate as costs can lead to inconsistent choices over time. For example, it could appear that delaying an investment in a technology makes it seem more cost-effective, thus leading to an indefinite delay. This is known as the Keeler-Cretin paradox. The following example of the paradox is adapted from CDC (1994).

Suppose that a technological investment of $100 today would result in saving ten lives (or one life saved per $10). If the market cost of capital were 10 percent, then the $100 investment in technology could be delayed and the money instead invested in the market, resulting in $110. In the next year, this $110 could be invested in the medical technology to save eleven lives. However, if the investment could be delayed for two years, the resulting $121 could then be invested in the medical technology in the third year to save twelve lives. Continuing with this logic, it seems that the investment in the technology should be delayed indefinitely if the health benefits are discounted at a rate less the discount rate used on the costs of the technology, which in this example is 10 percent. This is the paradox.

Therefore, the panel recommends that a real discount rate (adjusted for inflation) of 3 percent be used for both costs and QALYs. Moreover, the panel recommends that the CUA study be reevaluated using various real discount rates that range from 0 to 7 percent. With this in mind, we can discount the QALYs in equation (7.1) above in the following way to obtain the present value of the QALYs:

$$PV(QALY) = \sum_{t=1}^{T} F_t \, \delta^t \, \{p_a(t)w_a + p_b(t)w_b + p_c(t)w_c\}, \tag{7.5}$$

where $\delta = 1/(1 + r)$ is the discount factor with discount rate r (net inflation). We let the real discount rate r range from 0.00 to 0.07. Similarly, if the costs of all resources used in connection with the technology in period t are $C(t)$, then the total present value of the costs is

$$PV(C) = \sum_{t=1}^{T} C(t) \, \delta^t, \tag{7.6}$$

where $\delta = 1/(1 + r)$, with the inflation-adjusted discount rate r ranging from 0.00 to 0.07. We assume that all costs and health benefits occur at the end of each period (year). If we wanted to assume instead that they occur at the beginning of each period, then we would start the present value summations in equations (7.5) and (7.6) at $t = 0$ instead of $t = 1$.

The purchase of an expensive technology always involves a large capital outlay K. Instead of lumping K in as a cost included in $C(0)$ at the initial period $t = 0$, the outlay K is usually amortized (spread out over several time periods). Thus, we want to calculate the annual payment E that, over n periods, at real interest rate r, will be equal to K. (N is the life span of the technology itself, which may differ from the CUA's time horizon T.) Drummond, Stoddart, and Torrance (1987) recommend the following method to calculate the annual outlay E. If S is the resale value of the technology at period n, then

$$K = \sum_{t=1}^{n} E \, \delta^t + S \, \delta^n, \tag{7.7}$$

where $\delta = 1/(1 + r)$. Equation (7.7) can be further simplified to

$$K = E \cdot A(n,r) + \frac{S}{(1 + r)^n}, \tag{7.8}$$

where

$$A(n,r) = \frac{1 - (1 + r)^{-n}}{r}$$

is the annuity factor for the technology for n years at real interest rate r. Solving equation (7.8), we have

$$E = \frac{K - \dfrac{S}{(1 + r)^n}}{A(n,r)}.$$

This annual capital expense E should then be included in each cost factor $C(t)$ for periods 1 through n in the present value cost function of equation (7.6). (See Drummond, Stoddart, and Torrance 1987 for a discussion of other methods to include the depreciation rate of the technology.)

5. Comparing the Cost-Effectiveness of Technologies

Now we are at the point in the CUA study where we can compare the economic effectiveness of two technologies. Suppose that we have two technologies, *A* and *B*. First, we seek to compare their incremental or marginal cost-effectiveness—that is, how cost-effective they are when compared to their next best alternatives. Suppose that technology *A* has a standard baseline technology S_A, such that if technology *A* were not available for use in treating a particular medical condition, the provider would resort to using the standard baseline technology S_A. Similarly, assume that technology *B* has a standard baseline technology S_B. Using present value equations (7.5) and (7.6), we compute the incremental or marginal cost of technology *A* to be $PV_A(C) - PV_{S_A}(C)$, and the incremental or marginal effectiveness of technology *A* to be $PV_A(QALY) - PV_{S_A}(QALY)$. We can claim that technology *A* is more cost-effective than technology *B* if

$$\frac{PV_A(C) - PV_{S_A}(C)}{PV_A(QALY) - PV_{S_A}(QALY)} < \frac{PV_B(C) - PV_{S_B}(C)}{PV_B(QALY) - PV_{S_B}(QALY)}. \tag{7.9}$$

That is, technology *A* is more cost-effective than technology *B* if *A*'s marginal cost of producing a QALY is lower than that of *B*. If *A* is more cost-effective than *B* but technology *B* is not a viable, competing alternative to technology *A*, then technology *A*'s cost-effectiveness ratio, or CUA ratio, is quantified as

$$\frac{PV_A(C) - PV_{S_A}(C)}{PV_A(QALY) - PV_{S_A}(QALY)}.$$

However, if *B* is a viable alternative to *A* and if both technologies have the same standard baseline technology *S* (i.e., $S_A = S_B = S$), then technology *A*'s cost-effectiveness ratio is

$$\min\left\{ \frac{PV_A(C) - PV_S(C)}{PV_A(QALY) - PV_S(QALY)}, \frac{PV_A(C) - PV_B(C)}{PV_A(QALY) - PV_B(QALY)} \right\}. \tag{7.10}$$

That is, if both *B* and *S* are now alternatives to *A*, the cost-effectiveness ratio of *A* is the smaller ratio of the two considered in equation (7.10)—the ratio that provides the lower marginal cost per QALY for technology *A*. Because the CUA ratios in equation (7.10) are positive, technology *A* should be adopted for the good of society because it offers a comparative advantage over its alternatives, *B* and *S*—a more efficient means of using scarce health care resources to produce a desired health benefit.

6. Analyzing Uncertainties

CUA studies are often subject to uncertainty with regard to estimates of health states, disease probabilities, patient preferences, and costs. In the face of uncertainty, as with emerging medical technologies, interpretation of cost-effectiveness data should be accompanied by sensitivity analysis (see chapter 8) so that uncertain parameters may be varied systematically to determine what effect, if any, these variations might have on the analytic results (Warner and Luce 1982; Petitti 1994; M. Gold et al. 1996). The Panel on Cost-Effectiveness in Health and Medicine recommends that at a minimum, the CUA study should include a one-at-a-time sensitivity analysis of some of the key variables. For example, the CUA study should be repeated for different real interest rates ranging from 0 to 7 percent. Other key variables that should be varied one at a time are $p_a(t)$, $p_b(t)$, $p_c(t)$, w_a, w_b, and w_c in equation (7.5). The survival function F_t in equation (7.5) is often sensitive to the age and gender of patients. Thus, CUA studies should be repeated for specific patient subgroups where possible.

7. Addressing Noneconomic Issues

The preceding steps deal with quantifiable economic effects of technology. While CUA is purely economic in scope, no such analysis in practice would be complete without consideration of unquantifiable effects, economic or otherwise. Therefore, analytic findings should be interpreted in the light of other relevant, noneconomic issues, including social, ethical, legal, political, and organizational concerns that impinge on decision making (Warner and Luce 1982; Petitti 1994; M. Gold et al. 1996).

CBA

As discussed earlier in this chapter, the CUA method is very good for determining which of two technologies is more cost-effective. However, CUA does not help at all with the next step—determining whether the more cost-effective technology should be purchased. That is, even though we may have determined that a new technology is more cost-effective than the alternative technology, we still do not know whether society is willing to pay for that new technology. Society may instead wish to invest in education, child care, or job training, for example. CUA is not capable of ascertaining society's willingness to pay for new medical technology, but the method of CBA can assist us here because it explicitly elicits society's willingness to pay for such items.

Historically, CBA has not often been used in health care and medicine because many health care practitioners have raised ethical objections to evaluating life in monetary terms. CUA studies, in contrast, simply reveal the costs of extending length of life without making any monetary evaluation of health benefits. But as Uwe Reinhardt (1997) argues, someone in society must and will eventually place a monetary value on length of life. The only question is who will do it. In today's health care marketplace, many HMOs are going beyond CUA studies to do willingness-to-pay studies (Pauly 1995). HMOs need to know if their enrollees would be willing to pay higher premiums for new technologies. Since HMOs traditionally do not take the societal perspective in willingness-to-pay studies, Reinhardt argues that CUA studies must step in and become full-fledged CBA studies so that the societal perspective on willingness to pay for new technology will be fully analyzed.

The methods of CBA in medicine are still in their developmental stages. In this section, we provide a brief overview of the general methods of CBA to date. Both CUA studies and CBA studies value costs in monetary terms. Thus, the methods of valuing resource costs in the previous CUA section also hold for CBA. The key difference, however, is that CBA measures and values health outcomes in monetary terms.

There are two completely different approaches to valuing health outcomes monetarily: the human-capital approach and the willingness-to-pay approach. Following Nobel laureate Gary Becker's work (1964), it first became popular to quantify the value of a human life in monetary units based on a person's human capital, which is the discounted sum of that person's future labor income. It is calculated by aggregating the years of work loss that would occur if the technology were not used to extend life or enhance health status.

The human-capital approach has been criticized on several grounds, including (1) variation in lifetime earning streams (e.g., not accounting for periods of unemployment or different retirement ages); (2) inequities in life valuation by race or gender (e.g., undervaluing the lives of nonwhites and females compared to white males because of marketplace wage distortions); (3) undervaluation of unpaid labor (e.g., valuing homemakers' contributions according to wage rates for domestic servants); (4) zero valuation of premature death at the end of one's working life; and (5) inability to reflect an individual's satisfaction with a health benefit (Drummond 1980; M. S. Thompson 1980). Warner and Luce (1982, 88–89) also point out that this approach "measures the market value of livelihood rather than the value of life," and although this represents something of value to society, it is not "the full measure of the individual's self-valuation of life or of society's valuation of the individual's life."

The willingness-to-pay method was devised to overcome these problems by valuing nonmonetary effects in terms of what people would spend to obtain them (Acton 1973). To explain the willingness-to-pay method in detail, we employ a model by Zweifel and Breyer (1997). Suppose that p is the probability of dying within a given time period. We seek to determine the amount of money E that the individual is willing to pay for a small decrease δ in the risk of dying (e.g., 1 percentage point). The amount E is referred to as an equivalent variation. In contrast, the amount K that would be required to compensate the individual for an increase in p by the amount δ is called a compensating variation. As δ goes toward zero, the ratios E/δ and K/δ converge to a common value $m(y,p)$, which is the individual's marginal rate of substitution between wealth y and the risk of dying p. This rate $m(y,p)$ can be considered the individual's marginal willingness to pay for infinitesimal changes in the risk of dying.

Suppose that a total of n people may potentially benefit from a new technology in a given period. Suppose that the technology will affect each person differently—that is, the technology will reduce each individual i's risk of dying by δ_i. Next, assume that each person's equivalent variation for a fixed reduction in risk δ is E_i. Then, each person's equivalent variation for her actual reduction δ_i will be $\delta_i(E_i/\delta)$, which converges to $\delta_i m_i(y,p)$ as δ moves toward zero. Recall that m_i is the individual's marginal willingness to pay for a decrease in the risk of dying. Thus, the group of n individuals' aggregate willingness to pay for the technology is

$$B = \sum_{i=1}^{n} (\delta_i \frac{E_i}{\delta}) \approx \sum_{i=1}^{n} \delta_i m_i. \tag{7.11}$$

Thus, to compute the total monetary benefit B of the technology, we need to know each person's marginal rate of substitution m_i and the amount δ_i by which each person's risk of death is lowered by the technology. This is quite a large amount of information. However, using statistics, we can reduce equation (7.11) to the following form:

$$B \approx \sum_{i=1}^{n} \delta_i m_i = \bar{m} \sum_{i=1}^{n} \delta_i + n\text{Cov}(\delta_i, m_i), \qquad (7.12)$$

where $\bar{m}$ is the average marginal willingness to pay $(1/n)\sum_{i=1}^{n} m_i$ and where $\text{Cov}(\delta_i, m_i)$ is the covariance between the individual's amount of risk reduction and willingness to pay. If these two quantities are uncorrelated, then $\text{Cov}(\delta_i, m_i) = 0$, and equation (7.12) reduces to

$$B \approx \bar{m} \sum_{i=1}^{n} \delta_i. \qquad (7.13)$$

The quantity $\sum_{i=1}^{n} \delta_i$ is often referred to as the number of statistical lives saved by the technology. Thus, in equation (7.13), the total monetary benefit of the technology to the n people is approximated by the product of their average willingness to pay and the statistical number of lives saved by the technology.

The statistical number of lives saved by the technology can easily be obtained from RCTs. The average willingness to pay for the technology is usually elicited via a method called contingent valuation. This method involves a survey of the n people to elicit their equivalent and compensating variations contingent on the existence of a hypothetical market for the health benefits of the technology. The key to contingent valuation is the design of a questionnaire in such a way as to minimize response effect biases. A well-known bias occurs as a result of the free-rider problem, in which an individual may try to conceal her true willingness to pay to qualify for a lower price or copayment rate. (For a full discussion of contingent valuation, see Cummings, Brookshire, and Schulze 1986; Mitchell and Carson 1989; Johansson 1995; O'Brien and Gafni 1996.)

Finally, the results of a CBA study may be used to compare two technologies. If we have only one technology and the net benefits (discounted benefits minus discounted costs) $B - C$ are positive, then the technology should be purchased, since society is willing to pay for the benefits of the technology. This is often called the Kaldor-Hicks criterion. If we have two technologies, A and B, that are substitutes, then technology A should be purchased instead of B if $B_A - C_A > 0$ and $B_A - C_A >$

$B_B - C_B$. It is recommended that benefit-cost ratios (B/C) not be compared since they pose a problem when deciding whether to treat cost savings as a benefit or as a negative cost. This decision affects both the numerator and denominator of the B/C ratio but not the measure of the net benefit $B - C$.

Conclusion

There remains the question of which method of economic evaluation to use in assessing medical technology. CEA values costs monetarily but measures the health benefits of a technology in their natural units, such as number of lives saved, days of disability saved, or cases of disease prevented. CEA's principal shortcoming is that it measures health outcomes in a single unit—for example, life years saved. In reality, health outcomes often have multiple dimensions, such as mortality and morbidity, and calculation thus should also include a measure of the quality of those life years saved. CUA was designed specifically to solve this problem with CEA. By using societal preference ratings of the quality of various health states, CUA collapses all dimensions of a health outcome into a single index of QALYs. Because this QALY index allows any medical technology to be compared with another in terms of its incremental or marginal cost per QALY (its cost-effectiveness in producing one QALY unit when compared with its next best alternative), CUA has become the standard method for assessing the economic value of medical technology.

However, because CUA measures health benefits in terms of QALYs, the method does not allow one to decide whether to purchase a new medical technology or to invest instead in another sector of society, such as education or housing. CBA attempts to find out how much society is willing to pay for a new technology so that health benefits can be measured monetarily. This allows one to compare technological investments with investments in other sectors of the economy, but there are two drawbacks to CBA. First, it is exceedingly difficult to place a monetary value on human life. Second, because wealthy individuals are more willing to pay for technology, the measurement of benefits under CBA inherently favors the wealthy over the poor. Willingness to pay for technology, in many cases, may be more a reflection of an individual's socioeconomic status than of choice, leading to inequities in access to technology. This is evident, for example, in the current debate over prescription drug coverage under Medicare, in which elderly persons living on fixed incomes with limited assets must trade off needed medicine against such other necessities as food and rent. Thus, in conclusion, until the methods of CBA can be improved for use in health care and medicine, the Panel on Cost-Effectiveness in Health and Medicine recommends that the CUA method be used in major health policy decisions, such as in the ranking and prioritization of the uses of technology in medicine. Even so, one must weigh carefully the methodological assumptions on which such economic evaluations are based before making decisions to adopt and use new medical technology.

Recommended Reading

For a more complete treatment of the economic evaluation methods discussed in this chapter, the reader should consult M. Gold et al. 1996 and Drummond et al. 1997. A discussion of more advanced methods of cost-effectiveness analysis appears in Garber 2000.

A common criticism of economic evaluation methods is that they are theoretical in nature and have not been empirically tested. For a discussion of the recent empirical evidence on the methods of measuring health-related quality of life (e.g., QALYs), see P. Dolan 2000. Finally, for a good example of the interface between the evidence-based medicine methods of chapter 6 (the systematic reviews of the Cochrane Collaboration) and the economic evaluation methods of this chapter, see Vale et al. 2000, a case study of end-stage renal disease.

8

Clinical Decision Analysis
William E. Encinosa*

As we saw in the previous chapter on the economic evaluation of medical technology, the methods of medical technology evaluation usually involve comparing measures—such as the cost-effectiveness ratios—of two or more alternative technologies. However, each individual technology often presents the physician with a multitude of clinical options in treating the patient. Each clinical option may result in a different cost-effectiveness ratio for the same technology. Thus, it is of interest to the physician to find the optimal clinical strategy for using the technology. In this chapter, clinical decision analysis provides a framework for selecting the optimal clinical strategy for a given technology.

There are four basic steps to clinical decision analysis, as derived from a synthesis of major approaches described in the literature (Weinstein et al. 1980; Petitti 1994; Sonnenberg 1997):

1. develop a model that depicts all clinical options available under the technology, along with their potential health outcomes;
2. assign estimates of the probabilities and utility values of the health outcomes;
3. calculate the expected value of each clinical strategy (the clinical option with the highest expected value is the optimal strategy); and
4. conduct a sensitivity analysis of the model to determine how robust the optimal strategy is with respect to the accuracy of the probability and utility estimates obtained in step 2.

---

*The views herein do not necessarily reflect the views or policies of the AHRQ or the U.S. Department of Health and Human Services.

This chapter examines each of these steps in detail, beginning with an examination of different types of decision analysis models.

Decision Analysis Models

Four different models may be used in clinical decision analysis: (1) decision trees; (2) influence diagrams; (3) Markov processes; and (4) logical networks (Freund and Dittus 1992).

Decision Trees

Decision tree models are the simplest and most frequently used models in decision analysis (Sox et al. 1988). For each alternative clinical strategy, the downstream health outcomes and their probabilities of occurrence are listed sequentially and are displayed graphically along paths. Each path through the decision tree represents one possible sequence of chance and decision events, with the final endpoint (or terminal node) being a health outcome measured in terms of a utility— for example, a QALY (see chapter 7).

The decision tree begins with an initial decision node (represented by a square). Moving left to right, the decision node divides into multiple decision branches, with each branch indicating an alternative clinical strategy that may be selected. Each decision branch leads to a chance node (represented by a circle) that branches out into multiple chance events (or chance branches). Each chance event is outside the control of the decision maker and occurs after the clinical strategy represented in the parent decision branch has been implemented. The chance branches emanating from a single chance node must be mutually exclusive events that are collectively exhaustive (i.e., they must include all possible events). Thus, the probabilities of all chance branches coming out of a single chance node must sum to 1. Eventually, each chance branch either connects to a new decision node (creating a new layer of chance nodes and branches) or culminates in a terminal node (represented by a rectangle) that indicates a final health outcome, measured in utility terms). Figure 8.1 provides an illustration of a generic decision tree from Sonnenberg 1997.

Using a process known as averaging out and folding back (Weinstein et al. 1980; Petitti 1994), the clinical strategy selected at any decision node may then be assigned an expected utility. This expected utility is

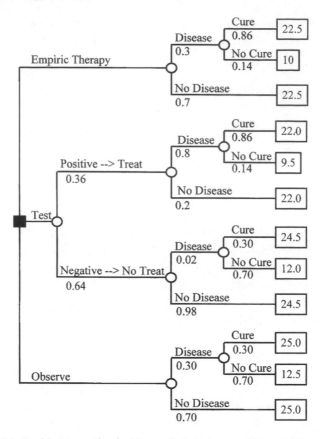

Fig. 8.1. Decision tree. The decision node is represented by a solid square, chance nodes by circles, and terminal nodes by rectangles containing numbers that represent utilities. The name of each branch appears above it; the probability of each branch of a chance node appears below the branch. (From Sonnenberg 1997.)

the average utility value (e.g., QALY) that the clinical strategy is expected to provide to the patient. Alternative clinical strategies may be compared with one another in terms of their expected utility.

To facilitate the construction and use of decision trees, several computer software programs have been developed, such as SMLTREE 2.9 (© 1989, J. Hollenberg, Roslyn, New York), DATA 4.0 (© 2003, TreeAge Software, Boston, Massachusetts), and DECISION MAKER (© 1993, Pratt Medical Group, Boston). In a primer on building decision trees, Detsky et al. (1997) recommend six tips for setting up decision trees for use in software packages.

First, the tree must have balance: each alternative clinical strategy must contain both risks (bad outcomes) and benefits (good outcomes). Second, the number of chance branches after each chance node should be limited to two. Thus, if there are three possible chance events at a chance node, it is best to combine two of the events into one and to follow that single event with a new chance node containing two chance branches, thereby decomposing the "bundled" event back into the two events. This method allows one to take full advantage of the software, which works optimally when there are only two branches after each node.

Third, decision nodes should not be embedded within one another. For example, suppose that at decision node 1, a physician must decide whether to use clinical strategy A. If A is not selected, the physician must decide between strategies B and C at decision node 2. Decision node 2 represents an embedded node because it is embedded within decision node 1. Embedded decision nodes of this kind should be removed by folding them back into the previous decision node. In the example given, this is accomplished by representing all three strategies (A, B, and C) at decision node 1 without any problem. This method is preferred since it allows the computer software to present sensitivity analyses that are easy to interpret.

Fourth, the branches must be linked. Suppose that two clinical strategies (1 and 2) have one possible health outcome in common, H. The probability of outcome H occurring under strategy 1 may be labeled as p_1. Similarly, p_2 may be used to represent the probability of H occurring under strategy 2. It is recommended that these two probabilities be linked since they both refer to the same outcome H. Thus, if $p_2 < p_1$, then p_2 could be linked to p_1 by rescaling p_2 as $p_2 = ep_1$, where $e \in (0,1)$ is an appropriate scaling factor. This scaling factor allows the computer to do more accurate sensitivity analysis.

Fifth, the tree must have symmetry. This means that all underlying initial health states that could affect outcomes are represented in all branches of the tree. Finally, the order of outcomes is not critical. There is often uncertainty about the order of outcomes within the structure of outcomes for each branch. For example, should the probability of disease occurrence be placed before or after a diagnostic test result? The key is that order does not matter since the expected utility for each branch is determined by folding back the tree. Mathematically, this involves multiplying all of the probabilities along the branches in a path until one obtains the probability of being in each state of the terminal nodes. Since the probabilities are multiplied together, their order does not matter.

Influence Diagrams

Influence diagrams have been in use for about thirty years but only recently have become popular alternatives to decision trees (Helfand and Pauker 1997). Although influence diagrams are mathematically equivalent to decision trees in that they yield the same expected utility, influence diagrams use a different graphical structure (Howard and Matheson 1984). Influence diagrams contain decision nodes (represented by rectangles) and chance nodes (represented as ellipses), as in decision trees, but there are no branches. Alternative events are represented as a joint probability distribution table associated with each chance node. The table specifies every possible combination of events represented by the chance node and its predecessors. In place of multiple terminal nodes, there is a single value node (usually represented by a diamond or sometimes by a double-rounded rectangle), together with a table indicating the values associated with all of the predecessor nodes. Thus, influence diagrams do not graphically display all of the chance outcomes and their probabilities. Instead, arcs connecting nodes graphically display the flow of information in the model. In contrast to a decision tree, in which the sequence of events is evident from the tree structure, an influence diagram relies on specific types of arcs to represent the sequence of events. An arc that leads (with an arrow) into a decision node from a chance node indicates that the chance event has occurred by the time the decision is made. This is called an informational arc. The absence of an arc from a chance node to a decision node reveals that the decision maker has not observed the outcomes of the chance event prior to making the decision. An arc from decision node 1 into decision node 2 indicates that decision 1 was made prior to decision 2. This type of arc is called a no-forgetting arc.

Arcs leading into chance nodes indicate influences on the probability of events represented by that node. The arcs may be drawn to reflect either of two orders of probabilistic conditioning. First, as in a decision tree, the order may reflect the order in which the events were observed. One advantage of the influence diagram, however, is that it can reflect the order of causality. This is called assessment ordering, arranging events from cause to effect, a very natural ordering. Through a method called arc reversal (Shachter 1990), influence diagrams also allow easy conversions back and forth between assessment ordering and the standard observational ordering of decision trees.

Arcs between chance nodes may be omitted only when events are assumed to be conditionally independent. Two events are conditionally independent, given a third event, if, after observing the third event, observing one of the two events gives no additional information about the likelihood of the other event. Influence diagrams allow this probabilistic independence to be easily noted in the diagram, whereas decision trees do not indicate probabilistic independence.

Finally, the arcs into the value node indicate the events that affect the values (QALYs) of the outcomes. The value node is the place to start in setting up the influence diagram's network of nodes and arcs. In particular, Nease and Owens (1997) offer five basic principles for setting up influence diagrams: (1) start at the value node and work back to the decision nodes, (2) draw the arcs in the direction that makes the probabilities easiest to assess, (3) use informational arcs to specify events that will have been observed at the time each decision is made, (4) ensure that missing arcs reflect intentional assertions about the conditional independence and timing of observations, and (5) ensure that there are no cycles in the influence diagram (i.e., there are no arcs that form a path from a node back to itself). Nease and Owens provide a nice illustration of how to construct an influence diagram for diagnosing and treating streptococcal infections (see figure 8.2).

Once an influence diagram is set up, it can be evaluated to compute the expected utilities of the alternative clinical decisions. An algorithm for evaluating influence diagrams is detailed in Owens, Shachter, and Nease 1997. Computer software has been developed to facilitate the construction and evaluation of influence diagrams. These programs include: Analytica 2.5 (© 2003, Lumina Decision Systems, Los Altos, California, www.lumina.com), DATA 4.0 (© 2003, TreeAge Software, Boston, www.treeage.com), DPL 4.0 (© 2000, Applied Decision Analysis, Menlo Park, California, www.adainc.com), and Precision Tree (© 2002, Palisade Corporation, Newfield, New York, www.palisade.com).

Influence diagrams are usually preferred over decision trees when the probability assessments in the decision tree require extensive Bayesian updating. Influence diagrams handle Bayesian updating automatically in their evaluation algorithms. One limitation of influence diagrams and decision trees is that they are not well suited to represent recurrent events that repeat over time. In chronic diseases, many health problems are confronted repeatedly during a lifetime. Rather than model each event as a separate branch of an extensive decision tree, the events can be more efficiently modeled as Markov processes.

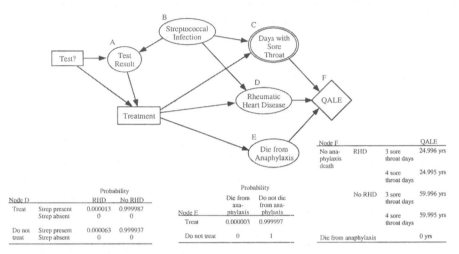

Node A

Node A		Test +	Test −	NA
Test	Strep present	0.90	0.10	0
	Strep absent	0.30	0.70	0
No test	Strep present	0	0	1
	Strep absent	0	0	1

Probability

Node B

Node B	Strep present	Strep absent
	0.60	0.40

Probability

Node C

Node C		Days with sore throat
Treat	Strep present	3
	Strep absent	4
Do not treat	Strep present	4
	Strep absent	4

Node D

Node D		RHD	No RHD
Treat	Strep present	0.000013	0.999987
	Strep absent	0	0
Do not treat	Strep present	0.000063	0.999937
	Strep absent	0	0

Probability

Node E

Node E	Die from anaphylaxis	Do not die from anaphylaxis
Treat	0.000003	0.999997
Do not treat	0	1

Probability

Node F

Node F			QALE
No anaphylaxis death	RHD	3 sore throat days	24.996 yrs
		4 sore throat days	24.995 yrs
	No RHD	3 sore throat days	59.996 yrs
		4 sore throat days	59.995 yrs
Die from anaphylaxis			0 yrs

Fig. 8.2. Influence diagram for the sore throat problem. Tables show the assessments required to specify fully the influence diagram. QALE = quality-adjusted life expectancy; Strep = streptococcal infection; RHD = rheumatic heart disease; NA = test result not available. (Data from Nease and Owens 1997. Tables are based on a decision analysis by Dippel, Touw-Otten, and Habbema [1992].)

Markov Processes

In a Markov process, events are modeled as transitions among a finite number of states occurring during fixed time intervals (Beck and Pauker 1983; Sonnenberg and Beck 1993; Sonnenberg 1997). States are represented by nodes. The arrows connecting states indicate which transitions may occur (see figure 8.3). In addition, each arrow is labeled with a transition probability, which indicates the probability that that transition will take place. An arrow from a state to itself indicates that patients may remain in a state for more than one time period. Transition probabilities are analogous to branch probabilities in a decision tree, with the difference that the probability represents the likelihood of transition only for the duration of one time period.

The states must include at least one absorbing state that the patient cannot leave after entering. The standard absorbing state is death. The

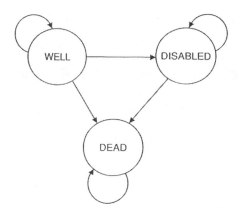

Fig. 8.3. Markov model. Each circle represents a Markov state. Arrows indicate allowed transitions. (From Sonnenberg and Beck 1993.)

Markov process usually cycles a cohort of patients through several time periods. Each state is given an incremental utility value for one time period (e.g., quality-adjusted life months, if the period is a month). As patients cycle through states, the incremental utility of each state is multiplied by the fraction of the cohort passing through that state and then summed across states to yield the total incremental utility. The cumulative utility essentially is a running tab of the total incremental utility generated during each period. The process is continued until all patients enter an absorbing state. Markov processes may be set up with some of the previously mentioned software, such as SMLTREE 2.9, DECISION MAKER, and DATA 4.0. Naimark et al. (1997) provide a primer on how to use the SMLTREE program to evaluate Markov processes.

Logical Networks

The major simplification made in Markov processes is that the transition probabilities are independent of what happened to the patient prior to entering the current state. However, many simulation methods using logical networks can deal with transition probabilities that are history dependent (S. D. Roberts and Klein 1984; Law and Kelton 1991). Two of the most interesting simulation models are the neural network and regression tree models.

Neural networks allow estimation of decision nodes that are impossible to model in standard linear and even nonlinear models such

Neural Network for Initial Clinical Data

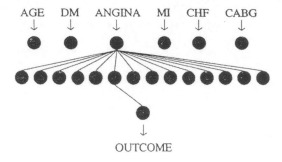

Neural Network for Dipyridamole Thallium Results

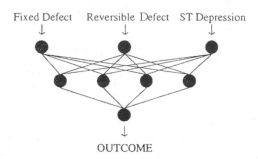

Fig. 8.4. Neural network. Each of the networks has three layers of interconnected processing elements (neurons). The interconnections (synapses) are modified throughout the training process in order to develop an effective model. Because of the number of neurons in the clinical data network, not all connections are shown. Inputs and outputs were coded as 1 or 0. (From Lapuerta et al. 1998.)

as logistic regression (Cross, Harrison, and Kennedy 1995; Lapuerta et al. 1998). Consider the following example from Phelps 1995. Suppose event *Y* happens when either *A* happens or *B* happens but does not occur when neither *A* nor *B* or both *A* and *B* occur. This situation, described in logic theory as an *or* gate, occurs often in medicine. For example, radiation therapy will be avoided when there is no cancer or when the cancer has spread to distant parts of the body. It will be used only when the cancer is localized. Neural network models are designed to handle such examples. Similarly, regression tree models allow variables to enter a model differently at different points in the tree in ways totally impossible in logistic models. As these new methods become more developed, they will inevitably play important roles in future clinical analyses. In fact, some software packages are now being used in clinical analyses specifically to develop neural networks, such as NeuralWorks Professional II/Plus 5.5 (© 2003, Neural-Ware, Pittsburgh, www.neuralware.com).

Assignment of Probabilities and Utilities

Many of the event probabilities in decision analysis are represented as conditional on patient characteristics, including age, gender, risk factors, and stage of disease. Data often are not available on the probabilities conditional on each of these subpopulations. As a result, the clinical decision analyst must estimate predictive models of the subpopulation-specific probability by assuming a statistical relationship between the probability event and the patient characteristic. These predictive models may be developed using logistic regression (Harrell et al. 1985), Poisson regression, neural networks (Cross, Harrison, and Kennedy 1995), proportional hazard models, or Bayesian belief nets (Howard 1990; Breese 1992). In some rare cases, the probability is highly dependent on very specific patient characteristics. In these situations, only expert opinion is available as an estimate of these probabilities.

The final step in the construction of the decision model is the assignment of values (e.g., QALYs) to the health states. As discussed in chapter 7, there are three methods for computing the QALY measure of a health state—the rating scale, the time trade-off, and the standard gamble. While the three methods usually yield different QALY weights, there is no theory or empirical evidence at present to indicate which method is most accurate. Thus, all three methods currently are well accepted and widely used.

Calculating Expected Utility

The primary goal of clinical decision analysis is to derive the utility that a clinical strategy is expected to provide to a patient. In all four modeling methods described here, the calculation of expected utility is quite complex and is usually carried out using one of the software packages mentioned earlier. However, to give an overview of the general method for calculating expected utility, we will demonstrate a very simple decision tree model from Phelps 1997.

Suppose that a physician faces two critical questions—whether to treat a patient with a given technology and whether to use a diagnostic test. For simplicity, assume that there are only four possible health states: sick and treated (S_T), sick and not treated (S_N), healthy and treated (H_T), and healthy and not treated (H_N). We will assume that $H_N \geq H_T$ (depending on the side effects of the treatment), that $S_T > S_N$, and that $H_T \geq S_T$. Thus, we can rank the health states: $H_N \geq H_T \geq S_T > S_N$. Let I be the income, or wealth, of the patient and let C be the cost of the treatment. Generally, patients value differently the trade-off between income and consumption of goods and services. If the patient has a value or utility function V with two arguments (health and remaining income), then the patient's value of each health state will be, respectively: $V(S_T, I - C)$, $V(H_T, I - C)$, $V(H_N, I)$, and $V(S_N, I)$. We will write these values more succinctly as V_{ST}, V_{HT}, V_{HN}, and V_{SN}. Note that $V_{HN} > V_{HT} > V_{ST} > V_{SN}$. Finally, let p be the patient's prior probability of having the disease.

First, suppose that no diagnostic test is available, so that the patient's expected utility under treatment is $pV_{ST} + (1 - p)V_{HT}$, and without treatment, the patient's expected utility is $pV_{SN} + (1 - p)V_{HN}$. Thus, the physician will decide to treat the patient when

$$pV_{ST} + (1 - p)V_{HT} > pV_{SN} + (1 - p)V_{HN}. \tag{8.1}$$

That is, the physician will choose to treat the patient if the patient's expected utility under treatment exceeds the patient's expected utility without treatment. The physician has only two options, to treat or not to treat—the physician must decide whether to use one technology or no technology. Thus, equation (8.1) is the physician's decision rule. This differs from the case studied in chapter 7, where the physician had to decide between two technologies. In that case, the physician's decision rule was to compare the cost-effectiveness ratios of the two technologies.

Next, let p_0 be the value of the prior probability p at which the two terms in equation (8.1) are equal. That is,

$$p_0 = \frac{\Delta V_H}{\Delta V_H + \Delta V_S}, \tag{8.2}$$

where $\Delta V_H = V_{HN} - V_{HT}$ and $\Delta V_S = V_{ST} - V_{SN}$. Thus, we can restate the physician's decision rule equivalently as follows: treat the patient if the patient's prior probability of illness p is greater than or equal to p_0; if $p < p_0$, do not treat the patient.

Diagnostic Testing

Suppose that the physician instead can perform a diagnostic test before treatment. This case, first analyzed by Pauker and Kassirer (1980), introduces three variables: the sensitivity, specificity, and cost of the diagnostic test. The sensitivity (*SN*) of the diagnostic test is defined as the probability that the patient tests positive for the disease when she does indeed have the disease. Thus, $1 - SN$ is the false-negative error rate of the test. The specificity (*SP*) of the diagnostic test is defined as the probability that the patient tests negative for the disease when she is indeed healthy. Hence, $1 - SP$ is the false-positive error rate of the diagnostic test.

To develop the decision rule for using the diagnostic test, we first need to compute the expected value of the diagnostic information revealed in the test. There are two cases to consider, depending on the physician's fallback strategy, absent the test.

Case 1: $p < p_0$, where p_0 is given in equation (8.2), so that no treatment would be provided in the absence of the diagnostic test. Suppose that the diagnostic test is indeed conducted in this case. If the test result is negative, then we have reason to believe that the patient is more likely to be healthy than previously thought. As a result, we still decide not to treat. Hence, the test turns out to be of no value in the case of a negative result. That is, the test result does not alter the physician's decision, since the physician was not going to treat the patient even before the test because $p < p_0$.

However, if the test result is positive, then the patient is more likely to be sick than previously thought. In fact, we can update the prior probability p with the new test information using Bayes's formula:

$$p_u \equiv P(S \mid +) = \frac{P(+ \mid S)p}{P(+ \mid S)p + P(+ \mid H)(1 - p)}, \tag{8.3}$$

where $P(S \mid +)$ is the probability of being sick conditional on a positive test result, $P(+ \mid S)$ is the probability of obtaining a positive test result when sick, and $P(+ \mid H)$ is the probability of obtaining a positive result when healthy. We will call p_u the updated (or posterior) probability of being sick (once a positive test result occurs). Often, p_u is also referred to as the predictive power of a positive test.

In our medical terminology of test sensitivity (*SN*) and specificity (*SP*), we can rewrite the updated probability in equation (8.3) as

$$p_u = \frac{pSN}{pSN + (1 - SP)(1 - p)}. \qquad (8.4)$$

Since a positive test result reveals that the patient is more likely to be sick than we had previously suspected, it is obvious that the updated (posterior) probability is greater than the prior probability p ($p_u > p$). In most cases, this positive test result generates an updated probability p_u large enough such that $p_u > p_0$, indicating that we should now treat the patient. Thus, the positive test result has tangible value in that the newly obtained information results in the decision to treat the patient, whereas the patient would not have been treated in the absence of the test. With treatment, the patient's expected utility becomes $p_u V_{ST} + (1 - p_u)V_{HT}$, which is equation (8.1) with the updated p_u replacing p. In the absence of the test, the patient would not have received treatment and instead would have an expected utility of $p_u V_{SN} + (1 - p_u)V_{HN}$. Thus, the value of the test is the incremental gain from receiving the treatment versus no treatment:

$$[p_u V_{ST} + (1 - p_u)V_{HT}] - [p_u V_{SN} + (1 - p_u)V_{HN}]. \qquad (8.5)$$

Equation (8.5) can be rewritten as $p_u \Delta V_S - (1 - p_u)\Delta V_H$. The test has this value only if it results in a positive finding. Thus, prior to the test, the expected value of the diagnostic test is

$$EV(\text{DIAG})_{NT} = P(+)[p_u \Delta V_S - (1 - p_u)\Delta V_H], \qquad (8.6)$$

where $P(+)$ is the probability that the test is positive and the NT subscript in $EV(\text{DIAG})_{NT}$ refers to the present case of there being no treatment in the absence of the test. From the theorem of total probabilities, we know that $P(+) = P(+ \mid S)p + P(+ \mid H)(1 - p)$. That is,

$$P(+) = pSN + (1 - SP)(1 - p). \qquad (8.7)$$

Using this expression of $P(+)$ in equation (8.7) and using the expression for p_u in equation (8.4), the expected value of the diagnostic information in equation (8.6) reduces to

$$EV(\text{DIAG})_{NT} = pSN\,\Delta V_S - (1 - p)(1 - SP)\Delta V_H. \qquad (8.8)$$

Case 2: $p \geq p_0$. In this case, the patient will undergo the treatment if not tested. Thus, the test will only be of value if it gives a negative test result, indicating that the patient should instead forgo treatment. Using a similar procedure to the one used in case 1, we derive the expected value of the diagnostic test to be

$$EV(DIAG)_T = -p(1 - SN) \Delta V_S + (1 - p)SP \Delta V_H. \tag{8.9}$$

With the value of the diagnostic test information firmly established in equations (8.8) and (8.9), we can develop the physician's decision rule for administering the diagnostic test. First, the cost of using the diagnostic test is C_D. Thus, the diagnostic test will be used whenever the expected value is greater than the cost: $EV(DIAG)_{NT} \geq C_D$ or $EV(DIAG)_T \geq C_D$. To analyze these conditions in greater detail, define p_1 to be the value of the prior probability p at which $EV(DIAG)_{NT} = C_D$. Similarly, define p_2 to be the value of p such that $EV(DIAG)_T = C_D$. Solving for p_1 and p_2, we have

$$p_1 = \frac{C_D + (1 - SP)\Delta V_H}{SN\Delta V_S + (1 - SP)\Delta V_H} \quad \text{and}$$

$$p_2 = \frac{SP\Delta V_H - C_D}{(1 - SN)\Delta V_S + SP\Delta V_{II}}.$$

With p_1 and p_2 thus defined, the physician's decision rule for both using the diagnostic test and treating the patient is as follows:

1. For $p < p_1$, do nothing: do not test and do not treat the patient.
2. For $p_1 \leq p \leq p_2$, test the patient and then treat according to the outcome of the test.
3. For $p > p_2$, treat the patient immediately without any testing.

These three steps give the physician's entire strategy for using the diagnostic test and properly treating the patient. The strategy depends only on the prior probability cutoff points, p_1 and p_2.

Sensitivity Analysis

In evaluating the physician's decision rule derived in the last section, the issue of uncertainty in the data must be addressed. Given that uncertainty, how confident can we be that the recommended testing and treatment strategy is really the best one? Sensitivity analysis attempts to answer this question by varying the values of one or more of the model's parameters and assessing the effect on the overall decision rule. Before discussing sensitivity analysis in detail, however, we must review the various sources of uncertainty possible in any model.

Model Uncertainty

The uncertainty in any analytic model arises primarily as a result of errors in measuring or estimating the true value of the model's parameters. In any given model, there are four main parameters that may contain errors (Phelps 1997). Using Phelps's model of the treatment decision rule in equation (8.1), when no diagnostic test is available, we see that the decision rule depends on (1) the prior probability of illness p; (2) the treatment efficacy and side effects, measured by the health states (H_T, S_T, S_N, and H_N); (3) the costs of treatment C; and (4) the patient's preferences for the health states, measured by the value or utility function V. If the diagnostic test is introduced, further errors may occur in the estimation of the diagnostic test's sensitivity (SN), specificity (SP), and costs (C_D).

In particular, the most common error in estimating the prior probability of an illness involves a systematic bias in which small probabilities get overstated. Viscusi (1989) has shown that in a standard Bayesian decision model, very small probability events necessarily get overemphasized by the clinician, while very high probability events get underemphasized. In addition, recent empirical evidence indicates that clinicians systematically overestimate very small probabilities (Sturdevant and Stern 1977; Poses, Cebul, and Collins 1985; J. G. Dolan, Bordley, and Mushlin 1986). This presents a problem since most diseases are rare, occurring at rates lower than one per 100,000 persons per year.

Performing Sensitivity Analysis

Now that we know what type of errors may appear in the analysis, we need to assess how sensitive the physician's decision rule is to these errors. Sensitivity analysis can determine whether the decision rule is robust over a range of parameter values or whether it hinges on the accuracy of a particular parameter.

In one-way sensitivity analysis, a single parameter (e.g., the prior probability p) is varied over its entire possible range of 0 to 1 (Krahn et al. 1997). The expected utility of each clinical strategy is calculated for each value of the parameter p. As the probability is varied, there may be a threshold value $\hat{p}$ of the probability for which one of the alternative clinical strategies yields the same expected utility as the baseline strategy. The baseline strategy is the recommended decision rule under the original values of the parameters—the baseline parameter values. Suppose that p_b is the baseline value used for the prior probability (in Phelps's model, $p_b = p_0$ from equation [8.2]). Thus, if the threshold value $\hat{p}$ is very close to the baseline p_b, then a small error in p_b may result in a different decision rule being recommended. In this case, the baseline strategy is very sensitive to the specification of the prior probability, or not very robust.

In two-way sensitivity analysis, two parameters are varied simultaneously (Petitti 1994). The threshold of each parameter is calculated for each value of the other parameter. A three-way sensitivity analysis performs a two-way threshold analysis for each value of a third parameter. To vary all parameters at the same time, one usually uses Monte Carlo simulation. In this method, the parameters are allowed to vary randomly within the constraints of given probability distributions (Doubilet et al. 1985). The evaluation is repeated thousands of times to generate many different combinations of the values for the parameters. The mean expected utility of each strategy will be the same as the expected utility in an ordinary sensitivity analysis. However, the Monte Carlo method allows uncertainty in parameters to be generated by a probability distribution, recognizing that not all values in the range used for sensitivity analysis are equally likely. Moreover, the Monte Carlo method provides a probability distribution of the expected utility values of each strategy (Sonnenberg 1997). The mean value of the distribution (not necessarily the peak) is equal to the expected utility of the strategy. The advantage of observing the distribution of the strategy is that it allows one to see the variance—not just the mean—of the expected utility for each strategy.

Performing Statistical Analysis

Interest has recently been increasing in applying statistical methods to examine parameter uncertainty when the source of the uncertainty is the sampling variation in the estimate of the parameter. When a parameter is determined in a clinical trial, a retrospective chart review, or a meta-analysis (see chapter 6), a measure of dispersion, such as the standard deviation or the standard error, is routinely computed. As a result, the 95 percent confidence interval of the parameter may also be calculated. This measure represents the interval in the range of the parameter that has a 95 percent chance of containing the true value of the parameter. (For a description of how to compute confidence intervals, see a standard statistics text, such as Mood, Graybill, and Boes 1974.)

One statistical approach that uses the confidence intervals of the parameters is rank-order stability analysis (Einarson, Arikian, and Doyle 1995). In rank-order stability analysis, if a parameter's 95 percent confidence interval lies within the threshold values of the one-way sensitivity analysis, then the baseline clinical strategy is said to be stable with respect to that parameter.

Instead of looking just at the confidence intervals of the parameters, as in rank-order stability analysis, we often need to examine the confidence interval of the final measure of the strategy, such as the cost-effectiveness ratio (C/E) of equation (7.10). O'Brien, Drummond, and Labelle (1994) were the first to attempt to compute the confidence interval of the C/E ratio. They use the delta method, a procedure based on the Taylor approximation that gives estimations for the means and variances of the ratios. Once the means and variances of the ratios are found, the confidence intervals can easily be computed.

The major problem with C/E ratios is that the means and ratios often do not exist because costs C and effects E are commonly assumed to be normally distributed. As a result, the C/E ratio is Cauchy distributed. The problem with Cauchy distributions is that as the effect E gets close to zero, the mean of the Cauchy distribution does not exist. For most distributions, the averages converge more and more to a common point as the number of observations increases. However, such a convergence does not occur for averages of Cauchy-distributed parameters. In fact, the average C/E ratio over any number of observations may exhibit the same degree of variation as a single observation. Since the mean of the Cauchy distribution does not exist, confidence intervals cannot easily be computed, and the delta method may produce a badly biased estimate of the true confidence interval. However, Van Hout et al. (1994) and Wakker and Klaassen (1995) developed other methods to accurately compute confidence intervals for C/E ratios. In addition, Mullahy and Manning (1994) developed a method that simulates a distribution for the C/E ratio, which then provides a consistent estimate of the C/E ratio's confidence interval.

Conclusion

When a medical technology is used to treat a patient for a specific disease, there is often more than one way in which the physician can proceed. Clinical decision analysis may be used to aid the physician in adopting the best clinical strategy for using the technology. There are four basic steps to using clinical decision analysis.

The first step is to select a model that depicts all of the clinical options. Decision trees and influence diagrams are the two simplest models to use. They offer equivalent results and allow a nice graphical representation of the sequence of chance events and clinical decisions. Influence diagrams are preferred if the decision trees involve probability assessments that require extensive Bayesian updating. A more complex model, such as a Markov model, will be required if the technology addresses a chronic disease that involves repeated treatments over the course of a lifetime. The most complex model, a logical network model, may be used to simulate the clinical use of the technology in highly complex situations involving history-dependent probabilities. Regardless of the model selected, all four models require the use of computer software packages.

The second step in the decision analysis is to estimate the probabilities and utilities for all health outcomes possible under the clinical strategy. Utility may be estimated using three different methods—the rating scale, the time trade-off, and the standard gamble.

The third step is to compute the expected value of the clinical strategies. The physician's decision rule is to select the clinical strategy with the highest expected value. If there is also an option of using a costly diagnostic test before treatment, the decision rule must take into account the diagnostic test's sensitivity and specificity. The sensitivity of the test is the probability that the patient tests positive for the disease when she does indeed have the disease, and the specificity is the probability that the patient tests negative for the disease when she does not have the disease.

The final step in the decision analysis is to conduct a sensitivity analysis that will reveal how robust the physician's decision rule is with respect to the accuracy of the estimates of the following model parameters: (1) the prior probability of disease, (2) the treatment efficacy, (3) the costs of treatment, and (4) the patient's preferences for health states as measured by the utility of various health outcomes. One-way sensitivity analysis varies a single parameter over its entire range and computes the expected value of the clinical strategy for each of these values. Monte Carlo sensitivity analysis simulates the case in which all parameters are randomly varied at the same time. More advanced statistical analyses allow the confidence intervals of the parameters to be computed.

A major thrust of clinical decision analysis today is the development of increasingly advanced statistical techniques that can compute more accurately the confidence interval of the cost-effectiveness ratio of a given technology. These methods will enable clinical decision analysis to measure just how sensitive clinical decisions are to the accuracy of the parameter data. More importantly, this will give society some assurance of the robustness of a medical technology's cost-effectiveness ratio in a health care environment in which medical data are constantly changing at an ever faster rate.

Recommended Reading

For a very applied treatment of the methods discussed in this chapter, see Gross 1999. The computer program used to run the analyses in Gross's book may be downloaded from www.med4th.com/BASIS/. For students and clinicians who may not have a mathematical background, Hammond, Keeney, and Raiffa 1999 offers a nice introduction to clinical decision analysis. For a more complete clinical treatment of the methods used in the diagnostic testing example found in this chapter, see Black et al. 1999.

9

Medical Technology Evaluation in the United States and Selected Other Countries
Alan B. Cohen and Ruth S. Hanft*

Medical technology evaluation (MTE)—also called health technology assessment (HTA) in many parts of the world—has proliferated globally during the past two decades, with nations varying in the intensity of their efforts, the degree of involvement by their governments, and the methods used (Perry, Gardner, and Thamer 1997). In 1985, an international survey by the Institute of Medicine (IOM 1985) found that efforts to evaluate the safety and efficacy of drugs were well established in most developed countries but that systematic assessment and regulation of devices occurred only in the United States, Sweden, Japan, and Canada. A survey conducted ten years later identified twenty-four countries with recognized technology evaluation programs (Perry, Gardner, and Thamer 1997). Of the 103 organizations performing ongoing evaluation in these nations, the United States led the way with 53 such organizations, followed by Canada with 17 (Perry, Gardner, and Thamer 1997; Fernandez et al. 1997).

In this chapter, we first examine MTE activities in the United States, with its myriad public and private organizations. We next look at international efforts in HTA, with particular emphasis on collaborative projects sponsored by the European Union. We then close with brief profiles of HTA programs in Sweden, Canada, the Netherlands, the United Kingdom, Spain, and Australia.

---

*With the research assistance of Catherine C. White and Shirley A. Stewart.

Medical Technology Evaluation in the United States

Organized efforts to assess health care technologies in the United States have been hampered by several factors over the years, including the diverse roles and agendas of the numerous organizations involved in evaluating technology, the absence of standardized priority-setting criteria for MTE, the lack of a reliable mechanism (e.g., a clearinghouse) for disseminating the results of technology evaluations, and deficient means for integrating results from multiple sources (Perry and Pillar 1990; Rettig 1997). To appreciate the fragmentation that presently exists in MTE efforts in the United States, we must examine the key players and their roles within the health care system.

The number of organizations involved in MTE activities has grown considerably since the mid-1970s. In its 1985 report, the IOM profiled twenty leading technology assessment programs, most of which resided in federal governmental agencies. A subsequent IOM publication (1988) listed more than 150 organizations, many of them governmental entities, engaged in some form of HTA activity. Private-sector involvement in MTE grew dramatically in the late 1980s and early 1990s, reflecting the huge demand for such information among third-party payers and purchasers of care created by the changing health care market conditions of the times (Rettig 1997). Today, a broad array of public and private organizations is active in MTE within the United States, including (1) federal governmental agencies, (2) state governmental agencies, (3) private insurers, (4) managed care organizations (MCOs), (5) professional and specialty societies, (6) provider associations, (7) technology industry groups, (8) disease-specific interest groups, and (9) private research groups, including academic medical centers, universities, and nonprofit as well as for-profit research organizations (Fernandez et al. 1997).

To place the MTE activities of these organizations in perspective, table 9.1 employs a framework based on definitions developed by Blumenthal (1983) and later refined by Foote (1987), in which MTE activities are divided into three types according to purpose or function: (1) knowledge development, (2) knowledge processing, and (3) regulation. Knowledge development covers a wide range of evaluation activities, from randomized controlled trials to case studies, and is directed toward increasing our understanding of the safety, effectiveness, and cost of a particular technology as well as the social, legal, and ethical implications of its adoption and use (see chapter 6). Knowledge processing

TABLE 9.1. Key Organizations in the United States Involved in Medical Technology Evaluation/Assessment

Sector[a]	Organization	Technology Evaluation/Assessment Activity[b]		
		Knowledge Development	Knowledge Processing	Regulation
Federal government (legislative)	OTA (ceased operations in 1995)	○	●	
	GAO		●	
Federal government (executive)	NIH—Institutes	●		
	NIH—OMAR, NLM		●	
	NSF, DoE, NASA	●		
	DoD	●		
	VA—MDRC, HSR&D programs	●	○	
	CDC—NCHS		●	
	AHRQ—CPTA, CERTs, NGC		●	
	AHRQ—EPCs, PORTs, MEDTEP	●	○	
	FDA	○	○	●
	CMS—Medicare		○	●
	MedPAC		●	
State government	Certificate of Need (CON)		○	●
	Medicaid		○	●
	Biomedical R&D Funds	●		
Private insurers	BCBSA, Aetna U.S. Healthcare, and others		○	●
Managed care organizations	KP, GHC, HPHC, United HealthCare, and others	○	○	●
Professional and specialty societies	AMA, ACP-ASIM, ACC, ACR, ACS, ACOG, and others	○	●	
Provider associations	AHA, AAHP, ACHP, and others	○	●	
Technology industry	Individual manufacturers/firms	●	○	
	Trade associations—AdvaMed, PhRMA, BIO, NEMA, MDMA, AMDM, and others		●	○
Disease-specific interest groups	American Heart Association, American Cancer Society, Arthritis Foundation, and others	○	●	○
Private research groups	Academic medical centers and universities—UHC and others	●	○	

(continued)

TABLE 9.1.—*Continued*

| Sector[a] | Organization | Technology Evaluation/ Assessment Activity[b] | | |
		Knowledge Development	Knowledge Processing	Regulation
	Nonprofit organizations—ECRI, MTPPI, RAND, and others	●	○	
	For-profit firms— Covance, Inc., Hayes, Inc., MEDTAP International,® and others	●	○	

Source: Based on table 3 in Cohen and Nichols 1993. Other sources of information include Rettig 1997, Fernandez et al. 1997, and various Web sites listed at the end of chapter 9.

Note: ● = principal technology-related activity; ○ = secondary technology-related activity (activities).
[a]Listed in the general order mentioned in the text.
[b]Definitions developed by Blumenthal (1983) and later refined by Foote (1987).

encompasses the activities used to gather, validate, interpret, and disseminate the information to public and private audiences (Foote 1987). Regulation involves the control of technology adoption and use through direct intervention in providers' and payers' decision-making processes. Although regulatory authority generally derives from the public sector, private insurers and MCOs in the United States also exert considerable control over decisions to purchase and use technology. In addition, industry trade groups and disease-specific special interests often influence regulatory policy and decision making.

The respective roles of the major players in MTE are described briefly here, with more detailed discussion appearing in later chapters. Except where noted in the text and in table 9.1, these organizations currently perform important MTE functions.

Federal Governmental Agencies

Within the legislative and executive branches of the U.S. federal government, multiple agencies are involved in MTE. For many years, the most visible and widely respected agency involved in technology assessment was a legislative branch agency, the U.S. Congress's Office of Technology Assessment (OTA) (see chapter 2). Accountable to a congressional oversight committee composed of six senators and six representatives who determined its research agenda, the OTA responded to requests from members of Congress for commissioned studies and reports containing syntheses of existing knowledge (knowledge processing) that were intended to inform policy-making (IOM 1985). Unfortunately, the agency ceased its operations in 1995, a victim of partisan politics and federal budget cuts (U.S. Congress, OTA 1995). However, the OTA's legacy lives on in the form of an on-line archive that contains all reports and assessments produced between 1974 and 1995 (see the listing of key informational Web sites at the end of this chapter).

At present, the principal legislative branch agency involved in MTE is the U.S. General Accounting Office (GAO). The GAO historically has focused on knowledge-processing activities that have included studies of the relationship between technology and health care cost growth (GAO 1992a, 1992b, 1994, 1995), analyses of the implementation of federal laws and regulations regarding technology (GAO 1989, 2000, 2001), and development of methods for evaluating technologies, such as cross-design synthesis (GAO 1992c). Like the OTA, the GAO's agenda in MTE is driven by congressional inquiries and requests, but GAO studies and reports tend to be narrower in scope and more short term in duration than the assessments and analyses produced by the OTA.

The executive branch—especially the Department of Health and Human Services—contains a number of agencies with well-defined roles in MTE. Of these, the National Institutes of Health (NIH) is the oldest and best known because of its prominent role as a primary funding source for basic biomedical research and clinical trials (knowledge development). The NIH also convenes consensus-development conferences on specific technologies and controversial issues in medicine through its Office of Medical Applications of Research. The conferences serve as the focal point for evidence-based assessments of clinical practices and contribute importantly to the development, processing, and transfer of scientific knowledge (see chapter 6). Since 2002, consensus-development conferences have been provided with the latest evidence-based reports developed by the Evidence-Based Practice Centers (EPCs) of the Agency for Healthcare Research and Quality (AHRQ) (see chapter 11). NIH consensus statements and state of the science statements are disseminated widely, with more than 120 produced since 1977 (NIH 2001). The NIH's National Library of Medicine maintains several databases relevant to MTE, including ClinicalTrials.gov, which is a publicly accessible Web site intended to inform patients and their families about clinical research studies (see information resources at the end of this chapter).

Outside the Department of Health and Human Services, several other federal agencies engage substantially in knowledge-development and -processing activities. The National Science Foundation, the Department of Energy, and the National Aeronautics and Space Administration all fund basic and applied research studies that often lead to the development of new technologies that may be applied within health care, while the Department of Veterans Affairs and the Department of Defense support extensive clinical testing of new drugs, devices, and surgical procedures within their respective patient populations. The Department of Veterans Affairs also supports major knowledge-processing activities—including economic analyses, decision analytic studies, and various syntheses of MTE information—through its Management Decision and Research Center in Boston and the regional health services research and development programs located throughout the department's extensive health care system.

Within the Department of Health and Human Services, the Centers for Disease Control and Prevention (CDC) and its constituent agency, the National Center for Health Statistics, are active in knowledge-processing activities, with responsibility for a wide range of data-gathering functions, including databases related to the utilization of various technologies (Foote 1987). The AHRQ performs several MTE-related functions in the realm of knowledge development and processing. The agency houses the Center for Practice and Technology Assessment, whose role is to review available evidence on specific health care technologies and to advise the Centers for Medicare and Medicaid Services (CMS) on technology coverage and payment decisions under the Medicare program (see chapter 12). The Center for Practice and Technology Assessment is responsible for (1) supporting the review and analysis of evidence-based medicine through twelve EPCs and (2) disseminating evidence-based clinical practice guidelines through a National Guideline Clearinghouse (NGC), conducted in partnership with the American Medical Association and the American Association of Health Plans. Between 1989 and 1999, the AHRQ was known as the Agency for Health Care Policy and Research, whose major role was to fund research on patient outcomes (through patient outcomes research teams) and on medical treatment effectiveness (through the Medical Treatment Effectiveness Program). The AHRQ continues to support outcomes and effectiveness research but also now plays a leadership role in fostering patient safety improvement and medical error reduction within health care. Since 1997, the agency has operated the Centers for Education and Research on Therapeutics, whose purpose is "to increase awareness of the benefits and risks of new, existing, or combined uses of therapeutics through education and research" (AHRQ 2001a). (The functions of the Center for Practice and Technology Assessment, the NGC, the EPCs, and the Centers for Education and Research on Therapeutics are detailed in chapter 11.)

The Food and Drug Administration (FDA), however, is the only federal agency with direct regulatory control over the introduction of new medical technology—specifically, drugs, biologics, and devices. While its principal MTE activity is regulation, the FDA also engages significantly in knowledge-processing and, in some cases, knowledge-development activities. (See chapter 10 for an extensive discussion of the FDA regulatory process for drugs, biologics, and devices.)

As the largest purchaser of health care, the CMS—formerly known as the Health Care Financing Administration—actively makes coverage decisions concerning new medical technologies under the Medicare program. Its MTE activities, therefore, include regulation and knowledge processing. In making these judgments, it relies heavily on data from other federal sources, such as the FDA, the NIH, and the AHRQ's Center for Practice and Technology Assessment, as well as from private professional societies and others. (Medicare payment policies affecting the adoption and use of technology are discussed in chapter 12.)

Finally, among federal agencies, the Medicare Payment Advisory Commission (MedPAC) serves as a bridge between the legislative and executive branches of government by advising both Congress and the CMS on Medicare payment policy for hospitals and physicians. The agency, whose principal activity is knowledge processing, was created by the Balanced Budget Act of 1997 to succeed the Prospective Payment Assessment Commission and the Physician Payment Review Commission in their roles regarding the setting of payment levels to hospitals and physicians, respectively, under the Medicare program. To fulfill its mandate, MedPAC maintains databases, performs analyses of trends in spending and the effects of technology-related factors on Medicare service use and costs, and issues reports in March and June of each year that contain specific recommendations for Congress and the CMS (see chapter 12).

State Governmental Agencies

State governmental agencies generally have played regulatory roles in MTE, with some elements of knowledge processing. Until recently, state roles have focused primarily on the review of technology purchases by hospitals and other health care providers and on the setting of Medicaid program payment policy. Certificate-of-need (CON) programs, for example, use information from technology evaluations to make determinations regarding (1) the need for new technologies, predominantly high-priced capital expenditure items, such as major diagnostic imaging equipment, special care units, and transplant surgery programs, and (2) the appropriate allocation of these resources among communities and subregions of a state. These CON functions are discussed at length in chapter 13. In making CON decisions, states typically rely on information gathered from federal agencies (e.g., the FDA, CMS, and AHRQ), private payers, and professional associations and specialty societies. As third-party payers for Medicaid program recipients, state governments also rely on these sources, especially the CMS, for information when making technology coverage decisions. As described in chapter 12, the state of Oregon has for many years employed a priority list of condition-treatment pairs to guide decision making for service coverage.

Many states historically have invested in biomedical research, principally through their university systems, but their investments have been modest when compared with those of federal agencies such as the NIH and the National Science Foundation. Recently, at least twelve states (Colorado, Florida, Illinois, Indiana, Kansas, Maryland, Michigan, New Mexico, Ohio, Oklahoma, Texas, and Utah) have created special funds earmarked for biomedical research and development to find cures for cancer, heart disease, and other tobacco-related illnesses (Demkovich 2000). These state set-aside funds were established with monies obtained from the landmark 1998 multibillion-dollar tobacco industry settlement that involved the recovery of state dollars spent on care for Medicaid recipients who had developed tobacco-related diseases. States are using these funds for knowledge-development purposes, particularly to cultivate and nurture the growth of biotechnology firms (Demkovich 2000). Unfortunately, only about 8 percent of the $246 billion settlement money has been used for these purposes, as many states have been channeling the proceeds toward other, nonhealth goals (Farragher 2001).

Private Insurers

Like their federal and state governmental counterparts, private insurers require MTE information to make technology coverage decisions;

thus, insurers' evaluation activities are fairly broad in scope (Fernandez et al. 1997; Rettig 1997). While private insurers generally confine their involvement in MTE to knowledge processing and to regulation of technology coverage, other payers—most notably, managed care companies and health maintenance organizations (HMOs)—undertake ambitious MTE programs that may include clinical trials and knowledge development (discussed later in this chapter).

Among private payers, the Blue Cross and Blue Shield Association has been a leader in using MTE information to guide coverage decisions. The organization established its Medical Necessity Program in 1977 to focus on the appropriateness of established medical and surgical procedures. Drawing heavily on the expertise of national medical specialty societies, the program issued and maintained guidelines on various tests and procedures. Those falling outside the program guidelines had to be justified by the physician to be covered as an insured benefit. In 1983, the Technology Evaluation and Coverage program was created as a companion to the Medical Necessity Program to evaluate the cost and effectiveness of new and emerging devices and procedures. As with the Medical Necessity Program, the Technology Evaluation and Coverage program relied on the literature and medical societies for information. The technology program provided recommendations regarding new technology to individual Blue Cross plans, which then used the information as they deemed appropriate (IOM 1985). The two programs eventually "converged analytically," and in 1993 Blue Cross and Blue Shield began to make its reports available to the public (Rettig 1997, 30). That same year, the Blue Cross and Blue Shield Association also joined Kaiser Permanente in a collaborative technology evaluation effort that drew on the analytic expertise of the former and the clinical population of the latter (L. Wagner 1993). Each organization contributed an initial $3 million to the effort, and the expanded program produced approximately forty assessments annually (L. Wagner 1993; Rettig 1997).

Over time, as private insurance companies increased their penetration of the managed care market through mergers and acquisitions, such companies became engaged more heavily in MTE. Prime examples have included Aetna and Prudential. Even before its 1996 purchase of U.S. Healthcare (a major managed care company), Aetna's Clinical and Coverage Policy Unit housed a well-established technology evaluation program that provided direct support for coverage decisions (Rettig 1997). MTE activities were limited to devices and procedures, while assessments of drugs were handled separately by a subsidiary, Aetna

Pharmacy Management. Coordination between drugs and devices was achieved through the chairmanship of the Aetna Pharmacy and Therapeutics Committee, which was headed by the chief of clinical and coverage policy. Prudential formally established its technology evaluation program in 1985 to support corporate policies on coverage and to guide local plans in making case-by-case decisions (Rettig 1997). Evaluations typically involved reviews of the literature, consensus statements, and assessments by public and private groups for approval by the Technology Assessment Advisory Committee, which issued Medical Technology Evaluation and Coverage Statements for dissemination to the five Prudential regions. Like Aetna U.S. Healthcare, Prudential maintained a separate pharmacy-benefits unit that assessed both new pharmaceuticals and off-label use of FDA-approved drugs. In December 1998, Aetna U.S. Healthcare acquired Prudential HealthCare, creating the nation's largest managed care company (Gemignani and Kurdas 1999a). The enlarged company retains a strong commitment to MTE.

MCOs

Among MCOs, Kaiser Permanente has a rich history of MTE. Founded in 1945, Kaiser Permanente is a nonprofit, group-practice HMO headquartered in Oakland, California, with more than 8 million enrolled members in nine states and the District of Columbia (Kaiser Permanente 2001). Its Northern California Plan established a department of medical methods research in 1961 to look at ways that technology could improve the delivery of medical care. The department examined the cost, effectiveness, and organizational impact of emerging, new, established, and obsolete technologies and employed methods that included case studies, epidemiologic methods, literature reviews, and consensus-development conferences (IOM 1985). The Southern California Kaiser Permanente Plan also has been a leader in MTE over the years, developing clinical policies and monitoring their implementation in terms of health outcomes and service utilization (Fernandez et al. 1997). At the national level, Kaiser Permanente introduced in the mid-1980s its Inter-Regional New Technologies Committee, which today continues to draw members from all Kaiser Permanente regions and advises the regional plans on the adoption of experimental technologies (Borzo 1996; Rettig 1997). There are currently seven regions, with each retaining authority and responsibility for making its own coverage policy decisions (Rettig 1997; Kaiser Permanente 2001).

Several other MCOs have implemented exemplary MTE programs, including Group Health Cooperative, Harvard Pilgrim Health Care, and United HealthCare (Fernandez et al. 1997; Rettig 1997). Group Health Cooperative, an early staff-model HMO founded in 1947, was a pioneer in employing MTE to guide technology adoption decisions and clinical practice policies. Within Group Health, three committees oversaw the plan's MTE activities (Rettig 1997). The Committee on Medically Emerging Technologies used secondary data from various sources to evaluate new medical devices, procedures, and practices. The Pharmacy and Therapeutics Committee managed Group Health Cooperative's drug formulary (see chapter 5 for a discussion of pharmacy and therapeutics committees) and used cost-minimization analysis—a rough form of cost-effectiveness analysis—to compare new drugs with other therapeutic agents (Rettig 1997). The Committee on Prevention focused on primary and secondary prevention and weighed in on decisions involving technologies with preventive potential for clinical conditions with significant mortality, morbidity, or cost. In 1997, Group Health Cooperative formed an alliance with Kaiser Permanente that allowed each to remain independent and separate but offered such benefits as the sharing of best clinical and administrative practices (including MTEs) and the ability to offer their members reciprocity for both routine and urgent care (Group Health Cooperative 2001; Kaiser Permanente 2001).

Harvard Pilgrim Health Care is a large Massachusetts MCO that was formed in the 1990s by the merger of the Harvard Community Health Plan (a combined staff-model/group-model HMO) with Pilgrim Health Care (an independent practice association). The current MTE program at Harvard Pilgrim stems from 1992, when the old Harvard plan established the Committee for Appropriate Technology to set policy for the HMO (Rettig 1997). The committee relies on the plan's physicians to perform technology evaluations, usually in partnership with major Boston teaching hospitals (e.g., Massachusetts General Hospital or Brigham and Women's Hospital), as well as on external assessments conducted by independent research organizations (Fernandez et al. 1997).

United HealthCare of Minneapolis, Minnesota, is a national managed care company composed of approximately twenty health plans whose formal MTE program in its central office provides support to medical directors in the individual plans (Rettig 1997). Like Harvard Pilgrim, United HealthCare supplements its internal evaluation efforts with extensive use of technology assessment reports from independent research groups.

In some communities, private payers have formed partnerships with local physician groups to perform MTE functions that would benefit technology adoption decision making community-wide. One such example is the Community Technology Assessment Advisory Board in Rochester, New York, which was established in 1993 by the local Blue Cross and Blue Shield plan in conjunction with the Rochester Community Individual Practice Association and is a community-based model for combining medical technology assessment with nonhospital capacity management (Berman 1993). The board consists of representatives from the hospital, physician, insurer, and business sectors of the community and from the general public, and the board addresses issues related to the assessment of new technology, new applications of existing technology, and proposals to acquire new capital-intensive service capacity (Community Technology Assessment Advisory Board 1993).

Professional and Specialty Societies

Professional and specialty societies have had long-standing involvement in MTE efforts, especially knowledge-processing activities that lead to publications in the medical literature. In fact, virtually every medical specialty society engages in knowledge processing and at times in knowledge-development activities related to medical technology. As interest in MTE has grown, especially among private insurers and MCOs, the research priorities of the professional associations and specialty societies have changed, in part to reflect the concerns and interests of these other players. Among the most active societies are the American College of Cardiology, the American College of Radiology, the American College of Surgeons, and the American College of Obstetricians and Gynecologists. However, the two professional organizations with the longest history and the most extensive programs in MTE are the American Medical Association and the American College of Physicians—American Society of Internal Medicine (ACP-ASIM).

The American Medical Association's Diagnostic and Therapeutic Technology Assessment Program was created in 1982 as a mechanism for providing prompt responses to inquiries from association members about the safety, effectiveness, and level of acceptance of various drugs, devices, and surgical procedures. Information from the literature and from expert opinion is used to evaluate new, established, and potentially obsolete technologies (IOM 1985; Rettig 1997). All opinions of the assessment program are published in the *Journal of the American Medical Association* and may appear in selected specialty journals as well. The American Medical Association also publishes the *Directory of Practice Parameters: Titles, Sources, and Updates,* which contains a comprehensive listing of practice parameters developed by leading national medical specialty societies and other groups. The American Medical Association also partners with the AHRQ and the American Association of Health Plans in supporting the NGC.

The Clinical Efficacy Assessment Project of the ACP-ASIM, a national society for internists and related medical subspecialists, was initiated in 1981 as an outgrowth of the American College of Physicians' early participation in Blue Cross's Medical Necessity Program. Early on, the Clinical Efficacy Assessment Project focused primarily on the evaluation of the safety and effectiveness of new medical and surgical procedures and on the development of guidelines for common diagnostic tests. Over time, however, the project expanded to include evaluations of procedures and therapies in clinical practice (Rettig 1997). As with the Diagnostic and Therapeutic Technology Assessment Program, the Clinical Efficacy Assessment Project synthesizes available literature and the expert opinions of its members in developing its recommenda tions (IOM 1985; Steinberg 1989). ACP-ASIM approved guidelines—and the background analyses on which they are based—are published in the *Annals of Internal Medicine* (Rettig 1997).

The ACP-ASIM also has developed guidelines outlining the knowledge, technical skills, and specific training considered necessary to establish competence for selected internal medicine procedures and has drawn on its large national network of physicians to accumulate data regarding the use and outcomes of procedures routinely employed in ambulatory care settings (Steinberg 1989).

Provider Associations

In addition to the physician specialty societies, three provider associations are active in knowledge processing for MTE—the American Hospital Association, the American Association of Health Plans, and the Alliance of Community Health Plans.

The American Hospital Association (AHA) historically has been a leader in MTE, but its focus predictably is more on hospital-management and capital-investment issues. AHA-sponsored technology evaluations typically have targeted new or established devices, instruments, and supplies and the systems needed to support them. The costs of new technology have been a prime consideration, and the AHA has relied on both literature synthesis and expert opinion for its reports (IOM 1985). Between 1982 and the early 1990s, the Hospital Technology Series program maintained active educational and publishing efforts, but organizational restructuring and changing priorities at the AHA led to a scaled-down effort in MTE that no longer includes educational programs for hospital managers (Rettig 1997).

The American Association of Health Plans is the principal organization representing the interests of the managed care industry. As a service to its member plans, the association works with the American Medical Association to encourage the development of clinical practice guidelines and partners with the American Medical Association and the AHRQ to support and maintain the National Guideline Clearinghouse. The Alliance of Community Health Plans was founded in 1984 as the HMO Group, an association of thirty health plans. During the 1980s, it established the Technology Management Information Exchange to assist its members in identifying emerging and new technologies and to provide members with evidence-based secondary evaluations (Rettig 1997). Today, the Alliance of Community Health Plans includes eighteen leading nonprofit and provider-based health plans serving more than 12 million enrollees in nineteen states and the District of Columbia (Alliance 2001). The Technology Management Information Exchange continues to provide evidence-based MTEs in partnership with Hayes, a for-profit research firm (discussed later in this chapter). In addition to this service, the Alliance of Community Health Plans offers its members benchmarking analyses and shared improvement projects involving evidence-based interventions and collaborates with the ACP-ASIM on the publication of *Effective Clinical Practice*, a thirty-thousand-subscriber journal (Alliance of Community Health Plans 2001).

Technology Industry Groups

Individual firms involved in the manufacture of new technology—whether pharmaceuticals, devices, or biotechnology—have a vested interest in both the content and the outcomes of technology assessment. Thus, most of their research may be characterized as either (1) research and development (R&D) activities designed to produce a marketable product or (2) clinical testing intended to satisfy regulatory requirements. (For a discussion of federal regulation of drugs and devices, see chapter 10.) Technology evaluations by pharmaceutical and device manufacturers typically are collaborative efforts, funded primarily by the manufacturer but carried out in clinical trials or in a practice setting by academic medical centers, universities, or contract research organizations.

Industry trade associations—such as the Advanced Medical Technology Association, the Pharmaceutical Research and Manufacturers Association (PhRMA), the Biotechnology Industry Organization, the National Electrical Manufacturers Association, the Medical Device Manufacturers Association, and the Association of Medical Diagnostics Manufacturers—do not sponsor or conduct technology evaluations per se. Rather, they engage in knowledge processing and are capable of wielding great political influence in policy circles that deal with governmental regulation of the adoption and use of technology. For example, the former director of the National Center for Health Care Technology has documented the role of the Advanced Medical Technology Association (when it was known as the Health Industry Manufacturers Association) in bringing about the agency's demise in the early 1980s (Perry 1982). Another example of the industry's political clout was its creation in 1992 of the nonprofit Health Care Technology Institute (HCTI), which was charged with "fostering a more informed climate for public and private decision making involving technology, particularly those related to health care reform" (HCTI 1993b, 49). Throughout the debate of the Clinton administration's proposed American Health Security Act, the HCTI produced evaluation reports favorable to the industry and to technology growth. However, as soon as the threat of health care reform—and its potentially negative financial implications for technology manufacturers—had evaporated in 1995, the HCTI was dissolved. More recently, PhRMA, the Medical Device Manufacturers Association, and the Association of Medical Diagnostics Manufacturers have been active in shaping legislation affecting the regulatory powers of the FDA, most notably the FDA Modernization Act of 1997 and the Medical Device User Fee and Modernization Act of 2002.

Other Private Groups and Organizations

Many other private organizations are actively involved in some aspect of MTE, including disease-specific interest groups, academic medical centers, universities, nonprofit research organizations, and for-profit research firms.

Disease-specific interest groups—such as the American Heart Association, the American Cancer Society, the Arthritis Foundation, the American Diabetes Association, the American Liver Foundation, the American Lung Association, and the Alzheimer's Association, to name just a few—concentrate primarily on the processing of knowledge obtained from clinical studies and the dissemination of research findings to professional as well as lay audiences. These groups at times also may contribute to knowledge development and the formulation of governmental regulatory policy (IOM 1988). Some are particularly adroit at influencing the legislative process, including lobbying Congress and state legislatures for research funding and for other programs that fulfill disease-specific goals.

Academic medical centers and universities, in contrast, are likely to participate primarily in knowledge-development activities (e.g., NIH-sponsored and/or industry-supported clinical trials and analyses) but also may engage in knowledge-processing activities. In some instances, individual academic medical centers have pooled their resources for undertaking MTE. One such organization is the University HealthSystem Consortium, which was founded in 1984 and represents approximately seventy academic medical centers (Rettig 1997; University HealthSystem Consortium 2001). The consortium maintains an ongoing technology evaluation program that provides members with such services as technology information resources (including a newsletter, *Clinical Practice Alert*); "value management," which includes benchmarking, clinical guidelines use, and outcomes assessment; "market management," which helps members analyze changes in local health market conditions; and group purchasing services for major capital equipment, pharmaceuticals, and various supplies (Rettig 1997; University HealthSystem Consortium 2001).

Finally, there are independent nonprofit and for-profit research groups that generate a great deal of MTE information for consumption by a wide range of audiences, including governmental agencies, private payers, MCOs, hospitals and other providers, and various pharmaceutical, biotechnology, and medical device manufacturers. These contract research organizations engage heavily in both knowledge-development and knowledge-processing activities. Knowledge-development activities include managing clinical trials and designing pharmacoeconomic studies, while knowledge-processing activities include conducting analyses to support coverage decisions by payers and adoption decisions by providers.

Examples of nonprofit research organizations include ECRI, the Medical Technology and Practice Patterns Institute, and the RAND Corporation. ECRI (established in 1955) operates the Health Technology Assessment Information Service, which assesses the safety and effectiveness of medical devices and the support systems required for their use (IOM 1985), and produces various online data services and published reports (e.g., the *Health Devices Sourcebook* and *Health Devices Alerts*) for use by hospitals, physician organizations, corporate health plans, MCOs, private insurers, and state governments (Fernandez et al. 1997; Rettig 1997; Lerner 1998; ECRI 2001). The Medical Technology and Practice Patterns Institute maintains the *Directory of Health Technology Assessment Organizations Worldwide* and focuses research efforts on areas that include pharmacoeconomics, health services research, and health policy analysis (Medical Technology and Practice Patterns Institute 1998). The RAND Corporation has been a leader in health services research and MTE for thirty years, producing numerous studies, database analyses, technical reports, and books on health care technology and MTE methods (Acton 1973; Brook et al. 1986, 1990; Rettig 1997).

In the for-profit sector, MEDTAP International, Hayes, and Covance are recognized names, providing MTE services to a wide range of audiences. MEDTAP is well known for its economic evaluations and cost-effectiveness analyses of medical technologies, including pharmacoeconomic studies. Hayes is a leading publisher of technology assessment reports for guiding payment coverage decisions of private payers (Rettig 1997); in addition, Hayes maintains the Technology Management Information Exchange in partnership with the Alliance of Community Health Plans. Covance is a premier contract research organization that specializes in comprehensive drug development services, including the management of phase 2 and phase 3 clinical trials for pharmaceutical and medical device companies. In addition, a multitude of management consulting firms—ranging from large companies (e.g., KPMG Peat Marwick, and Ernst and Young) to small specialty firms—have increased their involvement in MTE in recent years by offering contractual services to pharmaceutical and biotechnology manufacturers to design and to manage clinical trials of new drugs and biologics as part of new product development.

International Efforts in Health Technology Assessment

In the years following the 1985 publication of the IOM international survey, interest in the evaluation of medical technologies grew steadily throughout the world, with several organizations coming to the fore (Banta and Luce 1993; Perry, Gardner, and Thamer 1997). Two groups in particular helped to foster the early development of the field of HTA/MTE by championing the need for the assessment of all health care technologies, not just drugs and pharmaceuticals. The World Health Organization, through its designation of various collaborating centers on technology assessment, quality assurance, radiation medicine, health laboratory technology, and blood safety, gave visibility to HTA issues and provided a platform for the international exchange of expertise, methods, and assessment reports (Banta and Luce 1993). Among professionals, the International Society for Technology Assessment in Health Care advanced the development and application of methods and tools for HTA and promoted collegial interchange of information and ideas (Banta and Perry 1997). Established in 1985, the society stood as a major force within the field for many years, publishing the *International Journal of Technology Assessment in Health Care* and convening annual scientific meetings that contained state-of-the-art sessions on HTA methods, studies, and policies. In 2000, the society's mission was amended to embrace the principles of evidence-based medicine within HTA (President's Message 2000).

Financial difficulties in 2002, however, forced the society to disband. From its ashes, a new society—HTA International—was launched in 2003 to promote the exchange of information on HTA and to provide the key forum for all those interested in the science, development, and application of HTA (Granados 2003). For the first three years of its life, HTAi (Health Technology Assessment International) will be based at the Institute of Health Economics in Edmonton, Alberta, Canada (Granados 2003).

International commitment to and cooperation in HTA may be found in two networks established during the 1990s—the Cochrane Collaboration and the International Network of Agencies for Health Technology Assessment (INAHTA). Founded in Oxford, England, in 1993, the Cochrane Collaboration is a nonprofit organization that today has centers around the world that prepare, maintain, and disseminate systematic, up-to-date reviews of randomized controlled trials involving medical therapies. (See chapter 6 for a profile of the collaboration's databases.) Also founded in 1993, by representatives from twelve agencies in nine countries (Australia, Canada, France, the Netherlands, Spain, Sweden, Switzerland, the United Kingdom, and the United States), the INAHTA "provides a forum for the identification and pursuit of interests common to health technology assessment agencies" (INAHTA 2001). With growing health care spending in the 1990s placing intense pressure on gross national products virtually everywhere, the need to evaluate both new and established medical technologies became universal. Individual nations struggling with the challenge of mounting HTA activities and standardizing evaluation methods saw great benefit in sharing such information and in avoiding duplication of effort. Consequently, the membership of the INAHTA grew rapidly to thirty-six agencies and nonprofit organizations in eighteen nations and now includes members in Austria, Chile, Cuba, Denmark, Finland, Germany, Israel, New Zealand, and Norway (INAHTA 2001). Its headquarters is in Stockholm at the Swedish Council on Technology Assessment in Health Care (known as the SBU).

During the 1990s, the European Union sponsored several cooperative efforts across its member states. The 1994–97 collaborative project EUR-ASSESS was directed toward defining priorities for HTA, developing common methods for assessment, linking assessment results to insurance coverage, and identifying effective means of dissemination and implementation of results (Information 1996; Banta and Oortwijn 2000a). The spring 1997 issue of the *International Journal of Technology Assessment in Health Care* was devoted to the EUR-ASSESS project and its activities in the areas of priority setting, methodology development, dissemination and evaluation of impact, and insurance coverage policy (Report 1997). EUR-ASSESS was succeeded in 1996–98 by another European Union–financed study, the HTA-Europe Project, which produced detailed overviews of member nations' HTA efforts (see the spring 2000 issue of the *International Journal of Technology Assessment in Health Care*) and which called for the establishment of a permanent coordinating structure for HTA at the European level (Banta and Oortwijn 2000b). The HTA-Europe Project also recently produced an assessment of the state of the art in health screening and disease prevention in European Union countries, focusing specifically on mammography screening for breast cancer, screening for prostate cancer, and routine use of ultrasound in pregnancy (Banta, Oortwijn, and Cranovsky 2001)

A more recent effort is the European Collaboration for Assessment of Health Interventions (known as the ECHTA/ECAHI project), which was established by the European Commission in February 2000 for the purpose of generating and communicating a common evidence base regarding the effectiveness of various health interventions. Headquartered at the SBU in Stockholm, the project's six working groups facilitate information exchange and networking across the European Union's fifteen member states on topics that include methods development, assessments of interventions, dissemination of best practices, and education and support for decision making (European Collaboration 2001).

Other ongoing cooperative HTA efforts include (1) the Euroscan network, established in 1997 by Denmark, the Netherlands, Sweden, Switzerland, the United Kingdom, and the Basque region of Spain for the identification of emerging technologies requiring assessment (CCOHTA 2001a), and (2) the Technological Change in Health Care Research Network, in which investigators in clinical medicine, economics, and epidemiology from sixteen countries have found different patterns of technological change in the treatment of heart attacks that may be related to the underlying economic and regulatory incentives for providing treatments in each nation (McClellan and Kessler 1999, 2002; Technological Change in Health Care Research Network 2001).

A nonprofit international organization that has gained prominence in recent years is the International Society for Pharmacoeconomics and Outcomes Research. Formed in 1995 with headquarters in Lawrenceville, New Jersey, the society promotes the practice and science of pharmacoeconomics and health outcomes research. Its members include physicians, pharmacists, economists, and researchers from academia, the pharmaceutical industry, government, managed care, private research organizations, and the purchasers of care (International Society 2001).

Health Technology Assessment in Selected Countries

Historically, Europe and North America have been the hotbeds of HTA activity, with formal HTA programs strongest in nations whose health care systems either are tax financed (e.g., Sweden and Canada) or are employment based but significantly controlled by the national government (e.g., the Netherlands). During the 1980s and 1990s, various other nations established government-sponsored HTA programs, including Australia, Chile, Denmark, France, Hungary, Italy, New Zealand, Poland, Spain, and Switzerland. Today, many nations—including Argentina, Brazil, China, the Czech Republic, India, Latvia, Lithuania, Malaysia, Mexico, Pakistan, Peru, Romania, and Russia—are at some stage of institutionalizing formal HTA programs (President's Message 2000; President's Message 2001). Yet despite the strong advocacy of HTA over time by the Pan American Health Organization, efforts in Central and South American countries have been the slowest to develop (President's Message 2000; President's Message 2001). Although Brazil, Chile, and Mexico have been in the forefront of these nations, many of their neighbors have been less involved in technology assessment than in technology transfer—that is, purchasing new technologies that have been shown to be safe and efficacious (Perry, Gardner, and Thamer 1997). The governments of these nations face the daunting task of assessing their individual countries' ability to take full advantage of new health care technology. But without the basic health care delivery infrastructure in place (facilities, professionals, and other resources), technology alone cannot improve health care and health outcomes in those nations. To facilitate the dissemination of information on HTA activities and studies, both the International Society for Technology Assessment in Health Care and the INAHTA have published and circulated Spanish-language versions of their newsletters worldwide.

In the following sections, we profile three of the leading HTA programs in the world—those of Sweden, Canada, and the Netherlands. We also describe three HTA programs that developed rapidly since the late 1980s—those of the United Kingdom, Spain, and Australia.

Sweden

Technology assessment activities in Sweden have long enjoyed strong government support. Established by the Swedish government in 1968, the Swedish Planning and Rationalization Institute of Health Services became an early leader in technology assessment. It conducted some of the earliest studies on the use of CT scanners in the 1970s and was among the first to hold consensus-development conferences on an ongoing basis (IOM 1985; Banta and Luce 1993). In 1987, the SBU was created to assess health care technologies and to provide a focal point for such activities in Sweden. In 1992, the SBU became a permanent agency through an act of the Swedish parliament (Banta and Luce 1993). Two of the SBU's important activities have been convening international workshops on various technology-related topics (e.g., coronary artery revascularization, radiotherapy for cancer, and screening for prostate cancer) and issuing periodic reports of technology assessment studies (Information 1996). Examples of technology assessment reports include bone density measurement, estrogen treatment, and radiotherapy for cancer (Reports 1997; Carlsson et al. 2000). The SBU found in a 2002 study that its technology assessment reports have had moderate impacts on clinical practices, encouraging physicians to adopt evidence-based practices over time (Britton and Jonsson 2002). The SBU today serves as the organizational home base for the INAHTA and the ECHTA/ECAHI project. (For an excellent description of the SBU and its HTA activities, see Carlsson et al. 2000.)

Canada

Technology assessment in Canada is the responsibility of the Canadian Coordinating Office for Health Technology Assessment (CCOHTA), which was established in 1989 as a nonprofit organization funded by the provincial, territorial, and federal governments (Banta and Luce 1993). As one of its earliest activities, the CCOHTA in 1992 compiled a directory that included more than 300 technology assessment projects then in progress, together with the names and addresses of the organizations involved. Over the years, the CCOHTA has sponsored regional symposia on HTA, evaluated and disseminated numerous reports on individual technologies, and issued technology briefs and a quarterly newsletter, *Connection.* The CCOHTA also oversees the Canadian Health Technology Assessment Network, which includes government-funded organizations in several provinces, most notably the Agence d'Évaluation des Technologies et des Modes d'Intervention en Santé in Québec, the Alberta Heritage Foundation for Medical Research, the British Columbia Office of Technology Assessment, the Health Services Utilization and Research Commission in Saskatchewan, the Institute for Clinical Evaluative Sciences in Ontario, and the Manitoba Centre for Health Policy and Evaluation. In 1997, the CCOHTA initiated the Canadian Emerging Technology Assessment Program as a pilot project and made it a permanent and integral part of its research program the next year (CCOHTA 2001a). In 1999, the CCOHTA's operating budget more than doubled, enabling it to greatly expand the scope of its activities (CCOHTA 2000, 2001a). CCOHTA is a member of the Euroscan collaboration on emerging technologies (CCOHTA 2001a). Recent examples of technology assessment reports include drug treatments for Alzheimer's disease, economic evaluation of zanamivir for the treatment of influenza, and surveillance mammography after treatment of primary breast cancer (CCOHTA 2001b, 2001c).

The Netherlands

The diffusion of health care technology in the Netherlands has long been controlled through tight regulation of the introduction and use of new technologies. Article 18 of the Hospital Provisions Act authorizes the national government to license and regulate a number of technological services, including renal dialysis, various forms of organ transplants, radiotherapy, neurosurgery, cardiac angiography, cardiac surgery, interventional cardiology, neonatal intensive care, in vitro fertilization, CT, nuclear medicine, and genetic screening (Rigter 1993; Bos 2000).

Most health-related research in the Netherlands is funded by the government, particularly through the Ministry of Education, Culture, and Science, and is conducted primarily at the eight universities that have medical schools and affiliated hospitals (Bos 2000). HTA has high priority in government circles, and various university departments and institutes have received funding to conduct both empirical studies and literature reviews (Rigter 1993). Erasmus University in Rotterdam, for example, has several academic departments—including the Institute of Medical Technology Assessment—involved in collaborative technology assessment research. Other groups active in HTA include universities in Amsterdam, Maastricht, and Groningen as well as the Centre for Medical Technology of the Netherlands Organization for Applied Scientific Research, a member of the INAHTA (Rigter 1993; Bos 2000).

The Dutch Board for the Evaluation of Drugs is charged with responsibilities similar to those of the U.S. FDA: pharmaceutical firms must submit evidence of safety and effectiveness to the board for premarket approval to be given by the Ministry of Health, Welfare, and Sport. Once introduced into clinical practice, drugs and devices are monitored for their use by the Health Council of the Netherlands, an advisory body that counsels the government on the scientific state of the art with respect to health care (Rigter 1993). The council has responsibility for identifying emerging technologies and for recommending whether a new technology should be regulated under article

18 of the Hospital Provisions Act. (For a substantive discussion of HTA activities in the Netherlands, see Bos 2000.)

The United Kingdom

Compared with the preceding three HTA programs, the United Kingdom's HTA program is less centralized and coordinated (Woolf and Henshall 2000). The National Health Service always has maintained an active role in technology development and evaluation through its Research and Development Programme in conjunction with various British universities and academic medical centers. Interest in HTA, however, intensified greatly during the 1990s as the British government attempted to implement market-oriented reforms in the health service to contain rising health care costs. A new performance framework emphasizing effectiveness and outcomes was introduced in 1997, leading to the 1999 creation of the National Institute for Clinical Effectiveness, which was charged with conducting appraisals of the clinical effectiveness and cost-effectiveness of new and existing drug treatments and other interventions (Dobson 1999).

Within the National Health Service's Research and Development Programme, the Standing Group on Health Technology is responsible for (1) identifying and prioritizing technologies in need of assessment, (2) advising on the need for diffusion controls until better evidence becomes available, (3) identifying emerging technologies that have potentially major implications for the National Health Service, and (4) identifying and prioritizing the need for HTA methods development (Woolf and Henshall 2000). The National Co-ordinating Centre for Health Technology Assessment oversees the priority-setting process. Based at the University of Southampton, the centre works in partnership with the University of York's Centre for Health Economics and the Department of Health Sciences and Clinical Evaluation. Two other centers play complementary roles—the U.K. Cochrane Centre (based in Oxford) facilitates and coordinates systematic reviews of randomized controlled trials, and the Centre for Reviews and Dissemination (based at the University of York) conducts and commissions systematic reviews of effectiveness and cost-effectiveness.

Systematic reviews are disseminated widely to public and private organizations. Major users include the Medicines Control Agency, which is responsible for ensuring that all medicines on the U.K. market meet appropriate standards of safety, quality, and efficacy, and the

Medical Devices Agency, which is responsible for enforcing European Union directives on the safety and efficacy of medical devices (Medical Devices Agency 2001; Medicines Control Agency 2001). Other users include regional and local National Health Service decision makers, who sometimes conduct assessments to meet pressing policy decision needs (Woolf and Henshall 2000). Timely HTA information is also needed within the private sector of the health care system. A 1999 study of technology diffusion within the private sector strongly recommended that the National Health Service's HTA program link actively with private purchasers of health care to promote more rational diffusion and use of new medical technology (Doyle and McNeilly 1999). (For a comprehensive discussion of HTA activities in the United Kingdom, see Woolf and Henshall 2000.)

Spain

Formal HTA has grown rapidly in Spain, both nationally and regionally (Granados et al. 2000). In 1993, the Spanish government appointed a deputy director for technology assessment and made a commitment to establishing a new agency, the Agencia de Evaluación de Tecnologías Sanitarias in Madrid. In addition, three regional organizations play important roles in HTA—the Catalan Agency for Health Technology Assessment and Research, the Basque Office for Health Technology Assessment, and the Andalusian Agency for Health Technology Assessment. All four organizations are active participants in INAHTA, and each conducts independent technology assessment studies and issues periodic reports. Recent HTA reports have focused on the treatment of urinary incontinence, the treatment of hepatic tumors with radio frequencies, and the efficacy and costs of outpatient cataract surgery (Catalan Agency 2000). (For an informative review of HTA activities in Spain, see Granados et al. 2000.)

Australia

Australia was the first country to promote for government subsidy those drugs that produce cost-effective returns in health improvement (Drummond 1992; Freund et al. 1992; Commonwealth Department 1996). Before a new drug may be approved for government subsidy— that is, listed in the Pharmaceutical Benefits Scheme—an economic evaluation must be performed to assess the additional cost of the new drug for each additional benefit gained, compared to existing therapy. Mandated by legislation in 1987 and formally implemented in 1993, this review process is overseen by the Pharmaceutical Benefits Advisory Committee and requires drug manufacturers to conduct and submit cost-effectiveness analyses of new products. By March 1996, 205 economic evaluations had been assessed (Commonwealth Department 1996).

The principal responsibility for evaluating health technologies other than drugs rests with the Australian Health Technology Advisory Committee, which is a permanent subcommittee of the National Health and Medical Research Council (Perry, Hanft, and Chrzanowski 1993; Commonwealth Department 1996). The Australian Health Technology Advisory Committee (previously known as the National Health Technology Advisory Panel) was established specifically to coordinate HTA activities in Australia. The committee issues technology assessment reports that are used widely by governmental agencies for local planning purposes, for resource allocation, and for assessing the impact of new technologies on hospitals and other health services. The reports also are used to inform insurance coverage decisions and are employed by hospital managers in planning the introduction of new technologies.

One example of an early report by the National Health Technology Advisory Panel was a 1990 evaluation of MRI that included all public-sector imagers introduced since 1986 in five major teaching hospitals (Hailey and Crowe 1993). The report found that patient throughput at the sites increased by 50 percent, apparently in response to a National Health Technology Advisory Panel consensus statement that had been issued during the period and that called for more efficient use of MRI units. It is believed that this assessment helped to slow the diffusion of MRI in the public sector while increasing the productivity of units already in place. Examples of technology assessments by the Australian Health Technology Advisory Committee include colorectal cancer screening, minimal access (minimally invasive) surgery, diagnostic ultrasound, treatment of sleep apnea, and a clinical review of MRI. Since 1990, the government also has sponsored nationally funded centers for highly specialized technologies, such as liver and pancreas transplantation and cerebrovascular embolization units (Commonwealth Department 1996). Designation of these centers is awarded on a competitive basis, with regionalization goals in mind.

Conclusion

The panoply of MTE activities in the United States and elsewhere around the world is remarkable. However, a major difference between the United States and other nations lies in the extent to which technology evaluation activities are centralized. In most nations where the prevailing system of health care financing is either tax financed or government dominated, centralized HTA programs have been developed and institutionalized. Sweden, Canada, and the Netherlands, for example, have long been leaders in the international HTA movement, while the United Kingdom, Spain, Australia, and many other nations recently have established formal HTA programs. The United States, in contrast, stands alone with its highly decentralized and fragmented MTE activities mirroring the complexities of its pluralistic (and largely private) health care financing system. Without a comprehensive national policy toward MTE, the many public and private organizations engaged in MTE activities are likely to duplicate each other's efforts. While it is unlikely that the United States will adopt a centralized approach like its European counterparts in the near future, strategies such as a public-private partnership are by no means inconceivable and may hold promise for more rational evaluation of both emerging and established technologies. (See chapter 15 for a discussion of future evaluation strategies in the United States.)

Even in those countries where centralized HTA programs exist and where organizations such as INAHTA, IITAi, and the Cochrane Collaboration foster the sharing of evidence-based evaluation reports, it is unclear how different nations handle and resolve contradictory evaluation findings and/or policy recommendations. Indeed, with the continuing growth in databases containing clinical trials and meta-analyses, a major challenge for the international HTA community in the future will be to develop procedures for mediating disputes among evaluators and clinical investigators in the interpretation of technology evaluation findings.

Information Resources

The major organizations mentioned in this chapter all maintain active Web sites from which information about specific medical technologies and methods for evaluating technology may be obtained. The following is an alphabetical listing of key informational Web sites.

Organization/Source	Web Site
Advanced Medical Technology Association	www.advamed.org
Aetna U.S. Healthcare	www.aetnaushc.com
Agency for Healthcare Research and Quality	www.ahrq.gov
• Center for Practice and Technology Assessment	www.ahrq.gov/about/cptafact
• Centers for Education and Research on Therapeutics	www.certs.hhs.gov
• Evidence-Based Practice Centers	www.ahrq.gov/clinic/epc
• National Guideline Clearinghouse	www.guideline.gov
Alliance of Community Health Plans (formerly the HMO Group)	www.achp.org
Alzheimer's Association	www.alz.org
American Association of Health Plans	www.aahp.org
American Cancer Society	www.cancer.org
American College of Cardiology	www.acc.org
American College of Obstetricians and Gynecologists	www.acog.org
American College of Physicians– American Society of Internal Medicine	www.acponline.org
American College of Radiology	www.acr.org
American College of Surgeons	www.facs.org
American Diabetes Association	www.diabetes.org
American Heart Association	www.americanheart.org
American Hospital Association	www.aha.org
American Liver Foundation	www.liverfoundation.org
American Lung Association	www.lungusa.org

American Medical Association   www.ama-assn.org
Arthritis Foundation   www.arthritis.org
Association of Medical
   Diagnostics Manufacturers   www.amdm.org
Biotechnology Industry
   Organization   www.bio.org
Blue Cross and Blue
   Shield Association   www.bluecares.com
Canadian Coordinating Office for
   Health Technology Assessment   www.ccohta.ca
Centers for Disease Control
   and Prevention   www.cdc.gov
Centers for Medicare and
   Medicaid Services (formerly
   the Health Care Financing
   Administration)   www.hcfa.gov
Cochrane Collaboration   www.cochrane.org
Covance   www.covance.com
Department of Health and
   Human Services   www.dhhs.gov
Food and Drug Administration   www.fda.gov
ECRI   www.ecri.org
General Accounting Office   www.gao.gov
Group Health Cooperative   www.ghc.org
Harvard Pilgrim Health Care   www.hphc.org
Hayes   www.hayesinc.com
Health Technology
   Assessment International   www.htai.org
International Network of
   Agencies for Health
   Technology Assessment   www.inahta.org
International Society for
   Pharmacoeconomics and
   Outcomes Research   www.ispor.org
International Society for
   Technology Assessment in
   Health Care   www.istahc.org
Kaiser Permanente Health Plan   www.kp.org
Medical Device
   Manufacturers Association   www.medicaldevices.org

Medical Technology and Practice Patterns Institute	www.mtppi.org
Medicare Payment Advisory Commission	www.medpac.gov
MEDTAP International	www.medtap.com
National Center for Health Statistics	www.cdc.gov/nchs
National Electrical Manufacturers Association	www.nema.org
National Institutes of Health	www.nih.gov/health
• National Library of Medicine	www.nlm.nih.gov
• NIH Clinical Trials Database	www.clinicaltrials.gov
• NIH Consensus Development Conferences	www.consensus.nih.gov
• NIH Office of Medical Applications of Research	www.odp.od.nih.gov/omar
National Science Foundation	www.nsf.gov
Office of Technology Assessment Archive (The OTA Legacy	www.wws.princeton.edu/~ota
Pharmaceutical Research and Manufacturers of America	www.phrma.org
RAND Corporation	www.rand.org/health
Swedish Council on Technology Assessment in Health Care (includes the European Collaboration for Assessment of Health Interventions)	www.sbu.se
United HealthCare	www.uhc.com
University HealthSystem Consortium	www.uhc.org or www.uhc.edu
Veterans Health Administration	www.va.gov/vbs/health
World Health Organization	www.who.org

Policy Issues and Concerns

In part II of this book, we examined the methods of medical technology evaluation (MTE) and the organizations in the United States and selected other nations that are active in the development, analysis, synthesis, and dissemination of MTE information. In this third and final part (chapters 10–15), we focus on a series of public policy issues that relate to the effective evaluation and management of medical technology. Indeed, it might be argued that these policy issues define and frame the current debate over medical technology. These issues include

- safety and efficacy concerns regarding the introduction of medical technologies into clinical practice and the federal policies that govern the entry of technologies into the medical marketplace;
- quality concerns regarding the achievement of optimal patient outcomes and the public and private policies that influence evidence-based clinical practice and decision making concerning the use of technology;
- cost concerns regarding the adoption and use of medical technologies by hospitals and physicians and the public and private policies that determine coverage and payment for new technologies;
- access concerns regarding the equitable distribution and use of medical technologies among various population groups and the governmental policies that control the capacity of the health care system to provide technology-based services;
- social, ethical, and legal concerns regarding the application of MTE methods and the policies that govern the allocation of scarce health care resources and the development and enforcement of clinical practice standards; and
- evaluation concerns regarding future MTE strategies, especially in an environment that is increasingly dominated by aggressive managed care practices.

10

Safety and Efficacy Concerns: Medical Technology and Market Entry
Alan B. Cohen and Shirley A. Stewart

As various new technologies—pharmaceuticals, devices, and surgical procedures—have proliferated in recent years, concerns about their safety and efficacy have also grown. In some cases, regulatory approval for certain drugs or devices may have been premature, leading to product recalls or to removal from the market altogether. In this chapter, we focus on the public policies that govern the introduction (market entry) of new technologies into clinical practice. Such policies have centered generally on federal regulation of new drugs, biologics, and devices entering the medical marketplace. Various laws have established clear federal authority over the premarket approval of these technologies. The FDA regulatory processes for drugs, biologics, and devices are examined here with an eye toward understanding the processes' scope, fairness, effectiveness, and burden for manufacturers.

Federal Regulation of Drugs and Biologics

The federal government's involvement in the regulation of medical technology began with the Pure Food and Drugs Act of 1906, which provided for governmental control over the labeling and inspection of foods and patent medicines being sold through interstate commerce (Temin 1980). In 1938, the Food, Drug, and Cosmetic Act expanded federal authority, assigning the FDA responsibility for assuring the safety of new drugs and requiring drug companies to engage in premarket testing of new products. The FDA, however, did not specify standards for premarket testing, instead leaving such decisions to the drug manufacturers (Temin 1980; P. J. Feldstein 1988, 437–74).

In the late 1940s and 1950s, concerns arose that drug companies were profiting from aggressive marketing of high-priced drugs that appeared to offer little or no medical benefit. As a result, in 1962, the Kefauver-Harris Amendments were passed, (1) enabling the FDA to specify acceptable premarket testing procedures and (2) requiring drug companies to demonstrate the effectiveness as well as the safety of a new drug before obtaining approval to market it (Temin 1980; P. J. Feldstein 1988, 437–74).

As amended in 1962, the 1938 law for many years constituted the basis for the federal regulation of drugs. The law called for "substantial" evidence of effectiveness and safety, but the determination of what constituted substantial evidence was (and remains) an administrative decision made by the FDA (Hutt 1991). In practice today, the standards and procedures that form the new drug development process are complex and have been modified by the passage of the FDA Modernization Act of 1997 and the Prescription Drug User Fee Amendments of 2002 (discussed later in this chapter).

Within the FDA, responsibility for the evaluation of drugs (chemically synthesized compounds) resides with the Center for Drug Evaluation and Research (CDER). Biologics, in contrast, are derived from living sources (such as humans, animals, and microorganisms), and encompass blood products, vaccines, human tissue, allergenic materials and antitoxins, and cellular and gene therapies. Responsibility for the evaluation of biological products historically has rested with the Center for Biologics Evaluation and Research (CBER). Under the Medical Device User Fee and Modernization Act of 2002, the functions of the CDER and the CBER are being merged (FDA 2002d).

The New Drug Development Process

As displayed in figure 10.1, the new drug development process for pharmaceuticals contains three broad stages: preclinical research, clinical studies, and new drug application (NDA) review. The development process for new biologics is essentially similar except that it culminates in biologics license application (BLA) review. The FDA estimates that it takes approximately 8.5 years to study and test a new drug or biological product before it can be approved for the general public (FDA 2001). Industry sources assert that it takes at least 1.5 times

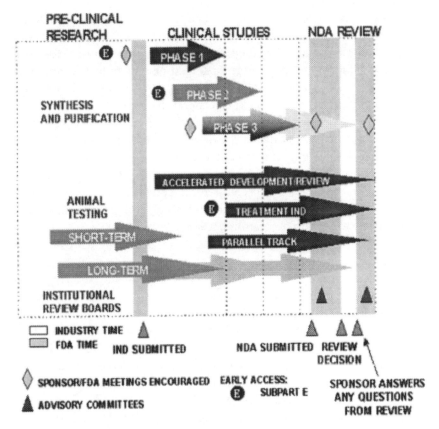

Fig. 10.1. The new drug development process: Steps from test tube to new drug application review. (From FDA 2001.)

longer than the FDA's estimate, an average of 12 to 15 years (PhRMA 2000).

Preclinical Research

During preclinical development, a sponsor of a new drug or biologic (the pharmaceutical or biotechnology company) evaluates the product's safety and biological activity through in vitro and in vivo laboratory animal testing. The FDA generally will ask, at a minimum, that the sponsor (1) develop a pharmacologic profile of the product's effects, (2) determine its acute toxicity in at least two species of animals (one rodent, one nonrodent), and (3) conduct short-term toxicity studies that range from two weeks to three months in duration (FDA 2001). On average, preclinical studies take approximately six years to complete before a new drug or biologic is ready for clinical testing (PhRMA 1998, 2000). Drug and biotechnology firms are increasingly using high-throughput screening methods and computer models (with computational forms of chemistry, biology, and genomics) to screen new chemical compounds and biological products against disease targets and to simulate the effects of these entities on animal subjects, in the hope of shortening the time necessary for discovery and preclinical testing. In some cases, long-term testing in animal models may extend for several years, continuing after human tests begin, to learn whether long-term use of the product may cause cancer or birth defects. Pharmaceutical industry data suggest that for every 5,000 chemical compounds screened for development, only 250 (5 percent) will enter preclinical testing, and only 5 of these will subsequently enter clinical testing (PhRMA 1998, 2000).

Before an application for an investigational new drug (IND) may be filed, however, the sponsor must submit data showing that the drug is reasonably safe for use in initial, small-scale clinical studies. The sponsor often requests preclinical meetings with the appropriate review division of the FDA to discuss testing phases, data requirements, and relevant scientific issues that need to be resolved prior to IND submission (FDA 2001). Under subpart E in section 312 of the *Code of Federal Regulations*, procedures may be invoked to expedite the development, evaluation, and marketing of new therapies that are intended to treat people with life-threatening or severely debilitating illnesses, especially where no satisfactory alternatives exist (FDA 2001). Institutional review boards also are used to ensure the rights and welfare of individuals participating in clinical trials both prior to and during their trial participation.

Clinical Studies

Once preclinical testing has been completed, the sponsor files an IND application, which is reviewed by the CDER (see figure 10.1). If IND status is granted, clinical studies in humans may commence. This stage of the new drug development process contains three phases of clinical investigation (see figure 10.1).

In phase 1 clinical trials, which normally involve limited numbers (usually between 20 and 80) of healthy volunteer subjects but may be conducted in patients, the prime objectives are to determine the metabolic and pharmacologic actions of the drug, ascertain safe dosage levels and gather information on potential side effects, and, if possible, collect early evidence on effectiveness (FDA 2001). In phase 1 trials, the

CDER can impose a clinical hold, either prohibiting a trial from starting or halting the progress of one that is under way. This phase takes an average of 1.5 years to complete and results in the elimination of about 20 percent of compounds entering this phase as a result of concerns about their safety, effectiveness, or economic feasibility (PhRMA 2000).

In phase 2 trials, human testing expands to include several hundred patients (often between 100 and 300) in well-controlled and closely monitored studies that are directed toward evaluating the drug's effectiveness in treating the disease or condition for which it is intended as well as toward determining common short-term side effects and risks (FDA 2001). The time involved in completing phase 2 is typically two years, and about 40 percent of the drugs entering this phase are eliminated from further review (PhRMA 2000). At the conclusion of phase 2, the FDA commonly meets with the drug's sponsor to determine whether it is safe to begin phase 3 testing and to plan the research protocols for phase 3 human studies (FDA 2001). These meetings set the ground rules, objectives, and data requirements for phase 3 trials and can avoid unnecessary effort and expense by the sponsor.

In phase 3 testing, clinical trials usually involve between one and five thousand patients, often in multiple clinical centers (including sites outside the United States). The purpose of this phase is to clarify the drug's therapeutic value, confirming its effectiveness and safety (including its potential toxicity and adverse effects) to evaluate its overall benefits and risks (PhRMA 2000; FDA 2001). Phase 3 studies serve as the basis for extrapolating results to the general population, for determining the information (indications and precautions) that will be included on the drug labels and package inserts, and for setting the bounds for marketing claims by the manufacturer. In this phase (as well as in phase 2), the CDER can impose a clinical hold if a study is unsafe or if the trial protocol has a design that is inadequate for meeting the stated objectives (FDA 2001). Phase 3 trials may take between 1 and 4 years and generally average 3.5 years.

The three phases of clinical investigation take almost seven years to complete for the average new drug. Once clinical trials have been completed successfully, the pharmaceutical manufacturer files a NDA with the FDA's CDER, seeking approval to market the new drug. However, before the NDA is submitted, it is customary for the FDA and the sponsor to meet to discuss the presentation of data in the NDA (FDA 2001). Because the NDA contains detailed and highly complex information, the pre-NDA meeting aids the sponsor by uncovering any major unresolved problems or issues that might interfere with the review of the application (FDA 2001). Once the NDA is filed, another meeting may be held within ninety days to discuss issues that are uncovered in the initial review. According to industry sources (PhRMA 2000), only one in five drugs that enter clinical testing ultimately receive FDA approval through the NDA process.

In the case of biologics, the sponsor files a biologics license application with the FDA's CBER, which has a review process similar to that of the CDER. The CBER has become increasingly active in recent years, as the number of new biological products entering the market has grown dramatically. Of the 40 new molecular entities approved by the FDA in 1999, 12 (30 percent) were biotechnological products (FDA 2001). More than half of the 133 biotechnological drugs that have been approved to date by the FDA were approved between 1997 and 2000 (FDA 2001; PhRMA 2001). As mentioned earlier, the FDA is merging the review processes of the CDER and the CBER (FDA 2002d).

Exceptions to the New Drug Development Process
To make promising new therapies available to desperately ill patients as early in the drug development process as possible, FDA policy allows for several exceptions to the standard review process under subpart E in section 312 of the *Code of Federal Regulations* (FDA 2001). First, if a drug offers significant benefit for a serious or life-threatening illness for which no therapy exists, the FDA may designate it for accelerated development/review. This mechanism may be employed in two specific circumstances: when approval of the drug is based on evidence of the drug's effect on a "surrogate endpoint" (a laboratory finding or physical sign that is not a measurement of how a patient feels, functions, or survives but is still likely to predict therapeutic benefit) or when the FDA determines that the safe use of the drug depends on restricting its distribution or use (FDA 2001). In either case, the manufacturer must continue testing the drug after approval to demonstrate that it indeed provides therapeutic benefit to the patient.

A second exception is the treatment IND in which the FDA permits an investigational drug to be used if there is preliminary evidence of drug efficacy and the drug is intended to treat a serious or immediately life-threatening disease (e.g., advanced cases of AIDS or herpes simplex encephalitis) or if there is no existing comparable alternative therapy to treat a particular stage of the disease in the intended patient population (FDA 2001). Treatment INDs are made available to patients before general marketing begins, usually during phase 3 studies. Thus, patients receiving a drug under a treatment IND are not eligible to be in the definitive clinical trials.

The third mechanism for permitting wider availability of experimental drugs is the parallel-track policy that was developed in response to the AIDS epidemic (FDA 2001). Under this mechanism, patients with AIDS whose condition prevents them from participating in controlled clinical trials can receive investigational drugs that preliminary studies have shown to be promising.

Until recently, Medicare beneficiaries did not have access to experimental drugs and therapies that had not yet been approved by the FDA, but a June 2000 presidential directive authorized Medicare payment for routine patient care costs and for costs due to medical complications associated with participation in clinical trials, thus opening yet another avenue for seriously ill individuals to gain access to experimental agents. (See chapter 12 for a discussion of Medicare coverage policy.)

The NDA Review Process

Upon receiving the NDA, the CDER initiates a comprehensive review of the drug that encompasses its chemistry, the results of the clinical investigations, the planned manufacturing process and manufacturing sites, and the proposed labeling of the product (see figure 10.2). The review may be performed by CDER staff or by approved external reviewers under contract to the FDA. The CDER, at its discretion, may use advisory committees to obtain outside expert advice and opinions regarding the new drug's safety and effectiveness, necessary labeling information, and special regulatory requirements that should be considered (FDA 2001). While advisory committee recommendations are not binding, the CDER weighs them carefully in making final agency decisions. Once the NDA review is complete, the FDA and the sponsor meet to discuss the agency's decision. A parallel process for reviewing biologics license applications is conducted by the CBER.

Postmarket Surveillance Studies and Monitoring Systems

Following the approval of a new drug, the FDA requires postmarket surveillance and monitoring of the drug's use in patient care. Use of the drug in day-to-day practice settings may reveal rare or delayed side effects, may provide information on long-term effectiveness, or even

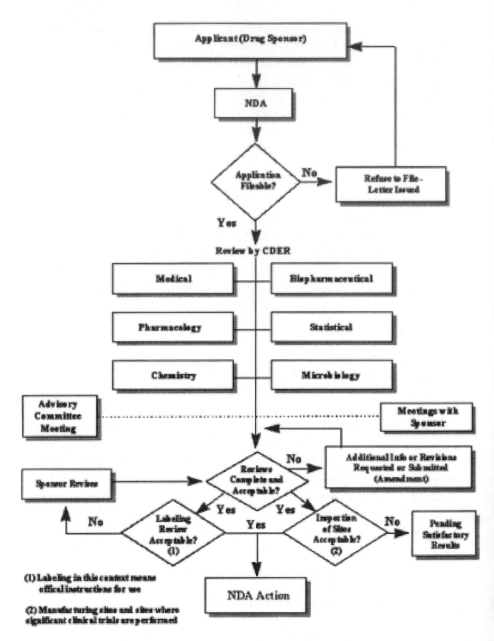

Fig. 10.2. The NDA review process. (From FDA 2001.)

may identify new indications for its use. Any of these events may lead the manufacturer to submit a request to the FDA for a labeling modification to include new indications or precautions. In some cases, the FDA also may instruct the manufacturer to perform additional studies of varying design and purpose, including clinical trials, observational studies, or epidemiologic studies (such as case-control or cohort studies), to gather information on the drug's long-term effects (PhRMA 2000).

The FDA's CDER currently operates two surveillance systems for monitoring and reporting adverse drug events.

- *Adverse Events Reporting System*—a mandatory reporting system in which manufacturers and distributors report adverse events involving drugs and therapeutic biologic products, including medication errors; expedited reports must be submitted for serious and unexpected adverse events, whereas quarterly or annual periodic reports must be submitted for all other serious and non-serious events.
- *MedWatch (FDA Medical Products Reporting Program)*—a voluntary reporting system in which health care professionals and consumers report adverse events involving medical products, including medical product errors; reports are triaged and transferred to the appropriate FDA center for evaluation and entry into the appropriate FDA database (FDA 2001).

The CBER operates two other surveillance systems for monitoring and reporting adverse events involving vaccines and biologics.

- *Vaccine Adverse Events Reporting System*—a voluntary reporting system (created as an outgrowth of the National Childhood Vaccine Injury Act of 1986) in which health care providers, manufacturers, and consumers report adverse events associated with U.S. licensed vaccines; the FDA jointly administers the system with the Centers for Disease Control and Prevention (FDA 2002a).
- *Biological Product Deviation Reporting System*—a mandatory reporting system in which licensed manufacturers of biological products, registered blood establishments, and transfusion services report errors and accidents in the manufacturing (including testing, processing, packaging, labeling, storage, and

distribution) of biological products or blood components that may affect the safety, purity, or potency of the distributed product (FDA 2001, 2002a).

FDA Drug Approval Times

For many years, the FDA was criticized severely for the long delays in the approval of new drugs for market entry. The average time for FDA review of a NDA was approximately two years until the mid-1980s, when the wait lengthened to almost three years, bringing the total time of drug development from synthesis to approval to almost fifteen years (PhRMA 1998). This caused an outcry among drug manufacturers, disease-specific interest groups, and patient advocacy groups, all of which wielded considerable influence with federal legislators. One such group, the AIDS Coalition to Unleash Power (ACT UP), was instrumental in pressuring the FDA to approve zidovudine (AZT), the first antiviral agent for the treatment of AIDS, and in influencing Congress to pass legislation that supported research, vaccine development, and resources for treating HIV-positive individuals (Carrns 2001). Under intense political pressure from Congress and these various groups, the FDA during the 1980s sought to reduce review times for NDAs through two administrative measures:

- a priority system for NDAs, in which new drugs were examined for their expected benefits to patients with a view toward identifying those worthy of expedited review (Gelijns 1990); and
- the codification of the treatment IND protocol, in which new investigational drugs that had not yet received FDA approval could be given to patients who had failed to respond to other therapies (Flannery 1986).

An early important test case of the treatment IND protocol involved AZT. As the first and only therapy for AIDS at the time, AZT was made available to more than 4,000 AIDS patients six months before it received final FDA approval. Because the drug's initial costs were prohibitively expensive ($10,000 per patient for a year's supply) and many AIDS patients either had no health insurance or were ineligible for Medicaid program coverage, the U.S. government also appropriated $30 million in 1987 to enable affected persons to gain access to the new drug (Penslar and Lamm 1989).

During the 1980s, Congress enacted two laws that encouraged the development and market entry—with expedited review—of generic equivalents and orphan drugs, respectively. The Drug Price Competition and Patent Restoration Act of 1984, also known as the Waxman-Hatch Act, expedited the approval of generic equivalents through an abbreviated NDA review process once the original drug patents had expired (Nightingale and Morrison 1987; Grabowski 1991). As a result, generic drugs more than doubled their share of the U.S. prescription drug market between 1984 and 2000, rising from 19 percent to 47 percent of all prescriptions (PhRMA 2001). Although a boon to consumers and health plans because of their lower costs, generic drugs are viewed with disdain by brand-name drug manufacturers, who fret about the inevitable erosion of their top-selling brand-name products' market shares once those patents have expired (Stolberg and Gerth 2000; PhRMA 2001). The Orphan Drug Act of 1983 offered drug and biologics manufacturers expedited review—plus several other incentives—to spur the development of orphan drugs and biologics for the treatment of rare diseases (discussed in the following section).

Orphan Drugs

Passed by Congress in 1983, the Orphan Drug Act sought to encourage the pharmaceutical industry to invest in research and development for new therapies to treat approximately 5,000 known rare diseases afflicting an estimated 20 million Americans (Asbury 1985; Nightingale 1986). As defined in the act, a rare disease or condition is one that either affects fewer than 200,000 persons or is not likely to have a drug or other therapy developed for it because prospective manufacturers would not be able to recover their development costs from sales in the United States. The act provided manufacturers with development incentives in the form of research grants, a 50 percent tax credit for expenses associated with clinical research, an expedited review process, and seven years of market exclusivity to the first company to reach the market with a new drug (Asbury 1991; FDA 1997; PhRMA 2001). Market exclusivity for a new orphan drug can be broken only if a subsequent version of the drug is demonstrated to be safer, more effective, or significantly more convenient for patients (Aoki 2001b). In the ten years preceding passage of the law, only 10 orphan drugs were developed without government support and were approved by the FDA (Asbury 1985). In the decade following enactment, more than 500 had been designated as orphans, and 99 of them had been approved for use in the treatment of rare diseases (Shulman et al. 1992; Arno, Bonuck, and Davis 1995; PhRMA 1998). The law was reenacted periodically throughout the 1980s and early 1990s and became permanent in 1997 (PhRMA 2001). By 2000, the cumulative number of approved orphan drugs had reached 220, with 800 more products under development or in testing (Aoki 2001b; PhRMA 2001). Examples of orphan drugs include Cerezyme for Gaucher's disease, Provigil for narcolepsy, and Avonex for multiple sclerosis (Aoki 2001b). After being removed from the market in the 1960s for causing birth defects, Thalidomide attracted new interest during the 1990s as a treatment for leprosy, thus qualifying for orphan drug status (Aoki 2001b).

While few would dispute the fact that the Orphan Drug Act clearly prodded drug companies to develop many true orphan drugs (those with limited commercial potential), one study found that the act contained weaknesses that enabled drug industry practices to "subvert the goals of the Act while usually adhering to the letter of the law," noting that sponsors of drugs for AIDS and other diseases were able to secure orphan drug designations—and market exclusivity—for fairly narrow indications, which they were then able to use to advantage in broader off-label markets for other indications that either existed or were likely to develop (Arno, Bonuck, and Davis 1995, 236). In some cases, sponsors "stacked" seven-year monopolies for the same drug on top of one another for marginally different indications or segmented patient populations into artificial subgroups to avoid the patient limit of 200,000. Also, as the experience with several AIDS-related drugs demonstrated, exclusive marketing rights generally have led to high drug prices, making the drugs hugely profitable for manufacturers but often unaffordable for patients with limited or no health insurance. Thus, while the act has been effective in speeding the market entry of orphan drugs, the pricing behavior of many companies and the lucrative profits of a few continue to stir controversy over the equity of access to such drugs for many Americans.

The Prescription Drug User Fee Act of 1992

Despite the introduction of various mechanisms for expedited review of NDAs, including the treatment IND protocol, the mean approval times for new drugs in the early 1990s still stood at 30 months, bringing the FDA under even greater fire from the industry and from Congress. To aid the agency in speeding up drug approval times, Congress enacted the Prescription Drug User Fee Act (PDUFA) of 1992. The act imposed "user fees" on pharmaceutical firms, generating $329 million in revenues over a five-year period to help cover the FDA's costs for its NDA review process and thereby enabling the agency to hire an additional 696 staff members and to shorten the review time for NDAs from an average of 30 months in 1987–92 to approximately 15 months in 1996–97 (FDA 1997; Neumann and Sandberg 1998).

The FDA Modernization Act of 1997 and Drugs

Even with PDUFA's apparent success, concerns about the review process and FDA efficiency still raged throughout the 1990s among pharmaceutical firms and patient advocacy groups alike, prompting Congress to pass the FDA Modernization Act of 1997. The new law contained many important provisions relating to the regulation of drugs and biologics (see table 10.1). Foremost among these provisions were: the reauthorization of the PDUFA for another five years (known as PDUFA II), the adoption of an accelerated review process, and the relaxation of rules in some circumstances regarding the basis for clinical evidence of drug safety and effectiveness (FDA 1997). Pharmaceutical and biotechnology firms hailed the FDA Modernization Act as a major step toward streamlining the FDA approval process (Rosenberg 1997). FDA review times for NDAs, which in 1997 had averaged approximately 15 months, dropped to just under 12 months by 1998 (PhRMA 1999; Stolberg and Gerth 2000). Fast-track "priority drugs" for HIV and AIDS had approval times that ranged from 1.4 months to 8.6 months, and new drugs for type II diabetes (Prandin and Rezulin), for the prevention of osteoporosis in postmenopausal women (Evista), and for atherosclerotic events (Plavix) all had approval times of seven months or less (Neumann and Sandberg 1998).

Although drug manufacturers were pleased with these results, many researchers and clinicians became alarmed that the 1997 legislation may have swung the pendulum too far in the direction of approving drugs before their health effects were adequately known. Between 1997 and 2001, the FDA had to remove at least twelve drugs (including Posicor and Baycol) from the U.S. market because of dangerous or fatal side effects (Neergaard 1998, 2001). In the case of the popular male impotence drug Viagra, revelations of adverse effects, including deaths, during its first year on the market sharply curtailed its initial meteoric

TABLE 10.1.   The FDA Modernization Act of 1997

<u>Major Provisions Pertaining to Drugs and Biologics</u>

Reauthorization of the Prescription Drug User Fee Act of 1992 (for another five years)

An accelerated review process for drugs and biological agents needed to treat serious, life-threatening diseases when no alternative treatments exist (the FDA must determine the eligibility for fast track status of a new drug within 30 days and complete the review within 120 days)

Codification of FDA regulations and practices to increase patient access to experimental drugs

An expanded FDA database on clinical trials of drugs, with improved access for patients

The requirement that manufacturers provide advance notice to patients of their intention to discontinue drugs on which the patients depend for life support or for the treatment of serious or debilitating diseases or conditions

Allowing as the basis for product approval, in certain circumstances, a single well-controlled clinical trial to establish sufficient evidence of drug safety and effectiveness

Permission for drug manufacturers to disseminate information about unapproved (i.e., "off-label") uses of their products; a firm may disseminate peer-reviewed journal articles about off-label indications provided that the firm commits to filing—within a specified time frame—a supplemental application based on appropriate research to establish the safety and effectiveness of the unapproved use; a firm also may provide economic information about the drug to formulary committees, managed care organizations, and similar large-scale buyers of health care products

Authorization of the Centers for Education and Research on Therapeutics (CERT) demonstration program, to be administered by the Agency for Health Care Policy and Research (now known as the Agency for Healthcare Research and Quality), for the improvement of quality of care and the reduction of costs by increasing public and professional awareness of the benefits and risks of new uses or combinations of medical products and also by improving the effectiveness of existing uses

Provision of an incentive—six months of additional marketing exclusivity—to encourage drug firms to conduct studies of the safety and effectiveness of drugs in children, when requested by the FDA

<u>Major Provisions Pertaining to Devices</u>

An expedited PMA review process for devices intended to diagnose or treat diseases for which there are no clinical alternatives

Exemption from 510(k) premarket notification any Class I device that poses little risk of illness or injury and is not intended for use in preventing health impairment in patients

Codification of FDA regulations and practices to increase patient access to investigational devices

An expanded FDA database on clinical trials of devices, with improved access for patients

Greater flexibility for manufacturers to alter devices and clinical protocols during clinical testing

Allowing as the basis for product approval, in certain circumstances, a single well-controlled clinical trial to establish sufficient evidence of device safety and effectiveness (similar to drugs and biologics)

TABLE 10.1.—*Continued*

Increased communication with FDA staff, including conferences early in the review
  process, to provide sponsors with information regarding the data requirements
  for clinical studies
Reduction of the review time for FDA approval of a humanitarian device exemption
  (from the statutorily required 180 days to 75 days)
Redirection of postmarket surveillance activities toward higher risk devices and toward representative sampling of user facilities
Expanded use of accredited third parties in the review of all Class I and some Class
  II devices (except those that are permanently implantable, life-supporting, or life-
  sustaining products)
Permission for device manufacturers to disseminate information about unapproved
  (i.e., "off-label") uses of their products (subject to the same conditions that apply
  to drugs and biologics)

Source: Data from Food and Drug Administration 1997.

rise in sales (Jeffrey and Langreth 1998). According to a survey conducted by the consumer advocacy group Public Citizen, the FDA's medical officers believed that safety and effectiveness standards had deteri-
orated under the pressure to accelerate the drug approval process
(Gemignani and Kurdas 1999b). Consequently, the FDA adopted a more
cautious stance in 2000, requiring drug companies to provide more extensive data on potential side effects before the FDA would approve
new products (Pollack 2001) and threatening to remove from the market some commonly prescribed drugs that predate the 1962 Kefauver-
Harris Amendments and thus never officially received FDA approval,
including the top-selling thyroid drug, Synthroid, which is thought to
be harmful for some patients (C. Adams 2001; Parker-Pope 2001). As a
result of this shift in FDA posture, the average approval time crept back
up to 17.6 months in 2000 (PhRMA 2001), but approval times for fast-
track drugs and biologics, such as Herceptin (for breast cancer) and
Gleevec (for chronic myeloid leukemia), were closer to three months
(FDA 2001).

The PDUFA III Amendments of 2002

Today, while the FDA appears to be genuinely committed to improving the efficiency of its NDA review process, the issue of optimal drug
approval time remains a source of contention between regulators anx-
ious to protect the public from premature diffusion of ineffective or
harmful drugs and pharmaceutical firms and patient advocacy groups

eager to bring new medications to the marketplace. In a study of 450 drugs reviewed by the FDA from 1977 to 2000, Carpenter (2001) found that political influence on FDA drug approvals appeared to work less through institutional oversight mechanisms (e.g., shifts in partisanship or ideology of congressional majorities, oversight committees, and the president) than through "salience signals" transmitted by advocacy groups and the media. For many diseases, media coverage appeared to be a mediating variable that amplified the effects of advocacy groups (e.g., AIDS activists or breast cancer lobbyists) working to secure faster approval of drugs for their diseases (Carpenter 2001; Mello and Brennan 2001).

Carpenter (2001) also analyzed the potential benefits of adding more staff to the CDER, finding that for every 10 percent increase in CDER staff, drug approval times would be reduced by 21–22 percent. This analysis had far-reaching policy implications for the ten-year-old PDUFA, which was renewed under the Public Health Security and Bioterrorism Preparedness and Response Act of 2002 in June 2002. Because neither the pharmaceutical industry nor the FDA wanted to see the law expire, the debate regarding another five-year extension of the act through 2007 turned not so much on the issue of whether it should be adopted as on what form it would take (C. Adams 2002). Under the new amendments known as PDUFA III, the FDA obtained a substantial increase in user fees—reaching as high as $533,400 for a drug application involving review of clinical data (FDA 2002c). The implementation of these fees is expected to generate more than $222 million in revenue in fiscal year 2003 and will allow the FDA to hire more staff and to expand its postmarket surveillance of drug safety and advertising. PDUFA III also reorganized the CDER and the CBER and set performance standards for FDA review of NDAs and BLAs (e.g., 90 percent of such applications must be acted upon within six months of receipt). The pharmaceutical and biotechnology industries initially opposed both the increase in drug application fees and the proposed change in their use for postmarket surveillance purposes but in the end saw the new law as facilitating product approval by the FDA (C. Adams 2002).

Federal Regulation of Medical Devices

Although the 1938 Food, Drug, and Cosmetic Act contained limited authority to regulate medical devices, such regulation did not occur until the passage of the Medical Device Amendments of 1976. Whereas the primary responsibility for regulating medical devices rests with the FDA's Center for Devices and Radiological Health (CDRH), the CBER regulates devices that are "involved in the collection, processing, testing, manufacture and administration of licensed blood, blood components and cellular products" (FDA 2002a). Even so, the review process for devices, whether conducted by the CDRH or the CBER, is governed by the medical device laws and regulations and includes both premarket review and postmarket surveillance. A *device* is defined broadly as any "instrument, apparatus, implement, machine, contrivance, implant, in vitro reagent, or other similar or related article" that is intended for use in the diagnosis, cure, mitigation, treatment, or prevention of disease and that "does not achieve any of its principal intended purposes through chemical action within or on the body of man" (FDA 1992, 2002b).

Classification of Devices

The FDA classifies medical devices into three groups, with different levels of premarket control necessary to assure that the devices are safe and effective (FDA 2002b). Class I devices pose little risk of illness or injury and require only general controls to assure that they are safe and effective for their intended use. Many instruments that are commonly found in a physician's office or are routinely used in a hospital nursing unit fall into this category, such as simple elastic bandages, examination gloves, and hand-held surgical instruments (FDA 2002b). Class I controls include premarket notification to the FDA (through the so-called 510[k] application process), registration and listing, record keeping, labeling, and good manufacturing practice standards (HCTI 1993a; FDA 2002b).

Class II devices pose moderate risk of injury and include such items as powered wheelchairs, infusion pumps, and surgical drapes (FDA 2002b). In addition to the general controls for Class I devices, these devices are subject to special controls, which usually include device-specific performance standards (FDA 2002b). In cases where the FDA has not developed specific performance standards for a device, existing national or international product standards may be used (Gelijns 1990).

Class III devices include products that "support or sustain human life" or that pose potential, unreasonable risk of illness or injury (FDA 2002b). Class III devices are subject to the most stringent form of FDA review, premarket approval, under which the device manufacturer must not only meet the requirements under general controls but also demonstrate the safety and effectiveness of the product before the device can be marketed (FDA 2002b). Any device that poses significant risk to humans is automatically considered to require the full Class III premarket approval review unless the manufacturer is able to demonstrate that the device is "substantially equivalent" to a legally marketed device. Examples of Class III devices include replacement heart valves, silicone gel–filled breast implants, and implanted cerebellar stimulators.

Development and Clinical Investigation of New Devices

Medical devices are developed and investigated clinically according to a process similar to that for new drug development. Each new device undergoes clinical testing and investigation through successively larger clinical trials intended to demonstrate its safety and effectiveness in human subjects. An individual or organization wishing to market Class I, Class II, or some Class III devices intended for human use in the United States must submit premarket notification (510[k]) to the FDA at least ninety days before marketing unless the device is judged to be exempt from 510(k) requirements (FDA 2002b).

Premarket Notification (510[k])

The 510(k) process derives its name from the section of the Food, Drug, and Cosmetic Act that governs its use. A 510(k) submission is required when (1) a device is introduced into commercial distribution (marketing) for the first time, (2) a different intended use is proposed for a device that already is in commercial distribution, or (3) a currently marketed device is changed or modified in a way that could significantly affect its safety or effectiveness (FDA 2002b). For a new device, the 510(k) submission must demonstrate that it is as safe and effective as a legally marketed device that is not subject to premarket approval. Thus, the applicant must compare the new device to one or more similar devices currently on the U.S. market and must support with data any claims of substantial equivalency (FDA 2002b). A "legally marketed" device is one that either was legally marketed prior to the 1976 amendments (in commercial distribution before May 28, 1976, and thus known as a preamendment device) or was approved after 1976 (a postamendment device) but has been reclassified from Class III to Class II or Class I (FDA 2002b). A new device is "substantially equivalent" to a legally marketed device if it has the same intended use and has either (1) the same technological characteristics or (2) different technological characteristics that do not raise new questions regarding safety and effectiveness and if the sponsor demonstrates that the new device is as safe and effective as the legally marketed device (FDA 2002b). The legally marketed device to which equivalence is drawn is known as the predicate device.

If the FDA determines the device to be substantially equivalent to a legally marketed device, then it can be marketed in the United States without undergoing the premarket approval process (see the following discussion of premarket approval requirements). However, if the FDA determines that the device is not substantially equivalent, the applicant has three options: (1) resubmit another 510(k) application with new data, (2) file a petition for reclassification, or (3) submit a premarket approval application (FDA 2002b). In general, though, the 510(k) process is intended to expedite the market entry of substantially equivalent new devices so that manufacturers face no greater regulatory burden than would have been the case prior to 1976. A 1989 GAO study found that 90 percent of medical devices were able to pass through the 510(k) review process, while only 10 percent required a full premarket approval review (GAO 1989). Examples of Class III devices that currently require only a premarket notification include implantable pacemaker pulse generators and endosseous implants (FDA 2002b).

Premarket Approval Process

The premarket approval application resembles an NDA in that it initiates the FDA's review process (FDA 2002b). Premarket approval requirements apply differently to three types of Class III devices.

- *Transitional devices* (those regulated by the FDA as new *drugs* prior to 1976) require premarket approval before they can be marketed. Examples include soft contact lenses and related lens care products, intraocular lenses, surgical sutures, bone cements, vascular grafts of animal origin, and absorbable homeostatic devices and dressings (FDA 2002b).
- *Nonsubstantially equivalent postamendment devices* (those introduced after 1976 and determined by the FDA not to be substantially equivalent to either preamendment devices or postamendment Class I or II devices) also require premarket

approval before being marketed in the United States. Examples include coronary angioplasty devices, implanted defibrillators, orthopedic prostheses for uncemented use, contraceptive cervical caps, synthetic ligaments, and implanted drug delivery systems (FDA 2002b).

- *Preamendment devices (and postamendment devices determined to be substantially equivalent to them)* can continue to be marketed without premarket approval until such approval is required by regulation. Examples include replacement heart valves, contraceptive intrauterine devices, contraceptive tubal occlusion devices, and implanted diaphragmatic/phrenic nerve stimulators (FDA 2002b).

The full premarket approval process involves the submission of the application with data supporting the safety and effectiveness of the new Class III device, the review of such data by the CDRH and an FDA advisory committee at a public hearing, the issuance of a recommendation by the committee either for or against approval of the application, and the publication of a decision by the FDA either approving or denying the premarket approval. While a device is undergoing full review, the manufacturer must obtain from the FDA an investigational device exemption, which allows the device to be used in clinical trials involving human subjects (FDA 2002b). For "significant risk" devices, both the FDA and an appropriate institutional review board must approve the exemption, whereas "non-significant-risk" devices require only FDA approval. In fiscal year 2000, the FDA reviewed 320 original exemption submissions and 4,335 supplements, with average review times of twenty-eight days and twenty days, respectively (FDA 2002b).

Exceptions to the Premarket Approval Process

To make promising new Class III devices available to desperately ill patients early in the premarket approval process, FDA policy allows for humanitarian device exemptions, applications for which are similar in form and content to those for premarket approval but are exempt from the effectiveness requirements for premarket approval (FDA 2002b). In fiscal year 2000, the CDRH approved six humanitarian device exemptions with an average elapsed time to approval of 216 days (FDA 2002b).

Postmarket Surveillance Studies and Monitoring Systems

Once a device has secured FDA approval under either the 510(k) process or the premarket approval process, the FDA may elect to order postmarket surveillance studies for any Class II or Class III device (1) that is intended to be implanted within the human body for more than one year, (2) that is a life-sustaining or life-supporting device used outside a device user facility, or (3) the failure of which is reasonably likely to have serious adverse health consequences (FDA 2002b). Within thirty days of receiving an order from the FDA to conduct a postmarket surveillance study, the manufacturer must submit, for approval, a plan for the required surveillance (FDA 2002b).

The Medical Device Reporting (MDR) regulation, which covers both user facilities and device manufacturers, provides a mechanism for the FDA to identify and monitor significant adverse events involving medical devices (FDA 2002b). The statutory authority for the reporting regulation stems from the 1938 act and the 1976 amendments, as modified by the Device Experience Network created in 1984 and by the Safe Medical Devices Act of 1990. Manufacturers of approved devices are required to report any deaths, injuries, or device malfunctions to the FDA within thirty days of becoming aware of such events. Under the Safe Medical Devices Act, user facilities—hospitals, nursing homes, outpatient treatment centers, and ambulatory surgery facilities—have ten workdays to report any device-related deaths to both the device manufacturer and the FDA and any device-related serious injuries to the manufacturer (FDA 2002b). Device distributors are not required to report adverse events but instead are ordered by the FDA Modernization Act of 1997 to maintain records of complaints and to make those records available to the FDA on request (FDA 2002b).

The FDA's CDRH currently operates one surveillance system and is designing a new one for monitoring and reporting adverse events involving medical devices.

- The *Manufacturer and User Device Experience (MAUDE) Database* combines voluntary reports on medical devices from the MedWatch medical products reporting system (discussed earlier in this chapter) and mandatory reports from device manufacturers and user facilities regarding device-related adverse events (see the Safe Medical Devices Act requirements described earlier in this section).

- The *Medical Product Surveillance Network Pilot Program* is a new national surveillance system based on a representative sample of medical device user facilities that eventually will replace the current mandatory reporting by all user facilities of device-related deaths and serious injuries; only those facilities selected to be in the program will be obligated to report to the CDRH (FDA 2001).

FDA Device Approval Times

During the early 1990s—concurrent with the criticism from drug manufacturers—the FDA also came under withering attack from device manufacturers and patient advocacy groups regarding the mounting backlog of premarket approval requests for new devices. The average time for CDRH review of 510(k) applications had increased from 69 days in 1987 to 102 days in 1991, and although the law required the FDA to process a premarket approval request within 180 days, the average elapsed time for approval review in 1991 was 633 days, up from 415 days during the previous year (HCTI 1993a). A 1992 congressional inquiry revealed a backlog of more than 1,100 device applications that had accumulated during that year alone (Firshein 1993). As in the case of drug approvals, the FDA embarked on an administrative strategy intended to streamline the device review process. A key change was the reclassification of certain Class III devices, such as daily-wear contact lenses, as Class II devices, which eliminated the need for these products to undergo full premarket approval review. Another change involved the implementation of a pilot program to outsource the initial review of Class I and low- to moderate-risk Class II devices to outside third-party experts accredited by the FDA. These and other changes led to substantial reductions in the mean approval time for premarket approval requests (from 14.6 months to 11.4 months) and in the backlog of reviews exceeding 180 days (from 45 to 17) during the period 1993–96 (Neumann and Sandberg 1998).

The FDA Modernization Act of 1997 and Devices

As with drug approval times, efficiency enhancements in device reviews during the mid-1990s were insufficient to guard against political pressure from the industry and from advocacy groups demanding that

Congress mandate further streamlining of the premarket approval process under the FDA Modernization Act of 1997. The act contained numerous provisions relating to the regulation of devices (see table 10.1). Prominent among these provisions were several that directed the FDA to focus its resources on medical devices posing the greatest risks to patients. Specifically, the law instructed the FDA to concentrate its postmarket surveillance activities on higher-risk devices and gave the agency wider latitude to employ a reporting system based on a representative sample of user facilities (see the earlier discussion of the Medical Product Surveillance Network) that experience deaths and serious injuries associated with the use of these devices (FDA 1997). The law also exempted from 510(k) premarket notification any Class I device that posed little risk of illness or injury and was not intended for a use that is substantially important in preventing health impairment in patients (FDA 1997). For all other Class I devices and for low- to moderate-risk Class II devices, the act authorized the expansion of an existing pilot program under which the FDA could accredit third-party experts to conduct the initial review of such devices but explicitly prohibited outside experts from reviewing devices that were permanently implantable, that were life supporting, that were life sustaining, or for which clinical data were required (FDA 1997).

In fiscal year 2000, the CDRH reviewed 4,397 510(k) submissions, with an average review time of 77 days (the shortest in a decade) and approved 43 original premarket approval requests and 474 premarket approval supplements, with average elapsed times to approval of 11.9 and 4.0 months, respectively (FDA 2002b). In March 2000 the FDA published a rule downgrading 28 well-understood preamendment devices, such as denture repair kits, from Class III to Class II (FDA 2002b). In August of that year, the FDA also invoked for the first time the modernization act's provision that allowed for reclassifications and certain other actions based on data contained in premarket requests that had been approved for at least six years. Using the six-year-data provision, the agency reclassified extracorporeal shock wave lithotriptors from Class III to Class II devices (FDA 2002b). Despite these attempts to improve the efficiency of premarket reviews, the FDA was not immune either to highly publicized recalls of unsafe and ineffective devices (e.g., pacemakers and implantable cardioverter-defibrillators during the 1990s) or to continuing criticism that premarket approval times still did not approach the statutorily required limit of 180 days (Barnard 2001;

FDA 2002b). Thus, after considerable debate by Congress, President Bush signed into law on October 26, 2002, the Medical Device User Fee and Modernization Act of 2002.

The Medical Device User Fee and Modernization Act of 2002

The Medical Device User Fee and Modernization Act of 2002 contained several key provisions aimed at improving the efficiency of CDRH review of medical devices. Drawing on the FDA's successful experience with user fees for the review of new drug applications, the law established a user fee structure to support the reviews of premarket approval applications as well as 510(k) submissions for new devices (FDA 2002d). Small businesses (i.e., those with sales and/or receipts of $30 million or less) were permitted to pay reduced fees. In addition, like PDUFA III, the new law set performance goals for more efficient review of devices and authorized inspections of device manufacturing establishments to be conducted by accredited third parties under carefully prescribed conditions. Other notable provisions of the act include

- new regulatory requirements for reprocessed single-use devices in which a new category of premarket submission—the premarket report—is to be submitted;
- expanded postmarket surveillance of medical devices; and
- the establishment of a new Office of Combination Products within the FDA, responsible for coordinating the review of products that involve a device in combination with a drug or biologic (FDA 2002d).

With these changes in the review process, the FDA today remains committed to improving its performance, but the long-term effects of both this law and the 1997 modernization act's device-related provisions likely may not be fully realized and assessed for some time.

The Introduction of Surgical Procedures

Unlike new drugs or devices, surgical procedures may be developed and introduced into clinical practice without undergoing regulatory scrutiny by the FDA or by any other federal agency. Presently, there are no prescribed standards or processes by which surgical procedures must demonstrate their safety and efficacy before entry into clinical use. Physicians, hospitals, and third-party payers rely instead on information from studies reported in the medical literature. Randomized controlled trials (RCTs) of surgical procedures are particularly difficult to mount, owing to the great expense involved and the investigator's inability to maintain double-blind experimental conditions. RCTs often are not mounted until several years after the procedure has begun to diffuse into practice, and several more years may pass before these trials' findings are published and disseminated in the medical literature. Information about the cost-effectiveness of surgical procedures is especially difficult to obtain, and payers often make insurance coverage decisions without the benefit of such information.

Consequently, as long as a procedure has potential medical benefit and third-party payment is available for its use, it is likely to (1) diffuse rapidly, even in the absence of rigorous evaluation of its medical effectiveness or cost-effectiveness compared to alternative therapeutic modalities, and (2) become so entrenched in standard clinical practice that physicians will offer great resistance to abandoning it or curtailing its use, despite legitimate concerns about its efficacy.

One example of rapid diffusion in the absence of good evaluative information was the dramatic growth during the 1980s in the number of U.S. patients undergoing coronary angioplasty, which by 1991 had eclipsed the number of patients receiving coronary artery bypass surgery (National Center 1993). Although several RCTs had been designed and implemented to compare the two procedures, these studies had not yet produced definitive information on comparative long-term effectiveness when these changes in utilization occurred. Laparoscopic cholecystectomy also was adopted rapidly with little evaluative information (Escarce et al. 1995). At the other extreme, examples of well-established surgical procedures that were slow to decrease in frequency of use despite mounting evidence supporting their reduction include hysterectomies, cesarean sections, and radical mastectomies.

The lack of a formal process for evaluating new surgical procedures as they enter clinical practice is a serious weakness in existing policy and warrants consideration of a review process parallel to that employed by the FDA for the regulation of drugs and devices. The implementation of such a process represents a formidable challenge, however, as surgical procedures differ from drugs, biologics, and devices in several important ways. First, surgical procedures are not products that can be sold to consumers or providers in the conventional ways that drugs, biologics, and devices are sold. Second, procedures cannot be patented like drugs or devices and thus may be adopted more freely by various parties without serious financial or legal constraints. Third, the surgical technique embedded within the procedure is likely to vary depending on the surgeon performing the procedure. Thus, for a review process for surgical procedures to succeed, the explicit cooperation of surgeons, hospitals, and other health care facilities would be necessary. However, rather than an FDA-style premarket approval review process, what should be explored is a well-designed and -coordinated voluntary process for the timely and appropriate evaluation of new surgical procedures before their widespread use in clinical practice.

11

Quality Concerns: Medical Technology Use and Evidence-Based Clinical Practice
Alan B. Cohen, Shirley A. Stewart, and Ruth S. Hanft

Historically, concerns regarding quality in the use of medical technology in American health care have been overshadowed by concerns about cost and access to such care (see chapters 12 and 13). Yet many important questions have arisen concerning the appropriate use of technology in health care, the variations in the use of technology among physicians, and the assessment of patient care outcomes. In recent years, as the principles, practices, and tools of quality improvement have grown in popularity throughout the health care system—particularly among cost-conscious managed care plans—various strategies and methods for quality improvement in health care have emerged. These approaches range from outcomes measurement and evidence-based practice research to the development of clinical practice guidelines, the design of health plan performance report cards, and the implementation of information-feedback systems and educational efforts intended to modify physicians' behavior and practice patterns.

In this chapter, we first discuss the relationship between medical technology evaluation (MTE) and quality improvement (QI) and the nature of utilization review (UR) and utilization management (UM) strategies. We also examine federal programs involving UR that have focused on quality of care and the use of medical technology, such as the Quality Improvement Organizations (QIOs) of the Centers for Medicare and Medicaid Services (CMS). We then explore the activities of the Agency for Healthcare Research and Quality (AHRQ) involving evidence-based medicine and clinical practice guidelines as well as private-sector strategies for UM (especially those that combine MTE with QI). We conclude by describing various private-sector initiatives intended to enhance consumer sovereignty over health care decisions and to improve patient safety.

MTE and QI

MTE and QI may be viewed as complementary, reinforcing processes. Avedis Donabedian, a physician and leading thinker in the field of health care quality assessment and improvement, saw these processes as differing more in their emphasis than in their substance. In an early paper that examined the intersection of MTE and quality assurance (QA) and QI, Donabedian (1988, 488) wrote that technology evaluation "passes judgment on the technology itself" by assessing the extent to which stated medical objectives are achieved and documenting the existence of unintended consequences, positive or negative, while quality assessment and improvement efforts assess how "judiciously, appropriately, and skillfully" the technology is used "in the health care of individuals and communities." QI thus takes a broader societal view, encompassing not only the evaluation of individual providers' performance but also the performance of teams and organizations.

Donabedian (1988) also contended that a partnership of technology evaluation and quality assessment is necessary to improve our ability to provide good health care—MTE establishes the criteria and standards of effective and efficient care, while QA/QI determines the degree to which the criteria and standards have been observed. Until the early 1990s, however, strategies and programs that were intended to control the use of medical technology tended to concentrate more on UR mechanisms than on QA/QI, as discussed later in this chapter.

UR and UM

UR and UM strategies often have been employed in conjunction with payment policies (see chapter 12) to reduce the use of health services and medical technologies. They have done so primarily by emphasizing the appropriateness of care in terms of both process and outcome. UR may be employed either prospectively or retrospectively and includes such mechanisms as preadmission certification of hospital stays and the use of specific technologies, concurrent review of hospital length of stay, second opinions for surgical procedures, mandates requiring the performance of certain procedures in outpatient rather than inpatient settings, and, more recently, the profiling of physician practice patterns against preestablished practice norms. UM is a subset of UR that prospectively controls the use of technologies through precertification of procedures or through case management of patients with severe or chronic high-cost conditions. Both UR and UM programs derive their power from third-party payers' ability to withhold payment for services not deemed to be essential to or appropriate for the care of individual patients.

Federal Programs Involving UR: From PSROs to PROs to QIOs

Federal programs involving UR date back thirty years to the Professional Standards Review Organization (PSRO) program, which was created by U.S. Public Law 92-603 in 1972 (Decker and Bonner 1973; Lohr 1990). Controlled by local physicians, the PSROs were nonprofit organizations charged with monitoring the hospital care delivered by local providers to beneficiaries of the Medicare, Medicaid, and Maternal and Child Health programs. Although supposedly intended to assure quality of care, the PSROs were designed to contain health care costs. They engaged largely in preadmission certification and concurrent review of hospital care and made determinations regarding the appropriateness of hospital admission and length of stay (Lohr 1990). In instances where admissions were denied or where preapproved lengths of stay were exceeded, providers risked forfeiting federal reimbursement for the costs of those services. An evaluation of the program concluded that the net impact of the PSROs on utilization and expenditures was unclear but that the PSRO program probably saved as many resources as it consumed (Lohr 1990).

With the introduction of the Tax Equity and Fiscal Responsibility Act of 1982, the PSROs were transformed into Utilization and Quality Control Peer Review Organizations (PROs), which had somewhat broader responsibilities for assuring quality of care, with enhanced powers and greater consumer representation in their governance structures (Lohr 1990). A 1990 Institute of Medicine (IOM) study found numerous weaknesses in the peer review organizations' ability to assure quality within the Medicare program and recommended sweeping changes in the structure of Medicare's quality assurance and UR efforts (Lohr

1990). Since then, the federal government has invested heavily in outcomes and effectiveness research and in the development and validation of clinical practice guidelines, not only for purposes of quality enhancement but also for cost containment and control of the use of technology (Gray 1992).

In December 2001, the CMS released its Seventh Contract Cycle Statement of Work,* outlining a three-year work plan (September 2002–September 2005), that effectively transformed the thirty-eight regional peer review organizations into quality improvement organizations (QIOs) with greatly expanded responsibilities for improving the quality of care delivered by nursing homes, home health care providers, and physician offices in addition to hospitals (Lovern 2001b; Sprague 2002). The new work plan also placed high priority on developing better public reporting of quality-measurement data for hospitals, nursing homes, and home health providers through consumer-accessible Web sites (Lovern 2001a).

The AHRQ

As described in chapter 2, the AHRQ was created through the Healthcare Research and Quality Act of 1999. The law reauthorized the existing Agency for Health Care Policy and Research (AHCPR) but renamed it the Agency for Healthcare Research and Quality to reflect both a shift in the agency's focus toward quality and patient-safety concerns and to correct the popular misperception that the agency was principally responsible for directing all federal health care policy and regulation. The AHRQ today is the lead federal government agency "charged with supporting research designed to improve the quality of healthcare, reduce its cost, improve patient safety, decrease medical errors, and broaden access to essential services" (AHRQ 1999). Its current priorities are to

- improve the quality of health care by coordinating, conducting, and supporting research, demonstrations, and evaluations related to the measurement and improvement of health care quality;

---

* There have been six previous statements of work, dating back to the PSROs.

- promote patient safety and reduce medical errors by developing research and by building partnerships with health care practitioners and health care systems to reduce such errors; and
- advance the use of information technology for coordinating patient care and for conducting quality and outcomes research (AHRQ 1999).

In addition to these priorities, the agency's existing commitment to support research on the cost and use of health care services and on access to services was expanded through the establishment of an Office of Priority Populations to ensure that the needs of these populations are addressed (AHRQ 1999). The following sections describe several key AHRQ programs that bear directly on the diffusion, evaluation, and use of medical technology in clinical practice, including some initiatives that originated under the former AHCPR.

The AHCPR's Medical Treatment Effectiveness Program

Through the Medical Treatment Effectiveness Program, the AHCPR examined the effects of variations in health care practices on patient outcomes and developed and disseminated scientific information to improve patient care (AHCPR 1991; Raskin and Maklan 1991). The Medical Treatment Effectiveness Program's activities fell into four broad categories: patient outcomes research, the development of clinical practice guidelines, the development of scientific data, and the dissemination of research (AHCPR 1991). Patient outcomes research was conducted through (1) twenty-two patient outcomes research team projects (multisite, multidisciplinary studies of variations in clinical practices and outcomes for specific medical conditions, using large databases for analysis) and (2) smaller-scale projects that focused on identifying or explaining practice variations, refining methods or measures of effectiveness research, and synthesizing or disseminating information (AHCPR 1991; Eisenberg 1998).

Clinical Practice Guideline Development in the AHCPR

Early in its history, the AHCPR also was responsible for the development of clinical practice guidelines that fell into three categories: diagnostic guidelines for the clinical evaluation of patients with particular symptoms or for screening asymptomatic, at-risk populations; management guidelines for the treatment of patients with specific illnesses or conditions; and service guidelines for the appropriate use of particular diagnostic or therapeutic procedures (Ginsburg, LeRoy, and Hammons 1990; Gray 1992). In 1995, however, congressional budget cuts and political pressure forced the agency to abandon guideline development in favor of becoming a "science partner" with private-sector groups (e.g., managed care companies and other health care purchasers), validating guidelines developed by others (Cotton 1996; C. N. Kahn 1998). Two years later, Congress restored funding for the AHCPR to a level that enabled it to establish the Center for Practice and Technology Assessment, which supports several major programmatic activities related to MTE, including the Evidence-Based Practice Program for the review and analysis of the scientific literature on health care effectiveness (AHCPR Names Evidence-Based Practice Centers 1997).

The Center for Practice and Technology Assessment

Although the Medical Treatment Effectiveness Program was the central activity of the AHCPR for much of the 1990s, MTE was and remains an important part of the agency's purview. Established in 1997, the Center for Practice and Technology Assessment plays the lead role in performing technology assessments to support the technology coverage policy decisions of the Centers for Medicare and Medicaid Services (see chapter 12). The role of the Center for Practice and Technology Assessment in MTE activities is described in chapter 9 and includes the functions of its organizational predecessors, the Center for Health Care Technology and the Office of Health Technology Assessment (Eisenberg 1998).

Evidence-Based Practice Centers
Having survived a "near death" experience in 1995 (in the words of the AHCPR's administrator, John Eisenberg [1998, 768]), the agency in 1997 awarded five-year Evidence-Based Practice Center (EPC) contracts to twelve academic and private research organizations (AHCPR 1997). The EPCs develop evidence reports and technology assessments on clinical topics that are common, expensive, and/or significant for the Medicare and Medicaid populations (AHRQ 2001b). The evidence reports and technology assessments are based on rigorous, comprehensive syntheses and analyses of relevant scientific literature, empha-

sizing detailed documentation of methods, rationale, and assumptions (AHRQ 2001b). Topics for evidence reports and technology assessments focus on specific aspects of prevention, diagnosis, treatment, and/or management of a particular condition or on an individual procedure, treatment, or technology (AHRQ 2001b).

By December 2001, forty-three evidence reports had been produced and made available to the public, covering such diverse topics as the diagnosis of sleep apnea, the evaluation of therapies for stable angina, and the management of chronic obstructive pulmonary disease (AHRQ 2001b). In January 2002, the AHRQ announced that it had formed a partnership with the NIH's Office of Medical Applications of Research to provide NIH consensus-development conferences with the latest scientific evidence available from the EPCs (AHRQ 2002a). Also in January 2002, the AHRQ announced the second phase of the EPC program (AHRQ 2002b). Funded under five-year contracts, the EPC II centers were to continue the work of the twelve original sites, updating prior evidence-based reports, expanding research on methodologically sound reviews, and providing technical assistance to various organizations for the translation of evidence report findings into QI tools, educational programs, and payment policies (AHRQ 2002b). Thirteen EPC II centers were selected in June 2002, of which ten had participated in the first phase (AHRQ 2002c). Table 11.1 lists all of the EPCs and their assigned topics. The Evidence-Based Practice Program, which is housed within the AHRQ's Center for Practice and Technology Assessment, had produced seventy-nine evidence reports by June 2003 (AHRQ 2003).

The National Guideline Clearinghouse

The Center for Practice and Technology Assessment also houses the National Guideline Clearinghouse (NGC), a publicly available database of evidence-based clinical practice guidelines that may be accessed via the Internet at http://www.guideline.gov. Launched in 1998, the NGC is a partnership of the AHRQ with the American Medical Association and the American Association of Health Plans. The NGC is updated weekly with new content and is administered by ECRI (see chapter 9 for a description of this nonprofit research organization) under contract with the AHRQ (AHRQ 2000). The NGC provides users with structured, standardized summaries of each guideline, along with a utility for comparing two or more guidelines in a side-by-side manner (AHRQ 2000). To be included in the NGC, a guideline (1) must contain systematically

TABLE 11.1. Evidence-Based Practice Centers and Their Assigned Topics

Blue Cross and Blue Shield Association, Technical Evaluation Center (TEC), Chicago, Illinois
  Testosterone suppression treatment for prostatic cancer—1997
  Use of erythropoietin in hematology and oncology—1998
  Management of chronic asthma—1999
  Role of endoscopic retrograde cholangiopancreatopography (ERCP) in clinical practice—2001
  Islet cell transplantation for diabetes—2002
Duke University, Durham, North Carolina
  Evaluation of cervical cytology—1997
  Management of acute chronic obstructive pulmonary disease—1998
  Treatment of pulmonary disease following spinal cord injury—1999
  Treatment of fibroids—1999
  Management of postterm pregnancy—2000
  Effect of seasonal allergies on working populations—2001
ECRI, Plymouth Meeting, Pennsylvania
  Diagnosis and treatment of dysphagia/swallowing problems in the elderly—1997
  Criteria for determining disability in patients with end-stage renal disease (ESRD)—1998
  Treatment of degenerative lumbar spinal stenosis—1999
  Repetitive motion disorders, diagnosis and treatment—2000
  Treatment-resistant epilepsy—2001
Johns Hopkins University, Baltimore, Maryland
  Evaluation and treatment of new onset of atrial fibrillation in the elderly—1997
  Treatment of acne—1998
  Anesthesia management during cataract surgery—1998
  Treatment of coexisting cataract and glaucoma—1999
  Bioterrorism: Training for rare public health event—2000
  Blood pressure monitoring, outside of clinic setting—2000
  Management of hepatitis C—2001
  Management of venous thrombosis—2001
  Use of glycohemoglobin and microalbuminuria in diagnosis and monitoring of diabetes mellitus—2001
  Training for rare public health events—update of prior report related to bioterrorism—2002
  Strategies for improving minority health care quality—2002
McMaster University, Hamilton, Ontario, Canada
  Treatment of attention deficit/hyperactivity disorder—1997
  Criteria for weaning from mechanical ventilation—1998
  Management of neurogenic/neuropathic pain following spinal cord injury—1999
  Impact of cancer-related decision aids—2000
  Diffusion and dissemination of evidence-based cancer control interventions—2001
  Dementia, treatment—2002
MetaWorks, Inc., Boston, Massachusetts (EPC I only)
  Diagnosis of sleep apnea—1997
  Criteria for the referral of patients with epilepsy—1999
  Management of breast disease—1999
  Diagnosis and management of Parkinson's disease—2000
  Medical and scientific research related to disability from chronic fatigue syndrome—2001

TABLE 11.1.—*Continued*

Oregon Health and Science University, Portland, Oregon
  Rehabilitation of persons with traumatic brain injury—1997
  Diagnosis and management of osteoporosis—1999
  Medical informatics and telemedicine coverage under the Medicare Program—1999
  Echocardiography and carotid ultrasound in evaluation and management of
    stroke—2000
  Hyperbaric oxygen therapy: Treatment for brain injury and stroke—2001
  Preventing adolescent criminal and other health-risking social behavior—2001
  Vaginal birth following cesarean section—2001
  Effect of health care working conditions on patient safety—2001
Research Triangle Institute and University of North Carolina at Chapel Hill,
  North Carolina
  Pharmacotherapy for alcohol dependence—1997
  Management of preterm labor—1998
  Efficacy of behavioral dietary interventions to reduce cancer risk—1999
  Methods to rate strength of scientific evidence—2000
  Criteria to determine disability for speech/language disorders—2000
  Management of bronchiolitis—2001
  Community-based participatory research—2002
  Distance learning program (phase I)—2002
  Health literacy: Impact on health outcomes—2002
Southern California Evidence-Based Practice Center—RAND,
  Santa Monica, California
  Prevention and management of urinary complications in paralyzed persons—1997
  Management of acute otitis media—1998
  Prevention of venous thromboembolism after injury—1998
  Otitis media with effusion—1999
  Mind-body interventions for gastrointestinal conditions—1999
  Ayurvedic treatments for diabetes mellitus—2000
  Diagnosis and treatment of congestive heart failure—2000
  Utilization of physician services—2000
  Clinical efficacy and side effects of ephedra—2001
  Obesity, pharmacological management—2002
Stanford University, Stanford and University of California, San Francisco, California
  Management of stable angina—1997
  Management of unstable angina—1998
  Refinement of HCUP Quality Indicators—1999
  Autopsy as ultimate outcome measure—2000
  Bioterrorism: Decision support systems in disease management—2000
  Management of coronary heart disease in women (phase 1)—2001
  Making health care safer: Critical analysis of patient safety practices—2001
  Effective payment strategies to support quality-based purchasing (phase I feasibility
    study)—2002
  Regional models for bioterrorism preparedness—2002
Tufts–New England Medical Center, Boston, Massachusetts
  Diagnosis and treatment of acute bacterial sinusitis—1997
  Management of cancer pain—1998
  Evaluation of technologies for identifying acute cardiac ischemia in the emergency
    department—1999
  Management of allergic rhinitis—2000

(continued)

TABLE 11.1.—*Continued*

    Criteria to determine disability for infant/childhood impairments—2000
    Management of clinically inapparent adrenal mass—2001
    Quality of life: Management of cancer-associated pain and related symptoms—2001
    Neonatal hyperbilirubinemia—2001
    Management of cancer symptoms—2002
University of Alberta, Edmonton, Alberta, Canada
    Biventricular pacing for congestive heart failure—2002
University of Minnesota, Minneapolis, Minnesota
    Total knee replacement—2002
    Efficacy of behavioral interventions to modify physical activity—2002
    Economic incentives: Impact on use/outcomes of preventive health services—2002
University of Ottawa, Ottawa, Canada
    Quality measures: Diagnosis and treatment of breast cancer in women—2002
    Sexuality and reproductive health following spinal cord injury (phase I feasibility
        study)—2002
University of Texas Health Science Center, San Antonio, Texas (EPC I only)
    Depression treatment with new drugs—1997
    Management of chronic hypertension during pregnancy—1998
    Use of garlic for cardiovascular disease—1999
    Use of silybum marianum in treatment of liver disease and cirrhosis—1999
    Defining and managing chronic fatigue syndrome—2000
    Medical harms workshop—2000

Source: Data from AHRQ 2001b, AHRQ 2002c.

developed recommendations or strategies to assist clinical decision making in specific circumstances; (2) must have been produced under the auspices of a relevant professional organization (e.g., medical specialty society, government agency, or health plan); (3) must include a verifiable, systematic literature search and review of existing evidence published in peer-reviewed journals; and (4) must be current and developed or revised within the past five years (AHRQ 2000).

The use of practice guidelines poses profound implications for the diffusion and use of technology in medicine. First, guidelines for technology use and appropriateness of care, if eventually linked to payment policies (as they likely may be under private plans and possibly under the Medicare + Choice program in the future), could conceivably affect the rate and extent of the diffusion of individual technologies throughout the health care system. Second, while the guidelines being reviewed, validated, and added to the NGC generally are being formulated in the private sector by physicians for physicians, their potential misuse by managed care plans and other payers to limit services and clinical choices in ways that stress cost considerations over those of quality could adversely influence physicians' decisions regarding the use of specific technologies. And, third, unlike the process employed in the NIH consensus-development conferences (see chapter 6), the development of practice guidelines in the private sector often does not include the participation of consumers, bioethicists, and epidemiologists.

While the AHRQ and its partners clearly do not intend to use the NGC as a tool for broad public dissemination of evidence-based information on practice guidelines, the question of how such information will be used remains a concern. Thus, initial "validation" of practice guidelines is not enough, and careful evaluation of a guideline's effects on the diffusion and use of technology, whether intended or unintended, ought to be incorporated into the overall QI process. Moreover, periodic updating of published guidelines with new evidence and expert judgment is critical if such guidelines are to remain useful to clinicians. A recent assessment of the current validity of seventeen clinical practice guidelines published by the AHRQ found that thirteen required substantial updating (Shekelle et al. 2001), but experts disagree on the method and frequency for updating the guidelines (Browman 2001).

Centers for Education and Research on Therapeutics

One of the ways in which the AHRQ promotes patient safety is through the Centers for Education and Research on Therapeutics program, which the agency administers in cooperation with the FDA (AHRQ 2001a). The concept of the centers grew out of the early 1990s experience of the AHCPR's Pharmaceutical Outcomes Program, which studied patient outcomes associated with pharmaceutical therapy. Congress authorized the Centers for Education and Research on Therapeutics program as part of the Food and Drug Modernization Act of 1997 (U.S. Public Law 105-115), with the goal of improving the quality of health care and reducing costs by increasing awareness of the benefits and risks of new, existing, or combined uses of therapeutics (i.e., drugs, medical devices, and biological products) through education and research (AHRQ 2001c). The centers focus specifically on reducing adverse drug reactions through research on the uses and risks of new drugs and drug combinations, biological products, and devices as well as mechanisms to improve their safe and effective use (AHRQ 2001a). The centers provide clinical information to patients and consumers, health care providers, pharmacists, pharmacy benefit managers and purchasers, health care delivery systems, managed care organizations

TABLE 11.2.   Centers for Education and Research on Therapeutics™

Duke University[a]
    Principal investigator: Judith Kramer, M.D.
    Approved drugs and therapeutic devices in cardiovascular medicine
University of Arizona
    Principal investigator: Raymond Woosley, M.D., Ph.D.
    Reduction of drug interactions, particularly in women
University of North Carolina at Chapel Hill
    Principal investigator: William Campbell, Ph.D.
    Rational use of therapeutics in the pediatric population
Vanderbilt University
    Principal investigator: Wayne Ray, Ph.D.
    Prescription medication use in the Medicaid managed care population
HMO Research Network (Harvard Pilgrim Health Care)
    Principal investigator: Richard Platt, M.D.
    Using large managed care databases to study prescribing patterns, dosing out-
        comes, and policy impact
University of Pennsylvania
    Principal investigator: Brian L. Strom, M.D.
    Antibiotic drug resistance, drug utilization, and intervention studies
University of Alabama at Birmingham
    Principal investigator: Kenneth Saag, M.D.
    Therapeutics for musculoskeletal disorders

Source: Data from AHRQ 2001a.
[a]Duke University also serves as the CERTs Coordinating Center, directed by Robert Califf, M.D.

and insurers, and government agencies. The program was implemented in September 1999 when the AHRQ awarded initial three-year cooperative agreements to support four centers. Three additional centers were funded in 2000 for a three-year period (AHRQ 2001c). Table 11.2 lists the seven existing centers.

The AHRQ's QI and Patient-Safety Initiatives

Within the AHRQ, the Center for Quality Improvement and Patient Safety conducts and supports research on the measurement, improvement, and reporting of health care quality and the enhancement of patient safety. The agency promotes the use of information technology and software tools for the assessment and dissemination of individual-provider and plan-level comparative performance measures and for the creation of effective linkages among sources of health information to enhance the delivery and coordination of evidence-based health services. The following are two long-standing initiatives:

- The Computerized Needs-Oriented Quality Measurement Evaluation System (CONQUEST), a QI database containing nearly 1,200 clinical performance measures and information on fifty-seven common or costly conditions affecting the general population, such as arthritis, asthma, cancer, cataracts, depression, diabetes, gallbladder disease, heart attack, hypertension, and pregnancy; access to the database is provided free to a broad array of users, including health care providers, managed care plans, health care purchasers, employers, policymakers and researchers (AHRQ 2001d).
- The Consumer Assessment of Health Plans (CAHPs), an easy-to-use kit of survey and report tools that provides reliable and valid information to help consumers and purchasers assess and choose among health plans; the surveys ask consumers about their experiences with their health plans; the information obtained from the surveys permits comparative assessment of the quality of care in health plans that may be used by plans to improve their programs and services; purchasers may also use the data to assess the value of the services they buy; and quality measurement organizations (e.g., accrediting organizations) can use the data to supplement their data collection and assessment activities (AHRQ 2001e).

Following the release of a 1999 IOM report (discussed later in this chapter), the Department of Health and Human Services established the Patient Safety Task Force to coordinate data-collection efforts on medical errors and adverse events, to coordinate research and analysis efforts, and to promote collaboration on reducing the occurrence of medical errors among public and private organizations (AHRQ 2001f). Composed of representatives from the AHRQ, the CDC, the FDA, and the CMS, the task force has focused on developing a coordinated reporting system on adverse events and errors and on producing patient-safety programs. The AHRQ, for its part, announced in 2000 a call for applications to establish Centers for Excellence for Patient Safety Research and Practice among academic institutions, nonprofit organizations, and delivery systems (AHRQ 2001c). The agency's patient-safety research program addresses themes culled from various sources, including the IOM, public and private national summits, and the federal Quality Interagency Coordination Task Force (AHRQ 2001c).

In October 2001, the AHRQ announced the commitment of $50 million to fund ninety-four new research grants and demonstrations to reduce medical errors and improve patient safety (AHRQ 2001c). The initiative represented the first phase of a multiyear effort to support projects in six major categories:

- demonstration projects to report medical errors data—twenty-four projects receiving $24.7 million to study different methods of collecting data on medical errors;
- use of computers and information technology to prevent medical errors—twenty-two projects receiving $5.3 million to develop and test the use of computers and information technology to reduce medical errors, improve patient safety, and improve quality of care;
- understanding the impact of working conditions on patient safety—eight projects receiving $3 million to examine how staffing, fatigue, stress, sleep deprivation, and other factors can lead to errors;
- innovative approaches to improving patient safety—twenty-three projects receiving $8 million to research and develop innovative ways to improve patient safety at health care facilities and organizations in geographically diverse locations;
- disseminating research results—seven projects receiving $2.4 million to educate clinicians and others about the results of patient-safety research; and
- patient-safety research initiatives—ten projects receiving $6.4 million to support other patient-safety research efforts (AHRQ 2001c).

A second initiative, called Partnerships for Quality, funded twenty-two projects in late 2002, to develop and promote partnerships among researchers, health plans, medical and nursing facilities and services, employers, consumer groups, and professional societies for testing prototype activities to accelerate the transfer of research findings into practice for quality improvement (AHRQ 2002d).

Private-Sector UM Efforts

Although private-sector efforts to manage the use of services—and of medical technology—generally have paralleled those of the federal government, many private insurers and managed care plans have done so with comparatively greater intensity and with stronger emphasis on cost-effectiveness concerns. Private payers such as Blue Cross and Blue Shield plans and commercial insurance companies have long been involved in UR and UM efforts. In fact, with support from large employers and other businesses, these groups pioneered many UM techniques, most notably second-opinion surgery programs and high-cost-illness case-management plans.

The literature on the UR experience is basically of two types: documented assessments of the programs themselves and population-based, epidemiologic studies assessing the prevalence of inappropriate applications of medical technology. Because UR programs, like many other cost-containment strategies, have concentrated most of their attention on hospital admissions and lengths of stay, the population-based studies may illustrate better the value of UR methods in constraining the inappropriate use of technology.

Wennberg (1984), for example, documented wide geographic variations in the incidence of surgical procedures such as tonsillectomies, hysterectomies, and cesarean deliveries, suggesting that physicians' practice styles may require modification toward some accepted norm or range of variation. Other efforts have focused on the inappropriate use of procedures and on the performance of "unnecessary surgery," defined as procedures that either provide no benefit to patients or provide small benefit that is outweighed by associated risks, morbidity, disability, or pain. It has been estimated that 13 to 32 percent of all surgical interventions may be inappropriate, with the percentage rising to 64 percent if "equivocal" cases are included (Leape 1989). Second-opinion surgery programs and precertification programs using established criteria and guidelines for specific procedures are the most frequently cited UM approaches aimed at limiting this volume.

Beginning in the early 1990s, however, nonsurgical procedures appeared to overtake their surgical counterparts in influencing rising health care costs (PPRC 1993). A study by Brook and his colleagues (1990), using Medicare data from five sites across the United States and appropriateness criteria developed with the aid of expert medical panels, found that two nonsurgical procedures (coronary angiography and upper gastrointestinal tract endoscopy) were inappropriately indicated in about 25 percent of cases. Carotid endarterectomy, a surgical procedure that had been the subject of fierce debate and controversy in the medical community, was found to be indicated inappropriately in two-thirds of cases. This procedure, after having fallen into disfavor in the late 1980s, underwent significant change in technique and experienced resurgent interest among vascular surgeons in the mid-1990s.

Commentary on appropriateness studies in the medical literature often has been critical (Kassirer 1993). Examining the methodologic foundations of the approach, Phelps (1993) cited several weaknesses that raised doubts about the validity of appropriateness studies, including a reliance on expert panel consensus (making global assessments of clinical practice far removed from actual patient encounters), data taken from secondary sources of questionable validity (hospital records), and the inability to control for other factors that might explain observed differences.

The increasing use of physician profiles has stirred similar controversy (Kassirer 1994). Although one analysis of inpatient practice patterns in Florida and Oregon (Welch, Miller, and Welch 1994) suggested that physician profiling may be useful for identifying and characterizing differences in practice style to which individual physicians or hospital staffs can legitimately respond, one observer (Kassirer 1994) cautioned that serious data flaws seemed to plague the commercial industry that markets practice profiles and that more research was needed on how to define the data required for valid profiles and how to collect and transmit the information while protecting patients' confidentiality.

A major private-sector effort during the 1990s was the development of health plan performance report cards that contain a core set of performance measures covering quality, access, and patient satisfaction (Corrigan and Nielsen 1993). Spearheaded by the National Committee for Quality Assurance (a nonprofit organization seeking to improve patient care quality in partnership with managed care plans and large employers), the Health Plan Employer Data and Information Set was developed and tested as a set of uniform reporting standards for managed care organizations. The data and information set includes several measures that are specific to well-established preventive services and technologies, such as childhood immunization, cholesterol screening, mammography screening, and Pap smears for cervical cancer (Corrigan and Nielsen 1993). Because employers, other purchasers, and consumers increasingly wish to know whether they are receiving the best value for their health care dollars, such performance report card systems are growing in influence. The Health Plan Employer Data and Information Set has undergone several revisions of its content and methods, and the National Committee for Quality Assurance, in conjunction with the CMS, has developed customized versions of the set for the Medicare and Medicaid populations. It is imperative that such systems contain valid and reliable measures that allow for clinically and financially meaningful comparisons across plans and providers.

Combining Medical Technology Evaluation with Quality Improvement

Throughout the 1980s and 1990s, as concerns over technology's contribution to rising health care costs grew and as interest in clinical practice guidelines and performance measurement increased, various programs that combined MTE with QI were established around the nation. Most of these programs were either hospital based or HMO based, but a few states adopted innovative approaches to improving quality of care by developing report card systems and integrated MTE/QI programs.

New York state, for example, pioneered the development and publication of report cards on hospitals and surgeons with its Cardiac Surgery Reporting System. The system produces annual reports on risk-adjusted hospital mortality rates for cardiac surgery and in 1991 generated the first physician-specific mortality report ever published in the United States (Green and Wintfeld 1995). Pennsylvania began publication in 1992 of a consumer's guide to coronary artery bypass graft surgery that listed annual risk-adjusted mortality rates for all hospitals and surgeons providing such surgery in the state (Schneider and Epstein 1996). Both reporting systems have been hailed as valuable information resources on patient outcomes, but concerns also have been voiced about the data and methods used to generate the reports, leading some observers to suggest that independent statistical evaluation may be needed to ensure that report cards offer fair and informative comparisons of providers (Green and Wintfeld 1995). In a review of the evidence regarding public release of performance data from seven U.S. reporting systems, M. N. Marshall and colleagues (2000) found that provider organizations—especially hospitals—make far greater use of available information from such systems than do consumers, purchasers, and physicians, raising doubts as to whether such standardized reporting indeed affords consumers with the information necessary to improve their health care decision making. Nevertheless, Epstein (2000, 1886) argues that while public reporting of health care quality data "may never be all things to all people," it promises to be an important part of the national QI agenda.

New York state also has been a leader in the area of integrated MTE/QI programs. In 1993, the state created the Task Force on Clinical Guidelines and Medical Technology Assessment as part of its existing prospective hospital reimbursement system to advise the governor, legislature, and commissioner of health on ways to best utilize clinical practice guidelines and MTE to improve health outcomes and the quality of care (Servis and Ferrara 1996). The task force endorsed the integrated use of guidelines and MTE as tools to inform and improve clinical decision making, reduce variation in clinical practice, measure and improve quality of care, guide coverage and payment decisions, increase patient participation in treatment decisions, and inform public policy-making (Servis and Ferrara 1996).

Hospital-based MTE/QI programs vary widely in structure and process. One early example was the Johns Hopkins Medical Institutions' Program for Medical Technology and Practice Assessment, which focused primarily on emerging technologies but also examined new and established technologies in terms of their clinical safety, efficacy, cost, and benefits relative to clinical alternatives, reimbursement, and use in clinical practice (Steinberg and Graziano 1990). Today, most academic medical centers and many large community hospitals operate integrated MTE/QI programs that enable them to identify and assess the development of new technologies, to make informed decisions regarding adoption and implementation, and to monitor the technology's applications within the hospital to provide appropriate information to health care professionals, patients, and the community. In many cases, the hospital combines this review of the technology's applications with analyses of its cost, of its medical appropriateness, and of the satisfaction patients and clinicians derive from its use.

Among HMOs and managed care plans, the approach undertaken by Kaiser Permanente is noteworthy both for its content and for its magnitude. In the early 1980s, Kaiser Permanente developed its Inter-Regional New Technologies Committee, with representatives from each of its regions and from its corporate office (McGuire 1990; Rettig 1997). The committee continues to review emerging technologies and makes recommendations regarding their adoption and use (Fernandez et al. 1997; Rettig 1997). Reviews typically incorporate current medical knowledge, government agency actions, viewpoints of system physicians, and information about coverage decisions made by other health plans and insurance companies. Final recommendations then become systemwide policy (McGuire 1990; Rettig 1997). Once adopted, use of the technology is monitored, with appropriate UR data shared within the system for QI purposes. As described in chapter 9, Kaiser Permanente joined the Blue Cross and Blue Shield Association in a 1993 collaborative effort that drew on Blue Cross's analytic expertise and Kaiser Permanente's clinical population (L. Wagner 1993). Each organization contributed significant funds to the effort, and the expanded program produces approximately forty assessments annually (Rettig 1997).

These combined or integrated structures for MTE and QI at the organizational level of hospitals and HMOs are popular today. Continuing competitive pressures in the health care marketplace leave providers and payers with little choice but to find better ways to determine how new technologies should be applied within patient populations and how these applications may affect costs, revenues, and quality of care. Such practice-level analysis can fill an important void in the field of MTE by offering better insight into and management of the final stage of technology diffusion—that is, providers' and payers' decisions on behalf of patients about the use of technologies.

Recent Private-Sector Initiatives in QI and Patient Safety

In the face of mounting public concern during the 1990s about health plan performance, potential medical errors, and adverse patient outcomes, a number of private-sector initiatives arose to enhance provider accountability, reduce medical errors, and improve patient outcomes. These efforts have been wide ranging and include informational, research-based, and practice-oriented QI approaches as well as public-private partnerships for quality measurement and reporting. Six such initiatives are profiled here—the Institute for Healthcare Improvement; the consumer-oriented Foundation for Accountability; the National Forum for Health Care Quality Measurement and Reporting; the research efforts of the IOM; the Robert Wood Johnson Foundation's Pursuing Perfection program; and the Leapfrog Group.

The Institute for Healthcare Improvement

For more than a decade, the nonprofit Institute for Healthcare Improvement (IHI) has been dedicated to leading the improvement of health care systems by continuously increasing their quality and value in terms of "improved health status, better clinical outcomes, lower cost, broadened access, greater ease of use, and higher satisfaction for individuals and their communities" (IHI 2001). The IHI's activities include an array of courses, professional conferences, collaborative series, networks, and specialized initiatives. The Breakthrough Series Collaboratives bring together health care organizations interested in achieving dramatic advances, such as lower costs and better outcomes, in a particular area of health services. Since 1995, more than 250 organizations in the United States and Canada have participated in more than twenty different collaboratives on such topics as adverse drug events, asthma care, cesarean section rates, delays and waiting times in the emergency department, efficiency and access to care, improving care at the end of life, improving care for people with chronic conditions, and improving care for children with attention deficit and hyperactivity disorders (IHI 2001). The IHI also sponsors two professional networks devoted to improving the quality and value of care in their member organizations: the Quality Management Network (comprising thirty-three provider organizations) and the Group Practice Improvement Network (consisting of fifty-two multispecialty group practices). In addition, the IHI has developed innovative schemes for the idealized design of clinical office practices, the intensive care unit, and the medication system, with plans to develop a new initiative for the idealized design of patient flow (IHI 2001). In 2001, the IHI was named the national program office for the Robert Wood Johnson Foundation's Pursuing Perfection program (described later in this chapter).

The Foundation for Accountability

In 1995, following the failure of national health care reform, an array of health care managers, policy analysts, and thinkers known as the Jackson Hole Group sponsored several meetings of large health care purchasers to form a nonprofit organization dedicated to helping Americans make better health care decisions and to holding the health care system accountable for quality. The organization came to be known as the Foundation for Accountability (FACCT) and was incorporated with a board of trustees composed of consumer, purchaser, and insurance organizations. FACCT creates tools that help consumers to understand and use quality information for making decisions about their health care. Early in its history, FACCT published its *Prototype Guidebook for*

Performance Measurement as well as performance measurement sets for such conditions as breast cancer, diabetes, and major depressive disorders. In addition to educating consumers about the use of quality measures, FACCT supports the collection and dissemination of quality information and encourages the formulation of health policy that empowers and informs consumers (FACCT 2001).

The organization conducts projects in four broad areas:

- tools for measuring and reporting on quality;
- educational and motivational messages for consumers;
- valid, comparative information for consumers so that they can make appropriate decisions; and
- decision support to consumers to help them sift through complex performance information (FACCT 2001).

In 2002, FACCT initiated its Compare Your Care project, which profiles individual primary care physician performance, and launched a comprehensive clearinghouse for consumer-centered health care materials, resources, and information (FACCT 2003).

The National Quality Forum

Incorporated in 1999 as the National Forum for Health Care Quality Measurement and Reporting, the National Quality Forum is a private, nonprofit entity whose mission is "to improve American healthcare through endorsement of consensus-based national standards for measurement and public reporting of healthcare performance data that pro vide meaningful information about whether care is safe, timely, beneficial, patient-centered, equitable and efficient" (National Quality Forum 2003). The forum has more than one hundred organizational members—including medical specialty societies, large companies, and trade associations—and is an open membership organization that seeks to develop consensus about standardized health care performance measures (Kizer 2001). A unique and specially convened Strategic Framework Board, composed of health policy experts, devotes significant time to carrying out the forum's stated mission (Kizer 2001; Sprague 2001). The forum also works closely with the AHRQ and other governmental agencies to coordinate its strategy with existing and planned quality measurement and reporting systems. Forum projects include hospital performance measures, nursing home measures, diabetes measures, mammography center quality, safe practices, and nursing care performance measures (National Quality Forum 2003).

The IOM's Reports on Quality of Care and Patient Safety

The IOM of the National Academy of Sciences has had long-standing interests in MTE and quality of care. The IOM's Committee on Quality of Health Care in America produced three major reports in recent years. In November 1999, *To Err Is Human* estimated that between 44,000 and 98,000 people die each year because of medical errors, dwarfing the mortality from highway accidents, breast cancer, and AIDS (IOM 1999). Although some researchers have questioned whether this estimate of preventable mortality resulting from medical errors is overstated, the numbers nonetheless are disturbingly high (Hayward and Hofer 2001). Moreover, the IOM report described a health care system that is highly fragmented, wasteful in its use of resources, and lacking in accountability for quality of care (IOM 1999). To improve patient safety, the committee called for numerous changes in the system, which included but were not limited to

- the creation of a Center for Patient Safety within the AHRQ (see the earlier discussion of the AHRQ in this chapter);
- a nationwide mandatory reporting system for the collection of standardized information by state governments about adverse events resulting in death or serious harm, with concomitant encouragement of voluntary reporting;
- performance standards and expectations for health care organizations and health professionals that focus greater attention on patient safety;
- increased FDA attention on the safe use of drugs in both premarket and postmarket review processes; and
- establishment of patient-safety programs by health care organizations and their professionals (IOM 1999).

The second IOM report, *Crossing the Quality Chasm,* was released in March 2001 and called for a revamped health care system in which health care providers and professionals adopt new perspectives on quality of care and new methods for achieving it (IOM 2001). It offered numerous recommendations for restructuring the health care system.

- Health care organizations, professionals, and purchasers should adopt as their main goal the continuous reduction of the burden of illness, injury, and disability and the improvement of the health and functioning of the American people.
- All health care organizations, professional groups, and private and public purchasers should work together to improve health care in six key areas: safety, effectiveness, patient centeredness, timeliness, efficiency, and equity. The secretary of the Department of Health and Human Services should monitor and track quality improvements in these areas and should report annually to Congress and the president on the progress made.
- Private and public purchasers, health care organizations, clinicians, and patients should work together to redesign health care processes in accordance with the following ten rules:

  care based on healing relationships,
  customization based on patient needs and values,
  the patient as the source of control,
  shared knowledge and the free flow of information,
  evidence-based decision making,
  safety as a system property,
  the need for transparency,
  anticipation of needs,
  continuous decrease in waste, and
  cooperation among clinicians.

- The AHRQ should identify fifteen or more priority conditions and, in collaboration with the National Health Care Quality Forum (described earlier in this chapter), develop strategies and action plans for improving quality for each condition over a five-year period.
- The AHRQ and private foundations should convene a series of workshops to address

  redesign of care processes based on best practices;
  the use of information technology to improve access to clinical information and to support clinical decision making;
  knowledge and skills management;
  development of effective teams;

coordination of care across patient conditions, services, and settings over time; and

incorporation of performance and outcome measurements for improvement and accountability.

- All interested parties should make a national commitment to build an information infrastructure to support health care delivery, consumer health, quality measurement and improvement, public accountability, clinical and health services research, and clinical education.
- Purchasers should review payment methods to remove barriers that impede quality improvement.

The third IOM report, *Leadership by Example*, was issued in October 2002. It argued that the federal government should lead the development of clinical standards for measuring care. The report also called for the development and use of financial incentives for organizations that improve the quality of care (Tieman 2002).

Pursuing Perfection, a Program of the Robert Wood Johnson Foundation

In October 2001, the Robert Wood Johnson Foundation awarded planning grants under its Pursuing Perfection program to twelve health care organizations to improve patient outcomes by "pursuing perfection in all of their major care processes" (Johnson Foundation 2001). The pursuit of perfection means striving to

- deliver all indicated preventive, acute, and chronic care services accurately and correctly;
- deliver the services in a timely manner;
- avoid services that are not helpful to the patient or are not reasonably cost-effective;
- avoid safety hazards and errors; and
- respect patients' needs and preferences.

With core technical assistance from the IHI (which serves as the national program office) and from a technical advisory group, program grantees during the planning phase each developed a business plan for improving health care in at least two illness-based care processes defined by national standard quality measures, a diffusion strategy for training clinical and administrative employees to redesign their processes based on lessons from the pilot studies, a strategy for building partnerships with outside organizations needed to pursue improved patient care, and an infrastructure-building strategy for organization-wide improvements (Johnson Foundation 2001). Seven of the twelve organizations were selected in April 2002 to receive major grants to support the implementation of their business plans over a two-year period in which their redesign of care processes is to be extended to at least five more diseases or conditions (IHI 2002).

The Leapfrog Group

Founded by the Business Roundtable, a national association of Fortune 500 business executives, the Leapfrog Group aims to mobilize the purchasing power of employers to initiate breakthrough improvements in patient safety. By providing market incentives to hospitals and health care providers that reward the adoption of new information technologies, such as computerized physician order entry systems and electronic medical records systems, the Leapfrog Group's 140 member organizations hope to reduce preventable medical errors and to enhance the quality and value of health care delivered to consumers. To become a Leapfrog member, health care purchasers (public and private) must subscribe to the group's purchasing principles to champion overall customer value and to focus on specific innovations that have been shown to produce "leaps" in patient safety (Leapfrog Group 2003).

12

Cost Concerns: Medical Technology and Health Care Payment Policies
Alan B. Cohen and Ruth S. Hanft*

As discussed in chapter 2, much of the rise in U.S. health care expenditures since 1970 has been attributed to system inefficiencies and to the intensive use of health services and medical technologies (Schwartz 1987; U.S. Congress, Congressional Budget Office 1991; GAO 1992b; Newhouse 1992; Peden and Freeland 1995; Chernew et al. 1998; P. E. Mohr et al. 2001; Levit et al. 2003). As a result, interest has grown sharply over time in devising cost-containment strategies that limit total service use and, more specifically, the use of expensive technology. Past efforts to control spending associated with service use have taken two forms: utilization review and management strategies (discussed in chapter 11) and payment policies. Both types of efforts attempt to encourage more cost-effective use of medical technology, but only payment policies also seek to influence the adoption of new technology indirectly through financial incentives. It should be borne in mind, however, that payment policies—as well as utilization review and utilization management strategies—have been designed primarily to reduce total spending, not just spending associated with the adoption and use of technology.

In this chapter, we first review the important post–World War II health policy changes in the United States that have affected health care spending and the adoption and use of medical technology, with emphasis on the incentives associated with payment methods in different time periods. We next look at payment policies and technology cover-

---

*With the research assistance of Shirley A. Stewart and Catherine C. White.

age policies of private payers, the federal Medicare program, and state Medicaid programs, examining how those policies may have affected the adoption and use of medical technology. We also briefly discuss some of the negative consequences of managed care payment policies on consumers and explore the experience with state-based hospital rate-setting systems.

Health Policy Changes, Health Care Spending, and the Adoption and Use of Medical Technology

In chapter 5, we examined the financial and professional incentives underlying the cost/quality trade-offs made by various stakeholders when deciding whether to adopt and use new medical technology in a managed-care-dominated health care system. Here we look once again at those complex incentive structures but do so within the context of major health policy changes over time and their effects on health care spending and on the adoption and use of medical technology.

Since the end of World War II, several major shifts in health policy have shaped the structure and resources of the U.S. health care delivery system. The postwar epoch may be divided into four time periods: 1945–65, an age of supply-side expansion; 1965–72, a time of distributive reform; 1972–94, an era of cost containment; and 1994 to the present, a period of market-driven competition. Throughout the entire half century, an overriding factor has been the unparalleled explosion in technological advances, most notably those in biology and genetics. Each time period is described below in terms of the major policy events (e.g., key legislation) and industry trends that influenced health care spending during that era, with particular regard to the payment policies of the time and the incentives that they fostered for the adoption and use of medical technology.

1945–1965: Supply-Side Expansion

The period from the end of World War II to the mid-1960s was a time of great supply-side expansion. This trend received impetus from advances in science and technology in general and from war-related advances specific to medical science and technology that were transferred to the civilian sector soon after the war's close. These advances included the development and use of radar and ultrasound, improved surgical techniques perfected on the battlefield, and the widespread use of antibiotics to control infection.

The immediate postwar period also witnessed congressional appropriation of large sums of federal funds for biomedical research. The National Institutes of Health experienced tremendous growth during this period, and rapid improvements in knowledge and technology led to increased specialization within the medical profession and to the expansion of residency training programs. The number of hospitals grew dramatically nationwide through an infusion of funds provided under the Hospital Survey and Construction Act of 1946 (known as the Hill-Burton Act), which enabled states to plan and construct hospitals and other facilities, especially in rural areas. The Veterans Administration's health care system also expanded during this era and was linked strongly to academic health centers.

During the 1950s and 1960s, concerns arose regarding the adequacy of the nation's supply of health care personnel, particularly physicians. Many states, with assistance from the federal government, expanded the numbers and class sizes of health professions schools within their borders. Along with this trend came considerable growth in private health insurance, which had originated with the establishment of Blue Cross in 1929 at Baylor University Hospital in Dallas, Texas, and which had taken hold in the form of employer-based health benefits offered to workers during World War II (Cunningham and Cunningham 1997). As Blue Cross and Blue Shield plans expanded, so did commercial indemnity insurance companies. By the early 1960s, approximately 70 percent of the U.S. population under age sixty-five was covered by health insurance, compared to only 20 percent before World War II. The advent of insurance for much of the population expanded access to health care and insulated people from the cost consequences of their private decisions to seek and to use health care. This phenomenon (which economists term "moral hazard") creates perverse incentives for the overuse of health services. Coupled with this were the dominant modes of payment for hospitals and physicians under private health insurance, which were cost based and fee for service (FFS), respectively. These policies generated strong incentives for providers to adopt and use new medical technology regardless of its cost.

1965–1972: Distributive Reform

The mid-1960s to the early 1970s marked a period of distributive reform in which the nation moved toward ensuring equal access to mainstream health care for all segments of the population. The Medicare and Medicaid programs were established in 1965, bringing elderly people and many low-income people under the health insurance umbrella. A major federal thrust to expand the availability of health care personnel and to increase the capacity of clinicians to intervene in disease treatment saw significant public investment in the training of various types of health professionals, in the expansion of NIH-based biomedical and clinical research, and in the transfer of scientific advances and technology from the laboratory to the field, with the Regional Medical Program a prime example of this technology transfer.

With the growth of public health insurance to complement the earlier growth in private health insurance, the hospital industry continued to expand. During this period, hospital revenues from the federal government nearly doubled, the value of hospital assets per bed almost tripled, and health care spending rose at a rate that was several percentage points higher than the general rate of economic inflation (Goddeeris 1987). The broad availability of health insurance also fueled hospital adoption of new medical technology, as the prevailing methods of cost-based and FFS payment for hospitals and physicians continued to provide neither disincentives against adopting new technology nor incentives for cost-sensitive adoption and efficient use of such resources (see table 5.8 for a description of the changing financial incentives for technology adoption and use over time). In fact, the introduction of new technology in the hospital setting was deemed economically rational because hospitals were reimbursed fully for their costs and could achieve economies of scale in the use of technology that were not possible for most individual physicians (Field 1987).

1972–1994: Cost Containment

Efforts at cost containment moved to the forefront of health policy in the early 1970s, as expenditures began to grow at nearly twice the rate of annual economic inflation and at least 25 percent of the annual rise was considered attributable to increased service intensity, particularly the expanding use of technology (HCFA 1991). Beginning with the 1972 Social Security Amendments, the federal government sought various ways to contain health care costs, including such mechanisms as prospective hospital payment demonstrations, the section 1122 capital expenditure review program (see chapter 13), and the professional standards review organizations, which focused on cost control through utilization review (see chapter 11). While all three strategies sought in some way to influence the adoption and use of medical technology, the section 1122 program was the most directly targeted in its review of capital equipment purchases by hospitals and other facilities. Coincidentally, the 1972 amendments also gave rise to the End-Stage Renal Disease Program, which, as an entitlement under Medicare for all Americans regardless of age, facilitated broad access to renal dialysis and transplantation services but which over time has had a clear inflationary effect on Medicare expenditures (Eggers 1988; Levinsky and Rettig 1991; E. A. Friedman 1996; Rettig 1996). In addition, in 1972 Congress established the Office of Technology Assessment (OTA) as an important advisory body on technology-related issues, including the economic impact of technology on health care.

Throughout the 1970s, the federal government took the lead in developing cost-control strategies, with market-based and regulatory approaches pursued simultaneously. The Health Maintenance Organization Act of 1973, for example, was intended to stimulate the growth of health maintenance organizations (HMOs) and prepaid group health plans in the medical marketplace. HMOs, which paid for patient care on a capitated (per person) rather than FFS basis, generally had lower hospitalization rates and smaller increases in annual premiums than traditional indemnity insurance plans of the time. By encouraging the development of prepaid plans, it was hoped that the market-oriented financial incentives that such plans engendered for greater efficiency would result in substantial cost reductions. At the same time, however, federal policymakers also looked toward regulatory controls, such as the National Health Planning and Resources Development Act of 1974, which created a nationwide system of state and local area health-planning agencies for the purpose of allocating health care resources more "rationally," including the control of system capacity (the supply of facilities, services, and capital-embodied technology) through state-based CON processes (see chapter 13). Although enacted for reasons other than cost containment, the Medical Device Amendments of 1976 nonetheless complemented these cost-control measures because it empowered the Food and Drug Administration (FDA) to expand its regulatory authority beyond drugs to include premarket approval of new medical devices, some of which might be costly to adopt and use (see chapter 10).

In many respects, the era of cost containment between 1972 and 1994 may be subdivided into two distinct periods. In the first period, 1972–84, payment methods remained relatively unchanged despite the implementation of the federal cost-containment strategies mentioned earlier and the efforts of some states to experiment with numerous forms of rate-setting systems (see table 5.8). Consequently, all providers still faced financial incentives that favored overwhelmingly the adoption and use of new technology but with capital expenditure review mechanisms, such as section 1122 and CON, serving as modest constraining influences. In contrast, the second period, 1984–94, was marked by major changes in federal and private payment policies that led to concurrent changes in the financial incentives for technology adoption and use by hospitals and physicians, as will be described subsequently in this chapter (see table 5.8).

Federal payment policies for health care under the Medicare program shifted radically during the 1980s from traditional, retrospective cost-based reimbursement to prospective case-based payment. Adopted in quick succession, two key laws—the Tax Equity and Fiscal Responsibility Act of 1982 and the Social Security Amendments of 1983—first set limits on Medicare payments to hospitals and then called for the design of a prospective hospital payment system. The creation of the Medicare Prospective Payment System (PPS) in 1984 was a watershed event in which hospitals henceforth would be paid for inpatient services based on prospectively set, case-adjusted rates. Under the PPS, a case-mix adjustment method known as diagnosis-related groups (DRGs) is used to set a price for all cases of a particular type (based on diagnosis, surgical procedures, and relevant risk factors). The payment system rewards hospitals for efficient behavior by allowing them to keep the surplus that accrues if they are able to keep the cost for that case below the fixed prospective payment but places them at risk for inefficient behavior in the event that the cost per case exceeds the prospective payment. As a result of this new payment method, the Medicare program began to exert considerable bargaining power in the marketplace, setting prices that it was willing to pay for inpatient services and forcing hospitals to recover their uncompensated costs by shifting those costs (charging higher prices) to the more lenient private payers and commercial insurers. Private payers eventually also began to adopt prospective payment methods—based either on DRG or on negotiated price—to contain hospital costs.

In 1986, the Medicare program began to explore prospective payment methods for physician services and over time developed a resource-based relative value scale approach that was later implemented in 1992 as part of the Medicare fee schedule for physicians. Private payers again followed suit, moving increasingly from traditional cost-based, FFS payment methods to prospective forms of payment for physicians, either negotiated discounts or capitated fees, by the early 1990s. These sweeping changes in payment method greatly altered the incentives for technology adoption and use, so that hospitals and physicians now had reasonably strong incentives to favor cost-saving technologies over cost-increasing technologies wherever possible (see table 5.8).

The adoption of aggressive managed care practices by private payers during the late 1980s and early 1990s reinforced this trend and signaled the beginning of a power shift between the public and private sectors in taking the lead in cost-containment efforts. Private payers increasingly resisted hospitals' efforts to charge higher prices for private patients, making it difficult for hospitals to recover the full cost of caring for Medicare and Medicaid patients. This, in turn, weakened the bargaining power of the public programs with hospitals, and they began to experience health care spending growth at rates that were much higher than private-sector spending growth. The short-lived prospect of national health care reform during 1992–94 further widened the disparity between private and public payers in cost-containment ability. The perceived regulatory threat posed by the Clinton administration's plan to reform the U.S. health care system through a combination of "managed competition" and expenditure controls (Starr 1992; Starr and Zelman 1993) caused the health insurance industry, including HMOs and managed care plans, to hold down premium increases and spending growth. Voluntary restraint by the pharmaceutical industry also led to minimal price increases for drugs during this period. By the time that the reform debate reached its conclusion in 1994, the threat of government intervention had evaporated, market forces had intensified as never before, and the balance of power within the system had shifted away from providers and toward purchasers and payers. The incentives for technology adoption and use were about to change dramatically as well.

1994 to the Present: Market-Driven Competition

The defeat of the Clinton health care reform plan (the American Health Security Act) ushered in a new age of market-driven competition. Since 1994, market forces within the health care system have intensified, producing the following changes:

- an enhanced role for employers and other purchasers/payers in all health care decisions, including choice of plans, services offered, and available technologies;
- increased enrollment in managed care plans and the expanded use of aggressive cost-reduction strategies to curtail costs and to limit access to expensive medical technologies;
- increased competition among health plans and providers for patients and clinicians;
- downsizing of many hospitals—and the closure of some—in response to financial and competitive pressures;
- increased consolidation among health plans and providers, including mergers, acquisitions, and the formation of strategic alliances and integrated delivery systems (leading in some areas to high market concentration);
- expanded interest among payers and consumers in the measurement, monitoring, and reporting of health plan performance;
- the shifting of many technology-based services out of the hospital inpatient setting into outpatient settings, including physicians' offices and the home;
- heightened consumer expectations regarding choice, access, and quality, concomitant with a backlash against the restrictive policies of managed care plans that has increasingly involved consumer resistance and litigation against plans and the enactment of legislation in some states to assure patients' rights; and
- increasingly negative reactions by consumers toward rapidly rising drug prices, managed care plans' multitiered copayment structures, and the lack of prescription drug coverage for Medicare beneficiaries.

These changes during the 1990s affected both private- and public-sector payment policies. In the private sector, managed care inspired health plans to employ prospective payment methods for hospitals and either capitated or discounted fees for physicians. In the public sector, states increasingly sought to enroll greater numbers of Medicaid recipients in managed care plans, and the Centers for Medicare and Medicaid Services (CMS) likewise encouraged Medicare beneficiaries to enroll in managed care plans under the Medicare + Choice program established under the Balanced Budget Act of 1997. However, since 2000, managed care plans have withdrawn from the Medicare + Choice program in increasing numbers, claiming that payments were insufficient to cover their costs, and those that remain have adopted more stringent cost-sharing arrangements and more restrictive drug coverage benefits that substitute lower-cost generic equivalents for brand-name pharmaceuticals (Achman and Gold 2002). Together, these various managed care practices and related policy developments since 1994 have created strong incentives for the adoption and use of cost-saving, quality-enhancing technologies above all others. (See chapter 5 for a detailed discussion of changing incentives under managed care.)

For reasons not fully understood—and therefore not necessarily attributable to the effects of managed care—the annual rate of growth in national health spending as a share of gross domestic product slowed greatly between 1995 and 1998 to levels not seen in almost thirty years (Levit et al. 2000). However, since 1999, clear signs have indicated that spending growth is again on the rise, driven in part by rapidly escalating pharmacy expenditures and hospital spending growth (Heffler et al. 2001; Levit et al. 2003). As a result, many private insurers and managed care organizations (MCOs), which had kept their premium levels low for competitive advantage during most of the 1990s, today are raising their premiums by as much as 15 to 20 percent per year. According to the CMS, premiums increased 10.5 percent nationally in 2001—the fourth consecutive year in which premiums rose (Levit et al. 2003). This growth in premiums has led some analysts to suggest that managed care may have had a "one-time only" impact on controlling spending growth (P. E. Mohr et al. 2001; Levit et al. 2003). Even so, market forces in health care are still likely to drive the technology decisions of various stakeholders for some time to come.

In the following pages, we examine the effectiveness of past cost-containment strategies and technology coverage policies, beginning with the private sector and concluding with the experiences of the federal government and the states.

Private Payment Strategies

As mentioned earlier in this chapter and elsewhere in the book (see chapters 2 and 5), private payers' retrospective, cost-based and FFS payment methods for hospitals and physicians contributed greatly to the swift diffusion of costly technologies and to the spiraling health care expenditures of the 1960s and 1970s (Goddeeris 1987; U.S. Congress, Congressional Budget Office 1991; GAO 1992b). Consequently, private payers increasingly became interested in alternative payment methodologies, such as competitively negotiated rates with preferred provider organizations (PPOs) and capitated (per patient) fee structures under HMOs and managed care networks.

Of these payment methodologies, PPO arrangements deviate the least from traditional FFS methods. Sponsored by insurers, hospitals, or physician groups, they build on provider discounts that have existed in the system for many years. However, by promoting selective contracting with limited numbers of providers (or even an exclusive provider), they seek even deeper discounts in exchange for steering patients to those providers (Rice et al. 1985). The proponents of PPOs have cited two major advantages: (1) by preserving much of the FFS structure, PPOs are less disruptive to providers than other payment changes; and (2) price negotiation with providers creates incentives for greater efficiency (Rice et al. 1985). Critics, however, have argued that PPOs have not achieved satisfactory cost savings. By negotiating on a unit price basis, they may actually create perverse incentives for providers to perform more tests, extend hospital lengths of stay, and increase the frequency of physician office visits. In addition, truly competitive price negotiation seems possible only in areas where multiple providers offer similar services (Boland 1987).

MCOs, especially those employing an independent practice association model, enjoyed rapid growth during the 1990s. Although MCOs vary structurally—from the looser independent practice association, network, and group models to the highly centralized, traditional staff-model HMO—many include gatekeeper physicians who manage and coordinate patients' care and determine access to specialists, hospitals, and other resources. Because physician payment in these plans is highly constrained—either through contractually negotiated or capitated fees or, in the case of staff-model HMOs, salaried arrangements—there are financial disincentives for physicians to use resources excessively and to make specialist referrals unnecessarily. Under some MCO structures, physicians may even incur financial penalties for inappropriate referrals (Eastaugh 1992).

Although MCOs in the late 1980s and early 1990s were heralded by some as having successfully decreased total health care costs in under-sixty-five populations, other analysts argued that the observed savings either reflected the low-risk (and hence low-use) characteristics of these fairly healthy populations or came primarily from reduced hospital admissions and inpatient days that may not be sustainable over time

(Chernew et al. 1998). During the mid-1990s, many MCOs kept their premiums artificially low to attract and capture greater market share in their areas, even as their costs, most notably pharmacy costs, rose precipitously (Heffler et al. 2001). National spending on prescription drugs increased 15.7 percent in 2001, marking the seventh consecutive year of double-digit growth (Levit et al. 2003). To stem rising pharmacy expenditures, MCOs have adopted multiple cost-containment strategies that include (1) strengthening the control of internal pharmacy and therapeutics committees over the list of approved drugs in their formularies (see chapter 5 for a description of such committees and their role in the adoption and use of new pharmaceuticals); (2) negotiating with pharmaceutical firms and major drug distributors to obtain more favorable prices for expensive prescription drugs; (3) instituting three-tiered copayment structures that encourage consumers to demand and physicians to prescribe generic equivalents or lower-cost variants of brand-name drugs; and (4) contracting out the management of pharmacy spending to specialized firms known as pharmacy benefits managers to undertake all of these activities and more.

As MCOs became increasingly competitive during the 1990s, they also began to limit or deny access to certain costly services, especially technology-intensive ones, thereby incurring patients' wrath in the process. Some MCOs (e.g., Kaiser Permanente of Northern California and Aetna U.S. Healthcare) instituted ongoing appeals processes—both internal and external to the plan—to handle denials of coverage (Daniels and Sabin 1998), but many did very little to address public concern, causing various states to pass legislation that (1) forced MCOs to make full disclosure of financial incentives within their payment structures for physicians, (2) lifted "gag rules" imposed by MCOs that prevented physicians from providing patients with full information about the range of clinical alternatives available to them, and (3) mandated coverage and minimum lengths of stay for certain services (e.g., childbirth and mastectomies). While the potential health benefits of mandated minimum stay legislation remain unclear, one study of Pennsylvania's maternal length-of-stay law found that as much as $20 million may have been added to the annual health care costs associated with births in Philadelphia (Webb et al. 2001). In the meantime, consumers nationwide have been choosing less restrictive forms of managed care, with the share covered by PPOs rising from 35 percent in 1998 to 41 percent in 2000 at the expense of conventional FFS and point-of-service plans (Levit et al. 2002).

Efforts by private payers, such as the Blue Cross and Blue Shield Association and various MCOs, including Kaiser Permanente, to gather and analyze information on emerging and new technologies are described in chapter 9. Technology reports issued by Blue Cross plans and other payers nationwide have served as the industry standard for guiding decisions about coverage and payment levels for diffusing technologies (Rettig 1997). Except for anecdotal accounts of denied coverage for some technologies, it is doubtful that these policies had significant cost-constraining effects under the old regime marked by retrospective cost-based and FFS payment (Cohen and Nichols 1993; M. Gold 1993). Conversely, evidence-based MTE reports may have greater value in the current environment of managed care, since MCOs face strong financial incentives to minimize unnecessary duplication of resources and excessive use of services. While some observers think that capitated fee arrangements create cost-consciousness conducive to MTE activities, it is unclear whether this situation translates into cost savings (Rettig 1997; Chernew et al. 1998), and in today's highly competitive marketplace, many plans are retreating from capitated fee structures because of intense resistance from physician groups, referral networks, and academic health centers with whom the plans maintain working relationships.

Medicare Prospective Payment for Hospitals and Physicians

Since 1983, prospective payment systems have been replacing cost-based and FFS systems for health care delivered to Medicare beneficiaries in nearly every sector of care. To date, Medicare prospective payment systems have been developed and implemented for hospital inpatient care, physician services, end-stage renal disease, ambulatory surgery centers, psychiatric facilities, skilled nursing facilities, home health care, hospital outpatient care, and post-acute-care inpatient services delivered in rehabilitation facilities and long-term hospitals (MedPAC 2001, 2003). Each of these payment systems is complex and is administered by the CMS, with analytic guidance and support from the Medicare Payment Advisory Commission (MedPAC). In advising the CMS on various aspects of Medicare payment policy, MedPAC monitors the financial performance of Medicare providers and makes recommendations regarding payment methods, updates, adjustments, and pass-throughs, taking into account the effects of new technologies as they diffuse into practice (MedPAC 2001).

Medicare payment policy has undergone sweeping change in recent years with the passage of three major federal laws—the Balanced Budget Act of 1997, the Balanced Budget Refinement Act of 1999, and the Medicare, Medicaid, and State Children's Health Insurance Program Benefits Improvement and Protection Act of 2000. For a detailed description of current Medicare payment policy, see MedPAC's report to Congress (2003), which is issued annually in March. We focus here on current Medicare payment policy and technology coverage processes as they relate to hospitals and physicians.

Medicare PPS for Hospital Inpatient Care

Structure of the Inpatient Payment System

The Medicare PPS for hospital inpatient care has long been the preeminent model of prospective payment, with hospitals receiving annually updated case-based payments for DRGs in a risk-reward structure (M. Gold et al. 1993). The DRGs represent a patient classification system in which hospital inpatient cases are (1) grouped according to similar clinical conditions that are treated with common medical or surgical treatment strategies and (2) priced separately because they are expected to require different amounts or types of providers' resources (MedPAC 2001, 2003). The inpatient PPS today consists of three core components:

- operating and capital base payment rates that reflect the average cost of Medicare cases nationwide, adjusted for the relative costliness of inputs (e.g., wages) in a hospital's local area;
- case weights that account for the relative costliness of each DRG compared with the national average Medicare case; and
- special adjustments that include outlier payments for unusually costly cases (patients with high resource use or long lengths of stay), an indirect medical education adjustment that reflects the higher costs of teaching hospitals, and a disproportionate share adjustment for hospitals that have a high burden of uncompensated care provided to low-income patients (MedPAC 2001, 2003).

Special allowances are also made to urban hospitals and to rural hospitals that are designated as sole community providers.

Expenses for capital investments and graduate medical education activities originally were not included in the DRG computations. Capital costs (building and equipment costs—largely debt service and depreciation—allocated to Medicare's inpatient services) instead were treated as fixed-percentage pass-through expenses in the early years of the PPS. Beginning in fiscal year 1992, however, a prospectively determined amount per hospital discharge was paid to hospitals for Medicare inpatient capital-related costs, so that the costs of actual equipment (e.g., MRI and lithotripters) were paid under this method, while the associated operating costs continued to be paid under the DRG-based system (GAO 1994). This form of Medicare capital PPS was phased in from 1992 to 2001, and all hospitals today are paid on the basis of national prospective rates (MedPAC 2000).

Graduate medical education expenses incurred by teaching hospitals traditionally were paid in two ways: (1) through a direct payment, separate from PPS payments, to cover Medicare's share of the direct costs related to graduate medical education (the salaries of residents and supervising physicians, office space, and other overhead expenses) and (2) through an indirect medical education adjustment to PPS payments to support the higher patient care costs associated with the training of residents (MedPAC 1998, 2001). For operating costs, the indirect medical education adjustment was based on the hospital's ratio of interns and residents to the number of beds; for capital costs, the adjustment was based on the hospital's ratio of interns and residents to average daily occupancy (MedPAC 2001). In 1999, however, MedPAC urged policymakers to view the two graduate medical education payments as compensation for patient care rather than training and recommended combining them into a single payment adjustment by folding the costs for inpatient direct graduate medical education into PPS rates through a revised indirect medical education adjustment to teaching hospitals' payments (MedPAC 2000).

Treatment of New Technology in the Inpatient Payment System
Historically, the costs of new technology in hospital inpatient care were addressed in the inpatient PPS through four principal mechanisms:

1. assignment of International Classification of Diseases—Ninth Revision—Case Mix codes to new technologies and periodic deletion of codes for outdated technologies;
2. periodic revision of the DRG classification system to reflect changes in the relative costliness of cases within DRGs, so that certain types of cases may be reassigned to a different DRG or

a particular DRG may be split into two or more new groupings and the case weights adjusted accordingly when circumstances warrant;

3. annual recalibration of the DRG case weights to reflect the costliness of cases in the previous year; and

4. annual updates in the base payment rates to adjust for increases in operating and capital costs associated with new technology (GAO 1994; MedPAC 2001).

The methods for updating the base payment rates, however, differed by type of expense, with Congress legislating updates for operating payments on an annual basis (and, more recently, on a three- to five-year basis) and the CMS, in conjunction with MedPAC, setting updates for capital payments through an annual rule-making process (MedPAC 2001).

The Benefits Improvement and Protection Act of 2000 changed the method of paying for new technology in the inpatient PPS, mandating that the CMS

- develop a process to incorporate new technologies expeditiously into the International Classification of Diseases—Ninth Revision—Case Mix coding system;
- collect data on the costs of new technologies for a period of two to three years and then assign cases that use the new technologies into new or existing DRGs whose case weights have been derived from the data collected; and
- provide for additional payment to cover the costs of each new technology, either in the form of "new technology" DRGs with case weights reflecting the average costs of patients using the technologies or as an add-on or adjustment to the "standard" DRG payment for cases in which the technology is used (MedPAC 2001).

The first two mandates formalized many of the procedures that had been used in the inpatient PPS for some time, but the third deviated significantly from past policy, paralleling the pass-through payment provision that was implemented in the new outpatient PPS (discussed later in this chapter).

To encourage hospitals to adopt new quality-enhancing but cost-increasing technologies that would benefit Medicare beneficiaries, Med-

PAC since 1999 has included an allowance for scientific and technological advances in its update framework for hospital payments (MedPAC 2001). The scientific and technological advances adjustment applies only to new technologies that have progressed beyond the experimental stage of development but have not yet diffused broadly in the hospital inpatient setting (MedPAC 2001). In deriving the allowance for fiscal year 2002, MedPAC examined new technologies in five categories (information systems, drugs and biologics, devices and diagnostics, imaging technology, and surgical/procedural techniques and other technological advances), estimated the net of the new and old technology costs for each, and calculated an aggregate scientific and technological advances adjustment to reflect the incremental increase in costs that would result from hospitals adopting new technologies or applying existing technologies in new ways beyond the costs automatically covered in the base payments received by the hospitals (MedPAC 2001).

The Effectiveness of the Inpatient PPS in Cost Containment
When introduced in 1983, the risk-reward structure of the hospital inpatient PPS was thought to provide incentives for minimizing the length of stay and for using resources more efficiently. Analysts at the time also thought it might create a perverse incentive for hospitals to increase admissions to maximize the number of profitable cases that could be treated (Goddeeris 1987; McCarthy 1988). However, admissions data for the period 1983 through 1987 indicated that hospital admissions for all patients declined and that for patients over age sixty-five, the average annual rate of decline was 2.2 percent, compared with an average annual increase of 5.2 percent during 1972–82 (McCarthy 1988). DRG-based prospective payment also was theorized to discourage the adoption of technology whose benefits were unproven while encouraging the adoption of cost-saving technology (Goddeeris 1987).

Whether the Medicare inpatient PPS had the desired effect on hospital expenditures is arguable (S. Altman and Young 1993; M. Gold et al. 1993). Overall, the inpatient PPS appeared to restrain the historical growth of Medicare Part A (hospital) expenditures by as much as 20 percent between 1983 and 1990 (Russell and Manning 1989; Coulam and Gaumer 1992). However, in doing so, the inpatient PPS also (1) eroded hospital Medicare profit margins during that period; (2) caused hospitals to shift costs to other payers, especially private payers; and (3) was associated with increases in postacute services, particularly nursing home care and home health services (Long et al. 1987; Morrissey, Sloan, and Valvona 1988), and in outpatient services, including preadmission testing and ambulatory surgery (M. Gold et al. 1993).

Medicare PPS inpatient margins for hospitals, which exceeded 13 percent in each of the program's first two years, fell to 3 percent by the fifth year and became negative in the seventh year. By 1991, the average margin had fallen to −2.4 percent (MedPAC 1998). Declining Medicare inpatient margins were thought to have diverted hospitals' attention away from efficiency-improvement strategies toward revenue-maximizing schemes involving the transfer of care (and costs) to outpatient settings and to nonhospital providers, where more lucrative FFS payment generally could be obtained. Technology-based services were among those affected by these shifts: prime examples included outpatient chemotherapy, enteral and parenteral nutrition, and respiratory therapy (Rollo 1987). Between 1980 and 1991, Medicare expenditures for hospital outpatient and clinical laboratory services increased 450 percent, and the number of ambulatory surgery procedures grew by more than 500 percent (ProPAC 1992). Although the inpatient PPS was not solely responsible for these trends, it clearly was a contributing factor.

Starting in 1992, Medicare PPS inpatient margins began to rise, reaching a healthy 11.1 percent by 1995 and climbing to an all-time high of 16.9 percent before declining thereafter (MedPAC 2001). Hospital total operating margins followed a similar pattern—after an initial decline from 7.3 percent in 1984 to about 3.6 percent between 1987 and 1990, they rose in the early 1990s, leading S. Altman and Young (1993) to conclude that hospitals had indeed shifted costs to private payers. By 1996, hospital total margins had risen to 6.1 percent, indicating that the hospital industry had adapted quite well to a highly competitive environment by changing practice patterns, reducing costs, and improving financial performance, at least for the time being (MedPAC 2001). However, with the Medicare payment cutbacks imposed by the Balanced Budget Act of 1997, Medicare hospital inpatient margins fell to 13.7 percent in 1998 and to 12.0 percent in 1999 (MedPAC 2001). Private payers also cut their payments during this period, placing great pressure on hospitals and causing total margins to decline markedly to 2.8 percent by 1999 (MedPAC 2001). Signs of improvement appeared in early 2000, however, with hospital total margins rebounding to a seasonally adjusted 5.1 percent for the first two quarters of the year (MedPAC 2001). Nonetheless, the financial status of many American hospitals in the early twenty-first century remains somewhat precarious.

Medicare PPS for Hospital Outpatient Care

Structure of the Outpatient Payment System
The Medicare PPS for hospital outpatient care is a relatively new pay-ment system, implemented in August 2000. In a manner analogous to the DRG classification system for inpatient care, outpatient services are classified into ambulatory payment classification (APC) groups. Ser-vices are grouped according to similar clinical characteristics and sim-ilar resource use, with the unit of payment being the individual serv-ice. If, however, a patient receives multiple services during the course of an outpatient visit, the hospital receives a separate payment for each service. Payment for a service in an APC group usually includes lim-ited bundling of ancillary services and supplies that are associated with the primary service; payment for outpatient surgery, however, contains extensive bundling, covering the hospital's costs for the operating and recovery rooms, anesthesia, most drugs, and most surgical supplies used during the surgery (MedPAC 2001).

Treatment of New Technology in the Outpatient Payment System
The outpatient PPS responds to the incremental costs of new technol-ogy in two ways: (1) by assigning a new service to a separate "new technology" APC group to ensure timely payment for a new technol-ogy that constitutes a new service that is similar in cost to an existing technology but is not necessarily clinically similar and (2) by making a cost-based, pass-through payment to supplement the standard APC payment when a specific technology is used as an input to an outpa-tient service but does not represent a distinct service (MedPAC 2001). A technology that is classified under a new technology APC remains in that grouping for two to three years while the CMS collects needed clinical and cost data before assigning it to an existing or new standard APC group. Pass-through payments for certain new drugs, biologics, and medical devices were authorized under the Balanced Budget Re-finement Act of 1999. For drugs and biologics, supplemental payments are set at 95 percent of the average wholesale price, while pass-through payments for medical devices are based on each hospital's costs. Be-cause such cost-based payments encourage hospitals to adopt new de-vices as long as their incremental costs are covered, these payments are potentially inflationary. Thus, they remain in effect for only two to three years until standard payment rates can be modified to include the costs of new devices (MedPAC 2001). To encourage the adoption and

use of quality-enhancing technologies in the outpatient setting, Med-PAC recommended in its March 2001 report to the CMS and Congress that

- a formalized procedure for expeditiously assigning service/ procedure codes and for updating the APC groups to reflect the costs of new and substantially improved technologies should be adopted;
- pass-through payments for specific technologies should be made only when a technology is new or substantially improved and adds substantially to the cost of care in an APC group; and
- pass-through payments should be made on a budget-neutral basis, and the costs of new or substantially improved technologies should be factored into the update to the outpatient conversion factor.

Physician Payment

In response to steeply rising Medicare Part B expenditures for physicians' services during the mid-1980s, Congress initiated physician payment reform in 1989, seeking to create incentives for greater efficiency through a prospective Medicare physician fee schedule that aligned payment more closely with actual resource costs (M. Gold et al. 1993). Specifically, the physician fee schedule contained a resource-based relative value scale that was intended to correct for the bias inherent in the existing payment structure that favored surgical and technological procedures relative to physicians' cognitive and consultative functions in patient care. The reform also placed limits on balance billing by physicians and called for the establishment of volume performance standards that would aid in setting expenditure targets for determining future fee increases (Ginsburg, LeRoy, and Hammons 1990; M. Gold et al. 1993; PPRC 1993). The payment method was not fully implemented within the physician fee schedule until 1992, and despite expectations that payments to specialists would decrease while payments to primary care physicians would increase, experience in the early 1990s suggested that structural flaws in the system were responsible for perpetuating the payment disparities between specialists and generalists (Hsiao, Dunn, and Verrilli 1993). Also, the physician fee schedule and the volume performance standards did not appear to have strong cost-containment effects on Medicare Part B expenditures for technology-related services, as both service volumes and expenditures continued to rise in the early 1990s (PPRC 1993).

In the late 1990s, the Medicare physician fee schedule was modified to take into account three types of resources used to provide physicians' services: physician work, practice expense, and malpractice insurance expense (MedPAC 1998). Up until 1999, only the physician work component was based on an assessment of the actual resources used to deliver care, with the remaining components based on historical charges (MedPAC 1998). The Balanced Budget Act of 1997, however, required that resource-based values be phased in for practice expense in 1999 and for malpractice insurance expense in 2000. To derive the payment for a given physician service, the relative value assigned to each component first was summed to create the total relative value for that service, and then the total relative value was multiplied by a dollar conversion factor that is updated annually (MedPAC 1998). Since 1999, updates have been determined by the sustainable-growth-rate system, which replaced the volume-performance-standards method as a means of holding spending growth in physicians' services to an expenditure target in line with that of the general economy (MedPAC 1998). The Balanced Budget Refinement Act of 1999 subsequently required the secretary of the Department of Health and Human Services—through the Agency for Healthcare Research and Quality (AHRQ)—to report to Congress by November 2002 on the use of physician services by Medicare beneficiaries, with specific consideration given to three factors: improvements in medical capabilities, advances in scientific technology, and demographic changes in the types of beneficiaries under the Medicare program (MedPAC 2000). Recently, however, MedPAC has called for the replacement of the sustainable-growth-rate system with an update method that better accounts for the costs of providing care (MedPAC 2001). (For a detailed description of current Medicare physician payment policy as well as changes mandated by the Balanced Budget Act of 1997 and the Balanced Budget Refinement Act of 1999, see MedPAC's recent reports [2001, 2003] to Congress.)

Medicare Coverage Policy for New Technology

Procedures and Criteria for Making Technology Coverage Decisions
The CMS is responsible for tracking emerging technologies and patterns of care to determine applicability of existing national Medicare coverage

policy and to assess the need for policy change (CMS 2001). Coverage for a technology is based on whether its use falls within the scope of Medicare-covered items and services; if so, payment levels for hospital and physician services that use the technology are set according to the methods described earlier in this chapter. The procedures for making Medicare coverage decisions are complex and may be found in the *Federal Register* or at the CMS's Web site, http://www.hcfa.gov/coverage. Each year, the CMS makes several national coverage decisions that are binding on all Medicare carriers, fiscal intermediaries, peer review organizations, Medicare + Choice organizations, and other contractors (Medicare Program; Criteria 2000). However, the CMS relies heavily on its Medicare intermediaries and contractors to make numerous local coverage decisions whenever the need arises (GAO 1994). In the case of national coverage decisions, the CMS collects information from multiple sources (e.g., the FDA and medical specialty societies) but places great importance on the technology assessments provided by the AHRQ's Center for Practice and Technology Assessment (see chapters 2, 9, and 11).

Historically, the criteria applied in making coverage determinations included the technology's safety and effectiveness (as evidenced by its approval by the FDA, in the case of a drug or device) and its appropriateness as a service for Medicare beneficiaries (whether it met the Medicare definition of a "reasonable and necessary" service). In a proposed rule published on January 30, 1989, in the *Federal Register*, the Medicare program broadened its criteria to include (1) safety and effectiveness, (2) experimental or investigational, (3) appropriateness, and (4) cost-effectiveness (Medicare Program; Proposed Rule 1989). The proposed addition of cost-effectiveness as a criterion to help guide Medicare coverage decisions was extremely controversial, generating extensive public debate and garnering strong opposition from the various technology industries. After a decade of deliberation, the CMS announced in the April 27, 1999, *Federal Register* its intention to withdraw the proposed rule and to propose instead a new rule that would include two criteria to govern national coverage decisions and local coverage decisions (Medicare Program; Procedures 1999; Medicare Program; Criteria 2000). To be covered, an item or service first must demonstrate evidence of medical benefit for a defined population; if beneficial, the item or service must then demonstrate added value to the Medicare population. An item or service would have added value if it (1) provides medical benefit when there is no similar Medicare-covered clinical alternative, (2) is substantially more beneficial than an existing Medicare-covered alternative, or (3) is equivalent in benefit to a Medicare-covered alternative but results in equivalent or lower total costs for the Medicare population than the Medicare-covered alternative (Medicare Program; Criteria 2000).

For many years, national coverage decisions were finalized with input from the CMS's Technology Advisory Committee, a twenty-six-member group that met quarterly and comprised mostly CMS physicians and medical directors from Medicare contractors (GAO 1994). In November 1998, the secretary of the Department of Health and Human Services chartered the Medicare Coverage Advisory Committee to advise the CMS on whether specific medical items and services were reasonable and necessary under Medicare law (CMS 2001). Although advisory in nature—the final decision on all issues rests with the CMS—the committee plays a critical role in supplementing the CMS's internal expertise on technology and science (CMS 2001). The committee consists of six medical specialty panels, each of which "evaluates medical literature, reviews technical assessments, and examines data and information on the effectiveness and appropriateness" of specific services that are covered or are eligible for coverage under Medicare (CMS 2001). Composed of experts from academia, industry, and consumer organizations, the six panels include diagnostic imaging; drugs, biologics, and therapeutics; durable medical equipment; laboratory and diagnostic services; medical and surgical procedures; and medical devices and prosthetics. An executive committee comprising the chairs of all panels, an at-large member, and representatives of consumer and industry interests provides overall guidance and coordination to the panels and reviews and ratifies panel recommendations (CMS 2001). In February 2001, the Medicare Coverage Advisory Committee's executive committee recommended that panels evaluate the effectiveness of a new technology, compared to established services or medical items, by placing it into one of seven categories, as shown in table 12.1.

Historically, the Medicare program did not pay for health care services provided as part of clinical trials because of their experimental nature. Thus, Medicare beneficiaries did not have access to any experimental drugs and therapies that had not yet been approved by the FDA. (See chapter 10 for descriptions of the FDA premarket approval processes for new drugs and devices.) However, on June 7, 2000, President Bill Clinton issued an executive memorandum directing the secretary of the Department of Health and Human Services to "explicitly authorize [Medicare] payment for routine patient care costs . . . and costs due to medical complications associated with participation in clinical trials" (CMS 2001). To implement this presidential directive, the CMS issued a national coverage decision specifying what constitutes "routine costs" in a clinical trial and setting forth a qualification process for clinical trials. Trials automatically deemed to qualify for Medicare coverage include those funded by federal agencies (NIH, CDC, AHRQ, CMS, the Department of Defense, and the Department of Veterans Affairs), those conducted under an investigational new drug application reviewed by the FDA, and those that are exempt from having an investigational new drug application (CMS 2001). The CMS also requested that the AHRQ form a multiagency federal panel to develop explicit qualifying criteria for scientifically sound clinical trials (CMS 2001).

Effects of Medicare Coverage Policy on the Adoption and Use of New Technology

The Medicare coverage process at times can be difficult and long, but there is little evidence to suggest that Medicare coverage policy has had a strong constraining or deterrent effect on the adoption and use of new technology. Decisions involving simple issues or expansion of ex-

---

TABLE 12.1. The Medicare Coverage Advisory Committee's Framework for Classifying New Technology on the Basis of Effectiveness

1. *Breakthrough technology:* The improvement in health outcomes is so large that the intervention becomes the standard of care.
2. *More effective:* The new intervention improves health outcomes by a significant, albeit small, margin as compared with established services or medical items.
3. *As effective but with advantages:* The intervention has the same effect on health outcomes as established services or medical items but has some advantages (convenience, rapidity of effect, fewer side effects, other advantages) that some patients will prefer.
4. *As effective and with no advantages:* The intervention has the same effect on health outcomes as established alternatives but with no advantages.
5. *Less effective but with advantages:* Although the intervention is less effective than established alternatives (but more effective than doing nothing), it has some advantages (such as convenience, tolerability).
6. *Less effective and with no advantages:* The intervention is less effective than established alternatives (but more effective than doing nothing) and has no significant advantages.
7. *Not effective:* The intervention has no effect or has deleterious effects on health outcomes when compared with doing nothing (e.g., treatment with placebo or patient management without the use of a diagnostic test).

Source: Data from Medicare Coverage Advisory Committee (MCAC) 2001.

isting coverage policy usually take two to twelve months to complete, whereas decisions involving more complex technologies or clinical issues often take several years. For example, the Medicare program took nearly five years to decide to cover liver transplants and more than ten years to withdraw coverage for thermography, a discredited diagnostic technique (GAO 1994). In the case of MRI during the 1980s, the Medicare program was slow to cover the new technology even though FDA approval had been obtained and private payers, such as Blue Cross plans and commercial insurers, were moving swiftly to cover it (Steinberg and Cohen 1984; GAO 1992a). Similarly, positron emission tomography (PET) diffused very slowly during the 1990s because hospitals waited for the Medicare program's coverage decision before investing in the technology. Although PET increasingly is becoming the key imaging modality for diagnosing many forms of cancer and holds promise for the diagnosis of Alzheimer's disease, Medicare coverage for the use of PET for several types of cancer was not granted until 2000 (C. Becker 2001).

Failure of the coverage process to encourage cost-effective diffusion of technology within the Medicare program has been documented in other cases, including those of hemodialysis (Maxwell and Sapolsky 1989) and cochlear implants (Kane and Manoukian 1989). Recent changes in Medicare coverage policy to broaden the criteria for review and in payment policy for both inpatient and outpatient services (as described earlier) address many of these shortcomings. However, the CMS still needs to revise its Medicare coverage and payment policies for new technology to allow for (1) more timely evaluation of emerging and new technologies, (2) more explicit consideration of cost-effectiveness as a criterion for review, and (3) more active ongoing assessment of the value of established (and possibly outdated) technologies that should be removed from coverage.

Medicaid Payment Policies

In making technology coverage and payment decisions, state Medicaid programs generally follow the lead of the Medicare program, covering new technologies when CMS national coverage decisions are available. In the absence of such national coverage decisions, Medicaid programs tend to rely on individual providers (e.g., hospitals, health plans, and physician groups) with whom the states have contractual relationships to identify new technologies that require coverage decisions. Two crite-ria are generally used in making a coverage determination. First, the medical necessity of the technology must be established—that is, the technology must offer a Medicaid recipient a medical service for which there is no other equally effective course of treatment available that is either more conservative or substantially less costly. Second, if medical necessity has been demonstrated, evidence of FDA approval for the technology must then be established so that it may be listed in the Med-icaid contract as a standard benefit. In some cases, individual plans un-dertake limited assessments of new technology to meet these criteria, but in other instances, the state Medicaid agency performs the review, turning to the CMS, the FDA, and other sources for information. Once coverage of a new technology has been approved, a payment level is set based on existing Medicaid policy in that particular state.

The state of Oregon received a federal waiver of Medicaid rules in 1993 to implement a new payment methodology in which a priority list of condition-treatment pairs (originally 714, but later reduced to 574) would guide decisions for covered services under a universal health care plan (Welch and Fisher 1992). The state developed its priority-ranking methodology based on values assigned by the public to a host of health states and treatments (Welch and Fisher 1992). After obtain-ing a five-year renewal of its federal waiver, the program appeared to improve access to care while quelling concerns that it would ration care to terminally ill and disabled persons (Demkovich 1998). Although some policymakers and observers remain concerned about the pro-gram's failure to deliver expected savings and about the access prob-lems faced by many poor individuals (Kilborn 1999), others have hailed it as a model for mobilizing political support in an inhospitable environment (Jacobs, Marmor, and Oberlander 1999; Leichter 1999).

The poor economic climate of the early twenty-first century presents state governments with severe fiscal challenges unseen in almost a decade (Pound 2002). With state revenues declining as part of the na-tional recession and total Medicaid spending in 2001 soaring by 10.8 percent nationally, many states are struggling to maintain their Medic-aid program budgets without cutting services to their low-income citi-zens (Levit et al. 2003; Pear and Toner 2002). The pressure to reduce costs already has made prescription drug spending a major target for cost control, and many states have united to form regional purchasing coalitions that leverage their bargaining power with drug firms (Gold, Hensley, and Caffrey 2001; National Conference 2001). One drug manufacturer, Pfizer, recently responded to pressure from consumers and politicians by announcing that it would sell its prescription drugs—including such top sellers as Lipitor (a cholesterol-lowering drug) and Zoloft (an antidepressant)—to low-income senior citizens at a flat fee of $15 per month (Hensley 2002).

State Rate-Setting Systems

State rate-setting programs for the prospective regulation of hospital payment rates originated in the 1970s (M. Gold et al. 1993) and were of three basic types: (1) Medicaid only, the least comprehensive form; (2) partial-payer systems, in which rates were usually set for Medicaid and private payers only; and (3) all-payer systems, in which service prices were set for all payers, including Medicare. By 1980, twenty-seven states had adopted rate setting (M. Gold et al. 1993), but most programs were voluntary and partial payer in nature. Only four states (Maryland, Massachusetts, New Jersey, and New York) implemented all-payer systems during the 1980s, and by 1998 all except Maryland had abandoned their programs as private payers moved to PPOs and MCOs and public payers (Medicare and Medicaid) sought to enroll greater numbers of their beneficiaries in managed care plans (G. F. Anderson 1992).

State rate-setting programs varied considerably in their approaches and methods, but incentives to reduce the adoption and use of technology always were secondary to the prime objective of hospital cost containment. For reasons similar to those described for the Medicare PPS, analyses of the effectiveness of rate-setting programs produced mixed and even conflicting results. Several studies found states with all-payer systems to be effective in constraining their spending growth, with mandatory programs more effective than voluntary programs (Coelen and Sullivan 1981; Sloan 1983; Schramm, Renn, and Biles 1986; Hadley and Swartz 1989). However, other studies challenged these findings, claiming that rate setting may have had a onetime effect and, by focusing on inpatient care, generally ignored the large shift in services from inpatient to outpatient settings (Finkler 1987; Rosko 1989).

There have been few studies of the effects of rate setting on the adoption and use of technology, but at least one analysis suggested that mandatory programs may have slowed the rate of technology adoption by hospitals (G. F. Anderson 1992). A second study found that complex technological services diffused at 75 percent of the national rate in states with mandatory programs but that these effects could not be disentangled from those of CON programs operating in those states (Cromwell and Kanak 1982). A third study—involving technology diffusion in Indiana, Maryland, and New York—found that New York's all-payer system had inhibited the diffusion of five little-ticket technologies but that no effect could be discerned for systems in the other two states (Romeo, Wagner, and Lee 1984)

While rate-setting systems might in theory hold promise for more rational adoption and use of technology, to be effective in the twenty-first century such systems would need to be mandatory, with all-payer structures that encompass ambulatory care as well as hospital care (Cohen and Nichols 1993). The sole remaining program (Maryland) is an example of how rate-setting systems might be configured to constrain systemwide costs (G. F. Anderson, Chaulk, and Fowler 1993). However, given the prevailing climate of market-driven competition in health care and the great interest in managed care exhibited by both private and public payers, it is highly unlikely that regulatory programs of this kind will be adopted anywhere else within the nation in the near future.

Managed care in both the private and public sectors provides clear incentives for the adoption of cost-saving, quality-enhancing technologies and, not surprisingly, disincentives for the adoption of technologies that are either cost increasing or quality decreasing. The gatekeeper mechanism within managed care is intended to constrain the overuse of technological services, while the use of capitated payment in provider contracts is designed to place providers at financial risk for their clinical decisions involving the management of patient care. The greatest challenge, then, for payers and providers will be to deal with cost-increasing but quality-enhancing technologies, which may well comprise the majority of biomedical innovations (see chapter 5). The expansion in recent years of federally supported research, especially by the AHRQ in the areas of patient outcomes, evidence-based practice, and patient safety, should produce more systematic evaluation of medical technologies, the results of which are likely to influence future payment policies.

13

Access and Equity Concerns: Medical Technology and System Capacity Controls
Alan B. Cohen and Ruth S. Hanft*

As described in chapter 12, various payment policies—public and private—have attempted to slow the rate of growth in health care spending as well as indirectly to influence the adoption of technology through financial incentives. Policies aimed directly at controlling the adoption of technology, however, have dealt either with its introduction into clinical practice (see chapter 10 regarding FDA regulation of drugs and devices) or with its distribution. Distribution refers to the physical allocation of a technology among providers (Cohen and Cohodes 1982) and, by definition, raises a host of concerns regarding impeded access and equity among populations and individuals.

In this chapter, we focus on distributional policies that have attempted to regulate technology adoption through system capacity controls, most notably capital expenditure review programs. Although the federal government at one time engaged in capital expenditure review (through the old section 1122 program), the principal policy instruments for controlling the capacity of the health care system today are state certificate-of-need (CON) programs. In this chapter, we trace the origins and early history of state CON programs; examine their goals, strategies, and effects; and discuss their current role in state regulatory policy. We then recount the disparate experiences of two technologies—both diagnostic imaging modalities—that emerged in different eras: X-ray computed tomography (CT) in the 1970s and magnetic resonance imaging (MRI) in the 1980s. We also address various financial,

---

*With the research assistance of Shirley A. Stewart and Catherine C. White.

geographic, and demographic barriers that may limit access to technology for some populations, and we conclude by exploring regulatory policies dealing with organ transplantation.

The Origins and History of State CON Programs

Historically, strategies to regulate the distribution of technology were focused primarily at the state level in the form of CON programs charged with performing capital expenditure review. The first such effort originated in 1964 with the passage of New York state's CON statute. In the ensuing ten years, twenty-six additional states adopted CON laws. The real impetus for this strategy, however, came from the unintended effects of several federal legislative initiatives (L. D. Brown 1983; Simpson 1985). With the 1946 Hill-Burton Act providing capital for hospital construction and the 1965 Medicare and Medicaid legislation promising expanded patient revenues as well as payment for capital costs, U.S. hospitals experienced a period of accelerated construction. Congress, however, was concerned about the cost and quality implications of this building boom and in 1966 enacted the Comprehensive Health Planning and Public Services Amendments to the Social Security Act to address this concern.

Federal Health Planning and Section 1122 Capital Expenditure Review

The federal health planning amendments provided funding to promote voluntary hospital participation in regional planning, with community leaders identifying health needs and coordinating public, private, and voluntary resources to meet these needs. However, the legislation contained few incentives for hospital compliance and spawned planning agencies that were dominated by physicians and hospital managers (Morone 1990; Jee 1993).

In the early 1970s, Congress strengthened the health planning legislation by enacting the Social Security Amendments of 1972, in which section 1122 called for planning agency review and approval of all proposals that involved hospital capital expenditures exceeding $100,000, changes in bed capacity, or substantial changes in services (Simpson 1985). The penalty for hospital noncompliance with the section 1122 capital expenditure review process was denial of federal reimbursement for the Medicare and Medicaid portions of the capital depreciation expenses associated with the unapproved project. Noncompliant states also were at risk of losing their federal Maternal and Child Health Program block grants. By 1975, forty-six states were conducting capital expenditure review under either or both of the section 1122 and state CON regulations (Simpson 1985).

The Rise and Fall of Federal Health Planning and State CON Programs

The Health Planning and Resources Development Act of 1974 created a national network of health systems agencies and state health planning and development agencies whose major roles were to develop comprehensive health plans for their communities and states, respectively, and to review proposed capital expenditures for congruence with these plans. The act also required state CON programs to be in conformance with federal standards for capital expenditure review as a condition for receiving Public Health Service funds. This meant that states without CON laws would have to enact federally compliant statutes, while states with active CON programs would have to review and if necessary amend their existing laws and regulations to comply with the federal standards.

A number of start-up problems delayed the implementation of the act, and by 1978 only eight states had passed CON statutes that met federal standards (J. B. Brown and Saltman 1985; Morone 1990; Mendelson and Arnold 1993). Nevertheless, by 1982, forty-nine states (the exception was Louisiana) and the District of Columbia had enacted CON statutes that regulated the capacity of hospitals, skilled nursing homes, intermediate care facilities, and renal dialysis centers to make capital purchases involving new construction, renovation, bed expansions, new or expanded services, and new technology (U.S. Congress, OTA 1984b). While they varied greatly in terms of their regulatory scopes and review methods, these programs—at minimum—called for the review of

- all capital expenditures exceeding $600,000,
- new services with annual operating expenditures exceeding $250,000, and
- purchases of medical equipment for inpatient hospital use exceeding $400,000 (Simpson 1985).

The federal health planning movement reached its zenith in the late 1970s and soon began to lose its broad base of support. Health care providers increasingly resisted government intrusion into their affairs, and many public leaders began to withdraw their support for the regulation of health care. A hospital-cost-containment bill proposed by President Jimmy Carter in 1979 would have placed caps on total hospital expenditures and would have required the health systems agencies and state health planning and development agencies to weigh proposed capital projects against one another and to look at the relative rather than absolute need for such projects. Many individuals in the hospital and technology industries viewed this as de facto rationing of facilities and equipment and persuaded Congress to rebuff the president's initiative.

Support for health planning declined further under President Ronald Reagan, whose administration was opposed philosophically to such regulation. Federal funds for health planning programs were reduced each year during the Reagan administration, shifting the fiscal burden for the planning structure to the states (C. Thomas 1993). Faced with dwindling federal support for health planning and with shrinking budgetary resources during a period of economic recession, many states had no choice but to reduce their financial support as well. In 1986 Congress repealed the 1974 federal health planning law, causing a number of states to follow suit either by abandoning their CON programs altogether or by relaxing their CON requirements (C. Thomas 1993). By 1988, a dozen states, including Arizona, Idaho, Kansas, Minnesota, New Mexico, Texas, and Utah, had repealed their CON statutes (Schwartz 1987; L. D. Brown 1992; C. Thomas 1992; Jee 1993).

In the absence of CON constraints, hospitals sought to inform their planning efforts with detailed data on patient origin and service utilization patterns to avoid overbuilding in a deregulated, competitive market (Larkin 1987). Some states eventually reinstated their federal section 1122 programs or instituted moratoria on new hospital construction and expansion projects as a result of fear of uncontrolled construction and rampant cost growth. Other states, however, preferred to maintain an unregulated environment even in the face of dramatic hospital growth: Utah, for example, repealed its law in 1984 and saw an 80 percent rise in hospital construction permits the following year, and Arizona experienced similar growth after the 1985 repeal of its CON program (AHA 1987).

The Role of CON Programs in Cost Containment

As cost-containment mechanisms, CON programs initially were intended to eliminate or prevent unnecessary duplication of facilities (Schwartz 1981). Although not specifically designed to constrain the diffusion of medical technology, CON programs became the major policy tool for controlling the introduction of new equipment-embodied technologies (Steinberg and Cohen 1984). Over time, CON programs were directed increasingly toward limiting the diffusion of such technology-based services as CT, MRI, renal lithotripsy, coronary care units, and various organ transplantation services (CT and MRI are discussed later in this chapter).

Supporters of CON have argued that the regulatory approach is sound but that political forces within the health care system have undermined or distorted its implementation. Community-based planning efforts during the 1970s and 1980s were rife with instances in which local decision makers faced conflicting desires to contain costs globally and to see health services expanded in their communities. Moreover, these local groups often saw their recommendations ignored or overridden by state agencies that were vulnerable to political pressures from other sources (Morone 1990; U.S. Congress, Congressional Budget Office 1991; L. D. Brown 1992). Proponents also have asserted that, in those few states (e.g., Maryland, Massachusetts, New Jersey, and New York) where CON programs were linked formally to hospital rate setting and to statewide (rather than local area) health planning efforts, the programs were effective in meeting cost-containment goals (U.S. Congress, Congressional Budget Office 1991). Opponents, conversely, have contended that costly application procedures and expensive legal challenges to CON approvals by competing hospitals led to higher systemwide expenses, a view supported by data from a 1987 Federal Trade Commission report that found hospital expenses in 1977 and 1978 to be 4 percent higher in states with CON programs than in those without CON (AHA 1987).

The Effectiveness of CON Programs in Cost Containment
Evidence regarding the effects of CON on health care spending is generally unrevealing. Limited data—combined with diverse program structures among states (different scopes, mandates, procedures, and sanctions)—have precluded definitive assessments of the value of CON programs (Jee 1993; C. Thomas 1993). Furthermore, many CON

programs sought to "balance multiple, competing goals related to cost, quality, and accessibility of services" (Simpson 1985, 1225). In some states, the potential deterrent or restraining effect of CON could never be measured during the program's tenure but seemed discernable from the sharp rise in new construction that occurred after the repeal of the CON statute (Jee 1993). Conversely, New York's strict CON approach led to major reductions in bed capacity and may have deterred new construction but also may have contributed to the crisis in access to hospital care for New York City's burgeoning HIV-infected population during the 1990s. The conventional wisdom, however, strongly points toward CON having had negligible impact on both aggregate spending and capital investment in hospitals, with numerous structural and political obstacles standing in the way of the desired outcome (L. D. Brown 1983; Simpson 1985; J. B. Brown and Saltman 1985; U.S. Congress, Congressional Budget Office 1991; Diller 1993).

Strategies Employed by CON Programs for Dealing with
New Technology
CON programs' specific effects on the adoption of technology are even more difficult to disentangle. At one time or another, states have employed five different CON strategies for dealing with the adoption of new technology under various circumstances (Cohen and Rock 1985):

- pro forma denial of CON applications, in which the burden of proof for demonstrating need for the technology rests with the applicant;
- uncontested approval of applications, in which the burden of proof for disproving need for the technology rests with the CON agency;
- formalized delay, in which a moratorium on accepting new CON applications for a specific technology is imposed, usually for a finite time but sometimes indefinitely;
- predetermined limits on diffusion, in which the CON agency decides in advance that a new technology may diffuse to a limited number of sites (usually academic medical centers or regional hospitals), with the stipulation that clinical and cost-effectiveness data be collected and analyzed to guide future CON decisions regarding subsequent diffusion of the technology; and
- shared service arrangements, in which two or more hospitals

enter into a joint venture or a sharing arrangement to acquire and operate the technology, which may be located at a fixed site (e.g., one of the hospital campuses or a freestanding site) or available on a mobile basis.

CON programs used the first three of these strategies primarily during the 1970s to handle applications for new technologies, most notably CT, while the latter two approaches evolved during the 1980s to deal with applications for MRI, renal lithotripsy, and organ transplantation (discussed later in this chapter). Together with the strategy of formalized delay, these two represent the principal strategies used by CON programs today to discourage unnecessary duplication of technological resources. However, the relative effectiveness of these strategies in controlling the adoption of new technology has not been adequately evaluated.

Resurgence of CON in the 1990s

Despite the lack of evidence regarding their effectiveness to meet cost-containment and technology-distribution goals, CON programs experienced mild resurgence as policy instruments during the national debate over President Bill Clinton's proposed Health Security Act of 1993 (see chapter 12). Following the defeat of the health care reform plan, states looked to CON programs with even greater interest as a result of lingering concerns about excess hospital bed capacity and the contribution of technology to rising health care spending (Diller 1993; Jee 1993; C. Thomas 1993). Some states passed new CON legislation, assiduously avoiding structural weaknesses of earlier-generation programs by including physicians' offices and ambulatory care settings in CON review and by giving data collection a more prominent role (C. Thomas 1992). But the lack of strong linkages to other controls, such as prospective payment systems, which work to constrain operating expenses, or expenditure caps/limits, which work to constrain total spending, continued to undermine the CON programs' effectiveness.

CON Programs Today

As of April 2003, thirty-six states and the District of Columbia still had CON statutes in force, with active review programs in operation

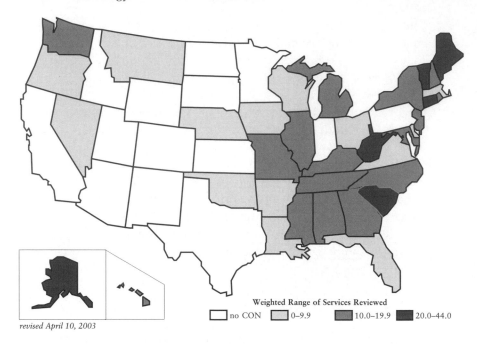

revised April 10, 2003

Fig. 13.1. CON regulation in the United States: Relative scope and threshold, 2003. (From American Health Planning Association 2003.)

(American Health Planning Association 2003). These programs are predominantly located in states found in the eastern half of the United States (see figure 13.1). According to a weighted ranking scheme developed by the American Health Planning Association (2002), the states with the most heavily regulated programs (those with the greatest number of services subject to CON review and with the most stringent review thresholds) are concentrated in the northeast and southeast (see figure 13.1).

The relative scope of CON regulation among the thirty-seven existing programs varies extraordinarily. As shown in figure 13.2, the six states (Alaska, Connecticut, Maine, South Carolina, Vermont, and West Virginia) whose programs have the broadest regulatory scope tend to be those with high numbers of regulated services—between nineteen and twenty-six—and with relatively lower dollar thresholds for triggering review of medical equipment—$400,000 to $2 million (American Health Planning Association 2003). In sharp contrast, the fourteen states with the least stringent programs tend to be those with substantially fewer regulated services and with higher thresholds for review. The most frequently reviewed technological services are either equipment-embodied

Fig. 13.2. table (service grid columns shown shaded; readable data reproduced below):

Rank (no. of svcs. x weight)	Categories	Other (items not otherwise covered)	Count (no. of svcs.)	Capital $ nrsg hm / hosp	Med Eqpt	New Svc	Weight
31.2	Maine		24	0.5M/2.0M	1,000,000	100,000	1.3
28.8	Connecticut		24	1,000,000	400,000	0	1.2
26.0	Alaska	Assisted living	26	1,000,000	1,000,000	1,000,000	1.0
21.6	Vermont		24	1.5/0.75M	500,000	300,000	0.9
20.9	South Carolina		19	1,000,000	600,000	400,000	1.1
20.7	West Virginia	Behavioral hlth	23	2,000,000	2,000,000	23 svcs	0.9
18.7	Georgia		17	1,250,199	694,556	any	1.1
18.4	North Carolina	IC & others	23	2,000,000	750,000	n/a	0.8
17.6	Tennessee	hospice, meth	22	2,000,000	1,500,000	any beds	0.8
17.0	Mississippi		17	2,000,000	1,500,000	any	1.0
16.8	Alabama	ESRD & ALC	21	3,200,000	1,500,000	any	0.8
16.1	Dist. of Columbia		23	2,000,000	1,300,000	600,000	0.7
15.2	Rhode Island		19	2,000,000	1,000,000	750,000	0.8
15.0	New York		25	3,000,000	3,000,000	any	0.6
5.0	Hawaii		25	4,000,000	1,000,000	any	0.6
4.4	Maryland	fed. swing bed	16	1,500,000	n/a	any	0.9
4.4	Michigan	Hosp & Surg	18	2,510,000	any	any clin.	0.8
4.4	Kentucky	Mobile svcs	18	1,831,594	1,831,594	n/a	0.8
3.3	Illinois	Other	19	6,326,066	6,175,751	any	0.7
2.8	Washington	Hospice	16	var. by svc.	n/a	any	0.8
2.6	New Hampshire		14	1,885,179	400,000	any	0.9
2.1	New Jersey		11	1,000,000	1,000,000	any	1.1
0.4	Missouri	New hosp.	13	0.6M/1.0M	0.4M/1.0M	1,000,000	0.8
8.1	Iowa		9	1,500,000	1,500,000	500,000	0.9
8.0	Virginia	MSI, SPECT	20	5,000,000	n/a	n/a	0.4
7.7	Florida	Hospice	11	none	none	any	0.7
7.0	Oklahoma	psych., chem.	5	500,000	n/a	any beds	1.4
.3	Montana		7	1,500,000	n/a	150,000	0.9
.0	Arkansas		5	500,000	n/a	hospice	1.2
.8	Massachusetts	ECMO	16	10,392,634	651,209	all	0.3
.8	Delaware	Birthing ctrs.	8	5,000,000	5,000,000	n/a	0.6
.4	Wisconsin	Others	4	1,000,000	600,000	any LTC	1.1
.5	Nevada		7	2,000,000	n/a	n/a	0.5
.0	Nebraska		2	any LTC	any LTC	any LTC	1.5
.4	Oregon		2	anyLTC/hs	n/a	LTC/hsp	1.2
.5	Ohio		1	2M renov	n/a	n/a	0.5
.4	Louisiana		2	n/a	n/a	LTC/MR	0.2

compiled by Thomas R. Piper
Missouri CON program
Jefferson City, MO
573-751-6403

Service grid column headers: Acute Care, Air Ambulance, Amb Surg Ctrs, Burn Care, Business Cmprs, Cardiac Cath., CT Scanners, Gamma Knives, Home Hlth, ICF/MR, Lithotripsy, Long Term Care, Med Off Bldg, Mobile Hi Tech, MRI Scnrs, Neo-ntl Int Care, Obstetric Svcs, Open Heart Svcs, Organ Transplnt, PET Scnrs, Psychiatric Svcs, Rad Therapy, Rehab, Renal Dialysis, Res Care Fac, Subacute, Substance Abuse, Swing Beds, Ultra-sound, Other (items not otherwise covered)

imer: Rank order relates to volume of items reviewed, NOT intensity of analysis or conclusions which are based on Criteria and Standards and decisions. Source: Updated April 10, 2003 using most recent information available information is summarized from the 2003 National Directory of Health Planning, Policy and Regulatory Agencies, the twelfthth edition published by the American Health Planning Association)

Fig. 13.2. Relative scope and review thresholds of CON-regulated services, by state, 2003. (From American Health Planning Association 2003.)

technologies or specialized surgical procedures. In descending order of frequency, they are: ambulatory surgery center (twenty-seven programs); open heart services (twenty-six programs); cardiac catheterization (twenty-five programs); positron emission tomography (PET, twenty-three programs); organ transplantation (twenty-one); MRI (twenty); renal lithotripsy (twenty); the gamma knife (eighteen); mobile high technology (seventeen); and CT (thirteen).

A Final Word about CON Programs

State CON programs today continue to have both supporters and detractors. As policy tools, CON programs are limited in their ability to constrain the introduction of new technology and to assure equitable distribution of technology among providers and communities for reasons that inhere in the programs' structural design and narrow regulatory foci.

1. *Focus on equipment*—by focusing primarily on expensive equipment-embodied technologies or highly specialized surgical procedures, many other technologies (including all pharmaceuticals, most surgical procedures, and many little-ticket devices) elude CON scrutiny (Cohen and Nichols 1993). Also, because CON programs concentrate on technology in fixed sites, hospitals use mobile technology to avoid the CON process (Hartley, Moscovice, and Christianson 1996).

2. *Focus on hospital and nursing home settings*—by restricting CON review in most states to hospitals and nursing homes, many technologies (e.g., CT, MRI, and other diagnostic imaging devices) are able to proliferate in unregulated settings, such as physicians' offices and ambulatory care centers (Jee 1993).

3. *Focus on capital expenditures*—by focusing solely on capital expenditures, CON programs lack control over the operating expenses associated with the use of technology (including the pricing of technological services), which contribute importantly to total health care spending (Mendelson and Arnold 1993).

4. *Focus on new projects*—by concentrating on capital expenditures only for new projects, CON programs may fail to take into account existing imbalances in technology distribution among health care providers and communities when making decisions, thereby possibly exacerbating those inequities (Jee 1993).

While CON may not be an effective cost-containment tool, one study found higher mortality rates for Medicare patients undergoing coronary artery bypass graft surgery in states without CON regulation than in states with such regulation, suggesting that CON regulation may be useful for ensuring higher quality and better patient outcomes (Vaughan-Sarrazin et al. 2002).

A Tale of Two Technologies and CON Review—CT and MRI

To illustrate past experience with CON policies, we examine here two case examples of equipment-embodied diagnostic technologies that posed unusual challenges for regulators, CT and MRI. Each, in its time, was hailed as a major technological breakthrough with enormous medical potential, and each diffused fairly swiftly in the absence of sound information regarding its efficacy (Banta 1980b; Steinberg and Cohen

1984). The CT case presented here relies primarily on the work of Banta (1980b), whereas the MRI case draws on multiple sources and builds on material presented in chapters 3 and 5.

CT: The Radiologic Marvel of the 1970s

CT was first introduced in the United States at the Mayo Clinic in 1973. By year's end, five more scanners had been installed, but few observers could have predicted what ensued—an unprecedented explosion of worldwide interest that resulted in the purchase and installation of 1,042 scanners in the United States alone by 1978 (Banta 1980b). In terms of distribution, this translated into 4.8 CT scanners per 1 million people. There was at least one CT in every state, ranging from one each in Rhode Island and Vermont to 196 in California. The District of Columbia had the highest density of CT to population, with 15.9 units per million, followed by Nevada, with 11.1 per million. California and Florida also had high rates—9.0 and 8.8 per million, respectively. One year later, in 1979, the number of CT installations had risen to 1,254, or 5.7 per million people nationwide (Banta 1980b).

Eighty-two percent of scanners were located in hospitals, many of them nonprofit, short-term community institutions. Of 1,780 public hospitals nationally, only 120 had obtained the technology by 1978. In fact, many large public hospitals serving predominantly poor people were without CT, including such institutions as Bellevue Hospital and Kings County Hospital in New York City, Charity Hospital in New Orleans, and Cook County Hospital in Chicago. In stark contrast, 73 percent of community hospitals with more than 500 beds had at least one scanner by 1978 (Banta 1980b).

The average purchase prices for both types of CT unit—head and body—were about $500,000, with average annual operating expenses ranging from about $260,000 to $400,000, based on 3,000 examinations per year. The average hospital fees in 1977 were $273 for a head scan and $286 for a body scan, yielding impressive profit margins of $86 (32 percent) to $126 (44 percent) per examination. By 1983, purchase prices differed little from 1977 (in real dollar terms), and fees for CT scans had declined slightly, but CT remained a profitable technology for a hospital or health center (B. J. Hillman 1986).

Banta (1980b) noted that CT technology diffused with unparalleled speed for reasons that are not entirely clear. An unquestionably exciting advance in diagnostic imaging, CT could not be shown initially to yield dramatic improvements in health outcome or in diagnosis of conditions not previously possible. Aside from its prestige-enhancing qualities and almost hypnotic allure to physicians, CT most likely proliferated rapidly in its early years because of its intrinsic profitability. Reimbursement for services was not a problem—the Health Care Financing Administration (HCFA, now the Centers for Medicare and Medicaid Services) approved CT for Medicare payment in 1976, virtually assuring that other third-party payers would soon follow suit. And with time, as evidence regarding its clinical value mounted, the only issue that remained was its possible overuse (Banta 1980b).

CON programs in many states were in their infancy around the time that CT emerged on the medical scene. Thus, such programs were hardly in a position to slow the spread of the technology at first. In fact, word of impending regulation by health planning agencies is thought to have triggered anticipatory behavior by some hospitals, encouraging them to accelerate plans for CT acquisition to avoid such restrictions (Banta 1980b; Steinberg and Cohen 1984). CON programs generally did not know how to respond to applications for CT scanners. Some granted uncontested approval in the face of local political pressures and the lack of evidence showing CT to be inefficacious or harmful. Others countered by denying specific proposals or by imposing blanket moratoria on all CT purchases. Still others invoked delay tactics until scientific information could be gathered (Cohen and Rock 1985). In many locales, private physicians' groups found ways to circumvent CON laws by purchasing CT units for installation in their offices (Banta 1980b; B. J. Hillman 1986). Invariably, an inequitable pattern of local distribution emerged, with the losers usually being public hospitals, whose technological disenfranchisement at the hands of CON programs Banta (1980a) termed "cost containment misdirected." The net effect of these experiences was a serious black mark on the regulatory record of state CON programs.

MRI: The Sensation of the 1980s

Originally called nuclear magnetic resonance imaging, MRI was introduced into a very different policy environment from that encountered by CT. The first unit in the United States was installed in December 1980 in a radiologist's private office. Two more were installed the next year, and by the end of 1984 108 units were in use nationwide, with another 110 on order (Steinberg, Sisk, and Locke 1985). This represented less than 20 percent of the total number of CT scanners installed within five years following the introduction of that imaging modality.

Several factors are hypothesized to account for the markedly slower growth in MRI placements, not the least of which were its more demanding purchase and installation requirements. Whereas early CT scanners generally cost between $300,000 and $600,000 to buy and about $50,000 to install, a MRI unit typically cost between $800,000 and $2 million to buy and $150,000 to $1 million to install, depending on the type and field strength of the magnet (Steinberg and Cohen 1984; B. J. Hillman 1986). Special site considerations also had to be taken into account, in some cases requiring the building of a structure specifically to house the unit (see chapter 5). Such requirements increased costs substantially and may have delayed installation of some units (Steinberg, Sisk, and Locke 1985). In addition, annual operating expenses for superconducting magnet systems averaged more than $840,000 (B. J. Hillman 1986).

MRI also entered a cost-containment environment filled with uncertainty about financing and payment for capital projects. The Medicare Prospective Payment System was poised to go into effect in 1984, and the volume of CT scans was declining (Banta 1980b; Steinberg 1985). Hospitals faced potentially declining inpatient revenues and were unsure of the expected volume of patients likely to utilize the new technology (Steinberg, Sisk, and Locke 1985). Initial reluctance by third-party payers to embrace MRI magnified the uncertainty. In 1984, four years after being introduced, MRI examinations were reimbursed routinely by only ten of thirty large commercial insurers, while the HCFA awaited findings from an analysis conducted by the Office of Health Technology Assessment (now the AHRQ's Center for Practice and Technology Assessment) before determining Medicare coverage of the technology (Steinberg 1985).

By this time CON programs had become well entrenched and had constrained the rate and extent of the diffusion of MRI. For example, Illinois, New York, and New Jersey each adopted predetermined limits on diffusion, restricting the total number of units statewide and dictating the locations and circumstances under which such units could be installed (Cohen and Rock 1985). Maryland took sixteen months before approving its first unit in March 1985 and denied at least thirty applications before doing so (Steinberg 1985).

CON laws clearly affected the distribution of MRI technology in two ways, by limiting its placement in hospital inpatient settings and by creating perverse incentives for providers to place the technology in unregulated care settings, such as physicians' offices and outpatient diagnostic imaging centers. Whereas CT scanners placed in physicians' offices accounted for 20 percent of the total supply seven years after introduction of the technology, MRI units in physicians' offices accounted for 39 percent of the total supply just four years after the technology's introduction (Steinberg, Sisk, and Locke 1985). Indeed, state CON authorities considered the existence of outpatient MRI installations as grounds for disapproving applications for inpatient placement (Steinberg 1985).

Ultimately, DRG payment to hospitals acted as another incentive to install MRI units in outpatient settings where unbundled MRI services could be billed separately. Also, unlike CT, MRI initially was suitable only for medically stable patients, making it more readily adaptable to outpatient settings. Interestingly, although MRI was subject to FDA premarket approval as a Class III device, this regulatory requirement had relatively little effect on its early diffusion, since most units installed by late 1983 had been granted investigational device exemptions (Steinberg, Sisk, and Locke 1985).

Unlike CT, MRI was not immediately profitable. One 1985 survey showed the average MRI site to be losing $500,000 per year. By 1987, however, a follow-up survey of seventy-two new MRI sites in operation since 1985 showed an average annual profit of $100,000 (Wilkinson 1987). Weekly patient volume increased and bad debt decreased as third-party payers increasingly came forward with coverage approvals (Wilkinson 1987). The advent of mobile MRI systems also augured well for the future of the technology, as hospitals unable to afford costly inpatient installations formed joint ventures with other institutions to purchase and operate such systems as shared services. As described in chapter 3, MRI diffused widely in the United States despite CON and other cost-containment strategies, so that by early 1998, approximately 4,000 units had been placed (Schrader 1998). One group of investigators (Baker 1997; Baker and Wheeler 1998) claimed to have found evidence of managed care's restraining effect on MRI diffusion, but the distributional effects of this influence—in terms of which types of organizations obtained or failed to obtain the technology—were unclear.

The growing number of MRI units in outpatient settings has posed access/equity problems for some populations dependent on hospitals for their primary care, especially individuals with limited financial resources and inadequate transportation services in geographically inaccessible locations. Also, because third-party coverage for MRI use in the outpatient setting often pays only 75 to 80 percent of the fee, fees on the order of $800 to $1,000 for an MRI study are nontrivial expenses for many people, not just low-income individuals (B. J. Hillman 1986).

In the early 1990s, another imaging technology, PET, emerged, posing challenges to CON programs similar to those previously posed by CT and MRI. The initial costs of acquiring PET were estimated at roughly $6 million for installation, with annual operating costs of more than $1 million and a cost per procedure of $1,500 to $2,000, depending on patient volume (Reiman and Mintun 1990). PET's ability to detect biochemical abnormalities before physical changes occur in the brain offers the promise of early diagnosis of various psychological and neurological conditions. In 1990, PET was available—as an investigational device—in only fifty large hospitals and medical centers in the United States (National Cancer Institute 1990). Unlike CT and MRI, though, PET did not sweep across the nation during the 1990s, as many hospitals were unwilling to invest in the technology because of its high financial requirements, the many unresolved questions about its clinical effectiveness, the dampening effect caused by the national health care reform debate of the mid 1990s, and the slowness with which the HCFA made national coverage decisions for disease-specific applications of the technology. This, however, has changed in recent years, and PET has diffused more rapidly since 2001 with expansion of Medicare coverage for scans to detect cancer. By mid-2003, there were an estimated 575 PET scanners operating in the United States (Rundle 2003).

Factors Impeding Access to Medical Technology

Health services researchers and health policymakers have long identified access to health care as a major problem within the American health care system. Factors affecting access to health care for populations and individuals—including specific types of barriers that may impede access—have been classified according to a framework first articulated by Aday and Andersen (1974; 1980), and subsequently modified and expanded by various authors (U.S. Congress, OTA 1992; IOM 1993; M. Gold 1998). Among such barriers are financial, geographic, and demographic obstacles that also have particular relevance for access to medical technology. We present here a discussion of these three types of barriers and how they may act to limit or interfere with an individual's ability to gain access to specialized medical technology.

Financial Access Barriers

Various financial access barriers to medical technology exist. The most common is the high cost of many new technologies, which is a formidable barrier for uninsured or underinsured individuals unless a health care provider is willing to deliver uncompensated (free) care. Over the past decade, financial access to health care declined greatly for many Americans despite economic growth unparalleled in the nation's history. Even with strong employment growth in service industries and in small businesses throughout the 1990s, the number of uninsured persons in the country rose to more than 44 million. The reasons for this seeming paradox are numerous. First, workers in service industries tend to be minimum-wage earners or part-time employees who either are not eligible to receive health insurance benefits or are unable to afford the premium. Second, employees in small businesses are less likely to receive health insurance either because their employers do not offer it or because the high-premium insurance products offered to them are unaffordable. Third, welfare reform during the 1990s caused many low-income individuals to lose their Medicaid eligibility, leading to a decline in Medicaid enrollment; because most former welfare recipients are minimum-wage earners employed in jobs where health insurance is either unavailable or unaffordable, these individuals and their dependents also joined the ranks of the uninsured. Although Congress enacted the State Child Health Insurance Program as part of the Balanced Budget Act of 1997 to increase health insurance coverage for children and many states have responded by enrolling high numbers of eligible children, the problem of uninsurance in America remains a serious one, costing the nation between $65 billion and $130 billion annually (IOM 2003).

The lack of health insurance for so many Americans clearly poses a major financial access barrier to many of the most advanced medical technologies available in the marketplace today. Even in cases where insurance provides access to health care, the exclusion from coverage of certain technologies erects significant access barriers for some individuals or populations. For example, the Medicare program presently does not provide outpatient coverage of prescription drugs for the elderly. Faced with high prices for new prescription drugs, many senior citizens are unable to afford such out-of-pocket expenses, essentially preventing them from gaining access to many of the latest medical advances and new therapies. Among private payers, managed care organizations make technology coverage decisions (see chapter 12) that are not always governed by objective assessment of the safety and effectiveness of a technology but instead are governed by financial considerations that in effect may deny consumers access to specific medical technologies for certain diseases. Such policies—and the denial-of-coverage decisions that they engender—have been the subject of intense debate and legal conflict between managed care organizations and consumers.

Another example of a financial access barrier is that of orphan drugs, which are beneficial to small population segments but which fail to reach the marketplace because their development costs cannot be recovered reasonably through sales. A celebrated case of an orphan drug was zidovudine (AZT), which was unavailable to many HIV-infected persons who could not afford its high cost and lacked insurance coverage for such therapy in the mid-1980s. AZT did not enjoy active development until the federal government intervened to subsidize its production and distribution. In its two decades of existence, the Orphan Drug Act of 1983 has encouraged the development and market entry of more than 220 new pharmaceuticals, thereby significantly minimizing access barriers associated with orphan drugs. (See chapter 10 for a discussion of orphan drugs.)

Geographic Access Barriers

Geographic barriers to technology also arise quite often because new technologies tend to be adopted first in academic health centers and major teaching hospitals before diffusing broadly across the health care system. Even so, geography may mean that some technologies remain chronically inaccessible to some populations, such as inner-city residents who use public hospitals (Banta 1980a; Pozen et al. 1984; Steinberg and Cohen 1984). In addition, rural populations historically have had limited access to certain technological services because of service cost-volume interdependencies and the maldistribution of physician specialists and other health professionals (Moscovice 1989). The lack of trained personnel to operate equipment or to perform surgical procedures often precludes rural community hospitals from adopting new technology, even when financial resources are available for purchasing such technology. Some observers have argued, therefore, that technologies requiring large capital investments and specialized personnel—

such as MRI, lithotripsy, and organ transplantation—should be located regionally, where expected patient volumes would be sufficient to cover both the capital and operating expenses associated with the technology and the availability of specialized personnel would assure adequate staffing of the services (A. L. Hillman and Schwartz 1985). In addition to the obvious economic advantages, regionalization of specialized services also may confer important quality-of-care benefits. For example, evidence-based meta-analyses performed by the Cochrane Collaboration have been used recently to support recommendations for the creation of dedicated primary stroke centers for improving outcomes associated with stroke (Alberts et al. 2000; Barnett and Buchan 2000).

Other approaches to overcoming geographic access barriers include the use of (1) portable technology, such as mobile CT scanners, MRI units, and other diagnostic equipment, and (2) various telehealth/telemedicine technologies to support long-distance health care in remote locations, including stereotactic robotic surgery. In one study of technology diffusion in rural community hospitals in eight states, mobile technology for CT, MRI, and mammography was found to be a key means of assuring that rural populations have access to these critical services (Hartley, Moscovice, and Christianson 1996). Telehealth initiatives, which include telemedicine, teleradiology, and telesurgery, use electronic information and telecommunications technologies to provide health care services and education (Health Resources and Services Administration 2001). The federal Health Resources and Services Administration has established an Office for the Advancement of Telehealth to promote the wider adoption of these advanced technologies (Health Resources and Services Administration 2001).

Demographic Access Barriers

Barriers also may exist in the form of inequitable access to technology on the basis of gender, race, ethnicity, or other demographic characteristics. For example, gender bias against females in the selection of diseases for study as well as in the selection of candidates for participation in NIH-sponsored clinical trials has been well documented (Healy 1992) and is a problem for which corrective action has only recently been undertaken by the NIH and affiliated groups. (See chapter 6 for a discussion of the NIH's efforts to include women and minorities in clinical trials.) Other factors that have been associated with differential access to technology include socioeconomic status (Epstein, Stern, and

Weissman 1990; Wenneker, Weissman, and Epstein 1990) and community characteristics (Goldberg et al. 1992).

The medical literature has been increasingly filled with reports of racial, ethnic, and gender disparities in the use of various therapeutic technologies, with African-Americans, Latinos, and other racial minorities less likely than whites and women less likely than men to receive such therapies, even though epidemiologic studies show disproportionately higher mortality and morbidity rates from heart disease, cancer, and stroke in minority populations (Teays and Purdy 2001). Racial and ethnic disparities have been reported in cardiac catheterization and bypass surgery (Maynard et al. 1986; Ford et al. 1989; Wenneker and Epstein 1989; Goldberg et al. 1992; Peterson et al. 1994; Hannan et al. 1999; Chen et al. 2001); reperfusion therapy for myocardial infarction (Canto et al. 2000); long-term hemodialysis and renal transplantation (Held et al. 1988; Kjellstrand 1988; Eggers 1995; Alexander and Sehgal 1998; Ayanian et al. 1999); liver and pancreas transplantation (Kasiske et al. 1991); curative surgery for early-stage lung cancer (Bach et al. 1999); and knee replacement surgery (B. P. Katz et al. 1996). In one study aimed at discerning whether differences in the use of cardiac catheterization according to the race and gender of the patient stemmed from differences in the clinical recommendations of physicians, Schulman and his colleagues (1999) found that African-American women were significantly less likely to be referred for catheterization than were white men and that the race and gender of a patient independently influence how physicians manage chest pain. Racial and ethnic disparities also have been shown to exist in access to various primary care services (Basu and Clancy 2001; Clancy and Stryer 2001), influenza vaccinations (Schneider et al. 2001), and outpatient pain management (R. S. Morrison et al. 2000). Moreover, the Institute of Medicine (2002) found that subtle racial prejudice and differences in the quality of care received by African-Americans and Latinos persisted even when they had the same insurance and income as white patients and may contribute to the minorities' higher death rates from cancer, heart disease, diabetes, and HIV infection.

It is important, therefore, to bear in mind that a delicate balance exists between access and cost considerations in health care. Awareness of and sensitivity to this relationship is needed when devising new policies to govern the introduction and distribution of medical technology, since stringent cost-containment efforts in some cases may create inequities in access to technology and in other cases may exacerbate already existing inequities. For example, it is quite possible that managed care policies and practices that limit consumers' choice of hospitals and physicians and restrict specialty referrals could create new inequities in access to certain technologies for some individuals and populations. Policymakers, health care managers, and health care providers thus must be vigilant about the potential technology-related access problems that may arise in the managed care marketplace.

The Supply and Distribution of Donor Organs for Transplantation

Perhaps one of the most vexing problems involving technology in U.S. health care over the years has been that of assuring an adequate supply of donor organs for transplantation and an equitable process for distributing them to transplant recipients. The National Organ Transplant Act of 1984, which governs U.S. policy in this area, grew out of a 1980 dilemma that the Medicare program faced: should it cover heart transplants as a reimbursable service? Liver, pancreas, and bone marrow transplants also were developing rapidly at the time, adding pressure to the situation. A federally commissioned study recommended coverage for heart transplants, but only if the procedures were performed in approved heart transplant centers meeting specified volume and quality standards set by the HCFA. However, no uniform standards existed at the time to assure safe, cost-effective transplant care.

Therefore, the National Organ Procurement and Transplantation Network was created to establish a national system for matching donor organs to recipients, to develop standards for the acquisition and transportation of donated organs, and to coordinate the transportation of organs. The act also established the national Scientific Registry of Transplant Recipients and the Task Force on Organ Procurement and Transplantation, which was to conduct studies of medical, legal, ethical, economic, and social issues related to the procurement and transplantation of organs. Within the Health Resources and Services Administration's Office of Special Programs, the Division of Transplantation was charged with managing the procurement and transplantation network and carrying out the act's mandate under a contract with the United Network for Organ Sharing, a private, nonprofit organization based in Richmond, Virginia.

For nearly two decades, the United Network for Organ Sharing has been active in managing the national transplant waiting list, which matches donors to recipients every hour of every day; monitoring every organ match to ensure adherence to the group's policy; setting standards for regional organ procurement organizations; working with the regional organizations to develop equitable policies for maximizing the supply of organs and for matching organs with recipients; setting professional standards for quality transplant care; and raising public awareness about organ donation and transplant policy. In 1999, the United Network for Organ Sharing implemented UNet, an Internet-based application for matching organs, and the organization is currently redesigning the Transplant Patient DataSource to be even more user-friendly to patients, the public, and the transplant community (United Network 2001).

In an attempt to address alleged inequities in the current regionally based transplantation system, the federal Division of Transplantation issued a proposed new rule in March 1998 for the national dissemination of organs based on common medical criteria, regardless of where patients live or the location where they await transplantation. The response to this proposed rule from transplant surgeons, states, and even some members of Congress was both immediate and negative. Not only did federal legislators introduce alternative bills, but several states also passed legislation that gave residents priority in receiving organs donated within the state. The controversy pointed out the ongoing tensions that exist between the transplant community and the federal government on the question of who should have authority over transplant policy (National Conference 2000).

Organ transplantation policy is unique in that the supply of donor organs is extraordinarily limited and both the cost and complexity of performing transplant procedures are very high. The designation of approved centers for transplantation eligible for Medicare payment, coupled with strict regulation of organ procurement and distribution, provides a means for controlling the cost, quality, and access associated with transplantation services. Some observers have argued that these policies offer valuable lessons for other technologies and may serve as potential bellwethers of future policy toward very high cost technologies, particularly as resources become increasingly constrained (Blumstein and Sloan 1989). However, given the current market-oriented environment in health care and the fact that system capacity control mechanisms, such as CON programs, have diminished in influence within this environment, it seems highly unlikely that more stringent regulatory approaches could begin to ascend in the near future.

14

Social, Ethical, and Legal Concerns: Experimentation, Rationing, and Practice Standards
Ruth S. Hanft and Stephanie M. Spernak

The quality of American medical technology has been and continues to be widely acknowledged as the best in the world, and there is little doubt that it contributes to both the high caliber and the high cost of American health care. The technological continuum that begins with basic research and biomedical innovation, flows through technology development and evaluation, and ends with technology adoption and use raises numerous social, ethical, and legal concerns at every step along the path.

These concerns have escalated in the United States since the 1960s (J. Katz 1993), stimulated by the rise of the civil rights and women's rights movements, by the rapidly rising costs of health care and the methods used to control them, by the medical malpractice crises (whether real or imagined) that have arisen periodically, by the occurrence of scandals and improprieties in human subjects research, and by the clash of managed care organizations with consumer groups over denial-of-coverage decisions. Various lifesaving and life-extending technologies as well as reproductive technologies have been at the core of many social, ethical, and legal rights debates. Yet despite these concerns, ten Have (1995) observed that systematic analysis of the ethical implications of technology development has not been an integral or substantial component of medical technology evaluation (MTE) programs because the prevailing conceptualization of MTE has tended to separate technology from the social context in which it operates and has dealt only secondarily with the impact of technology on society. Technology, in his opinion, is not only embedded within a society's culture but is in fact a "producer of culture" (ten Have 1995, 19).

In this chapter, we first explore the social and ethical concerns that revolve around questions of when and how to evaluate and use medical technology, with particular emphasis on five issues: (1) experimentation and evaluation, (2) the role of the patient in clinical decision making, (3) the ethics of MTE, (4) distributive justice and the rationing of health care resources, and (5) conflicts among social, cultural, and religious values. We then examine the legal implications of government efforts to control medical decision making and to establish standards of care through the use of clinical practice guidelines.

Experimentation and Evaluation

While advances in basic research often occur through intellectual endeavor and the development of models or paradigms, clinical advances generally are determined only after testing has been completed on animal and human subjects. Issues of human subjects research fall into three general categories: informed consent of the subject, the inclusion and exclusion of certain population groups in clinical trials, and the ethics of withholding treatment from control-group subjects once efficacy has been established.

Informed Consent

The public horror over the gruesome medical experiments inflicted on concentration camp prisoners that came to light in the Nuremberg trials at the end of World War II spurred the beginnings of policies on informed consent. But not until about thirty years ago, with the revelation of the Tuskegee study involving poor African-American men in rural Alabama, was significant progress made toward ending policies of uninformed consent in human subjects research in the United States. In this study, which began in 1932 to determine the natural history of untreated syphilis, four hundred poor black men with syphilis were denied antibiotic therapy after it became evident in the 1940s that penicillin was a safe and effective agent against the disease. When the study's existence was publicly disclosed in 1972, it was cited as an example of unethical experimentation and was quickly terminated (Caplan 1992; Savitt 2001).

The release of information about the denial of treatment led to congressional hearings, which in turn resulted in the passage of the National Research Act of 1974, which required institutional review board approval of all proposed federally funded research on human subjects. Congress also created the National Commission for the Protection of Human Subjects of Biomedical and Behavioral Research (Caplan 1992). The commission developed policies to guide researchers in human subjects research and promoted public dialogue on the autonomy of patients, standards for informed consent, and measurement of risks and benefits (Jonsen 1993).

The issues of institutional review and of what constitutes informed consent have stimulated growth of an extensive literature on patient autonomy, the meaning of "informed" consent, and the use of surrogate decision makers when the patient or subject is incapable of providing truly informed consent. While the Tuskegee study is an extreme example of the absence of informed consent, ethical concerns also abound in cases involving surrogate decision making (e.g., when study subjects have diminished mental capacity to make informed choices) or in instances of potential coercion (e.g., when prisoners are subjects in clinical research). Debate continues about what constitutes informed consent for children and the mentally disabled (Ross 1997).

Inclusion/Exclusion Criteria in Clinical Trials

For many years, women, minorities, elderly people, and children frequently were excluded from clinical research, particularly randomized controlled trials (Healy 1992). A 1990 General Accounting Office report indicated that although a 1986 policy required the inclusion of women and minorities in federally funded human subjects research, women were substantially underrepresented (Dresser 1992). The failure to include women, minorities, and elderly people leads to imperfect research findings on the diagnosis and treatment of many diseases that affect people regardless of age, race, or gender (see the discussion in chapter 6). We know, for example, that the physiological and genetic characteristics of different groups may result in different responses to patterns of disease and treatment, making findings generalized from studies of white males inappropriate for such groups. We also know that elderly individuals respond differently to certain drug dosage levels than do younger persons, yet elderly people have rarely been included in clinical studies. The NIH in 1994 promulgated new guidelines for inclusion of these groups in clinical trials (see chapter 6 for a discussion of the methodological implications of these guidelines).

Withholding Treatment from Control-Group Subjects Once
Efficacy Has Been Established

The Tuskegee study raised the dual issues of informed consent and
withholding an efficacious treatment to collect research data. A somewhat similar situation arose in the randomized controlled trial to determine the efficacy of AZT in treating AIDS. In the case of AZT, however, the trial was discontinued once efficacy had been established so
that the therapy could be provided to those who might benefit.

In striving for greater sensitivity to ethical concepts in research,
there is potential risk for limiting the researcher's ability to test the
safety, efficacy, and effectiveness of given treatment modalities. For example, the efficacy of bone marrow transplants in the treatment of advanced breast cancer was unclear for many years. Some people considered clinical trials that would compare this treatment to standard
therapies to be unethical because such trials would pose an obstacle to
patients desperately desiring this therapy. Yet without such randomized controlled trials, the efficacy of bone marrow transplantation
might have remained unclear, and patients would have continued to
experience raised expectations, pain, and significant costs with an ineffective treatment. In such cases of serious life-threatening illness,
whether advanced cancer or AIDS, there is clearly increasing tension
between the unproven promise of new therapies whose effectiveness
must be assessed appropriately and the understandable human desire
to palliate symptoms and to delay death and disability. These conflicts
almost certainly will increase as society explores strategies that ration
health care.

The Patient's Role in Clinical Decision Making

The role of the patient in clinical decision making has changed dramatically during the past thirty years. Two opposing ethical concepts of autonomy—the physician's professional autonomy and the patient's autonomy—have met, challenged each other, and moved to a new balance
(Starr 1982; Beauchamp and Childress 1983). Medical technology and
MTE raise a series of questions about physician autonomy and patient
choice/autonomy.

Until the late 1960s, patients rarely questioned their physicians' decisions. The lack of technical information available to consumers, the

image of the physician as expert, and the role of the physician as the patient's agent all led to reliance on the physician rather than to patient involvement in decision making. However, three factors—the civil rights movement, the women's rights movement, and technological breakthroughs—combined with emerging bioethics debates to change the paradigm. Most recently, direct-to-consumer advertising of pharmaceuticals and increased media coverage of medical advances have caused consumers to place even greater demands on physicians.

In contrast, technological advances have raised issues concerning a patient's right to abstain from treatment, to terminate life-support systems, and to select unproven or marginal technology. Conflicts have arisen between families and physicians that increasingly have had to be resolved in the courts. The core issue revolves around various questions: Whose decision is it to make? Who decides whether a very premature infant with serious neurologic damage should be placed on and continued on life support? Can the family override a competent patient's instruction not to resuscitate and not to use artificial nutrients to sustain life? In the past fifteen years, patients increasingly have asserted their wishes through living wills and durable powers of attorney; in addition a growing number of court interventions have occurred (*In the Matter of Nancy Ellen Jobes*, 108 N.J. 394, Supreme Court of New Jersey). There also has been a growing popular movement for patients to choose, based on risks and benefits, to undergo certain diagnostic tests or treatment modalities even before there is clear evidence regarding efficacy.

MTE also has raised serious questions about the efficacy and cost-effectiveness of many procedures, including the routine use of electronic fetal monitoring, diagnostic ultrasound, magnetic resonance imaging, and coronary artery bypass surgery. Yet physicians' practice behavior has been slow to change, as has consumer demand for these technologies. Consumers increasingly have raised questions about the safety and efficacy of drugs and procedures, such as Halcion and surgical treatments for cancer, but nevertheless continue to pressure physicians for access to such treatments. It should be noted, however, that the outcome of MTE for specific technologies can change as the technologies are refined and new information comes to light, such as the emergence of immunosuppressive drugs for organ transplants and the use of multiple drugs in combination to treat AIDS.

Systematic, large-scale MTE has the potential to provide consumers with information to make informed choices and to reduce the physician's agent role. At the same time, however, private payers and managed care organizations are increasingly using MTE and evidence-based research to review physicians' practice patterns and to restrain physician autonomy in determining hospital admissions, lengths of stay, and diagnostic and treatment patterns. These utilization review techniques are limiting consumer decision making, particularly in the area of new or emerging technologies.

The Ethics of MTE

Numerous ethical issues are related to the technology evaluation process itself. How rigorous must an evaluation be? For how long should testing be conducted before a technology is deemed safe and effective for generalized use? How much risk is acceptable, and for how much benefit (given that no technology is risk free)? How frequently should a technology be reassessed, especially if it is in a relatively early stage of diffusion and there may be long-term health and social consequences associated with its use?

In recent years, reports have circulated widely about the risks of di-ethylstilbestrol, silicone breast implants, and Halcion. Vaccines that are safe and effective for 97 or 98 percent of recipients may pose severe side effects for a few. Who should make the determination of clinical safety? What success rate should be used as a guide for introducing an expensive technology into common practice? How meaningful is 50 percent survival for five years as a measure of successful transplantation? Why not 40 percent or 60 percent?

Technologies change over time—refinements are made, and costs may increase or decrease. At what point should decisions be made regarding a technology's cost-effectiveness? Should cost-effectiveness be a major determinant of whether a technology becomes available to the public, or should cost-effectiveness be balanced against other criteria, such as distributive justice or the quality of life? Is it ethical for physicians to use emerging technologies before they have been fully tested outside a research protocol? Is it ethical to withhold a promising technology before the full clinical trial has been completed, as was the case with AZT for AIDS and autologous bone marrow transplants for advanced breast cancer? Is it ethical to use a drug, device, or procedure for purposes other than its initially approved application?

The use of effective technologies for marginal indications is controversial. Utilization rates for cesarean section, electronic fetal monitoring, magnetic resonance imaging, ultrasound, and coronary artery bypass surgery are substantially higher in the United States than in other developed countries. Is it ethical for the physician and/or consumer to demand these technologies when their clinical value in specific cases or applications may be questionable?

Distributive Justice and the Rationing of Health Care Resources

Distributive justice issues thread throughout MTE, from the distribution of resources for basic research to decisions regarding technology development and diffusion. Federal efforts to address issues of distributive justice in MTE date back to April 1978, when after many discussions about the allocation of research resources for various missions and diseases, the secretary of the Department of Health, Education, and Welfare established a task force to develop a comprehensive five-year research plan for the department's health-related agencies that explicitly took into account the distribution of disease as a factor for guiding resource allocation decisions (IOM 1979). Examples of efforts to assure that consideration is given to the needs of all groups within the general population include the Orphan Drug Act of 1983 and the recent changes in policy regarding the way in which organs are distributed geographically (see the discussion in chapter 13). However, the influence of powerful special interest groups, including technology manufacturers, patient advocacy groups, and even academic groups, can distort the allocation of resources in basic research.

The lack of universal health insurance in the United States and the geographic maldistribution of facilities and professionals raise serious questions about distributive justice and the rationing of health care. Health care rationing always has occurred in one form or another, often in an ad hoc manner based on ability to pay and the accident of one's residence. The current Oregon Medicaid experiment and the health care reform debate of 1993–94 have brought this issue more prominently into the public eye. Rationing of care in the United States generally has been more implicit than explicit (Merrill and Cohen 1987) and often has been imposed through such mechanisms as

- price—lack of financial access to care by poor and uninsured persons;
- cost control—lack of access to care by decisions of insurers and managed care plans;

- physical access—maldistribution of services and personnel;
- technologic availability—inequitable access to technology because of the poor financial status of institutions that traditionally care for uninsured and poor patients;
- medical condition—lack of access to highly specialized services, such as organ transplants; and
- social support systems—lack (or inadequacy) of support for patients in the community following technological procedures, such as in the case of organ transplants early in their development (Churchill 1987).

Other nations ration care in different ways, most commonly by controlling the general supply of services, which then requires microrationing by age, cost-effectiveness, and medical condition. Aaron and Schwartz (1984) studied the British health care system and found that rationing occurred on the basis of age, visibility of disease, aggregate cost, capital cost, and the cost of alternatives. In the British system, the physician plays a key role in microrationing.

The major difference between the United States and nations that have national health insurance plans is the other nations' stringent control of the supply of physician specialists and capital investments in technology, combined with a global or relatively fixed budget for health care. Even under multiple-payer systems, as in France and Germany, there are system capacity controls and limits on total expenditures for health care. In the United States, we have relied instead on ad hoc insurance arrangements and a quasi market with multiple points for capital and workforce decisions.

Social, Cultural, and Religious Issues

The development and diffusion of technology affect and are affected by social, cultural, and religious attitudes toward human life. Profound social change can occur through technological development. Theologians, bioethicists, and social scientists have been concerned with issues ranging from the allocation of resources to decisions at the beginning and end of life to the implications of the human genome project and its potential demographic and societal consequences. Theologians also have played a major role in developing the field of bioethics and continue to play an important role in discussions ranging from abortion to gene therapy (Hanson 1997). The recent approval of RU-486 again raises issues of abortion and choice. Religious and moral values are interwoven throughout discussions of starting and removing life support for severely damaged infants, the disabled, and elderly. Stem cell and embryonic research decisions also are affected by these values.

Although not as preeminent, social issues permeate the development, diffusion, and evaluation of technology. As noted in chapter 2, the decision to determine gender in utero is thought to have affected the gender balance of children in China, with broader implications for population demographics and family formation. The potential for genetic manipulation may well prevent a number of serious genetic diseases, thereby extending life expectancy and creating implications for demographic and societal productivity. The potential for genetic manipulation, however, also raises the specter of eugenics.

Cultural differences across nations also can affect technology development and diffusion, as in the case of the different policies for the distribution of renal dialysis treatment in England and the United States. The recent debate within the deaf community on the use of cochlear implants is another example of cultural influence in the United States. Proponents of "deaf culture" oppose the implants as invasive, of possibly dubious efficacy, and as a threat to deaf culture (Tucker 1998).

Practice Guidelines and the Legal Control of Physician Decision Making

Litigation plays a key role in the development and diffusion of medical technology, from gene patenting to conflicts over the denial of investigational or newly emerging technology by insurers and managed care organizations. The discussion of practice guidelines and legal control of physician decision making is presented here as an example of the role of the courts in MTE. The issue is a major one in the patients' rights debate.

Until about ten years ago, relatively little attention was paid to the role of physician decision making in delivering good-quality health care. The physician's clinical judgment generally served as the patient's gateway to the full panoply of medical technology. However, unless the physician exercised accurate judgment in diagnosing and treating the patient's problems, the application of medical technology to the patient could be useless or even harmful.

The development of clinical practice guidelines, based on medical effectiveness research and evidence-based medicine, was undertaken to enhance clinical decision making, thereby improving the quality of medical care and reducing unnecessary costs associated with substandard care (Freund et al. 1999). MTE provides the underlying support for recommending guidelines (see chapter 11). Efforts to develop clinical practice guidelines raise several important questions about the nature of medical decision making and its effects on the quality and cost of care. What factors and standards generally have guided physician judgment? Health care providers typically have relied on their medical training, the medical literature, peer practices, and informal clinical protocols in determining how to care for patients.

The development of practice guidelines also raises larger societal issues, particularly regarding whether the proper locus of medical decision making, with its power to control life and death through resource allocation, should remain solely within the objective realm of medicine and science (Eddy 1994). For example, a person making a scientifically based decision might conclude that there is a one in a thousand chance of benefit from a procedure. But a value judgment remains necessary to determine whether to go forward with this very low chance of benefit. Patients near death or suffering severe pain would likely view the odds as being worth the risk.

It is believed that patients can use science based guidelines to in form their decision making about medical options, and public and private payers can use them to reach rational social judgments about what level of care to provide (IOM 1992). The desire for objective, science-based decision making in health care is exemplified by Etzioni's (1991) conclusion that the slippery slope of withdrawing care can be avoided if withdrawal decisions are based on the judgment of two physicians who, in turn, base their decision on clear guidelines that can be legitimized by legal means.

Reasonable Standards of Care

The legal system governs the quality of medical decision making through a "reasonable standard of care" mechanism. Under the law, all physicians who provide health care have a duty to provide care that meets a reasonable standard. The legal system does not develop specific rules dictating the substance of patient care decisions, such as whether to perform surgery or to prescribe a drug regimen for a patient's medical condition, but rather governs medical decision making by relying on a physician's professional training and experience to determine whether surgery or drug treatment is most appropriate in a particular case. Physicians whose care falls below the reasonable standard may be held liable for breach of duty and must compensate the patient for injuries caused by failure to exercise the requisite care. Such liability for breach of duty is known as medical malpractice.

Defining Reasonable Care

Whether a physician has met the standard of care in any particular instance may be determined objectively. A patient who alleges that the physician breached the duty of reasonable care has the burden of producing the testimony of a medical expert who can articulate the standard and indicate how the physician in question has failed to meet this standard.

The courts have held that this standard requires only that the physician exercise "ordinary and reasonable care" rather than the highest degree of care. This view has become known as the customary-practice rule and is the legal rule that faces the most scrutiny in the light of research on practice variation and the development of practice guidelines. Whether guidelines should embrace customary practices or set forth new practices—at higher or lower levels of care—is perhaps the most controversial issue related to the development of practice guidelines (Bovbjerg 1975; Eddy 1997). The medical community's growing use of clinical practice guidelines will have significant legal implications as evidence of care standards (Leahy 1989; Hyams, Shapiro, and Brennan 1996). Moreover, the development and application of practice guidelines by managed care organizations and other payers raise the issue of whether cost containment and related financial incentives are appropriate factors for determining whether standards of care are reasonable (Havighurst 1986; Shuman 1997; Larson 1999).

In most states, the standard of care is described for a jury by introducing evidence of what other reasonably competent practitioners with similar training would have done under the circumstances. The customary-practice rule has been criticized as being based largely on a combination of limited clinical studies, unverified beliefs, and professional traditions rather than on reliable data (Leahy 1989).

The Locality Rule

The standard of care embodies several other important rules, including the locality rule, the school rule, and the best-judgment rule. Only the locality factor in the traditionally articulated standard of care has undergone substantial change in recent years. Some claim that judicial change in the locality rule has been a contributing factor to the widespread perception of a medical malpractice crisis.

The locality rule has two important components: (1) the standard against which physicians will be compared is based on the customary practices of reasonably competent physicians in their local area, and (2) in a medical malpractice case, medical evidence could be obtained only from physicians practicing in the local area who are familiar with local customary practices. This traditionally has conferred an important advantage on physicians sued for malpractice. Injured patients have had to seek the assistance of other local physicians (colleagues of the accused), thus creating a situation that critics charge has led to the medical community's "conspiracy of silence" (Robinson 1984).

In 1985, the Mississippi Supreme Court rejected the locality rule in favor of a national standard of care (see *Hall v. Hilbun,* 466 So. 2d 856 [Miss. 1985]). Most other states also have subsequently rejected the locality rule.

The School Rule

The school rule holds that physicians who have received training in a specialty will be held to a standard that reflects this additional training and experience. Thus, if a general practitioner and a specialist treat the same patient, the general practitioner would be obligated to provide the level of care expected of a reasonably competent general practitioner, whereas the specialist would be obligated to provide the level of care expected of a reasonably competent specialist.

A significant implication of the school rule for general practitioners or primary care physicians, particularly in a managed care setting, is that a general or primary care physician may be liable for failure to refer a case that is beyond his or her training or experience to an appropriate specialist. Whether and how practice guidelines are developed to address potential differences in the use of medical technology by general practitioners and specialists will be an important aspect of their development and use.

The Best-Judgment and Minority-View Rules

The best-judgment rule is often referred to as the honest-error-judgment rule, an unfortunate phrasing that leads to confusion about its meaning. The minority-view rule states that where one or more recognized courses of treatment exist, the physician will not be penalized if the chosen course results in an adverse patient outcome. The physician needs to show only that the choice of treatment is supported by some reasonably competent members of the medical profession. There is no consensus among the courts regarding the size of the minority required. Both rules recognize the diversity and uncertainty that exist in medical opinion and are designed to protect the physician from liability for an adverse outcome where appropriate care was provided.

The best-judgment rule pertains to the physician's decision-making process in selecting among multiple recognized treatment approaches. Where there is legitimate but minority support for a given course of treatment, the physician still fails to meet the requisite standard of care if reasonably competent judgment is not exercised in selecting the treatment approach. The court determines whether a physician's decision-making process is reasonable by determining whether other similarly trained physicians under similar circumstances would make the same choice.

As discussed here, courts routinely rely on members of the medical profession for information about standards of medical care. It is important to recognize, however, that the legal system has the last word regarding the level of quality required of physicians. The question of medical negligence is ultimately one of law, and the courts have been known to take it on themselves to define standards of care (see *Hellinger v. Carey*, 518 P.2d 987 [Wash. 1974]).

Legal Standards of Care and the Quality of Physician Decision Making

Despite the law's heavy reliance on recognizable medical standards of care, research on physician practice variation and outcomes effectiveness has raised disturbing doubts. Eddy (1993, 521) stated that the "credibility of clinical judgment, whether exercised individually or collectively, has been severely challenged by observations of wide variations in practice, inappropriate care, and practitioner uncertainty." The Institute of Medicine (1992) noted that several studies of outcomes effectiveness found that (1) there were major unexplained variations in physicians' practice patterns, (2) many procedures were believed to be unnecessary or inappropriate for patients' conditions, and (3) many procedures are characterized by the uncertainty surrounding their effectiveness.

Regarding the customary-practice rule, Eddy (1993, 521) noted that "the presumption that a treatment that is widely used must have some benefit has been shaken not only by reports that many common treatments have no supporting evidence of effectiveness, but by actual trials that have overturned some common benefits." As examples, he pointed to research showing that there was no value to drugs (encainide and flecainide) commonly prescribed for heart attack.

Despite the fundamental importance of good decision making for ensuring the quality of medical care, little is known about how physicians arrive at complicated diagnoses and treatments for particular patients or how they develop their practice styles in general (Eisenberg 1986). Many factors undoubtedly affect physician decision making. Geoffrey Anderson (1993) argued that the factor most relevant to guideline use is how physicians incorporate research evidence into their practices. According to Anderson, Lomas and colleagues' (1989) passive-diffusion model is based on three highly questionable assumptions: that physicians seek out new evidence, that they know how to assess it, and that they either incorporate this knowledge into existing practice patterns or adopt new ones. Lomas and his coauthors stated that the failure of this model to produce appropriate care is a driving force behind the development of guidelines.

Physicians often cite lack of resources as a contributing factor to substandard care. However, other observers have cited additional factors, including "ignorance, incompetence, poor management, and deliberate disregard of established knowledge" (Delamonthe 1993, 218).

15

Evaluation Concerns: Medical Technology Evaluation in the Future
Alan B. Cohen and Ruth S. Hanft

Our journey through the various issues, methods, and policy concerns pertaining to medical technology is nearing its end. No text on this subject would be complete, however, without a concluding chapter on the future of medical technology evaluation (MTE), especially in the changing U.S. health care financing and delivery environment.

In this final chapter, we offer closing thoughts and reflections regarding the key questions raised in chapter 2 and addressed throughout the text. We then discuss future considerations in MTE, focusing on issues of evaluative purpose, priority setting, methods, and the role of government, particularly as they relate to the United States. We conclude by examining how the current managed care environment is likely to affect the development, diffusion, and evaluation of medical technology and by identifying areas that require further study.

Concluding Thoughts on Key Questions

Throughout the book, we have attempted to examine questions of central importance to the development, diffusion, and evaluation of medical technology. In each case, we have endeavored to illuminate the salient issues surrounding the question and to offer the reader a clearer understanding of the nature of the problems that exist. Because these questions are weighty and complex, their treatment in preceding chapters likely has generated as many—if not more—questions than answers. In this section, we attempt to bring closure to those issues where closure may be possible and to share additional insight into others where it may not.

Technology and Rising Costs

For more than two decades, medical technology has been characterized in some quarters as the culprit behind rising health care costs. While there is little doubt that the adoption and use of new technology is indeed a major driver of health care cost growth (Newhouse 1992; Chernew et al. 1998; P. E. Mohr et al. 2001), technology does not deserve to be portrayed in such negative terms, lest we forget its tangible benefits or lose sight of the myriad economic, social, ethical, cultural, and professional forces that influence and mediate its role in medicine as well as its effects on health care spending. In fact, some innovations looming on the technological horizon, such as the impending revolution in genomics and proteomics for the treatment of various diseases, are being hailed as "saviors" of medicine because they promise to transform health care scientifically, economically, and socially (Ellis 1998). Therefore, rather than vilifying technology, it would be far more productive to (1) understand the factors behind health care providers' decisions to adopt and use new technology, (2) develop strategies for improving the decision-making process and associated outcomes, and (3) recognize that MTE is vital to future cost-containment efforts. This last point is especially crucial. If we are to succeed as a nation in controlling our spending on health care and in reallocating our resources judiciously, then substantial investment in MTE is needed to assist in targeting the most promising technologies to develop, adopt, and use (McGregor 1989; Fuchs and Garber 1990). Moreover, MTE will need to move beyond its traditional focus on the technical and economic effects of technology to consider the profound societal changes that are presaged by the genetic revolution (Kitcher 1996).

The Pace of Technology Diffusion

The pace of technology diffusion inspires contentious debate between those who believe that it is too fast and those who perceive it as being too slow. Where one stands on this question ultimately depends on where one sits—that is, whether one is a manufacturer of technology, a health care provider, a payer or purchaser of care, a regulator (e.g., the FDA), or a consumer. For obvious reasons, each of these stakeholders has a different point of view, which in most cases may be at variance with the societal view. What, then, would be an appropriate rate of technology diffusion from a broad societal perspective? Perhaps the answer lies in how much is known about a specific technology and its effects at the point in time when decisions must be made about its adoption and use. As a general rule, a technology should diffuse at a pace that is appropriate to the level of available evidence about its effects. Just as the old dictum "No wine before its time" suggests that wine should not be uncorked before it has reached an acceptable level of maturity, so too should no technology diffuse widely into clinical practice without clear and sufficient knowledge of its risks, benefits, and costs. In many cases, though, the societal impact of a technology cannot be determined for many years. One example of premature diffusion involved the antihypertension drug Posicor, which was removed from the market just ten months after receiving FDA approval because of serious interactions with more than twenty-five other drugs, raising questions about why the drug had been approved (Neergaard 1998).

The Timing of Evaluation

In an ideal world, the evaluation of a given medical technology should be both timely and strategic—timely in relation to the stage of the technology's development and diffusion, and strategic in terms of satisfying the information needs of potential adopters, third-party payers, and regulators. Where possible, the risks, benefits, and costs of the technology should be assessed early in its development and preferably before it has diffused to any appreciable extent. Early MTE, however, is a challenging task, particularly when an emerging technology (e.g., a device or drug) is in a state of flux concerning its ultimate design or formulation for commercial introduction and use (Blume 1998). Historically, the process for evaluating the effects of a new technology generally has proceeded in discrete stages to meet specific information needs that arise over time: first an assessment of safety and efficacy (to satisfy FDA requirements), followed by various assessments of effectiveness (under "average" conditions of use) and by analyses of cost-effectiveness (to meet the demands of health care purchasers seeking cost savings). The changing health care marketplace, with its competitive forces and cost-containment pressures, has altered this dynamic in recent years, making it imperative that cost-effectiveness information be obtained much earlier in the evaluation process, preferably concurrent with assessments of safety, efficacy, and effectiveness (Fuchs and Garber 1990). As a result, many pharmaceutical firms (as well as other technology manufacturers) increasingly are mounting rigorous clinical trials that have cost-effectiveness measures incorporated directly within the study design.

The Need for Reassessment of Technology

Even when safety, efficacy, and cost-effectiveness studies conducted in the earliest stages of a technology's diffusion provide reasonably comprehensive information about its effects, it is important to recognize that these studies are only initial assessments at a single point in time. Further assessment of the technology may be warranted as a result of such factors as continuing concerns about safety, effectiveness, and long-term effects; the emergence of new clinical applications of the technology; and evolutionary changes in the technology itself. The monitoring of new products for safety purposes (to identify adverse effects, drug interactions, technology-induced injuries, and so forth) is essential to the protection of patients, and the FDA currently has in place postmarketing surveillance and reporting systems for drugs and devices that can signal potential problems, as in the cases of Posicor; Baycol, a cholesterol-reducing statin that was withdrawn from the market in 2001 (see chapter 10); and Viagra, the popular impotency drug for males whose growing use has revealed unanticipated drug interactions (Jeffrey and Langreth 1998; Neergaard 2001).

The emergence of new clinical applications for an established technology years after its introduction is not uncommon in medicine. For example, when MRI first began to diffuse in the early 1980s, few physicians envisioned the breadth and diversity of its future applications in clinical practice. Thus, early evaluations focused narrowly on MRI's use in imaging the brain and central nervous system. Over time, as MRI evolved to include imaging of cardiac blood flow and of various tissues, evaluating its diagnostic effectiveness in each new application became important. In addition, there have been instances in which a technology has been discredited as either harmful or inefficacious for a given clinical purpose but later has reemerged for a different purpose, requiring an independent assessment. One example is the drug Thalidomide, whose use in treating morning sickness in pregnancy was abandoned in the 1960s when it was found to have harmful teratogenic effects on fetuses but which now may have potential therapeutic benefit in treating several conditions, including chronic graft-versus-host disease and leprosy (NIH 1997; Annas and Elias 1999; Aoki 2001b). Another example involves the internal mammary artery, which in the 1970s was demonstrated to be inefficacious in treating angina pectoris (Barsamian 1977) but which attracted renewed interest in the 1980s when studies showed it to be superior to the saphenous vein in coronary artery by-pass graft surgery (Spencer 1986).

Formal reassessment of established technologies generally does not occur, however, because the vast majority of regulatory attention and MTE resources are focused instead on assessing new technologies. As Banta and Thacker (1990, 239) have noted, "there is a comparable if not greater need to emphasize periodic reassessment of existing technologies." Thus, the operative rule should be that once is not enough, and both monitoring and reassessment of technology should be part of an ongoing evaluative process.

The Evaluation of Surgical Procedures

As noted in chapter 10, the introduction of new surgical procedures is not regulated at present by any government entity. Unlike drugs and devices, which must be approved by the FDA before market entry, new surgical procedures may diffuse easily and swiftly into clinical practice with little evaluation of their risks, benefits, and costs. From time to time, there have been calls for regulatory oversight of surgical innovations, the principal argument being that such untested procedures may be costly and potentially hazardous and thus should be subjected to the same evaluative scrutiny as pharmaceuticals and devices. Opponents of such control argue on philosophical grounds that it would be detrimental to surgical innovation and would add unnecessary expense to the R&D process. A procedure, by definition, is a combination of surgical technique with a drug and/or a device (or instrument). Controlled trials of surgical procedures, on average, are more difficult and costly to design and to mount than similar trials involving pharmaceuticals or devices as a result both of the complex nature of the procedures themselves and of the need to involve multiple clinical centers in the study design. The bureaucratic apparatus required to regulate the introduction of new surgical procedures likely would be burdensome. Thus, while surgical procedures undoubtedly would benefit from more rigorous MTE in the early stages of diffusion, the costs of a regulatory approach might well outweigh its benefits. Instead, the medical profession—particularly the specialty societies—should assume greater leadership in setting priorities for the evaluation of surgical procedures and in formulating standards for the use of such procedures in clinical practice (Frazier and Mosteller 1995).

Future Considerations in MTE

As described in chapter 9, the process of MTE varies remarkably across nations. In the United States, for example, MTE involves a host of public and private organizations that do not work in concert with one another. In considering how the generic process of MTE in health care may be strengthened and improved—particularly in the United States—we present a prescriptive outline that concentrates on four parameters: evaluative purpose, priority setting, methods, and the role of government.

Evaluative Purpose of MTE

Technology evaluation may be used for one or more of the following evaluative purposes:

- to assess the safety, efficacy, and effectiveness of a technology when applied for a specific medical purpose (whether preventive, diagnostic, therapeutic, or rehabilitative);
- to provide information to providers, payers, and consumers regarding the marginal or incremental cost-effectiveness of a technology compared with existing clinical alternatives;
- to provide information on appropriate strategies for using a technology to achieve favorable health outcomes and to assure quality of care;
- to illuminate issues relating to the social, ethical, and legal implications of adopting and using a technology; and
- to assist in making policy decisions regarding resource allocation at national, state, local, and institutional levels.

In most cases, MTE is undertaken to satisfy multiple objectives on this list. The relative emphasis placed on each depends on a nation's specific political, cultural, ethical, economic, and social characteristics as well as on different stakeholders' particular information needs. However, the generic MTE approach employed is similar across widely diverse systems of financing and delivery of care. In an ideal process, the evaluative purpose(s) of MTE should always be clearly specified in advance.

Priority Setting in MTE

The early identification of a technology as potentially safe/valuable or as harmful/inefficacious is a challenging task. With literally thousands of scientists and physicians experimenting with medical innovations at many basic and applied research levels and with no established priority-setting method for MTE, the current process tends to be haphazard, with some technologies introduced swiftly and others stymied in the early stages of development for lack of adequate evaluation.

An ideal system would scan basic and applied research in progress (much of it funded by government sources) and would identify potentially promising technologies for formalized assessment at relatively early stages of development (preferably at the stage of translation from basic research to applied research). Even under the best circumstances, no priority-setting system will be able to identify all existing technology development or be able to handle the volume and cost of assessing every identified technology. Nevertheless, a priority-setting process in MTE is greatly needed to guide individual organizations and agencies in determining which technologies should be assigned high priority for assessment given resource constraints. The Institute of Medicine (1992) recommends that a priority-setting process be

- consistent with the mission of the organization that will use it (e.g., for health outcome improvement);
- consistent with the information needs of users (e.g., clinicians);
- efficient in using scarce resources available for MTE; and
- capable of operating in the real world (i.e., sensitive to the political, economic, and social context in which it is used and thus accountable to the public).

Several systems for selecting technologies for evaluation have been proposed, with differing criteria and weights. The criteria listed here have been culled and synthesized from several sources (Eddy 1989; Phelps and Parente 1990; IOM 1992). A technology should be given priority for MTE if one of the following parameters is met:

- it addresses a high-prevalence disease or condition;
- it addresses a disease or condition with a high burden of illness (severity, urgency);
- either it or the health problem that it addresses has high unit or aggregate costs;
- its use in clinical practice is marked by substantial variation;
- it possesses high potential to improve health outcomes;
- it has high potential to decrease the cost of care;
- it has high potential to inform ethical, legal, or social issues;
- its use is surrounded by scientific, professional, or public controversy;
- there is a need to make a regulatory decision about its adoption; or
- there is a need to make a payment decision about its use.

The specific weight assigned to each parameter will vary according to the interests and information needs of an individual stakeholder. Yet even when agreement exists about the relative importance of these priority-setting criteria, questions remain concerning the methodology of MTE.

The Methodology of MTE

While there is reasonable agreement among analysts regarding economic evaluation methods (M. Gold et al. 1996), controversy continues to surround the issue of whether randomized controlled trials (RCTs) or database analyses should be the method of choice in evaluating the clinical safety and efficacy of technologies. The more prominent questions include: Should all technologies be subjected to the gold standard of RCTs? How safe is safe, and how effective is effective? When should a trial be stopped on the basis of early findings? Is demonstrated cost-effectiveness under RCT conditions more (or less) meaningful than cost-effectiveness under nonexperimental conditions? How comprehensive in scope should MTE be?

Despite divergent professional opinions on these and other methodological questions, some clear lessons and recommendations emerge.

- There is a need to design simpler clinical trials that may be conducted with greater ease, efficiency, and timeliness (Frazier and Mosteller 1995). One way to accomplish this may be to encourage the expanded use of the "firm system" in large hospitals—that is, setting up "firms" of patients to act as comparison groups in clinical trials (Neuhauser 1992).

- There is a need to design better economic evaluations within the context of clinical trials (M. Gold et al. 1996). Cost-effectiveness studies of new technologies should be conducted at the earliest possible stages of development and diffusion, and greater emphasis should be placed on measuring quality of life (Fuchs and Garber 1990; Frazier and Mosteller 1995). As technologies diffuse and their service volumes increase, their unit costs may decrease as a result of economies of scale. Under such circumstances, new cost-effectiveness studies might be warranted.
- The results of clinical trials and economic evaluations should be organized in a common database available to all users of the information. Through the evolving Cochrane Collaboration, data from clinical trials presently are being archived and synthesized (Cochrane Collaboration 2001), but this effort should be expanded to include relevant economic (cost-effectiveness) and quality-of-life information.
- Appropriateness studies and clinical practice guidelines should become integral parts of any MTE system. The failure of health care providers and consumers to adopt the findings of evaluations may be attributable in many cases to poor dissemination strategies that lack practical information on the appropriate use of technology. Practice guidelines reinforced by MCOs and other organizations, together with better consumer information, may lead to more rational diffusion of new technologies over time.
- An ongoing system of postmarket surveillance and periodic reassessment of the effects of technologies should be devised and implemented. In particular, the safety, effectiveness, and cost-effectiveness of drugs and devices should be reevaluated as they diffuse and are applied for new clinical purposes.
- Wherever possible, MTE should be comprehensive in scope and method, with ethical, legal, and social issues identified early in the diffusion process and addressed accordingly within the assessment design.

The Role of Government in MTE

Technology evaluation in the United States presently is fragmented among an array of public and private organizations (see chapter 9). The federal government plays multiple roles regarding medical technology—as a promoter of technology development, as a regulator of technology diffusion, as an evaluator of technological impact and effectiveness, and as a purchaser of technological goods and services (see chapter 2). Specifically, these roles are carried out through the following agency activities:

- The FDA has regulatory oversight for premarket approval and postmarket surveillance of drugs, biologics, and devices, with individual evaluations financed by the pharmaceutical, biotechnology, and device industries and often performed in academic health centers (see chapter 10).
- Within the National Institutes of Health, the Office of Medical Applications of Research convenes consensus-development conferences, while individual institutes support biomedical research that often leads to the development of new technologies as well as clinical research (including multicenter RCTs) that evaluates the effects of technologies (see chapter 6).
- The Department of Veterans Affairs and the Department of Defense conduct clinical trials and other evaluations of technology and purchase technological goods and services for their constituencies.
- The Centers for Medicare and Medicaid Services (CMS) make technology coverage policy decisions for the Medicare program that result in decisions to purchase technological goods and services for Medicare beneficiaries (see chapter 12).
- The Medicare Payment Advisory Commission is responsible for advising Congress on payment policies concerning the Medicare program, including issues related to factors affecting program expenditures and methods for paying providers for technologically based services (see chapter 12).
- The Agency for Healthcare Research and Quality (AHRQ) evaluates available evidence regarding new technology and advises the CMS on Medicare coverage policy, funds Evidence-Based Practice Centers and Centers for Education and Research on

Therapeutics, supports research on medical effectiveness and patient safety and cosponsors the National Guideline Clearing-house (see chapter 11).

In addition to these federal activities, state governments engage in limited MTE activities for state Medicaid programs, with Oregon perhaps the most active in terms of assessing the benefits of specific technologies and developing a priority listing of covered services (see chapter 12). In the private sector, many large HMOs conduct MTE studies and develop practice guidelines. Various groups, such as the American Medical Association, the American Hospital Association, the American College of Physicians—American Society of Internal Medicine, and diverse medical specialty societies, as well as numerous academic health centers and private research organizations, conduct a wide array of MTE activities for manufacturers, insurers, HMOs, hospital systems, and others.

Never before in American history has so much collective activity—public and private—occurred in technology evaluation. However, the efforts are uncoordinated and diffuse, producing in some cases conflicting information about specific technologies that confuses consumers and providers alike and arguably creates more chaos than order in the health care system. Most important, there exists no central locus of control or coordination for priority setting in MTE, for developing methodological standards, and for policy-making regarding the systemwide diffusion and coverage of medical technology. Unlike most industrialized countries, which have national policies toward medical technology and where the national government provides leadership in MTE, the United States lacks both a coherent national policy and a recognized national leader in MTE. For some stakeholders in the American health care system, the current situation is not only tolerable but in fact may be preferred in an economic environment that highly values free enterprise and minimal government interference. Indeed, prior efforts to establish a national policy and an organizational locus for MTE (in the form of the National Center for Health Care Technology) were quashed by industry and professional groups seeking to maintain their hegemony over technology and medicine (Perry 1982). Many other stakeholders, however, see the absence of a comprehensive national policy as a threat to public safety, consumer sovereignty, and cost containment in a resource-constrained health care system. What roles, then, should government play in MTE, and how extensive should those roles be?

It is fair to assume that the federal government will continue in its roles as a promoter and a purchaser of technology as a result of its public mandate to support biomedical and clinical research and of its internal need to purchase technological goods and services for diverse populations that include Medicare beneficiaries, military personnel and their families, veterans, federal employees, and Native Americans. Its roles as a regulator and an evaluator, however, require strengthening, especially in view of the systemwide deficiencies noted previously. Alternative policy models have been advanced as proposals to remedy this situation, including (1) restrictive rationing strategies (Aaron and Schwartz 1984), (2) a national institute for health care evaluation (Egdahl and Gertman 1978; Bunker, Fowles, and Schaffarzick 1982; Mosteller and Burdick 1989), and (3) a comprehensive national program of MTE (Perry and Pillar 1990). All three models represent public-sector solutions, with federal agencies residing at the core of activities in each case, although their respective policy purviews vary in scope. None has been adopted, most likely because key stakeholders in the private sector have been unwilling to cede control over such activities to public agencies. Thus, with these harsh political realities in mind, we offer the following suggestions for improving existing policy for MTE.

- Establish a public-private partnership among all relevant stakeholders to set priorities and to pool resources for conducting MTE. A partnership among the many public and private organizations holding a stake in technology-related decisions is highly desirable. Assuming that federal antitrust laws would not be violated by such an alliance, activities should include (1) development and implementation of a priority-setting system that would identify and select emerging technologies for MTE; (2) pooling of resources (expertise, data, and funding) to support evaluation activities for selected high-priority technologies; (3) development and implementation of methodological standards for MTE; and (4) sharing and dissemination of data and information from alliance-sponsored MTE activities to support decision making in all aspects of technology development and diffusion. If adopted, this public-private partnership could maximize the use of limited resources for MTE and could result in more efficient and timely exchange of valuable information for decision making by all concerned parties. For these reasons, the membership should include representatives of: relevant federal agencies (FDA, AHRQ, CMS, the Medicare Payment Advisory Commission, the Department of Veterans Affairs, the Department of Defense, and the National Institutes of Health); appropriate state agencies (Medicaid programs, CON programs); private insurers and payers; HMOs and managed care organizations; technology manufacturers (especially the pharmaceutical, biotechnology, and device industries); professional and specialty groups (medicine, nursing, and others); the hospital industry; the home care industry; academic research centers and private research organizations; and consumer groups. Even under the best circumstances, a partnership of this kind will face severe political and legal challenges. Members will need to assiduously avoid engaging in collusive activity (e.g., using the information from technology evaluations to set common payment rates or prices for services), and the partnership will need to comply with existing laws and regulations governing restraint of trade and antitrust. It is also safe to assume that stakeholder politics will threaten to compromise, if not thwart, rational decision making, so the partnership will need to establish well-developed rules of behavior for all participants.

- Make cost-effectiveness an explicit review criterion in CMS technology coverage policy decisions for the Medicare program. At present, FDA regulation of pharmaceuticals, biologics, and medical devices is based solely on evidence of safety and effectiveness, and the CMS does not engage formally in determinations of cost impact when making technology coverage policy decisions for the Medicare program. With growing pressures for cost reduction in the health care system (sometimes at the expense of health care quality), it is time for the CMS to incorporate cost-effectiveness as an explicit review criterion within its policy purview. It is hoped that this change will lead to more appropriate technology coverage decisions under the Medicare program.

- Expand federal efforts to disseminate information regarding medical technology. Information about what works (and what does not) in health care is essential both to providers and to well-informed consumers. Unfortunately, few public sources of such information exist, and the demise of the U.S. Congress's

Office of Technology Assessment, after a distinguished twenty-three year career of sponsoring and publishing numerous research reports on health care technology for professionals and laypersons, left a serious void (U.S. Congress, OTA 1995). The AHRQ, particularly through its Evidence-Based Practice Centers, its National Guideline Clearinghouse, and its Centers for Education and Research on Therapeutics, is attempting to fill this void, but there remains a clear need for the federal government to increase the level of its dissemination efforts.

Today's Managed Care Environment

The U.S. health care system presently is dominated by competitive market forces. National health expenditures continue to rise. After a brief respite during the late 1990s, the pace of spending once again has quickened (Heffler et al. 2001; Levit et al. 2003). Purchasers of health care, particularly employer groups, have assumed an increasingly important role in decision making that directly affects the adoption and use of medical technology (J. B. White and Rundle 1998). Continuing uncertainty also remains about managed care's ability to control costs that increasingly seem to be driven by technological advances, especially in the fields of pharmaceuticals and biotechnology.

In a scholarly review of the economic and policy literatures, Chernew and his colleagues (1998) examined the relationships among managed care, medical technology, and health care cost growth and concluded that managed care may have reduced the rate of health care cost growth in selected markets during the 1980s and early 1990s, largely because of spillover effects on the entire market, but that the magnitude of these reductions appeared insufficient to stabilize or reduce the percentage of gross domestic product devoted to health care. Moreover, these managed-care-induced reductions in cost growth may at best have been only transitional and not indicative of a long-term trend. The authors also concluded from the evidence that new medical technologies were indeed key drivers of rising health care expenditures and that managed care's ability to control technology diffusion in the future was unclear.

Taken together, these conclusions pose important implications for future policy, practice, and research. Indeed, the finding that managed-care-induced reductions in cost growth may be only transitional and are of insufficient magnitude to stabilize or reduce the percentage of the gross domestic product devoted to health care is troubling for several reasons. It suggests that managed care may not be the magic bullet for cost containment that its proponents believe it to be. It also raises serious policy questions about the long-term prospects for controlling national health care spending and about the wisdom of policy decisions by federal and state governments to enroll vulnerable populations, such as the elderly, the poor, and the disabled, in managed care plans under the Medicare and Medicaid programs (Cohen 1998). If managed care is to have a long-term constraining effect on health care spending, then it must be able to manage the costs associated with technology adoption and use.

What then are the likely effects of managed care and market forces on the development and diffusion of new technology? In view of the changing financial incentives affecting technology decisions under managed care (see chapter 5), three future scenarios seem plausible:

- an optimistic vision in which managed care yields net positive effects by generating appropriate incentives that foster the development, adoption, and use of cost-effective innovations, that encourage the design of more rigorous evaluation studies, and that empower purchasers and consumers to demand better information to support their decision making;
- a pessimistic outlook in which managed care produces net negative effects by creating perverse incentives that work to stifle the development of beneficial but unprofitable innovations, that promote the adoption of cost-saving technologies at the expense of health care quality, and that create inequities in access to technology because of restrictive gatekeeper practices and limits imposed on consumers' choice of providers; and
- a neutral view in which managed care has little or no overall effect on technology, allowing the current technological imperative of medicine to continue driving management decisions about the nature and types of innovations to be developed and adopted.

The first scenario might be called the health care manager's fantasy, whereas the second may represent the consumer's dilemma. It is difficult to imagine either of these polar opposites becoming the dominant scenario in the near term. Some have argued that the third scenario is most likely to prevail, at least in the short run, while managers and policymakers continue to aspire to the goals engendered by the first and strive to avoid the pitfalls of the second (S. H. Altman 1997). The only certainty at present is how little we know about the impact of managed care on health care cost growth and on medical technology diffusion (Chernew et al. 1998). A need clearly exists for further research in a variety of areas.

Areas for Future Research

Further research into managed care and medical technology is needed in at least four broad areas (Cohen 1998). First and foremost, studies are needed of the general effects of managed care in diverse markets, geographic areas, and populations, particularly as managed care practices evolve over time and as managed care plans penetrate new markets and populations, most notably the Medicare population. For example, the Balanced Budget Act of 1997 fostered enrollment of Medicare beneficiaries in managed care plans under the Medicare + Choice program. However, many plans either have withdrawn from the program since 2000, citing low payment levels, or have adopted aggressive cost-reduction practices that include higher cost sharing for beneficiaries and substitution of generic drugs for brand-name prescription drugs (M. Gold 2001; Achman and Gold 2002). Thus, research is needed on the effects of these changes on Medicare populations' access to new technology. In addition, we need to overcome the limitations of previous studies by looking at the effects of managed care on cost growth outside the hospital, such as in the ambulatory and home care settings, where many services are being shifted for cost-reduction purposes and where new technologies are being used with increasing frequency. Studies of the effects of these service and technology shifts on total cost growth and of managed care's ability to control such expenditures are vital to our understanding of managed care.

A second area for further exploration involves physician behavior under managed care. While physicians appear to employ treatment patterns for their fee-for-service patients that mirror the patterns for their managed care patients, suggesting the existence of spillover effects from managed care (Chernew et al. 1998), we really do not know the extent to which physicians are aware of patients' insurance status when making clinical decisions and how this information may influence those decisions. As the managed care picture becomes even more diverse and complex, will individual physicians be able to continue managing all of their patients in the same uniform practice style, or will they be increasingly pressured to manage patients differently depending on the specific practice guidelines or protocols of the patients' managed care plans? Studies of such decision-making behavior would be illuminating.

Third, numerous research questions abound with regard to the effects of managed care on technology diffusion. For example, studies of the incentives for technology adoption and use are needed to gain a better understanding of the dynamics inherent in the technology R&D process (Weisbrod 1991, 1994) and to determine how these incentives influence the behavior of providers, consumers, payers, and manufacturers. As hospitals continue to form integrated delivery systems and as decisions to adopt and use new technologies in those systems come under the control of managers in parent organizations, it becomes imperative that we study how these organizational changes—in concert with managed care incentives—affect technology adoption and use decisions. Studies within market areas are particularly valuable to assess the effects of technology adoption decisions by providers on their competitors ("first mover" effects) and to understand the benefits and risks of different adoption strategies. Similarly, research into how managed care specifically affects physicians' decisions to adopt and use new technology will be important to our overall understanding of managed care.

The incentives under managed care clearly favor the adoption of substitutive technologies, but this is not always possible, and medicine has a long history of producing expensive "halfway" innovations (L. Thomas 1977) that often are additive and labor increasing. Thus, the extent to which managed care may be able to control the adoption and use of complementary technologies will be crucial, and studies that analyze a specific technology—especially relative to its competing clinical alternatives within a cost-effectiveness context—are needed and represent a fourth major area of inquiry. For example, managed care plans have looked to various pharmaceuticals as potential cost-saving alternatives to expensive hospitalizations, but dramatic growth in drug spending has caused many plans to reevaluate the management of their pharmacy benefits within the context of their premium structures (J. B. White and Rundle 1998). Broader application of cost-effectiveness analysis and pharmacoeconomic studies would provide both managers and health care practitioners with useful information on these kinds of questions.

In addition to these four areas of research on the effects of managed care, studies of the social impacts of medical technology and of access to new technology by various racial and ethnic population groups are needed. While racial and ethnic disparities in health care, particularly with regard to access and use of various medical technologies, are well documented (see chapter 13), new evidence recently has come to light suggesting that subtle racial prejudice and differences in the quality of care received by African-Americans and Latinos may contribute to their higher death rates from cancer, heart disease, diabetes, and HIV infection (IOM 2002). The IOM found that the disparities in access to care persisted even when minority and white patients had the same insurance and income, and the study recommended further research to identify sources of racial and ethnic disparities, especially the prevalence and influence of bias, prejudice, and stereotyping on the part of clinicians and health care providers.

Conclusion

In conclusion, advances in medical science and technology continue to proliferate at a staggering pace. It has never been more important to evaluate those innovations—objectively, comprehensively, and expeditiously—in terms of their potential value to health care and to communicate the findings of such evaluations to a broad set of audiences. The field of MTE, although continuously evolving and maturing, is still relatively young. Its future role in health care seems indisputable. It will become an invaluable endeavor in society, vital both to our understanding of what constitutes effective health care and to our sustained efforts to make wise and efficient use of our resources. Numerous challenges lie ahead—some methodological, others political, and many either ethical or social in nature.

The road to health care reform in the United States has been and remains a long and arduous one, fraught with controversial issues of prescription drug coverage, cost containment, workforce shortages, and managed care "abuses" dominating the current policy discussions. Whether we ultimately reach the goal of universal access to high-quality, affordable health care for our citizens will depend not only on political forces at work but also on our ability to harness technological change in a positive and constructive way. As health professionals interested in the evaluation and management of medical technology, we bear responsibility for assuring that the field of MTE progresses and that it leads to better-informed decision making in our health care system. Without MTE and the valuable knowledge that it produces, the health care system will suffer and the goal of reform will remain elusive. With it, decision makers will benefit and the possibilities for improved health care may indeed be virtually limitless.

Appendix: List of Acronyms

AAHP	American Association of Health Plans
ACC	American College of Cardiology
ACHP	Alliance of Community Health Plans
ACOG	American College of Obstetricians and Gynecologists
ACP-ASIM	American College of Physicians–American Society of Internal Medicine
ACR	American College of Radiology
ACS	American College of Surgeons
AHA	American Hospital Association
AHCPR	Agency for Health Care Policy and Research
AHPA	American Health Planning Association
AHRQ	Agency for Healthcare Research and Quality
AMA	American Medical Association
AMDM	Association of Medical Diagnostics Manufacturers
APC	Ambulatory payment classification
CBA	Cost-benefit analysis
CBER	Center for Biologics Evaluation and Research
CCOHTA	Canadian Coordinating Office for Health Technology Assessment
CDC	Centers for Disease Control and Prevention
CDER	Center for Drug Evaluation and Research
CDRH	Center for Devices and Radiological Health
CEA	Cost-effectiveness analysis
CMS	Centers for Medicare and Medicaid Services
CON	Certificate of need
CONSORT	Consolidated Standards of Reporting Trials
CT	Computed tomography
CUA	Cost-utility analysis
DEALE	Declining exponential approximation of life expectancy

383

DRG	Diagnosis-related group
EFM	Electronic fetal monitoring
EPCs	Evidence-Based Practice Centers
FACCT	Foundation for Accountability
FDA	Food and Drug Administration
FFS	Fee for service
GAO	U.S. General Accounting Office
GHC	Group Health Cooperative
HCFA	Health Care Financing Administration
HCTI	Health Care Technology Institute
HCUP	Healthcare Cost & Utilization Project
HMO	Health maintenance organization
HPHC	Harvard Pilgrim Health Care
HTA	Health technology assessment
IHI	Institute for Healthcare Improvement
INAHTA	International Network of Agencies for Health Technology Assessment
IND	Investigational new drug
IOM	Institute of Medicine
KP	Kaiser Permanente
MCO	Managed care organization
MDMA	Medical Device Manufacturers Association
MDRC	Management Decision and Research Center
MedPAC	Medicare Payment Advisory Commission
MRI	Magnetic resonance imaging
MTE	Medical technology evaluation
MTPPI	Medical Technology and Practice Patterns Institute
NDA	New drug application
NEMA	National Electrical Manufacturers Association
NGC	National Guideline Clearinghouse
NIH	National Institutes of Health
NLM	National Library of Medicine
OTA	U.S. Congress, Office of Technology Assessment
PDUFA	Prescription Drug User Fee Act
PET	Positron emission tomography
PhRMA	Pharmaceutical Research and Manufacturers of America
PMA	Premarket approval
PPO	Preferred provider organization
PPRC	Physician Payment Review Commission
PPS	Prospective Payment System

ProPAC	Prospective Payment Assessment Commission
PSRO	Professional Standards Review Organization
QA	Quality assurance
QALY	Quality-adjusted life year
QI	Quality improvement
R&D	Research and development
RCT	Randomized controlled trial
SBU	Swedish Council on Technology Assessment in Health Care
UHC	University HealthSystem Consortium
UM	Utilization management
UR	Utilization review

References

Aaron, H. J. 1991. *Serious and Unstable Condition: Financing America's Health Care.* Washington, DC: Brookings Institution.

Aaron, H. J., and W. B. Schwartz. 1984. *The Painful Prescription: Rationing Hospital Care.* Washington, DC: Brookings Institution.

Achman, L., and M. Gold. 2002. *Medicare + Choice: Beneficiaries Will Face Higher Cost-Sharing in 2002.* New York: Commonwealth Fund.

Acton, J. P. 1973. *Evaluating Public Programs to Save Lives: The Case of Heart Attacks.* Report no. R950RC. Santa Monica, CA: RAND.

Adams, C. 2001. FDA Questions Safety and Efficacy of Abbott's Popular Thyroid Drug. *Street Journal,* June 1.

Adams, C. 2002. FDA Is Seeking a 60% Increase in User Fees for Drug Reviews. *Wall Street Journal,* February 7.

Adams, M. E., N. T. McCall, D. T. Gray, M. J. Orza, and T. C. Chalmers. 1992. Economic Analysis in Randomized Controlled Trials. *Medical Care* 30:231–43.

Aday, L. A., and R. Andersen. 1974. A Framework for the Study of Access to Medical Care. *Health Services Research* 9:208–20.

Aday, L. A., and R. Andersen. 1980. Equity to Access to Medical Care: A Conceptual and Empirical Overview. *Medical Care* 19 (supplement): 4–27.

Advanced Medical Technology Association. 2003. *AdvaMed: About the Organization.* Available at http://www.advamed.org.html.

AHA. 1987. Law: Fear of Expansion Keeps CON Alive. *Hospitals,* June 20, p. 76.

AHA. 1997. *Summary of State Certificate of Need Laws, September 9, 1997.* Chicago: American Hospital Association.

AHCPR. 1991. *Report to Congress: Progress of Research on Outcomes of Health Care Services and Procedures.* AHCPR publication no. 91-0004. Rockville, MD: U.S. Department of Health and Human Services.

AHCPR. 1994. *Magnetic Resonance Angiography: Vascular and Flow Imaging.* AHCPR publication no. 95-0004. Rockville, MD: U.S. Department of Health and Human Services.

AHCPR. 1997. AHCPR Announces First Evidence Report Topics. Media advisory, October 17.

AHCPR Names Evidence-Based Practice Centers. 1997. *Health Technology Assessment* 9 (3): 6.

AHRQ. 1999. *Reauthorization Fact Sheet.* AHRQ publication no. 00-P002, December. Available at http://www.ahrq.gov/news/ahrqfact.

AHRQ. 2000. *The National Guideline Clearinghouse Fact Sheet.* AHRQ publication no. 00-DP004, July. Available at http://www.ahrq.gov/clinic/ngcfact.

AHRQ. 2001a. *Centers for Education and Research on Therapeutics.* Available at http://www.ahrq.gov/clinic/certsovr.

AHRQ. 2001b. *Evidence-Based Practice Centers.* Overview. October. Available at http://www.ahrq.gov/clinic/epc.

AHRQ. 2001c. *About AHRQ.* Available at http://www.ahrq.gov.

AHRQ. 2001d. *CONQUEST Fact Sheet.* Available at http://www.ahrq.gov/qual /conquest.

AHRQ. 2001e. *Consumer Assessment of Health Plans (CAHPS): Fact Sheet.* Available at http://www.ahrq.gov/qual/cahpfact.

AHRQ. 2001f. *Patient Safety Task Force Fact Sheet.* Available at http://www .ahrq.gov/qual/taskforce.

AHRQ. 2002a. AHRQ and NIH Form Partnership to Broaden Evidence Used in Consensus Development Conferences. Press release, January 14. Available at http://www.ahrq.gov/news/press.

AHRQ. 2002b. AHRQ Seeks Request for Proposals for Evidence-Based Practice Centers II. Press release, January 18. Available at http://www.ahrq.gov /news/press.

AHRQ. 2002c. New Evidence-Based Practice Center (EPC II) Awards. Press release, June 21. Available at http://www.ahrq.gov/news/press.

AHRQ. 2002d. New AHRQ Initiative Will Move Research into Practice More Quickly. Press release, November 15. Available at http://www.ahrq.gov /news/press.

AHRQ. 2003. Evidence-Based Practice Centers. Available at http:/www .ahrq.gov/clinic/epcII.

Alberts, M. J., G. Hademenos, R. E. Latchaw, A. Jagoda, J. R. Marler, M. R. Mayberg, R. D. Starke, H. W. Todd, K. M. Viste, M. Girgus, T. Shephard, M. Emr, P. Shwayder, and M. D. Walker. 2000. Recommendations for the Establishment of Primary Stroke Centers. *Journal of the American Medical Association* 283:3102–9.

Alexander, G. C., and A. R. Sehgal. 1998. Barriers to Cadaveric Renal Transplantation among Blacks, Women, and the Poor. *Journal of the American Medical Association* 280:1148–52.

Alliance of Community Health Plans. 2001. *About CHP.* Available at http://www.achp.org.

Altman, L. K. 1990. New Method of Analyzing Health Data Stirs Debate. *New York Times,* August 21.

Altman, S. H. 1988. Impact of the Changing Medical Payment System on Technological Innovation and Utilization. In *New Medical Devices: Invention, Development, and Use,* ed. K. B. Ekelman, 93–103. Washington, DC: National Academy Press.

Altman, S. H. 1997. Closing Remarks. Conference on Health System Change and the Development and Diffusion of Health Care Technology, Council on the Economic Impact of Health System Change, Washington, DC, June 22.

Altman, S. H., and S. S. Wallack. 1979. Technology on Trial—Is It the Culprit behind Rising Health Costs? The Case for and Against. In *Medical Technology: The Culprit behind Health Care Costs?* ed. S. H. Altman and R. J. Blendon, 24–38. Washington, DC: National Center for Health Services Research.

Altman, S. [H.], and D. Young. 1993. A Decade of Medicare's Prospective Payment System: Success or Failure? *Journal of American Health Policy* 3:11–19.

American Health Planning Association. 2003. *2003 Relative Scope and Review Thresholds of CON Regulation.* Available at http://www.ahpanet.org.

Anders, G. 1993. Vital Statistic: Disputed Cost of Creating a Drug. *Wall Street Journal,* November 9.

Anderson, G. 1993. Implementing Practice Guidelines. *Canadian Medical Association Journal* 148:753–55.

Anderson, G. F. 1992. All-Payer Ratesetting: Down but Not Out. *Health Care Financing Review* (1991 annual supplement) 14:35–41.

Anderson, G. F., P. Chaulk, and E. Fowler. 1993. Maryland: A Regulatory Approach to Health System Reform. *Health Affairs* 12:40–47.

Anderson, G. [F.], and E. Steinberg. 1984. To Buy or Not to Buy: Technology Acquisition under Prospective Payment. *New England Journal of Medicine* 311:182–85.

Anderson, G. F., and E. P. Steinberg. 1994. Role of the Hospital in the Acquisition of Technology. In *Adopting New Medical Technology,* ed. A. C. Gelijns and H. V. Dawkins, 61–70. Washington, DC: National Academy Press.

Anderson, G. [F.], E. Steinberg, and R. Heyssel. 1994. The Pivotal Role of the Academic Health Center. *Health Affairs* 13:146–58.

Andreasen, B. 1988. Consensus Conferences in Different Countries. *International Journal of Technology Assessment in Health Care* 4:305–8.

Angell, M. 1985. Cost Containment and the Physician. *Journal of the American Medical Association* 254:1203–7.

Annas, G. J., and S. Elias. 1999. Thalidomide and the *Titanic:* Reconstructing the Technology Tragedies of the Twentieth Century. *American Journal of Public Health* 89:98–101.

Aoki, N. 2000. Boom to Bust to Boom: Biotech Industry Growing Stronger but No End Is Seen to Pendulum Swing. *Boston Globe,* October 25.

Aoki, N. 2001a. Health's Price Tag: Soaring Cost of Drugs Spurs Numerous Debates on Insurance, Care for All. *Boston Globe,* March 28.

Aoki, N. 2001b. The Price of Success: Orphan Drug Act Has Spurred Advances—and Disputes. *Boston Globe,* July 25.

Arno, P. S., K. A. Bonuck, and M. Davis. 1995. Rare Diseases, Drug Development, and AIDS: The Impact of the Orphan Drug Act. *Milbank Quarterly* 73:231–52.

Arno, P. S., K. A. Bonuck, and R. Padgug. 1994. The Economic Impact of High-Technology Home Care. *Hastings Center Report* 24 (special supplement): S15–19.

Asbury, C. H. 1985. *Orphan Drugs: Medical versus Market Value.* Lexington, MA: Lexington Books.

Asbury, C. H. 1991. The Orphan Drug Act: The First 7 Years. *Journal of the American Medical Association* 265:893–97.

Ayanian, J. Z., P. D. Cleary, J. S. Weissman, and A. M. Epstein. 1999. The Effect of Patients' Preferences on Racial Differences in Access to Renal Transplantation. *New England Journal of Medicine* 341:1661–69.

Bach, P. B., L. D. Cramer, J. L. Warren, and C. B. Begg. 1999. Racial Differences in the Treatment of Early-Stage Lung Cancer. *New England Journal of Medicine* 341:1198–1205.

Baird, K. L. 1999. The New NIH and FDA Medical Research Policies: Targeting Gender, Promoting Justice. *Journal of Health Politics, Policy, and Law* 24: 531–65.

Baker, L. C. 1997. *Managed Care and Technology Adoption in Health Care: Evidence from Magnetic Resonance Imaging.* Stanford, CA: Stanford University.

Baker, L. C., and S. K. Wheeler. 1998. Managed Care and Technology Diffusion: The Case of MRI. *Health Affairs* 17:195–207.

Banta, H. D. 1980a. Computed Tomography: Cost Containment Misdirected. *American Journal of Public Health* 70:215–16.

Banta, H. D. 1980b. The Diffusion of the Computed Tomography (CT) Scanner in the United States. *International Journal of Health Services* 10:251–69.

Banta, H. D., C. J. Behney, and J. S. Willems. 1981. *Toward Rational Technology in Medicine: Considerations for Health Policy.* New York: Springer.

Banta, H. D., and B. Luce. 1993. *Health Care Technology and Its Assessment: An International Perspective.* Oxford: Oxford University Press.

Banta, [H.] D., and W. Oortwijn. 2000a. Introduction: Health Technology Assessment and the European Union. *International Journal of Technology Assessment in Health Care* 16:299–302.

Banta, [H.] D., and W. Oortwijn. 2000b. Conclusion: Health Technology Assessment and Health Care in the European Union. *International Journal of Technology Assessment in Health Care* 16:626–35.

Banta, H. D., W. Oortwijn, and R. Cranovsky. 2001. Health Policy, Health Technology Assessment, and Screening in Europe. *International Journal of Technology Assessment in Health Care* 17:409–17.

Banta, H. D., and S. Perry. 1997. A History of ISTAHC: A Personal Perspective on Its First 10 Years. *International Journal of Technology Assessment in Health Care* 13:430–53.

Banta, H. D., and S. B. Thacker. 1979. Policies toward Medical Technology: The

Case of Electronic Fetal Monitoring. *American Journal of Public Health* 69: 931–35.

Banta, H. D., and S. B. Thacker. 1990. The Case for Reassessment of Health Care Technology: Once Is Not Enough. *Journal of the American Medical Association* 264:235–40.

Banta, H. D., and S. B. Thacker. 2002. Electronic Fetal Monitoring: Lessons from a Formative Case of Health Technology Assessment. *International Journal of Technology Assessment in Health Care* 18:762–70.

Barfield, C. E., and C. Beltz. 1995. *Balancing and Rebalancing the National Interest in the Patent System.* Washington, DC: American Enterprise Institute, October.

Barnard, A. 2001. Pacemaker Study Finds Warnings and Recalls Are Up. *Boston Globe,* August 15.

Barnett, H. J. M., and A. M. Buchan. 2000. The Imperative to Develop Dedicated Stroke Centers. *Journal of the American Medical Association* 283:3125–26.

Barsamian, E. M. 1977. The Rise and Fall of Internal Mammary Artery Ligation in the Treatment of Angina Pectoris and the Lessons Learned. In *Costs, Risks, and Benefits of Surgery,* ed. J. P. Bunker, B. A. Barnes, and F. Mosteller, 212–20. New York: Oxford University Press.

Basu, J., and C. M. Clancy. 2001. Racial Disparity, Primary Care, and Specialty Referral. *Health Services Research* 36 (6), pt. 2: 64–77.

Battelle Columbus Laboratories. 1976. Analysis of Selected Biomedical Research Programs. In *Report of the President's Biomedical Research Panel,* appendix B. DHEW publication no. (OS) 76-502. Washington, DC: Department of Health, Education, and Welfare.

Battista, R. N. 1989. Innovation and Diffusion of Health Related Technologies: A Conceptual Framework. *International Journal of Technology Assessment in Health Care* 5:227–48.

Bayot, J. 2001. Drugs' Costs Called Too High. *Boston Globe,* July 24.

Beauchamp, T. L., and J. F. Childress. 1983. *Principles of Biomedical Ethics.* New York: Oxford University Press.

Beck, J. R., J. P. Kassirer, and S. G. Pauker. 1982. A Convenient Approximation of Life Expectancy (The "DEALE"): Part 1, Validation of the Method. *American Journal of Medicine* 73:883–88.

Beck, J. R., and S. G. Pauker. 1983. The Markov Process in Medical Prognosis. *Medical Decision Making* 3:411–58.

Becker, C. 2000a. Imaging: The Next Generation—New Scanners Blend PET with CT for Faster, More Accurate Cancer Diagnoses. *Modern Healthcare,* November 27, pp. 48–52, 61.

Becker, C. 2000b. When Giants Ruled—Industry Powerhouses Use RSNA Meeting to Showcase New Acquisitions and Products. *Modern Healthcare,* December 4, pp. 14, 16.

Becker, C. 2001. PET Proponents Bite Nails. *Modern Healthcare,* December 17, pp. 12–13.

Becker, G. 1964. *Human Capital.* New York: Columbia University Press.

Behney, C., and H. D. Banta. 1979. Is Medical Technology Safe? *Hospitals* 53: 110–12.

Bennett, I. L., Jr. 1977. Technology as a Shaping Force. *Daedalus* 106:125–33.

Bennett, J. C., and the Board on Health Sciences Policy of the Institute of Medicine. 1993. Inclusion of Women in Clinical Trials—Policies for Population Subgroups. *New England Journal of Medicine* 329:288–92.

Benson, K., and A. J. Hartz. 2000. A Comparison of Observational Studies and Randomized Controlled Trials. *New England Journal of Medicine* 342:1878–86.

Berland, G. K., M. N. Elliott, L. S. Morales, J. I. Algazy, R. L. Kravitz, M. S. Broder, D. E. Kanouse, J. A. Munoz, J. A. Puyol, M. Lara, K. E. Watkins, H. Yang, and E. A. McGlynn. 2001. Health Information on the Internet: Accessibility, Quality, and Readability in English and Spanish. *Journal of the American Medical Association* 285:2612–21.

Berman, H. 1993. Rochester Health Care: An Epilogue. *Health Affairs* 12:213–14.

Berman, H., S. F. Kukla, and L. E. Weeks. 1994. *The Financial Management of Hospitals.* 8th ed. Ann Arbor, MI: Health Administration Press.

Bero, L., and D. Rennie. 1995. The Cochrane Collection: Preparing, Maintaining, and Disseminating Systematic Reviews of the Effects of Health Care. *Journal of the American Medical Association* 274:1935–38.

Bero, L., and D. Rennie. 1996. Influences on the Quality of Published Drug Studies. *International Journal of Technology Assessment in Health Care* 12: 209–37.

Biotechnology Industry Organization. 2003. *BIO Guide to Biotechnology.* Available at http://www.bio.org.html.

Black, E. R., D. R. Bordley, T. G. Tape, and R. J. Panzer. 1999. *Diagnostic Strategies for Common Medical Problems.* 2d ed. Philadelphia: American College of Physicians.

Blendon, R. J., K. Donelan, R. Leitman, A. Epstein, J. C. Cantor, A. B. Cohen, I. Morrison, T. Moloney, C. Koeck, and S. W. Levitt. 1993. Physician Perspectives on Caring for Patients in the United States. *New England Journal of Medicine* 328:1011–16.

Bloom, B. S. 1979. Stretching Ideology to the Utmost: Marxism and Medical Technology. *American Journal of Public Health* 69:1269–71.

Blume, S. 1998. Early Warning in the Light of Theories of Technological Change. *International Journal of Technology Assessment in Health Care* 14: 613–23.

Blumenthal, D. 1983. Federal Policy toward Health Care Technology: The Case of the National Center. *Milbank Quarterly* 61:584–613.

Blumenthal, D., J. Reuter, and S. Thier. 2001. *A Shared Responsibility: Academic Health Centers and the Provision of Care to the Poor and Uninsured.* New York: Commonwealth Fund.

Blumstein, J. F., and F. A. Sloan. 1989. *Organ Transplantation Policy: Issues and Prospects.* Durham, NC: Duke University Press.

Boden, W. E., and R. McKay. 2001. Optimal Treatment of Acute Coronary Syndromes—An Evolving Strategy. *New England Journal of Medicine* 344: 1939–42.

Boland, P. 1987. Commentary: Trends in Second Generation PPOs. *Health Affairs* 6:75–81.

Booth, W. 1991. When Medical High Tech Isn't Necessarily Better: Fetal Monitors Widely Used, Often Unneeded. *Washington Post,* October 29.

Borzo, G. 1996. Managed Care and Technology Assessment: Who Should Pay? *American Medical Association Technology News* 9:3–5.

Bos, M. 2000. Health Technology Assessment in the Netherlands. *International Journal of Technology Assessment in Health Care* 16:485–519.

Boston Consulting Group. 1996. *Sustaining Innovation in U.S. Pharmaceuticals: Intellectual Property Protection and the Role of Patents.* Boston: Boston Consulting Group, January.

Bovbjerg, R. 1975. The Medical Malpractice Standard of Care: HMOs and Customary Practice. *Duke Law Journal* (6):1375–1414.

Bradley, T. B., and G. F. Kominski. 1992. Contributions of Case Mix and Intensity Change to Hospital Cost Increases. *Health Care Financing Review* 14: 151–63.

Breese, J. S. 1992. Construction of Belief and Decision Networks. *Computational Intelligence* 8:624–47.

Brennan, T. A. 1996. What Role for Hospitals in the Health Care Endgame? *Inquiry* 33:106–9.

Britton, M., and E. Jonsson. 2002. Impact of Health Technology Assessments: Some Experiences of SBU. *International Journal of Technology Assessment in Health Care* 18:824–31.

Brook, R. H., F. A. Chassin, A. Fink, D. H. Solomon, J. Kosecoff, and R. E. Park. 1986. A Method for the Detailed Assessment of the Appropriateness of Medical Technologies. *International Journal of Technology Assessment in Health Care* 2:53–63.

Brook, R. H., R. E. Park, M. R. Chassin, D. H. Solomon, J. Keesey, and J. Kosecoff. 1990. Predicting the Appropriate Use of Carotid Endarterectomy, Upper Gastrointestinal Endoscopy, and Coronary Angiography. *New England Journal of Medicine* 323:1173–77.

Browman, G. P. 2001. Development and Aftercare of Clinical Guidelines: The Balance between Rigor and Pragmatism. *Journal of the American Medical Association* 286:1509–11.

Brown, J. B., and R. B. Saltman. 1985. Health Capital Policy in the United States: A Strategic Perspective. *Inquiry* 22:122–31.

Brown, L. D. 1983. Common Sense Meets Implementation: Certificate of Need in the States. *Journal of Health Politics, Policy, and Law* 8:480–94.

Brown, L. D. 1992. Political Evolution of Federal Health Care Regulation. *Health Affairs* 11:17–37.

Bryce, C. L., and K. E. Cline. 1998. The Supply and Use of Selected Medical Technologies. *Health Affairs* 17:213–24.

Bucci, V. A., J. B. Reiss, and N. C. Hall. 1985. New Obstacles in the Path of Marketing New Medical Devices: The Stream of Regulation. *Journal of Health Care Technology* 2:81–96.

Bunker, J. P., J. Fowles, and R. Schaffarzick. 1982. Evaluation of Medical Technology Strategies: Proposal for an Institute for Health-Care Evaluation. *New England Journal of Medicine* 306:687–92.

Burda, D. 1996. Doc Income Falls 3. 65 in '94. *Modern Healthcare* 26:10.

Buring, J. E. 2000. Women in Clinical Trials—A Portfolio for Success. *New England Journal of Medicine* 343:505–6.

Canto, J. G., J. J. Allison, C. I. Kiefe, C. Fincher, R. Farmer, P. Sekar, S. Person, and N. W. Weissman. 2000. Relation of Race and Sex to the Use of Reperfusion Therapy in Medicare Beneficiaries with Acute Myocardial Infarction. *New England Journal of Medicine* 342:1094–1100.

Caplan, A. L. 1992. When Evil Intrudes. Twenty Years After: The Legacy of the Tuskegee Syphilis Study. *Hastings Center Report* 22 (6):29–32.

Carlsson, P., E. Jonsson, L. Werkö, and D. Banta. 2000. Health Technology Assessment in Sweden. *International Journal of Technology Assessment in Health Care* 16:560–75.

Carpenter, D. P. 2001. *Groups, the Media, and Agency Waiting Costs: The Political Economy of FDA Drug Approval.* Ann Arbor: University of Michigan, June.

Carrns, A. 2001. Twenty Years of AIDS in America. *Wall Street Journal,* May 30.

Catalan Agency for Health Technology Assessment and Research. 2000. Notes on Recent Work: Research. *Informatiu* 20:4–5, 10–11.

Caves, R. 1972. *American Industry: Structure, Conduct, and Performance.* Englewood Cliffs, NJ: Prentice-Hall.

CCOHTA. 2000. A Turning Point for CCOHTA! *Connection* 5:1–2.

CCOHTA. 2001a. *About CCOHTA.* Available at http://www.ccohta.ca.

CCOHTA. 2001b. CCOHTA Activities: New Releases. *Connection* 7: 4.

CCOHTA. 2001c. CCOHTA Activities: New Releases. *Connection* 8:2.

CDC. 1994. *A Practical Guide to Prevention Effectiveness: Decision and Economic Analyses.* Atlanta: U.S. Department of Health and Human Services.

Center for Studying Health System Change. 2000. *Tracking Health Care Costs: An Upswing in Premiums and Costs Underlying Health Insurance.* Data bulletin no. 20. Washington, DC: Center for Studying Health System Change.

Chalmers, I. 1991. The Work of the National Perinatal Epidemiology Unit: One Example of Technology Assessment in Perinatal Care. *International Journal of Technology Assessment in Health Care* 7:430–59.

Chalmers, I., M. W. Enkin, and M. J. N. C. Keirse, eds. 1989. *Effective Care in Pregnancy and Childbirth.* Oxford: Oxford University Press.

Chalmers, T. C. 1974. The Impact of Controlled Trials on the Practice of Medicine. *Mount Sinai Journal of Medicine* 41:753–59.

Chang, S. W., and H. S. Luft. 1991. Reimbursement and the Dynamics of Surgical Procedure Innovation. In *The Changing Economics of Medical Technology*,
ed. A. C. Gelijns and E. A. Halm, 96–122. Washington, DC: National Academy Press.

Chen, J., S. S. Rathore, M. J. Radford, Y. Wang, and H. M. Krumholz. 2001.
Racial Differences in the Use of Cardiac Catheterization after Acute Myocardial Infarction. *New England Journal of Medicine* 344:1443–49.

Chernew, M., A. M. Fendrick, and R. A. Hirth. 1997. Managed Care and Medical Technology: Implications for Cost Growth. *Health Affairs* 16:196–206.

Chernew, M., R. Hayward, and D. Scanlon. 1996. Managed Care and Open-
Heart Surgery Facilities in California. *Health Affairs* 15:191–201.

Chernew, M., R. A. Hirth, S. S. Sonnad, R. Ermann, and A. M. Fendrick. 1998.
Managed Care, Medical Technology, and Health Care Cost Growth: A Review of the Evidence. *Medical Care Research and Review* 55:259–88.

Christensen, C. M., R. Bohmer, and J. Kenagy. 2000. Will Disruptive Innovations Cure Health Care? *Harvard Business Review* (Sept./Oct.):102–12.

Churchill, L. R. 1987. *Rationing Health Care in America: Perceptions and Principles
of Justice.* South Bend, IN: University of Notre Dame Press.

Clancy, C. M., and D. B. Stryer. 2001. Racial and Ethnic Disparities and Primary
Care Experience. *Health Services Research* 36:979–86.

Cleverley, W. O. 1997. "Capital Project Analysis. " In *Essentials of Health Care Finance*, 4th ed., 334–69. Gaithersburg, MD: Aspen.

CMS. 2001. *Medicare Coverage Policy.* Available at http://www.hcfa.gov
/coverage.

Cochrane, A. L. 1972. *Effectiveness and Efficiency: Random Reflections on Health
Services.* London: Nuffield Provincial Hospitals Trust.

Cochrane Collaboration. 2001. *The Cochrane Collaboration. Brochure.* Available at
http://www.cochrane.org.html.

Coelen, C., and D. Sullivan. 1981. An Analysis of the Effects of Prospective
Reimbursement Programs on Hospital Expenditures. *Health Care Financing
Review* 2:1–40.

Cohen, A. B. 1983. Decision and Policy Analysis for Electronic Fetal Monitoring. Ph.D. diss., Harvard University.

Cohen, A. B. 1996. *Medical Technology Development and Diffusion: Changing Incentives under Managed Care.* Report to the Robert Wood Johnson Foundation
(grant no. 26077). Boston: Boston University School of Management.

Cohen, A. B. 1998. Commentary. *Medical Care Research and Review* 55:289–97.

Cohen, A. B., and D. R. Cohodes. 1979. *Certificate of Need and Low Capital Cost
Technology: The Case of Electronic Fetal Monitoring.* Cambridge, MA: Urban
Systems Research and Engineering.

Cohen, A. B., and D. R. Cohodes. 1982. Certificate of Need and Low Capital-
Cost Medical Technology. *Milbank Memorial Fund Quarterly* 60:307–28.

Cohen, A. B., and S. S. Nichols. 1993. *Cost Containment Strategies Involving*

Medical Technology: An Overview of the Issues. Report to the Robert Wood Johnson Foundation (grant no. 21335). Waltham, MA: the Heller School, Brandeis University.

Cohen, A. B., and R. C. Rock. 1985. Changing Health Policies and Clinical Laboratory Services. *Journal of Health Care Technology* 1:237–55.

Cole, G. (president and CEO, Emerson Hospital, Concord, MA). 1995. Personal communication, October 30.

Coleman, J. S., E. Katz, and H. Menzel. 1966. *Medical Innovation: A Diffusion Study.* Indianapolis: Bobbs-Merrill.

Collins, F. S., and V. A. McKusick. 2001. Implications of the Human Genome Project for Medical Science. *Journal of the American Medical Association* 285:540–44.

Committee on Technology and Health Care. 1979. *Medical Technology and the Health Care System: A Study of the Diffusion of Equipment-Embodied Technology.* Washington, DC: National Academy of Sciences.

Commonwealth Department of Health and Family Services. 1996. *Assessing Health Care Technology in Australia.* Canberra, Australia: Commonwealth Department of Health and Family Services.

Community Technology Assessment Advisory Board. 1993. *Community Technology Assessment Advisory Board: A Background Paper.* Rochester, NY: Blue Cross and Blue Shield of the Rochester Area.

Comroe, J. H., Jr., and R. D. Dripps. 1977. *The Top Ten Clinical Advances in Cardiovascular-Pulmonary Medicine and Surgery, 1945–1975.* DHEW publication no. (NIH) 78-1521. Washington, DC: U.S. Department of Health, Education, and Welfare.

Comroe, J. H., Jr., and R. D. Dripps. 1981. Scientific Basis for the Support of Biomedical Science. In *Biomedical Innovation,* ed. E. B. Roberts et al., 101–22. Cambridge: MIT Press.

Concato, J., N. Shah, and R. I. Horwitz. 2000. Randomized, Controlled Trials, Observational Studies, and the Hierarchy of Research Designs. *New England Journal of Medicine* 342:1887–92.

Corrigan, J. M., and D. M. Nielsen. 1993. Toward the Development of Uniform Reporting Standards for Managed Care Organizations: The Health Plan Employer Data and Information Set (Version 2.0). *Journal of Quality Improvement* 19:566–75.

Cotton, P., ed. 1996. No More Guidelines for AHCPR. *Medicine and Health* 50:1.

Coulam, R., and G. Gaumer. 1992. Medicare's Prospective Payment System: A Critical Appraisal. *Health Care Financing Review* (1991 annual supplement) 14:45–77.

Cowan, C. A., H. C. Lazenby, A. B. Martin, P. A. McDonnell, A. L. Sensenig, C. E. Smith, L. S. Whittle, M. A. Zezza, C. S. Donham, A. M. Long, and M. W. Stewart. 2001. National Health Expenditures, 1999. *Health Care Financing Review* 22:77–110.

Cowley, G., and A. Underwood. 2000. A Revolution in Medicine. *Newsweek,* April 10.

Crater, R. (chief executive officer, Massachusetts General Hospital, Boston). 1995. Personal communication, October 16.

Cromwell, J., P. Ginsburg, D. Hamilton, and M. Sumner. 1975. *Incentives and Decisions Underlying Hospitals' Adoption and Utilization of Major Capital Equipment.* Cambridge, MA: Abt Associates.

Cromwell, J., and J. R. Kanak. 1982. The Effects of Prospective Reimbursement Programs on Hospital Adoption and Service Sharing. *Health Care Financing Review* 4:67–88.

Cross Design Synthesis: A New Strategy for Studying Medical Outcomes? 1992. *Lancet* 340:944–46.

Cross, S. S., R. F. Harrison, and R. L. Kennedy. 1995. Introduction to Neural Networks. *Lancet* 346:1075–79.

Crowley, W. F., Jr. (director of clinical research, Massachusetts General Hospital, Boston). 2003. Personal communication, March 25.

Cummings, R. G., D. S. Brookshire, and W. D. Schulze. 1986. *Valuing Environmental Goods: A State of the Art Assessment of the Contingent Valuation Method.* Totowa, NJ: Rowman and Allanheld.

Cunningham, R., III, and R. M. Cunningham Jr. 1997. *The Blues: A History of the Blue Cross and Blue Shield System.* De Kalb: Northern Illinois University Press.

Cutler, D. M., and E. R. Berndt. 2001. *Medical Care Output and Productivity.* Chicago: University of Chicago Press.

Cutler, D. M., and M. McClellan. 1996. *The Determinants of Technological Change in Heart Attack Treatment.* NBER Working Paper Series no. 5751. Cambridge, MA: National Bureau of Economic Research.

Cutler, D. M., and M. McClellan. 2001. Is Technological Change in Medicine Worth It? *Health Affairs* 20 (5): 11–29.

Cyert, R. M., and J. G. March. 1963. *A Behavioral Theory of the Firm.* Englewood Cliffs, NJ: Prentice-Hall.

Daniels, N., and J. E. Sabin. 1998. Last Chance Therapies and Managed Care: Pluralism, Fair Procedures, and Legitimacy. *Hastings Center Report* 28 (2): 27–41.

Davis, K. 1974. The Role of Technology, Demand, and Labor Markets in the Determination of Hospital Costs. In *The Economics of Health and Medical Care,* ed. M. Perlman. New York: John Wiley.

Deber, R. B. 1992. Translating Technology Assessment into Policy. *International Journal of Technology Assessment in Health Care* 8 (1): 131–37.

Decker, B., and P. Bonner. 1973. *PSRO: Organization for Regional Peer Review.* Cambridge, MA: Ballinger.

Delamonthe, T. 1993. Wanted: Guidelines That Doctors Will Follow. *British Medical Journal* 307:218.

Dembner, A. 2001. Drug Firms Woo Doctors with Perks. *Boston Globe,* May 20.

Demkovich, L. 1998. No Rationing: The Oregon Health Plan Gets High Marks. *State Health Notes* 19 (280): 1.

Demkovich, L. 2000. Biomedical Research: States Seek a Piece of the Action in a Booming Field. *State Health Notes* 21 (328): 1.

Detsky, A. S. 1989. Are Clinical Trials a Cost-Effective Investment? *Journal of the American Medical Association* 262:1795–1800.

Detsky, A. S., G. Naglie, M. D. Krahn, D. A. Redelmeier, and D. Naimark. 1997. Primer on Medical Decision Analysis: Part 2. *Medical Decision Making* 17: 126–35.

Diemunsch, J. 1990. Desktop Reference: Manufacturers of Magnetic Resonance Imagers. *Healthweek,* November 19.

Diller, W. 1993. States Show New Interest in Regulated Health Planning. *Business and Health* 11 (2): 20–24.

DiMasi, J. A., R. W. Hansen, and H. G. Grabowski. 2003. The Price of Innovation: New Estimates of Drug Development Costs. *Journal of Health Economics* 22:151–85.

Dippel, D. W. J., F. Touw-Otten, and D. F. Habbema. 1992. Management of Children with Acute Pharyngitis: A Decision Analysis. *Journal of Family Practice* 34:149–59.

Dobson, F. 1999. Modernizing Britain's National Health Service. *Health Affairs* 18 (3):40–41.

Dolan, J. G., D. R. Bordley, and A. I. Mushlin. 1986. An Evaluation of Clinicians' Subjective Prior Probabilities. *Medical Decision Making* 6:216–23.

Dolan, P. 2000. The Measurement of Health-Related Quality of Life for Use in Resource Allocation Decisions in Health Care. In *Handbook of Health Economics,* ed. A. J. Culyer and J. P. Newhouse. Amsterdam: Elsevier.

Donabedian, A. 1988. The Assessment of Technology and Quality: A Comparative Study of Certainties and Ambiguities. *International Journal of Technology Assessment in Health Care* 4:487–96.

Dorfman, R. 1972. *Prices and Markets.* Englewood Cliffs, NJ: Prentice-Hall.

Doubilet, P. M., C. A. Begg, M. C. Weinstein, P. Braun, and B. J. McNeil. 1985. Probabilistic Sensitivity Analysis Using Monte Carlo Simulation: A Practical Approach. *Medical Decision Making* 5:157–77.

Doyle, Y. G., and R. H. M. McNeilly. 1999. The Diffusion of New Medical Technologies in the Private Sector of the U. K. Health Care System. *International Journal of Technology Assessment in Health Care* 15:619–28.

Dresser, C. K. 1992. Wanted: Single, White Male for Medical Research. *Hastings Center Report* 22 (1): 24–29.

Droitcour, J., G. Silberman, and E. Chelimsky. 1993. Cross-Design Synthesis: A New Form of Meta-Analysis for Combining Results from Randomized Clinical Trials and Medical-Practice Databases. *International Journal of Technology Assessment in Health Care* 9:440–49.

Drummond, M. F. 1980. *Principles of Economic Appraisal in Health Care.* Oxford: Oxford University Press.

Drummond, M. F. 1992. Basing Prescription Drug Payment on Economic Analysis: The Case of Australia. *Health Affairs* 11:191–96.

Drummond, M. F., B. O'Brien, G. L. Stoddart, and G. W. Torrance. 1997. *Methods for the Economic Evaluation of Health Care Programmes.* 2d ed. Oxford: Oxford University Press.

Drummond, M. F., G. L. Stoddart, and G. W. Torrance. 1987. *Methods for the Economic Evaluation of Health Care Programmes.* Oxford: Oxford University Press.

Durenberger, D. F. 1993. Brave New World: Medical Technology in the Age of Managed Competition. *Academic Medicine* 68:540–41.

Durenberger, D. F., and S. B. Foote. 1993. Medical Technology Meets Managed Competition. *Journal of American Health Policy* 2:23–28.

Eastaugh, S. R. 1992. *Health Economics: Efficiency, Quality, and Equity.* Westport, CT: Auburn House.

Ebert, R. H. 1979. Effectiveness and Efficiency—How Well Are We Doing? *American Journal of Medicine* 66:191–92.

ECRI. 2001. *Who We Are.* Available at http://www.ecri.org.

Eddy, D. M. 1989. Selecting Technologies for Assessment. *International Journal of Technology Assessment in Health Care* 5:485–501.

Eddy, D. M. 1993. Clinical Decision-Making: From Theory to Practice. Three Battles to Watch in the 1990s. *Journal of the American Medical Association* 270.520–26.

Eddy, D. M. 1994. Health System Reform: Will Controlling Costs Require Rationing of Services? *Journal of the American Medical Association* 272:324–28.

Eddy, D. M. 1997. Breast Cancer Screening in Women Younger Than 50 Years of Age: What's Next? *Annals of Internal Medicine* 127:1035–36.

Egdahl, R. H., and P. M. Gertman. 1978. *Technology and the Quality of Health Care.* Germantown, MD: Aspen Systems.

Egger, M., P. Jüni, C. Bartlett, and the CONSORT Group. 2001. Value of Flow Diagrams in Reports of Randomized Controlled Trials. *Journal of the American Medical Association* 285: 1996–99.

Eggers, P. W. 1988. Effect of Transplantation on the Medicare End-Stage Renal Disease Program. *New England Journal of Medicine* 318:223–29.

Eggers, P. W. 1995. Racial Differences in Access to Kidney Transplantation. *Health Care Financing Review* 17 (2): 89–103.

Einarson, T., S. R. Arikian, and J. J. Doyle. 1995. Rank-Order Stability Analysis (ROSA). *Medical Decision Making* 15:367–72.

Eisenberg, J. M. 1986. *Doctors' Decisions and the Cost of Medical Care: The Reasons for Doctors' Practice Patterns and Ways to Change.* Ann Arbor, MI: Health Administration Press.

Eisenberg, J. M. 1998. Special Report: AHCPR Focuses on Information for Health Care Decision Makers. *Health Services Research* 33:767–81.

Eisenberg, J. M. 2000. The Agency for Healthcare Research and Quality: New Challenges, New Opportunities. *Health Services Research* 35:xi–xvi.

Elixhauser, A., B. R. Luce, W. R. Taylor, and J. Reblando. 1993. Health Care CBA/CEA: An Update on the Growth and Composition of the Literature. *Medical Care* 31 (supplement): JS1–11.

Ellenberg, S. S. 1997. Informed Consent: Protection or Obstacle? *Controlled Clinical Trials* 18:628–36.

Ellis, J. 1998. Ending Hypertension. *Boston Globe,* July 18.

Emanuel, E. J., D. Wendler, and C. Grady. 2000. What Makes Clinical Research Ethical? *Journal of the American Medical Association* 283:2701–11.

Emmitt, R. B., and J. W. Lasersohn. 1983. *Company Report on Diasonics.* New York: F. Eberstadt, May 26.

Epstein, A. M. 1995. U.S. Teaching Hospitals in the Evolving Health Care System. *Journal of the American Medical Association* 273:1203–07.

Epstein, A. M. 2000. Public Release of Performance Data: A Progress Report from the Front. *Journal of the American Medical Association* 283:1884–86.

Epstein, A. M., R. S. Stern, and J. S. Weissman. 1990. Do the Poor Cost More? A Multihospital Study of Patients' Socioeconomic Status and the Use of Hospital Resources. *New England Journal of Medicine* 322:1122–28.

Escarce, J. J., B. S. Bloom, A. L. Hillman, J. A. Shea, and J. S. Schwartz. 1995. Diffusion of Laparoscopic Cholecystectomy among General Surgeons in the United States. *Medical Care* 33:256–71.

Esmond, T. H., Jr. 1982. *Budgeting Procedures for Hospitals.* 3d ed. Chicago: American Hospital Association.

Etzioni, A. 1991. Health Care Rationing: A Critical Evaluation. *Health Affairs* 10:88–95.

European Collaboration for Health Technology Assessment. 2001. *The European Collaboration for Assessment of Health Interventions (ECAHI).* Available at http://www.sbU.Se.

Evans, R. W. 1983. Health Care Technology and the Inevitability of Resource Allocation and Rationing Decisions, Part II. *Journal of the American Medical Association* 249:2208–19.

Evens, R. G. 1996. Contempo 1996: Radiology. *Journal of the American Medical Association* 275:1854–55.

Ewigman, B. G. 1989. Should Ultrasound Be Used during Pregnancy? An Opposing View. *Journal of Family Practice* 29:660–64.

Ewigman, B. G., J. P. Crane, F. D. Frigoletto, M. L. LeFevre, R. P. Bain, and D. McNellis. 1993. Effect of Prenatal Ultrasound Screening on Perinatal Outcomes. *New England Journal of Medicine* 329:821–27.

FACCT. 2001. *About FACCT.* Available at http://www.facct.org.

FACCT. 2003. *About FACCT.* Available at http://www.facct.org.

Farragher, T. 2001. Little of $246b Deal Fights Tobacco. *Boston Globe,* August 9.

FDA. 1997. *The FDA Modernization Act of 1997.* November 21. Available at http://www.fda.gov.

FDA. 2001. *The New Drug Development Process.* Available at http://www.fda .gov/cder/handbook.

FDA. 2002a. *About CBER.* Available at http://www.fda.gov/cber.

FDA. 2002b. *The Center for Devices and Radiological Health: Device Advice.* Available at http://www.fda.gov/cdrh/devadvice.

FDA. 2002c. *The Prescription Drug User Fee Amendments of 2002.* June 12. Available at http://www.fda.gov/oc/pdufa.

FDA. 2002d. *The Medical Device User Fee and Modernization Act of 2002.* October 26. Available at http://www.fda.gov/oc/mdufma.

Feldstein, M. S., and A. K. Taylor. 1977. *The Rapid Rise of Hospital Costs.* Report to the Council on Wage and Price Stability. Washington, DC: U.S. Government Printing Office.

Feldstein, P. J. 1988. *Health Care Economics.* 3d ed. New York: Wiley.

Fendrick, A. M., J. J. Escarce, C. McLane, J. A. Shea, and J. S. Schwartz. 1994. Hospital Adoption of Laparoscopic Cholecystectomy. *Medical Care* 32: 1058–63.

Fenn, P., A. McGuire, M. Backhouse, and D. Jones. 1996. Modelling Programme Costs in Economic Evaluation. *Journal of Health Economics* 15:115–26.

Fernandez, A. M., J. J. Schrogie, W. W. Wilson, and D. B. Nash. 1997. Technology Assessment in Healthcare: A Review and Description of a "Best Practice" Technology Assessment Process. *Best Practices and Benchmarking in Healthcare* 2:240–53.

Field, M. G. 1987. Reflections on Medical Technology as a Special Type of Capital: Some Implications for the Hospital. *International Journal of Technology Assessment in Health Care* 3:275–80.

Fineberg, H. V. 1979. Gastric Freezing—A Study of Diffusion of a Medical Innovation. In *Medical Technology and the Health Care System: A Study of the Diffusion of Equipment-Embodied Technology,* 173–200. Washington, DC: National Academy of Sciences.

Fineberg, H. V., and H. H. Hiatt. 1979. Evaluation of Medical Practices: The Case for Technology Assessment. *New England Journal of Medicine* 301: 1086–91.

Finkelstein, S. N., S. B. Schectman, E. J. Sondik, and D. Gilbert. 1981. Clinical Trials and Established Medical Practice: Two Examples. In *Biomedical Innovation,* ed. E. B. Roberts, R. I. Levy, S. N. Finkelstein, J. Moskowitz, and E. J. Sondik, 200–215. Cambridge: MIT Press.

Finkler, M. D. 1987. State Rate Setting Revisited: Commentary. *Health Affairs* 5:82–89.

Firshein, J., ed. 1993. Problems Plague FDA Device Office. *Medicine and Health* 47:3.

Flannery, E. J. 1986. Should It Be Easier or Harder to Use Unapproved Drugs and Devices? *Hastings Center Report* 16 (1): 17–23.

Fletcher, R. H. 1989. The Costs of Clinical Trials. *Journal of the American Medical Association* 262: 1842.

Foote, S. B. 1987. Assessing Medical Technology Assessment: Past, Present, and Future. *Milbank Quarterly* 65:59–80.

Foote, S. B. 1991. The Impact of Public Policy on Medical Device Innovation: A Case of Polyintervention. In *The Changing Economics of Medical Technology*, ed. A. C. Gelijns and E. A. Halm, 69–88. Washington, DC: National Academy Press.

Ford, E., R. Cooper, A. Castaner, B. Simmons, and M. Mar. 1989. Coronary Arteriography and Coronary Bypass Surgery among Whites and Other Racial Groups Relative to Hospital-Based Incidence Rates for Coronary Artery Disease: Findings from NHDS. *American Journal of Public Health* 79:437–50.

Frazier, H. S., and F. Mosteller, eds. 1995. *Medicine Worth Paying For: Assessing Medical Innovations*. Cambridge: Harvard University Press.

Freeland, M. S., and C. E. Schendler. 1983. National Health Expenditure Growth in the 1980s: An Aging Population, New Technologies, and Increasing Competition. *Health Care Financing Review* 4:1–58.

Freund, D. A., and R. S. Dittus. 1992. Principles of Pharmacoeconomic Analysis of Drug Therapy. *PharmacoEconomics* 1:20–32.

Freund, D. A., D. Evans, D. Henry, and R. S. Dittus. 1992. Implications of the Australian Guidelines for the United States. *Health Affairs* 11:202–6.

Freund, D. A., J. Lave, C. Clancy, G. Hawker, V. Hasselblad, et al. 1999. Patient Outcome Research Teams: Contributions to Outcomes and Effectiveness Research. *Annual Review of Public Health* 20:337–59.

Friedman, E. A. 1996. End-Stage Renal Disease Therapy: An American Success Story. *Journal of the American Medical Association* 275:1118–22.

Friedman, L. H., and J. Jorgensen. 1994. Physicians' Influence on the Decision to Acquire Magnetic Resonance Imagers in Acute Care Hospitals. *International Journal of Technology Assessment in Health Care* 10:667–74.

Friedman, L. M., C. D. Furberg, and D. L. DeMets. 1981. *Fundamentals of Clinical Trials*. Boston: John Wright/PSG.

Friend, T. 2000. Genome Projects Complete Sequence. *USA Today*, June 23–25.

Fuchs, V. R. 1968. The Growing Demand for Medical Care. *New England Journal of Medicine* 279:190–95.

Fuchs, V. R. 1972. *Essays in the Economics of Health and Medical Care*. New York: Columbia University Press.

Fuchs, V. R. 1984. The "Rationing" of Medical Care. *New England Journal of Medicine* 311:1572–73.

Fuchs, V. R. 1986. *The Health Economy*. Cambridge: Harvard University Press.

Fuchs, V. R. 1993. *The Future of Health Care Policy*. Cambridge: Harvard University Press.

Fuchs, V. R., and A. M. Garber. 1990. The New Technology Assessment. *New England Journal of Medicine* 323:673–77.

GAO. 1989. *Medical Devices: FDA's Implementation of the Medical Device Reporting Regulation*. Report to House Subcommittee on Health and the Environment, GAO/PEMD-89-10. Washington, DC: GAO.

GAO. 1992a. *Excessive Payments Support the Proliferation of Costly Technology.* Report to House Ways and Means Committee, GAO/HRD-92-59. Washington, DC: GAO.

GAO. 1992b. *Hospital Costs: Adoption of Technologies Drives Cost Growth: Report to Congressional Requesters.* GAO/HRD-92-120. Washington, DC: GAO.

GAO. 1992c. *Cross-Design Synthesis: A New Strategy for Medical Effectiveness Research: Report to Congressional Requesters.* GAO/PEMD-92-18. Washington, DC: GAO.

GAO. 1994. *Medicare: Technology Assessment and Medical Coverage Decisions: Fact Sheet for the Subcommittee on Technology, Environment and Aviation, Committee on Science, Space, and Technology, House of Representatives.* GAO/HEHS-94-195FS. Washington, DC: GAO.

GAO. 1995. *Prescription Drug Prices: Official Index Overstates Producer Price Inflation: Report to the Chairman, Special Committee on Aging, U.S. Senate.* GAO/HEHS-95-90. Washington, DC: GAO.

GAO. 2000. *Women's Health: NIH Has Increased Its Efforts to Include Women in Research: Report to Congressional Requesters.* GAO/HEHS-00-96. Washington, DC: GAO.

GAO. 2001. *Women's Health: Women Sufficiently Represented in New Drug Testing, but FDA Oversight Needs Improvement: Report to Congressional Requesters.* GAO-01-754. Washington, DC: GAO.

Garber, A. 2000. Advances in Cost-Effectiveness Analysis of Health Interventions. In *Handbook of Health Economics,* ed. A. J. Culyer and J. P. Newhouse, Amsterdam: Elsevier.

Garber, A., and C. E. Phelps. 1997. Economic Foundations of Cost-Effectiveness Analysis. *Journal of Health Economics* 16:1–32.

Garber, A., M. C. Weinstein, G. W. Torrance, and M. S. Kamlet. 1996. Theoretical Foundations of Cost-Effectiveness Analysis. In *Cost-Effectiveness in Health and Medicine,* ed. M. R. Gold, J. E. Siegel, L. B. Russell, and M. C. Weinstein, 25–53. Oxford: Oxford University Press.

Garrison, L. P., and E. M. Brown. 1991. *Assessing the Impact of Changes in Technology on Medicare Expenditures for Physician Services: Background, Issues, and Options.* Prepared under Cooperative Agreement no. 99-C-99168/3-03 for the Health Care Financing Administration. Millwood, VA: Project HOPE Center for Health Affairs.

Gaus, C. R., and B. S. Cooper. 1976. Technology and Medicare: Alternatives for Change. Paper presented at the Conference on Health Care Technology and Quality of Care, Boston University Health Policy Center, November 19–20.

GE Medical Systems Introduces First-of-Its-Kind Imaging System Available to Help Doctors Better Diagnose Cancer. 2000. *PR Newswire,* June 6. Available at http://proquest.umi.com.html.

Geisler, E. 1999. Multiple-Perspectives Model of Medical Technology. *Health Care Management Review* 24:55–63.

Gelijns, A. C. 1990. Appendix B: Comparing the Development of Drugs,

Devices, and Clinical Procedures. In *Modern Methods of Clinical Investigation,* ed. Gelijns, 147–201. Washington, DC: National Academy Press.

Gelijns, A. C., and N. Rosenberg. 1994. The Dynamics of Technological Change in Medicine. *Health Affairs* 13:28–46.

Gemignani, J., and C. Kurdas. 1999a. Aetna Adds PruCare to Its Empire. *Business and Health* 17:8.

Gemignani, J., and C. Kurdas. 1999b. Is the FDA Approving Drugs Too Easily? *Business and Health* 17:12–13.

Gerth, J., and S. G. Stolberg. 2000. Drug Makers Reap Profits on Tax-Backed Research. *New York Times,* April 23.

Ginsburg, P. B., L. B. LeRoy, and G. T. Hammons. 1990. Medicare Physician Payment Reform. *Health Affairs* 9:178–88.

Glanz, J. 2001. Scientists Bring Light to Full Stop, Hold It, Then Send It on Its Way. *New York Times,* January 18.

Glass, G. V. 1976. Primary, Secondary, and Meta-Analysis of Research. *Educational Researcher* 5:3–8.

Goddeeris, J. H. 1987. Economic Forces and Hospital Technology. *International Journal of Technology Assessment in Health Care* 3:223–40.

Gold, M. 1998. Beyond Coverage and Supply: Measuring Access to Healthcare in Today's Market. *Health Services Research* 33:625–52.

Gold, M. 2001. Medicare + Choice: An Interim Report Card. *Health Affairs* 20:120–38.

Gold, M., K. Chu, S. Felt, M. Harrington, and T. Lake. 1993. Effects of Selected Cost-Containment Efforts: 1971–1993. *Health Care Financing Review* 14:183–225.

Gold, M., J. E. Siegel, L. B. Russell, and M. C. Weinstein, eds. 1996. *Cost-Effectiveness in Health and Medicine.* Oxford: Oxford University Press.

Gold, R., S. Hensley, and A. Caffrey. 2001. Industry Headache: States Square Off against Drug Firms in Crusade on Prices. *Wall Street Journal,* December 7.

Goldberg, K. C., A. J. Hartz, S. J. Jacobsen, H. Krakauer, and A. A. Rimm. 1992. Racial and Community Factors Influencing Coronary Artery Bypass Graft Surgery Rates for All 1986 Medicare Patients. *Journal of the American Medical Association* 267:1473–77.

Goldsmith, M. F. 1994. Realizing Potential of MR Coronary Angiography May Ease Patients' Test Load and Diagnosis Costs. *Journal of the American Medical Association* 271:256.

Gordon, G., and G. L. Fisher, eds. 1975. *The Diffusion of Medical Technology: Policy and Research Planning Perspectives.* Cambridge, MA: Ballinger.

Gordon, G., A. E. MacEachron, and G. L. Fisher. 1975. Perspectives on Diffusion Research. In *The Diffusion of Medical Technology: Policy and Research Planning Perspectives,* ed. G. Gordon and G. L. Fisher, 197–232. Cambridge, MA: Ballinger.

Grabowski, H. 1991. The Changing Economics of Pharmaceutical Research and Development. In *The Changing Economics of Medical Technology,* ed. A. C. Gelijns and E. A. Halm, 35–52. Washington, DC: National Academy Press.

Granados, A. L. (chair, Committee for a New International Society for Health Technology Assessment). 2003. Personal communication, April 16.

Granados, A., L. Sampietro-Colom, J. Asua, J. Conde, and R. Vazquez-Albertino. 2000. Health Technology Assessment in Spain. *International Journal of Technology Assessment in Health Care* 16:532–59.

Grant, A. 1989. Monitoring the Fetus during Labour. In *Effective Care in Pregnancy and Childbirth,* ed. I. Chalmers, M. W. Enkin, and M. J. N. C. Keirse, 846–82. Oxford: Oxford University Press.

Gray, B. H. 1992. The Legislative Battle over Health Services Research. *Health Affairs* 11:38–65.

Green, J., and N. Wintfeld. 1995. Report Cards on Cardiac Surgeons: Assessing New York State's Approach. *New England Journal of Medicine* 332:1229–32.

Greer, A. L. 1977. Advances in the Study of Diffusion of Innovation in Health Care Organizations. *Milbank Memorial Fund Quarterly* 55:505–32.

Greer, A. L. 1985. Adoption of Medical Technology: The Hospital's Three Decision Systems. *International Journal of Technology Assessment in Health Care* 1:669–80.

Greer, A. L. 1988. The State of the Art versus the State of the Science: The Diffusion of New Medical Technologies into Practice. *International Journal of Technology Assessment in Health Care* 4:5–26.

Greer, A. L., and A. A. Zakhar. 1977. *Hospital Adoption of Medical Technology: A Preliminary Investigation into Hospital Decision Making.* Milwaukee, WI: Urban Research Center.

Greer, A. L., and A. A. Zakhar. 1979. Patient Leverage Theory Proves to Be False. *Hospitals* 53:98–106.

Griffith, J. R. 1972. *Quantitative Techniques for Hospital Planning and Control.* Lexington, MA: D. C. Heath.

Grimes, D. A. 1993. Technology Follies: The Uncritical Acceptance of Medical Innovation. *Journal of the American Medical Association* 269:3030–33.

Grimes, D. A., and K. F. Schulz. 1992. Randomized Controlled Trials of Home Uterine Activity Monitoring: A Review and Critique. *Obstetrics and Gynecology* 79:137–42.

Griner, P. F. 1992. New Technology Adoption in the Hospital. In *Technology and Health Care in an Era of Limits,* ed. A. C. Gelijns, 37–50. Washington, DC: National Academy Press.

Gross, R. 1999. *Making Medical Decisions: An Approach to Clinical Decision Making for Practicing Physicians.* Philadelphia: American College of Physicians.

Group Health Cooperative. 2001. *About Group Health.* Available at http://www.ghc.org.

Gurwitz, J. H., N. F. Col, and J. Avorn. 1992. The Exclusion of the Elderly and

Women from Clinical Trials in Acute Myocardial Infarction. *Journal of the American Medical Association* 268:1417–22.

Gutzwiller, F., and R. Chrzanowski. 1986. Technology Assessment: Impact on Medical Practice. *International Journal of Technology Assessment in Health Care* 2:99–106.

Guyatt, G. H., P. X. Tugwell, D. H. Feeny, M. F. Drummond, and R. B. Haynes. 1986. The Role of Before-After Studies of Therapeutic Impact in the Evaluation of Diagnostic Technologies. *Journal of Chronic Diseases* 39:295–304.

Hadley, J., J. C. Cantor, R. J. Willke, J. Feder, and A. B. Cohen. 1992. Young Physicians Most and Least Likely to Have Second Thoughts about a Career in Medicine. *Academic Medicine* 67:180–90.

Hadley, J., and K. Swartz. 1989. The Impacts on Hospital Costs between 1980 and 1984 of Hospital Rate Regulation, Competition, and Changes in Health Insurance Coverage. *Inquiry* 26:35–47.

Hage, J., and M. Aiken. 1970. *Social Change in Complex Organizations.* New York: Random House.

Hailey, D. M., and B. L. Crowe. 1993. The Influence of Health Technology Assessment on the Diffusion of MRI in Australia. *International Journal of Technology Assessment in Health Care* 9:522–29.

Halm, E. A., and A. C. Gelijns. 1991. An Introduction to the Changing Economics of Technological Innovation in Medicine. In *The Changing Economics of Medical Technology,* ed. Gelijns and Halm, 1–20. Washington, DC: National Academy Press.

Hammond, J., R. L. Keeney, and H. Raiffa. 1999. *Smart Choices: A Practical Guide to Making Better Decisions.* Boston: Harvard Business School Press.

Hannan, E. L., M. van Ryn, J. Burke, D. Stone, D. Kumar, D. Arani, W. Pierce, S. Rafii, T. A. Sanborn, S. Sharma, J. Slater, and B. A. DeBuono. 1999. Access to Coronary Artery Bypass Surgery by Race/Ethnicity and Gender among Patients Who Are Appropriate for Surgery. *Medical Care* 37:68–77.

Hanson, M. J. 1997. Religious Voices in Biotechnology: The Case of Gene Patenting. *Hastings Center Report* 27 (6): 1–21.

Hanson, M. J. 1999. A Xenotransplantation Protocol. *Hastings Center Report* 29 (6): 1–23.

Harrell, F. E., K. L. Lee, D. B. Matchar, and T. A. Relchert. 1985. Regression Models for Prognostic Prediction: Advantages, Problems and Suggested Solutions. *Cancer Treatment Report* 69:1071–77.

Harris, D. J., and P. S. Douglas. 2000. Enrollment of Women in Cardiovascular Clinical Trials Funded by the National Heart, Lung, and Blood Institute. *New England Journal of Medicine* 343:475–80.

Harris, G. 2001. Cost of Developing Drugs Found to Rise. *Wall Street Journal,* December 3.

Hartley, D., I. Moscovice, and J. Christianson. 1996. Mobile Technology in Rural Hospitals: The Case of the CT Scanner. *Health Services Research* 31:213–34.

Hatlie, M. J. 1993. Climbing "The Learning Curve": New Technologies, Emerging Obligations. *Journal of the American Medical Association* 270:1364–65.

Havighurst, C. C. 1986. Altering the Applicable Standard of Care. *Law and Contemporary Problems* 49:265–75.

Hayward, R. A., and T. P. Hofer. 2001. Estimating Hospital Deaths due to Medical Errors: Preventability Is in the Eye of the Reviewer. *Journal of the American Medical Association* 286:415–20.

HCFA. 1991. *Health Care Financing Review* 13:31.

HCTI. 1993a. *Measuring Factors That Contribute to Rising Health Care Costs.* Alexandria, VA: HCTI.

HCTI. 1993b. *1993 Reference Guide for the Health Care Technology Industry.* Alexandria, VA: HCTI.

HCTI. 1993c. *The Role of Medical Equipment and Supplies in the Prices of Inputs and Outputs of Medical Care.* Alexandria, VA: HCTI.

The Health Effect. 2000. *Economist,* June 3.

Health Industry Manufacturers Association. 1992. *Health Industry Manufacturers Association Report,* vol. 1, July.

Health Resources and Services Administration. 2001. *Office for the Advancement of Telehealth.* Available at http://telehealth.hrsa.gov.

Healy, B. 1992. The Yentl Syndrome. *New England Journal of Medicine* 325:274–76.

Heffler, S., K. Levit, S. Smith, C. Smith, C. Cowan, H. Lazenby, and M. Freeland. 2001. Health Spending Growth Up in 1999; Faster Growth Expected in the Future. *Health Affairs* 20:193–203.

Held, P. J., M. V. Pauly, R. R. Bovbjerg, J. Newmann, and O. Salvatierra Jr. 1988. Access to Kidney Transplantation: Has the United States Eliminated Income and Racial Differences? *Archives of Internal Medicine* 148:2591–2600.

Helfand, M., and S. G. Pauker. 1997. Influence Diagrams: A New Dimension for Decision Models. *Medical Decision Making* 17:351–52.

Hellman, S., and D. S. Hellman. 1991. Of Mice but Not Men: Problems of the Randomized Clinical Trial. *New England Journal of Medicine* 324:1585–89.

Hennekens, C. H., and J. E. Buring. 1987. *Epidemiology in Medicine.* Boston: Little, Brown.

Henney, J. E. 2000. New System for Monitoring Intrapartum Fetal Oxygen Saturation. *Journal of the American Medical Association* 284:33.

Hensley, S. 2002. Pfizer Offers Seniors a Flat-Fee Drug Plan. *Wall Street Journal,* January 16.

Heudebert, G. R., R. M. Centor, J. C. Klapow, R. Marks, L. Johnson, and C. M. Wilcox. 2000. What Is Heartburn Worth? A Cost-Utility Analysis of Management Strategies. *Journal of General Internal Medicine* 15:175–82.

Hillman, A. L., and J. S. Schwartz. 1985. The Adoption and Diffusion of CT and MRI in the United States: A Comparative Analysis. *Medical Care* 23:1283–94.

Hillman, B. J. 1986. Government Health Policy and the Diffusion of New Medical Devices. *Health Services Research* 21:681–711.

Hillman, B. J. 1992. Physicians' Acquisition and Use of New Technology in an Era of Economic Constraints. In *Technology and Health Care in an Era of Limits*, ed. A. C. Gelijns, 133–49. Washington, DC: National Academy Press.

Hirsch, L. (chairman and CEO, U.S. Surgical Corporation, Norwalk, CT). 1995. Personal communication, November 15.

Hirth, R. A., M. E. Chernew, and S. M. Orzol. 2000. Ownership, Competition, and the Adoption of New Technologies and Cost-Saving Practices in a Fixed-Price Environment. *Inquiry* 37:282–94.

Holtzman, N. A., and T. M. Marteau. 2000. Will Genetics Revolutionize Medicine? *New England Journal of Medicine* 343:141–44.

Howard, R. A. 1990. From Influence to Relevance to Knowledge. In *Influence Diagrams, Belief Nets, and Decision Analysis*, ed. R. M. Oliver and J. Q. Smith, 3–24. Chichester: Wiley.

Howard, R. A., and J. E. Matheson. 1984. Influence Diagrams. In *The Principles and Applications of Decision Analysis*, ed. Howard and Matheson, vol. 2. Menlo Park, CA: Strategic Decisions Group.

Howell, J. D. 1996. *Technology in the Hospital: Transforming Patient Care in the Early Twentieth Century.* Baltimore: Johns Hopkins University Press.

Howell, J. D. 1999. The Physician's Role in a World of Technology. *Academic Medicine* 74:244–47.

Hsiao, W., D. Dunn, and D. Verrilli. 1993. Assessing the Implementation of Physician-Payment Reform. *New England Journal of Medicine* 328:928–33.

Hutt, P. B. 1991. The Impact of Regulation and Reimbursement on Pharmaceutical Innovation. In *Medical Innovation at the Crossroads*, vol. 2, *The Changing Economics of Medical Technology*, 169–80. Washington, DC: National Academy Press.

Hyams, A. L., D. W. Shapiro, and T. A. Brennan. 1996. Medical Practice Guidelines in Malpractice Litigation: An Early Retrospective. *Journal of Health Politics, Policy, and Law* 21:289–313.

Iglehart, J. K. 1977. The Cost and Regulation of Medical Technology: Future Policy Directions. *Milbank Memorial Fund Quarterly* 55:25–59.

Iglehart, J. K. 1979. Looking Ahead at Technology. *Hospitals* 53:88–90.

Iglehart, J. K. 2001. Medicare and Prescription Drugs. *New England Journal of Medicine* 344:1010–15.

IHI. 2001. *About IHI.* Available at http://www.ihi.org.

IHI. 2002. Pursuing Perfection: Raising the Bar for Health Care Performance. Available at http://www.ihi.org.

Illich, I. 1976. *Medical Nemesis: The Expropriation of Health.* New York: Random House.

INAHTA. 2001. *INAHTA Member Information.* Available at http://www.inahta.org.

Information from SBU: Synthesizing the Evidence. 1996. *Medical Science and Practice* 96:2.

International Society for Pharmacoeconomics and Outcomes Research. 2001. *About ISPOR*. Available at http://www.ispor.org.

Ioannidis, J. P. A., and J. Lau. 1999. Pooling Research Results: Benefits and Limitations of Meta-Analysis. *Joint Commission Journal on Quality Improvement* 25:462–69.

IOM. 1979. *A Review of DHEW's Research Planning Principles*. Washington, DC: National Academy of Sciences.

IOM. 1985. *Assessing Medical Technologies*. Washington, DC: National Academy Press.

IOM. 1988. *Medical Technology Assessment Directory*. Washington, DC: National Academy Press.

IOM. 1989. *Assessment of Diagnostic Technology in Health Care: Rationale, Methods, Problems, and Directions*. Monograph of the Council on Health Care Technology. Washington, DC: National Academy Press.

IOM. 1990. *Consensus Development at the NIH: Improving the Program*. Washington, DC: National Academy Press.

IOM. 1991. *Guidelines for Clinical Practice: From Development to Use*. Washington, DC: National Academy Press.

IOM. 1992. *Setting Priorities for Health Technology Assessment: A Model Process*. Washington, DC: National Academy Press.

IOM. 1993. *Access to Health Care in America*. Washington, DC: National Academy Press.

IOM. 1999. *To Err Is Human: Building a Safer Health System*. Washington, DC: National Academy Press.

IOM. 2001. *Crossing the Quality Chasm: A New Health System for the 21st Century*. Washington, DC: National Academy Press.

IOM. 2002. *Unequal Treatment: Confronting Racial and Ethnic Disparities in Health Care*. Washington, DC: National Academy Press.

IOM. 2003. Hidden Costs, Value Lost: Uninsurance in America. Washington, DC: National Academies Press.

Jacobs, L., T. Marmor, and J. Oberlander. 1999. The Oregon Health Plan and the Political Paradox of Rationing: What Advocates and Critics Have Claimed and What Oregon Did. *Journal of Health Politics, Policy and Law* 24 (1): 161–80.

Jacoby, I. 1985. The Consensus Development Program of the National Institutes of Health: Current Practices and Historical Perspectives. *International Journal of Technology Assessment in Health Care* 1:420–32.

Jacoby, I., and M. Rose. 1986. Transfer of Information and Its Impact on Medical Practice: The U.S. Experience. *International Journal of Technology Assessment in Health Care* 2:107–15.

Janowsky, E. C., L. L. Kupper, and B. S. Hulka. 2000. Meta-analysis of the

Relation between Silicone Breast Implants and the Risk of Connective-Tissue Diseases. *New England Journal of Medicine* 342:781–90.

Jee, M. 1993. Perspectives: States Rediscover Certificate-of-Need Laws. *Medicine and Health* 47:1–4.

Jeffrey, N. A., and R. Langreth. 1998. Viagra's Lesson: New Drugs, Unknown Risks. *Wall Street Journal*, June 10.

Jennings, J. R, and A. Weinstein. 1991. Technology Assessment: Why Hospitals Must Get Serious. *Decisions in Imaging Economics* 4:31–35.

Johannesson, M., J. S. Pliskin, and M. C. Weinstein. 1994. A Note on QALY's, Time Tradeoff, Issues in the Design and Analysis of Stochastic Cost-Effectiveness Studies in Health Care. *Medical Care* 32:150–63.

Johansson, P. 1995. *Evaluating Health Risks.* Cambridge: Cambridge University Press.

Johnson, G. 2001. All Science Is Computer Science. *New York Times,* March 25.

Johnson Foundation. 2001. *Pursuing Perfection: Raising the Bar for Health Care Performance.* Call for Proposals. Princeton, NJ: Robert Wood Johnson Foundation. Available at http://www.rwjf.org.

Jonsen, A. 1993. The Birth of Bioethics. *Hastings Center Report* 23 (special supplement): S1–4.

Kahn, A. 1991. The Dynamics of Medical Device Innovation: An Innovator's Perspective. In *The Changing Economics of Medical Technology,* ed. A. C. Gelijns and E. A. Halm, 89–95. Washington, DC: National Academy Press.

Kahn, C. N. 1998. The AHCPR after the Battles. *Health Affairs* 17:109–10.

Kaiser Permanente. 2001. *About Kaiser Permanente.* Available at http://www.kp.org.

Kane, N. M., and P. D. Manoukian. 1989. The Effect of the Medicare Prospective Payment System on the Adoption of New Technology: The Case of Cochlear Implants. *New England Journal of Medicine* 321:1378–83.

Kanouse, D. E., ed. 1989. *Changing Medical Practice through Technology Assessment: An Evaluation of the NIH Consensus Development Program.* Ann Arbor, MI: Health Administration Press.

Kasiske, B. L., J. F. Neylan, R. R. Riggio, G. M. Danovitch, L. Kahana, S. R. Alexander, and M. G. White. 1991. The Effect of Race on Access and Outcome in Transplantation. *New England Journal of Medicine* 324:302–7.

Kassirer, J. P. 1992. Clinical Trials and Meta-Analysis: What Do They Do for Us? *New England Journal of Medicine* 327:273–74.

Kassirer, J. P. 1993. The Quality of Care and the Quality of Measuring It. *New England Journal of Medicine* 329:1263–65.

Kassirer, J. P. 1994. The Use and Abuse of Practice Profiles. *New England Journal of Medicine* 330:634–36.

Katz, B. P., D. A. Freund, D. A. Heck, R. S. Dittus, J. E. Paul, J. Wright, P. Coyte, E. Holleman, and G. Hawker. 1996. Demographic Variation in the Rate of Knee Replacement: A Multi-Year Analysis. *Health Services Research* 31: 125–40.

Katz, D., and R. Kahn. 1966. *The Social Psychology of Organizations.* New York: Wiley.

Katz, J. 1993. Ethics and Clinical Research Revisited: A Tribute to Henry K. Beecher. *Hastings Center Report* 23 (5): 31–39.

Katz, S. J., W. P. Welch, and D. Verrilli. 1997. The Growth of Physician Services for the Elderly in the United States and Canada: 1987–1992. *Medical Care Research and Review* 54:300–319.

Keeler, E., and R. Bell. 1992. New DEALEs: Other Approximations of Life Expectancy. *Medical Decision Making* 12:307–11.

Kennedy, E. M. 1997. Investing in America's Good Health. *Boston Globe,* July 15.

Kilborn, P. T. 1999. Oregon Falters on a New Path to Health Care. *New York Times,* January 3.

Kim, W. Y., P. G. Danias, M. Stuber, S. D. Flamm, S. Plein, E. Nagel, S. E. Langerak, O. M. Weber, E. M. Pedersen, M. Schmidt, R. M. Botnar, and W. J. Manning. 2001. Coronary Magnetic Resonance Angiography for the Detection of Coronary Stenoses. *New England Journal of Medicine* 345: 1863–69.

Kitcher, P. 1996. *The Lives to Come: The Genetic Revolution and Human Possibilities.* New York: Simon and Shuster.

Kizer, K. W. 2001. Establishing Health Care Performance Standards in an Era of Consumerism. *Journal of the American Medical Association* 286:1213–17.

Kjellstrand, C. M. 1988. Age, Sex, and Race Inequality in Renal Transplantation. *Archives of Internal Medicine* 148:1305–9.

Klarman, H. E., J. O. Francis, and G. D. Rosenthal. 1968. Cost Effectiveness Analysis Applied to Treatment of Chronic Renal Disease. In *Health Economics,* ed. M. H. Cooper and A. J. Culyer, 230–40. Harmondsworth: Penguin.

Klein, R., and H. Sturm. 2002. Viagra: A Success Story for Rationing? *Health Affairs* 21:177–87.

Knox, R. A. 1995. More Drug Firms Pitching Ads Directly to Consumers. *Boston Globe,* March 13.

Koelemay, M. J. W., J. G. Lijmer, J. Stoker, D. A. Legemate, and P. M. M. Bossuyt. 2001. Magnetic Resonance Angiography for the Evaluation of Lower Extremity Arterial Disease: A Meta-Analysis. *Journal of the American Medical Association* 285:1338–45.

Kolata, G. 1992. When Doctors Say Yes and Insurers No. *New York Times,* August 16.

Krahn, M. D., G. Naglie, D. Naimark, D. A. Redelmeier, and A. S. Detsky. 1997. Primer on Medical Decision Analysis: Part 4. *Medical Decision Making* 17: 142–51.

Kranish, M. 2002. Breakthroughs in Effort to Map Body's Proteins. *Boston Globe,* February 6.

Kuntz, K. M., and M. C. Weinstein. 1995. Life Expectancy Biases in Clinical Decision Modeling. *Medical Decision Making* 15:158–69.

Lamas, G. A., M. A. Pfeffer, P. Hamm, J. Wertheimer, J. L. Rouleau, and E. Braunwald. 1992. Do the Results of Randomized Clinical Trials of Cardiovascular

Drugs Influence Medical Practice? *New England Journal of Medicine* 327: 241–47.

Lander, E. S. 2000. After Deciphering the Map, the Next Task Is a Guidebook for the Human Genome. *New York Times*, September 12.

Langreth, R., M. Waldholz, and S. D. Moore. 1999. DNA Dreams: Big Drug Firms Discuss Linking Up to Pursue Disease-Causing Genes. *Wall Street Journal*, March 4.

Lapuerta, P., G. J. L'Italien, S. Paul, R. C. Hendel, J. A. Leppo, L. A. Fleisher, M. C. Cohen, K. A. Eagle, and R. P. Giugliano. 1998. Neural Network Assessment of Perioperative Cardiac Risk in Vascular Surgery Patients. *Medical Decision Making* 18:70–75.

Larkin, H. 1987. Deregulation Spurs Market Information Demand. *Hospitals* 61:58.

Larson, E. B. 1999. Evidence-Based Medicine: Is Translating Evidence into Practice a Solution to the Cost-Quality Challenges Facing Medicine? *Joint Commission Journal on Quality Improvement* 25:480–85.

Lave, J. R., C. L. Pashos, G. F. Anderson, D. Brailer, T. Bubolz, D. Conrad, D. A. Freund, S. H. Fox, E. Keeler, J. Lipscomb, H. S. Luft, and G. Provenzano. 1994. Costing Medical Care: Using Medicare Administrative Data. *Medical Care* 32:JS77–89.

Law, A. M., and W. D. Kelton. 1991. *Simulation Modeling and Analysis.* New York: McGraw-Hill.

Leahy, R. E. 1989. Rational Health Policy and the Legal Standard of Care: A Call for Judicial Deference to Medical Practice Guidelines. *California Law Review* 77:1483–1528.

Leape, L. L. 1989. Unnecessary Surgery. *Health Services Research* 24:351–407.

Leapfrog Group. 2003. About the Leapfrog Group. Available at http://www.leapfroggroup.org.

Lee, D. W. 1991. Estimating the Cost of New Technology on Medicare Program Outlays: Do Related Procedures Matter? Draft paper, American Medical Association, Center for Health Policy Research, March 18.

Leichter, H. M. 1999. Oregon's Bold Experiment: Whatever Happened to Rationing? *Journal of Health Politics, Policy and Law* 24 (1): 147–60.

Lerner, J. C. 1998. Buying Medical Technology for Ambulatory Care. *Journal of Ambulatory Care Management* 21:78–91.

Levin, H. M. 1983. *Cost-Effectiveness: A Primer.* Beverly Hills, CA: Sage.

Levinsky, N. G., and R. A. Rettig. 1991. The Medicare End-Stage Renal Disease Program: A Report from the Institute of Medicine. *New England Journal of Medicine* 324:1143–48.

Levit, K., C. Cowan, H. Lazenby, A. Sensenig, P. McDonnell, J. Stiller, A. Martin, and the Health Accounts Team. 2000. Health Spending in 1998: Signals of Change. *Health Affairs* 19:124–32.

Levit, K., C. Smith, C. Cowan, H. Lazenby, A. Sensenig, and A. Catlin. 2003. Trends in U.S. Health Spending, 2001. *Health Affairs* 22:154–64.

Lewin Group. 2000. Report 1: The State of the Industry. Report to the Health Industry Manufacturers Association, March 24.

Lewontin, R. 2000. *The Triple Helix: Gene, Organism, and Environment.* Cambridge: Harvard University Press.

Lippman, M. E. 2000. High-Dose Chemotherapy Plus Autologous Bone Marrow Transplantation for Metastatic Breast Cancer. *New England Journal of Medicine* 342:1119–20.

Littell, C. L. 1994. Innovation in Medical Technology: Reading the Indicators. *Health Affairs* 13:226–35.

Littenberg, B. 1992. Technology Assessment in Medicine. *Academic Medicine* 67: 424–28.

Lohr, K. N., ed. 1990. *Medicare: A Strategy for Quality Assurance.* Vol. 1. Washington, DC: National Academy Press.

Lomas, J., G. M. Anderson, K. Dominick-Pierre, E. Vayda, M. W. Enkin, and W. J. Hannah. 1989. Do Practice Guidelines Guide Practice? *New England Journal of Medicine* 321:1306–11.

Long, M. J., J. D. Chesney, R. P. Ament, S. I. Desharnais, S. T. Fleming, E. J. Kobrinski, and B. S. Marshall. 1987. The Effect of PPS on Hospital Product and Productivity. *Medical Care* 25:528–38.

Lovern, E. 2001a. "Gotcha" Gives Way to Guidance: Quality Improvement behind Plan to Change Medicare Review Groups' Image. *Modern Healthcare,* December 17, p. 20.

Lovern, E. 2001b. QIOs Eye Mission: Better Reporting. *Modern Healthcare,* December 10, p. 12.

Lutz, S. 1996. Merger, Acquisition Activity Hits Record in 1st Quarter. *Modern Healthcare,* May 27, pp. 2–3.

Mannebach, M. A., F. J. Ascione, C. A. Gaither, R. P. Bagozzi, I. A. Cohen, and M. L. Ryan. 1999. Activities, Functions, and Structure of Pharmacy and Therapeutics Committees in Large Teaching Hospitals. *American Journal of Health Systems Pharmacy* 56:622–28.

Mansfield, E. 1975. *Microeconomics: Theory and Applications.* New York: Norton.

March, J. G., and H. A. Simon. 1958. *Organizations.* New York: Wiley.

Mark, D. B., M. A. Hlatky, R. M. Califf, C. D. Naylor, K. L. Lee, P. W. Armstrong, G. Barbash, H. White, M. L. Simoons, C. L. Nelson, N. Clapp-Channing, J. D. Knight, F. E. Harrell Jr., J. Simes, and E. J. Topol. 1995. Cost Effectiveness of Thrombolytic Therapy with Tissue Plasminogen Activator as Compared with Streptokinase for Acute Myocardial Infarction. *New England Journal of Medicine* 332:1418–24.

Markoff, J. 2002. The Increase in Chip Speed Is Accelerating, Not Slowing. *New York Times,* February 4.

Marshall, A. K. M. 1994. Manufacturers' Responses to the Increased Demand for Outcomes Research. In *Adopting New Medical Technology,* ed. A. C. Gelijns and H. V. Dawkins, 152–71. Washington, DC: National Academy Press.

Marshall, M. N., P. G. Shekelle, S. Leatherman, and R. H. Brook. 2000. The

Public Release of Performance Data: What Do We Expect to Gain? A Review of the Evidence. *Journal of the American Medical Association* 283:1866–74.

Matherlee, K. 1999. *The Public Stake in Biomedical Research: A Policy Perspective.* Washington, DC: George Washington University, National Health Policy Forum, November.

Maxwell, J. H., and H. M. Sapolsky. 1989. Prospective Payment in the ESRD Program: Implications for Technology and Program Administration. In *Health Care, Technology, and the Competitive Environment*, ed. H. P. Brehm and R. M. Mullner, 135–53. New York: Praeger.

Maynard, C., L. D. Fisher, E. R. Passamani, and T. Pullum. 1986. Blacks in the Coronary Artery Surgery Study (CASS): Race and Clinical Decision Making. *American Journal of Public Health* 76:1446–48.

McCarthy, C. M. 1988. DRGs: Five Years Later. *New England Journal of Medicine* 318:1683–86.

McClellan, M. 1996. Are the Returns to Technological Change in Health Care Declining? *Proceedings of the National Academy of Sciences USA* 93:12701–8.

McClellan, M., and D. Kessler. 1999. A Global Analysis of Technological Change in Health Care: The Case of Heart Attacks. *Health Affairs* 18:250–55.

McClellan, M. B., and D. P. Kessler. 2002. *Technological Change in Health Care: A Global Analysis of Heart Attack.* Ann Arbor: University of Michigan Press.

McDermott, W. 1977. Evaluating the Physician and His Technology. *Daedalus* 106:135–57.

McGlynn, E. A., J. Kosecoff, and R. H. Brook. 1990. Format and Conduct of Consensus Development Conferences: Multinational Comparison. *International Journal of Technology Assessment in Health Care* 6:450–69.

McGregor, M. 1989. Technology and the Allocation of Resources. *New England Journal of Medicine* 320:118–20.

McGuire, P. 1990. Kaiser Permanente's New Technologies Committee: An Approach to Assessing Technology. *Quality Review Bulletin* 16:240–42.

McKinlay, J. B. 1981. From "Promising Report" to "Standard Procedure": Seven Stages in the Career of a Medical Innovation. *Milbank Memorial Fund Quarterly* 59:233–70.

McLean, R. A. 1997. *Financial Management in Health Care Organizations.* Albany, NY: Delmar.

McPeek, B., F. Mosteller, and M. McKneally. 1989. Randomized Clinical Trials in Surgery. *International Journal of Technology Assessment in Health Care* 5:317–32.

Medical Devices Agency. 2001. *Medical Devices Agency—MDA.* Available at http://www.medical-devices.gov.uk.

Medical Technology and Practice Patterns Institute. 1998. *Institute Overview.* Washington, DC: MTPPI.

Medicare Coverage Advisory Committee. 2001. *Medicare Coverage Policy— MCAC. Recommendations for Evaluating Effectiveness.* Available at http://www.hcfa.gov/coverage.

Medicare Program; Criteria for Making Coverage Decisions. 2000. *Federal Register*, May 16.

Medicare Program; Procedures for Making National Coverage Decisions. 1999. *Federal Register*, April 27.

Medicare Program; Proposed Rule for Making Coverage Decisions. 1989. *Federal Register*, January 30.

Medicines Control Agency. 2001. *About the Agency*. Available at http://www .mca.gov.uk.

MedPAC. 1998. *Report to the Congress: Medicare Payment Policy*. Vols. 1 and 2. Washington, DC: MedPAC, March.

MedPAC. 2000. *Report to the Congress: Selected Medicare Issues*. Washington, DC: MedPAC, June.

MedPAC. 2001. *Report to the Congress: Medicare Payment Policy*. Washington, DC: MedPAC, March.

MedPAC. 2003. *Report to the Congress: Medicare Payment Policy*. Washington, DC: MedPAC, March.

Meenan, R. F. 1982. The AIMS Approach to Health Status Measurement: Conceptual Background and Measurement Properties. *Journal of Rheumatology* 9:785–88.

Mello, M. M., and T. A. Brennan. 2001. The Controversy over High-Dose Chemotherapy with Autologous Bone Marrow Transplant for Breast Cancer. *Health Affairs* 20:101–17.

Mendelson, D. N., R. G. Abramson, and R. J. Rubin. 1994. State Involvement in Medical Technology Assessment. *Health Affairs* 13:83–98.

Mendelson, D. N., and J. Arnold. 1993. Certificate of Need Revisited. *Spectrum: The Journal of State Government* 66:36–44.

Meredith, E. B., and S. B. Steever. 1996. Mergers and Acquisitions: What's Going On? In *1996 Healthcare Financial Management Resource Guide*, 12–16. Westchester, IL: Healthcare Financial Management Association.

Merkatz, R. B., R. Temple, S. Sobel, K. Feiden, D. A. Kessler, and the Working Group on Women in Clinical Trials. 1993. Women in Clinical Trials of New Drugs: A Change in Food and Drug Administration Policy. *New England Journal of Medicine* 309:292–96.

Merrill, J. C., and A. B. Cohen. 1987. The Emperor's New Clothes: Unraveling the Myths about Rationing. *Inquiry* 24:105–9.

Miao, L. L. 1977. Gastric Freezing: An Example of the Evaluation of Medical Therapy by Randomized Clinical Trials. In *Costs, Risks, and Benefits of Surgery*, ed. J. P. Bunker, B. A. Barnes, and F. Mosteller, 198–211. New York: Oxford University Press.

Miller, R. H. 1996. Competition in the Health Care System: Good News and Bad News. *Health Affairs* 15:107–20.

Miller, R. H., and H. S. Luft. 1994. Managed Care Plan Performance since 1980. *Journal of the American Medical Association* 271:1512–19.

Mishan, E. J. 1976. *Cost-Benefit Analysis*. New York: Praeger.

Mitchell, R. C., and R. T. Carson. 1989. *Using Surveys to Value Public Goods: An Assessment of the Contingent Valuation Method.* Washington, DC: Resources for the Future.

Moher, D., C. S. Dulberg, and G. A. Wells. 1994. Statistical Power, Sample Size, and Their Reporting in Randomized Controlled Trials. *Journal of the American Medical Association* 272:122–24.

Moher, D., A. Jones, L. Lepage, and the CONSORT Group. 2001. Use of the CONSORT Statement and Quality of Reports of Randomized Trials. *Journal of the American Medical Association* 285:1992–95.

Moher, D., and I. Olkin. 1995. Meta-Analysis of Randomized Controlled Trials: A Concern for Standards. *Journal of the American Medical Association* 274: 1962–64.

Moher, D., K. F. Schulz, D. Altman, and the CONSORT Group. 2001. The CONSORT Statement: Revised Recommendations for Improving the Quality of Reports of Parallel-Group Randomized Trials. *Journal of the American Medical Association* 285:1987–91.

Mohr, L. 1969. Determinants of Innovation in Organizations. *American Political Science Review* 63:111–26.

Mohr, P. E., C. Mueller, P. Neumann, S. Franco, M. Milet, L. Silver, and G. Wilensky. 2001. *The Impact of Medical Technology on Future Health Care Costs.* Report to the Health Insurance Association of America and the Blue Cross and Blue Shield Association, March 13. Bethesda, MD: Project Hope.

Moloney, T. W., and D. E. Rogers. 1979. Medical Technology—A Different View of the Contentious Debate over Costs. *New England Journal of Medicine* 301: 1413–19.

Mood, A. M., F. A. Graybill, and D. C. Boes. 1974. *Introduction to the Theory of Statistics.* New York: McGraw-Hill.

Moore, J. 1996. *The Pharmaceutical Industry.* Washington, DC: George Washington University, National Health Policy Forum, January.

Morin, K., H. Rakatansky, F. A. Riddick, L. J. Morse, J. M. O'Bannon, M. S. Goldrich, P. Ray, M. Weiss, R. M. Sade, and M. A. Spillman. 2002. Managing Conflicts of Interest in the Conduct of Clinical Trials. *Journal of the American Medical Association* 287:78–84.

Morone, J. A. 1990. *The Democratic Wish.* New York: Basic Books.

Morrison, L. J., P. R. Verbeek, A. C. McDonald, B. V. Sawadsky, and D. J. Cook. 2000. Mortality and Prehospital Thrombolysis for Acute Myocardial Infarction. *Journal of the American Medical Association* 283:2686–92.

Morrison, R. S., S. Wallenstein, D. K. Natale, R. S. Senzel, and L. L. Huang. 2000. "We Don't Carry That"—Failure of Pharmacies in Predominantly Nonwhite Neighborhoods to Stock Opioid Analgesics. *New England Journal of Medicine* 342:1023–26.

Morrissey, M. A., F. A. Sloan, and J. Valvona. 1988. Shifting Medicare Patients out of the Hospital. *Health Affairs* 7:52–64.

Moscovice, I. 1989. Rural Hospitals: A Literature Synthesis and Health Services Research Agenda. *Health Services Research* 23:891–930.

Moses, L. 1986. Data Acquisition for Assessment of Medical Technology: Methods Other Than Technical Trials. *International Journal of Technology Assessment in Health Care* 2:27–37.

Moskowitz, J., S. N. Finkelstein, R. I. Levy, E. B. Roberts, and E. J. Sondik. 1981. Biomedical Innovation: The Challenge and the Process. In *Biomedical Innovation*, ed. E. B. Roberts, R. I. Levy, S. N. Finkelstein, J. Moskowitz, and E. J. Sondik, 1–17. Cambridge: MIT Press.

Mosteller, F., and E. Burdick. 1989. Current Issues in Health Care Technology Assessment. *International Journal of Technology Assessment in Health Care* 5: 123–36.

Mowery, D., and N. Rosenberg. 1979. The Influence of Market Demand upon Innovation: A Critical Review of Some Recent Empirical Studies. *Research Policy* 8:102–53.

Moxley, J. H., and P. C. Roeder. 1988. How Trends Will Interact: The Perspective of the Hospital. In *New Medical Devices: Invention, Development, and Use*, ed. K. B. Ekelman, 127–37. Washington, DC: National Academy Press.

Much Ado about Mergers and Acquisitions. 1996. *Business and Health* 14:9.

Mullahy, K. M., and W. G. Manning. 1994. Statistical Issues in Cost-Effectiveness Analyses. In *Valuing Health Care: Costs, Benefits, and Effectiveness of Pharmaceuticals and Other Medical Technologies*, ed. F. Sloan. New York: Cambridge University Press.

Murphy, K., and R. Topel. 2000. *Exceptional Returns: The Economic Value of America's Investment in Medical Research.* Chicago: University of Chicago Business School, May.

Mushkin, S. J., and J. S. Landefeld. 1979. Health Expenditures and Biomedical Research. In *Biomedical Research: Costs and Benefits*, 345–361. Cambridge, MA: Ballinger.

Mushkin, S. J., L. C. Paringer, and M. M. Chen. 1977. *Returns to Biomedical Research, 1900–1975: An Initial Assessment of Impacts on Health Expenditures.* Mimeograph. Washington, DC: Georgetown University Public Services Laboratory.

Myers, S., and D. G. Marquis. 1969. *Successful Industrial Innovations.* NSF 69-17. Washington, DC: National Science Foundation.

Naimark, D., M. D. Krahn, G. Naglie, D. A. Redelmeier, and A. S. Detsky. 1997. Primer on Medical Decision Analysis: Part 5. *Medical Decision Making* 17:152–59.

National Cancer Institute Workshop Panel. 1990. Advances in Clinical Imaging Using Positron Emission Tomography. *Archives of Internal Medicine* 150:735–39.

National Center for Health Statistics. 1993. *National Hospital Discharge Survey, 1992.* Washington, DC: NCHS.

National Conference of State Legislatures. 2000. Transplant Policy: States' Response to Federal Rule Is Keep Organs "at Home. " *State Health Notes* 21 (325): 1, 6.

National Conference of State Legislatures. 2001. Prescription Drug Costs: States Unite to Strengthen Their Bargaining Power. *State Health Notes* 22 (361): 1, 5–6.

National Quality Forum. 2003. About the National Quality Forum. Available at http://www.qualityforum.org.

National Science Board. 1993. *Science and Engineering Indicators, 1993.* Washington, DC: U.S. Government Printing Office.

Nease, R., and D. Owens. 1997. Use of Influence Diagrams to Structure Medical Decisions. *Medical Decision Making* 17:263–75.

Neergaard, L. 1998. Questions Raised in Heart Drug Debacle. *Boston Globe,* June 10.

Neergaard, L. 2001. Cholesterol Drug Tied to Deaths Is Pulled Back. *Boston Globe,* August 9.

Nelson, K. B., J. M. Dambrosia, T. Y. Ting, and J. K. Grether. 1996. Uncertain Value of Electronic Fetal Monitoring in Predicting Cerebral Palsy. *New England Journal of Medicine* 334:613–18.

Nelson, R. R., and S. G. Winter. 1977. In Search of Useful Theory of Innovation. *Research Policy* 6:36–76.

Neuhauser, D. 1992. Progress in Firms Research. *International Journal of Technology Assessment in Health Care* 8:321–24.

Neumann, P. J., and E. A. Sandberg. 1998. Trends in Health Care R&D and Technology Innovation. *Health Affairs* 17:111–19.

Neumann, P. J., and M. C. Weinstein. 1991. The Diffusion of New Technology: Costs and Benefits to Health Care. In *The Changing Economics of Medical Technology,* ed. A. C. Gelijns and E. A. Halm, 21–34. Washington, DC: National Academy Press.

Newhouse, J. P. 1992. Medical Care Costs: How Much Welfare Loss? *Journal of Economic Perspectives* 6:3–21.

Newhouse, J. P. 1993. An Iconoclastic View of Health Cost Containment. *Health Affairs* 12:152–71.

Nightingale, S. L. 1986. Orphan Drugs. *American Family Practitioner* 33:235–36.

Nightingale, S. L., and J. C. Morrison. 1987. Generic Drugs and the Prescribing Physician. *Journal of the American Medical Association* 258:1200–1204.

NIH. 1984. *Diagnostic Ultrasound Imaging in Pregnancy.* NIH Consensus Development Conference Statement. Washington, DC: NIH.

NIH. 1992. *Basic Data Relating to the National Institutes of Health.* Washington, DC: U.S. Department of Health and Human Services.

NIH. 1997. *Consensus Development Conference on Thalidomide: Potential Benefits and Risks.* Bethesda, MD: NIH, September 9–10.

NIH. 2001. *NIH Consensus Development Program.* Available at http://odp.od.nih.gov/consensus.

Norkin, J. 1993. New Imaging Techniques and Early Treatment. *HEADlines,* July–August, pp. 10–11.

Nowicki, M. 1999. Capital Budgeting. In *The Financial Management of Hospitals and Healthcare Organizations,* 187–99. Chicago: AUPHA/HAP.

O'Brien, B., and A. Gafni. 1996. When Do the "Dollars" Make Sense? *Medical Decision Making* 16:288–99.

O'Brien, B., M. F. Drummond, and R. J. Labelle. 1994. In Search of Power and Significance: Analysis of Medical Decision Problems with Influence Diagrams. *Medical Decision Making* 17:241–62.

Omnibus Budget Reconciliation Act of 1989, Public Law 101-239. *Health Care Financing Review* 12:105–15.

Owens, D. K., R. D. Shachter, and R. F. Nease. 1997. Representation and Discounting. *Medical Decision Making* 14:188–93.

Parham, P. 2000. Review of *The Triple Helix: Gene, Organism, and Environment,* by Richard Lewontin. *New England Journal of Medicine* 343:667.

Parker-Pope, T. 2001. Some Prescribed Drugs Slip onto the Market without FDA Approval. *Wall Street Journal,* December 7.

Passamani, E. 1991. Clinical Trials—Are They Ethical? *New England Journal of Medicine* 324:1589–91.

Patrick, D. L., and P. Erickson. 1996. Applications of Health Status Assessment to Health Policy. In *Quality of Life and Pharmacoeconomics in Clinical Trials,* 2d ed., ed. B. Spilker, 140–53. Philadelphia: Lippincott-Raven.

Pauker, S. G. 1986. Decision Analysis as a Synthetic Tool for Achieving Consensus in Technology Assessment. *International Journal of Technology Assessment in Health Care* 2:83–97.

Pauker, S. G., and J. P. Kassirer. 1980. The Threshold Approach to Clinical Decision Making. *New England Journal of Medicine* 302:1109–17.

Pauly, M. V. 1995. Valuing Health Care Benefits in Money Terms. In *Valuing Health Care,* ed. F. A. Sloan. New York: Cambridge University Press.

Pear, R. 2001. Drug Spending Grows Nearly 19%. *New York Times,* May 8.

Pear, R., and R. Toner. 2002. States Face Hard Choices on Medicaid Cuts. *New York Times,* January 14.

Peden, E. A., and M. S. Freeland. 1995. A Historical Analysis of Medical Spending Growth, 1960–1993. *Health Affairs* 14:235–47.

Penslar, R. L., and R. D. Lamm. 1989. Who Pays for AZT? *Hastings Center Report* 19 (5): 30–32.

Perrow, C. 1972. *Complex Organizations: A Critical Essay.* Glenview, IL: Scott, Foresman.

Perry, S. 1982. The Brief Life of the National Center for Health Care Technology. *New England Journal of Medicine* 307:1095–1100.

Perry, S. 1987. The NIH Consensus Development Program: A Decade Later. *New England Journal of Medicine* 317:485–88.

Perry, S., E. Gardner, and M. Thamer. 1997. The Status of Health Technology

Assessment Worldwide: Results of an International Survey. *International Journal of Technology Assessment in Health Care* 13:81–98.

Perry, S., R. Hanft, and R. Chrzanowski. 1993. Report from the Australian Institute of Health and Welfare—Perceptions of Australian Health Technology Assessments: Report of a Survey. *International Journal of Technology Assessment in Health Care* 9:588–90.

Perry, S., and B. Pillar. 1990. A National Policy for Health Care Technology Assessment. *Medical Care Review* 47:401–17.

Peterson, E. D., S. M. Wright, J. Daley, and G. E. Thibault. 1994. Racial Variation in Cardiac Procedure Use and Survival Following Acute Myocardial Infarction in the Department of Veterans Affairs. *Journal of the American Medical Association* 271:1175–80.

Petitti, D. B. 1986. Competing Technologies: Implications for the Costs and Complexity of Medical Care. *New England Journal of Medicine* 315:1480–83.

Petitti, D. B. 1994. *Meta-Analysis, Decision Analysis, and Cost-Effectiveness Analysis: Methods for Quantitative Synthesis in Medicine.* Oxford: Oxford University Press.

Phelps, C. E. 1993. The Methodologic Foundations of Studies of the Appropriateness of Medical Care. *New England Journal of Medicine* 329:1241–45.

Phelps, C. E. 1995. Perspectives in Health Economics. *Health Economics* 4: 335–54.

Phelps, C. E. 1997. Good Technologies Gone Bad. *Medical Decision Making* 17: 107–17.

Phelps, C. E., and S. T. Parente. 1990. Priority Setting in Medical Technology and Medical Practice Assessment. *Medical Care* 28:703–23.

PhRMA. 1998. *Pharmaceutical Industry Profile 1998.* Washington, DC: PhRMA.

PhRMA. 1999. *Pharmaceutical Industry Profile 1999.* Washington, DC: PhRMA.

PhRMA. 2000. *Pharmaceutical Industry Profile 2000: Research for the Millennium.* Washington, DC: PhRMA.

PhRMA. 2001. *Pharmaceutical Industry Profile 2001.* Washington, DC: PhRMA.

PhRMA. 2002. *Pharmaceutical Industry Profile 2002.* Washington, DC: PhRMA.

PhRMA. 2003. *Pharmaceutical Industry Profile 2003.* Washington, DC: PhRMA.

Pocock, S. J., and D. R. Elbourne. 2000. Randomized Trials or Observational Tribulations? *New England Journal of Medicine* 342:1907–09.

Pollack, A. 2001. Two Companies Get Bad News from FDA on New Drug. *New York Times*, July 11.

Poses, R. M., R. D. Cebul, and M. Collins. 1985. The Accuracy of Experienced Physicians' Probability Estimates for Patients with Sore Throats: Implications for Decision Making. *Journal of the American Medical Association* 254: 925–29.

Pound, W. T. 2002. The Fiscal State of States. *New York Times*, January 14.

Pozen, M. W., D. J. Lerner, R. B. D'Agostino, H. W. Strauss, and P. M. Gertman. 1984. Cardiac Nuclear Imaging: Adoption of an Evolving Technology. *Medical Care* 22:343–48.

PPRC. 1992a. *Annual Report to Congress, 1992.* Washington, DC: PPRC.

PPRC. 1992b. *Fee Update and Medicare Volume Performance Standards for 1993.* Report no. 92-4. Washington, DC: PPRC.

PPRC. 1993. *Fee Update and Medicare Volume Performance Standards for 1994.* Report no. 93-1. Washington, DC: PPRC.

The President's Message. 2000. *Health Technology Assessment* 12 (2): 4.

The President's Message. 2001. *Health Technology Assessment* 13 (1): 4.

Prince, T. R. 1998. A Medical Technology Index for Community Hospitals. *Health Care Management Review* 23:52–63.

ProPAC. 1992. *Medicare and the American Health Care System, Report to the Congress.* Washington, DC: ProPAC.

Raskin, I. E., and C. W. Maklan. 1991. Medical Treatment Effectiveness Research: A View from inside the Agency for Health Care Policy and Research. *Evaluation and the Health Professions* 14:161–86.

Read, J. L., and K. B. Lee Jr. 1994. Health Care Innovation: Progress Report and Focus on Biotechnology. *Health Affairs* 13:215–25.

Reiman, E. M., and M. A. Mintun. 1990. Positron Emission Tomography. *Archives of Internal Medicine* 150:729–31.

Reinhardt, U. 1997. Making Economic Evaluations Respectable. *Social Science and Medicine* 45:555–62.

Reiser, S. J. 1978. *Medicine and the Reign of Technology.* Cambridge: Cambridge University Press.

Report from the EUR-ASSESS Project. 1997. *International Journal of Technology Assessment in Health Care* 13:133–340.

Reports from the Swedish Council on Technology Assessment in Health Care. 1997. *International Journal of Technology Assessment in Health Care* 13:488–94.

Rettig, R. A. 1994. Medical Innovation Duels Cost Containment. *Health Affairs* 13:7–27.

Rettig, R. A. 1996. The Social Contract and the Treatment of Permanent Kidney Failure. *Journal of the American Medical Association* 275:1123–26.

Rettig, R. A. 1997. *Health Care in Transition: Technology Assessment in the Private Sector.* Santa Monica, CA: RAND.

Rice, T., G. de Lissovoy, J. Gabel, and D. Ermann. 1985. The State of PPOs: Results from a National Survey. *Health Affairs* 4:25–40.

Rigter, H. 1993. Assessment of Health Care Technology in the Netherlands. In *Health Care Technology and Its Assessment: An International Perspective,* ed. D. Banta and B. Luce, 213–22. Oxford: Oxford University Press.

Roberts, E. B. 1981. Influences on Innovation: Extrapolations to Biomedical Technology. In *Biomedical Innovation,* ed. E. B. Roberts, R. I. Levy, S. N. Finkelstein, J. Moskowitz, and E. J. Sondik, 50–74. Cambridge: MIT Press.

Roberts, E. B. 1982. The Development of Biomedical Technologies. In *Critical Issues in Medical Technology,* ed. B. J. McNeil and E. G. Cravalho, 3–22. Boston: Auburn House.

Roberts, S. D., and R. W. Klein. 1984. Simulation of Medical Decisions: Applications of SLN. *Simulation* 43:234–41.

Robinson, J. 1984. Why the Conspiracy of Silence Won't Die. *Medical Economics* 61:180.

Robinson, J., D. W. Garnick, and S. J. McPhee. 1987. Market and Regulatory Influences on the Availability of Coronary Angioplasty and Bypass Surgery in U.S. Hospitals. *New England Journal of Medicine* 317:85–90.

Rogers, E. M. 1962. *Diffusion of Innovations.* New York: Free Press.

Rogers, E. M. 1981. *Diffusion of Innovations: An Overview.* In *Biomedical Innovation,* ed. E. B. Roberts, R. I. Levy, S. N. Finkelstein, J. Moskowitz, and E. J. Sondik, 75–97. Cambridge: MIT Press.

Rogers, E. M. 1995. *Diffusion of Innovations.* 4th ed. New York: Free Press.

Rogers, E. M., and F. F. Shoemaker. 1971. *Communication of Innovations: A Cross-Cultural Approach.* New York: Free Press.

Rollo, F. D. 1987. Adopting New Technologies under the DRGs. In *Health Care Technology under Financial Constraints: Government Perspectives, Industry Perspectives, Health Care Institution Perspectives,* ed. R. M. F. Southby, W. Greenberg, and B. Luce. Columbus, OH: Battelle Press.

Romeo, A. A. 1988. Private Investment in Medical Device Innovation. In *New Medical Devices: Invention, Development, and Use,* ed. K. B. Ekelman, 62–72. Washington, DC: National Academy Press.

Romeo, A. A., J. L. Wagner, and R. H. Lee. 1984. Prospective Reimbursement and the Diffusion of New Technologies in Hospitals. *Journal of Health Economics* 3:1–24.

Rosenberg, R. 1997. Biotech Firms Praise FDA Legislation. *Boston Globe,* November 11.

Rosenberg, R. 2001a. Bioinformatics: Drug Firms Turning to Simulated Tests, Computer Models Speed Drug Testing. *Boston Globe,* March 26.

Rosenberg, R. 2001b. Stock Prices Have Biotechs' Backs to Wall. *Boston Globe,* March 28.

Rosenberg, R., and R. Mishra. 2000. The Beginning of a New Science. *Boston Globe,* June 27.

Rosenthal, G. 1979. Anticipating the Costs and Benefits of New Technology: A Typology for Policy. In *Medical Technology: The Culprit behind Health Care Costs?* ed. S. H. Altman and R. J. Blendon, 77–87. DHEW publication no. (PHS) 79-3216. Washington, DC: National Center for Health Services Research.

Rosko, M. D. 1989. A Comparison of Hospital Performance under the Partial-Payer, Medicare PPS, and State All-Payer Rate-Setting Systems. *Inquiry* 26:48–61.

Ross, L. F. 1997. Health Care Decision Making by Children: Is It In Their Best Interest? *Hastings Center Report* 27 (6): 41–45.

Rossi, P. H., and H. E. Freeman. 1985. *Evaluation: A Systematic Approach.* 3d ed. Beverly Hills, CA: Sage.

Rothman, K. J., and K. B. Michels. 1994. The Continuing Unethical Use of Placebo Controls. *New England Journal of Medicine* 331:394–98.

Rundle, R. L. 2003. PET Scanners Become New Rx for Diagnostics. *Wall Street Journal*, May 6.

Russell, L. B. 1976. The Diffusion of New Hospital Technologies in the United States. *International Journal of Health Services* 6:557–80.

Russell, L. B. 1977. The Diffusion of Hospital Technologies: Some Econometric Evidence. *Journal of Human Resources* 12:482–502.

Russell, L. B. 1979. *Technology in Hospitals: Medical Advances and Their Diffusion*. Washington, DC: Brookings Institution.

Russell, L. B., and C. Manning. 1989. The Effect of Prospective Payment on Medicare Expenditures. *New England Journal of Medicine* 320:439–43.

Russell, L. B., and J. E. Sisk. 1988. Medical Technology in the United States: The Last Decade. *International Journal of Technology Assessment in Health Care* 4: 269–86.

Sacks, H. S., J. Berrier, D. Reitman, V. A. Ancona-Berk, and T. C. Chalmers. 1987. Meta-Analyses of Randomized Controlled Trials. *New England Journal of Medicine* 316:450–55.

Saltus, R. 2000. Decoding of Genome Declared. *Boston Globe*, June 27.

Sanders, C. A. 1982. Adoption of New Technologies in Hospitals. In *Critical Issues in Medical Technology*, ed. B. J. McNeil and E. G. Cravalho, 25–36. Boston: Auburn House.

Savitt, T. L. 2001. The Use of Blacks for Medical Experimentation in the Old South. In *Bioethics, Justice, and Health Care*, ed. W. Teays and L. Purdy, 215–25. New York: Wadsworth.

Schersten, T. 1986. Some Reflections on Randomized Controlled Trials. *International Journal of Technology Assessment in Health Care* 2:39–52.

Schneider, E. C., and A. M. Epstein. 1996. Influence of Cardiac-Surgery Performance Reports on Referral Practices and Access to Care. *New England Journal of Medicine* 335:251–56.

Schneider, E. C., P. D. Cleary, A. M. Zaslavsky, and A. M. Epstein. 2001. Racial Disparity in Influenza Vaccination. Does Managed Care Narrow the Gap between African Americans and Whites? *Journal of the American Medical Association* 286:1455–60.

Schrader, E. (KPMG Peat Marwick, Boston). 1998. Personal communication, March 16.

Schramm, C. J., S. C. Renn, and B. Biles. 1986. Controlling Hospital Cost Inflation: New Perspectives on State Rate Setting. *Health Affairs* 5:22–33.

Schroeder, S., and L. Sandy. 1993. Specialty Distribution of U.S. Physicians: The Invisible Driver of Health Care Costs. *New England Journal of Medicine* 328: 961–63.

Schulman, K. A., J. A. Berlin, W. Harless, J. F. Kerner, S. Sistrunk, B. J. Gersh, R. Dubé, C. K. Taleghani, J. E. Burke, S. Williams, J. M. Eisenberg, and J. J.

Escarce. 1999. The Effect of Race and Sex on Physicians' Recommendations for Cardiac Catheterization. *New England Journal of Medicine* 340:618–26.

Schulz, K. F., I. Chalmers, D. A. Grimes, and D. G. Altman. 1994. Assessing the Quality of Randomization from Reports of Controlled Trials Published in Obstetrics and Gynecology Journals. *Journal of the American Medical Association* 272:125–28.

Schwartz, W. B. 1981. The Regulation Strategy for Controlling Hospital Costs: Problems and Prospects. *New England Journal of Medicine* 305:1249–55.

Schwartz, W. B. 1987. The Inevitable Failure of Current Cost-Containment Strategies: Why They Can Provide Only Temporary Relief. *Journal of the American Medical Association* 257:220–24.

Scitovsky, A. A. 1985. Changes in the Costs of Treatment of Selected Illnesses, 1971–1981. *Medical Care* 23:1345–57.

Scitovsky, A. A., and N. McCall. 1976. Changes in the Costs of Treatment of Selected Illnesses, 1951–1964–1971. Publication no. (HRA) 77-3161. Rockville, MD: U.S. Department of Health, Education, and Welfare.

See, W. A., C. S. Cooper, and R. J. Fisher. 1993. Predictors of Laparoscopic Complications after Formal Training in Laparoscopic Surgery. *Journal of the American Medical Association* 270:2689–92.

Serruys, P. W., F. Unger, J. E. Sousa, A. Jatene, H. J. R. M. Bonnier, J. P. A. M. Schönberger, N. Buller, R. Bonser, M. J. B. van den Brand, L. A. van Herwerden, M-A. M. Morel, and B. A. van Hout for the Arterial Revascularization Therapies Study Group. 2001. Comparison of Coronary-Artery Bypass Surgery and Stenting for the Treatment of Multivessel Disease. *New England Journal of Medicine* 344:1117–24.

Servis, K. W., and E. P. Ferrara. 1996. The New York State Task Force on Clinical Guidelines and Medical Technology Assessment. *Joint Commission Journal on Quality Improvement* 22:134–40.

Shachter, R. D. 1990. An Ordered Examination of Influence Diagrams. *Networks* 20:535–63.

Shadid, A. 2001. U.S. Funding Tilts Science Landscape. *Boston Globe,* March 5.

Shalala, D. 2000. Protecting Research Subjects—What Must Be Done. *New England Journal of Medicine* 343:808–10.

Shearer, M. 1991. Maternity Patients' Advocates in the 1990s: Changing Debates and New Debaters. *International Journal of Technology Assessment in Health Care* 7:517–29.

Sheils, J. F., G. J. Young, and R. J. Rubin. 1992. O Canada: Do We Expect Too Much from Its Health System? *Health Affairs* 11:7–20.

Shekelle, P. G., E. Ortiz, S. Rhodes, S. C. Morton, M. P. Eccles, J. M. Grimshaw, and S. H. Woolf. 2001. Validity of the Agency for Healthcare Research and Quality Clinical Practice Guidelines: How Quickly Do Guidelines Become Outdated? *Journal of the American Medical Association* 286:1461–67.

Shepard, D., and R. J. Zeckhauser. 1976. Where Now for Saving Lives? *Law and Contemporary Problems* 40:5–45.

Shine, K. I. 1997. Low-Cost Technologies and Public Policy. *International Journal of Technology Assessment in Health Care* 13:562–71.

Shortell, S. M., R. R. Gillies, and K. J. Devers. 1995. Reinventing the American Hospital. *Milbank Quarterly* 73:131–60.

Showstack, J. A., M. H. Stone, and S. A. Schroeder. 1985. The Role of Changing Clinical Practices in the Rising Costs of Hospital Care. *New England Journal of Medicine* 313:1201–7.

Shulman, S. R., B. Bienz-Tadmor, P. S. Seo, et al. 1992. Implementation of the Orphan Drug Act. *Food and Drug Law Journal* 47:363–403.

Shuman, D. W. 1997. The Standard of Care in Medical Malpractice Claims, Clinical Practice Guidelines, and Managed Care: Toward a Therapeutic Harmony? *California Western Law Review* 34:99.

Siegel, J. E., M. C. Weinstein, L. B. Russell, and M. R. Gold. 1996. Recommendations for Reporting Cost-Effectiveness Analyses. *Journal of the American Medical Association* 276:1339–41.

Silvers, J. B., W. Zelman, and C. N. Kahn, eds. 1983. *Health Care Financial Management in the 1980s: Time of Transition.* Ann Arbor, MI: AUPHA Press.

Simon, H. 1957. *Administrative Behavior.* New York: Macmillan.

Simpson, J. B. 1985. State Certificate-of-Need Programs: The Current Status. *American Journal of Public Health* 75:1225–28.

Skolnick, A. 1996. Technologies Described at Radiology Meeting Someday May Be Deployed in War against Cancer. *Journal of the American Medical Association* 275:92–93.

Sloan, F. A. 1983. Rate Regulation as a Strategy for Hospital Cost Control: Evidence from the Last Decade. *Milbank Memorial Fund Quarterly* 61:195–220.

Sonnenberg, F. 1997. Decision Analysis in Disease Management. *Disease Management and Clinical Outcomes* 1:20 34.

Sonnenberg, F., and J. R. Beck. 1993. Markov Models in Medical Decision Making: A Practical Guide. *Medical Decision Making* 13:322–38.

Soper, M., and D. Ferriss. 1992. The Growth of Managed Care in the Private Sector. In *Technology and Health Care in an Era of Limits,* ed. A. C. Gelijns, 37–50. Washington, DC: National Academy Press.

Sox, H. C., M. A. Blatt, M. C. Higgins, and K. I. Marton. 1988. *Medical Decision Making.* Stoneham, MA: Butterworth.

Spencer, F. C. 1986. The Internal Mammary Artery: The Ideal Coronary Bypass Graft? *New England Journal of Medicine* 314:50–51.

Sprague, L. 2001. *Quality in the Making: Perspectives on Programs and Progress.* Washington, DC: George Washington University, National Health Policy Forum, April.

Sprague, L. 2002. *Contracting for Quality: Medicare's Quality Improvement Organizations.* Washington, DC: George Washington University, National Health Policy Forum, June.

Stadtmauer, E. A., A. O'Neill, L. J. Goldstein, P. A. Crilley, K. F. Mangan, J. N. Ingle, I. Brodsky, S. Martino, H. M. Lazarus, J. K. Erban, C. Sickles, J. H.

Glick, and the Philadelphia Bone Marrow Transplant Group. Conventional-Dose Chemotherapy Compared with High-Dose Chemotherapy Plus Autologous Hematopoietic Stem-Cell Transplantation for Metastatic Breast Cancer. 2000. *New England Journal of Medicine* 324:1069–76.

Starr, P. 1982. *The Social Transformation of American Medicine.* New York: Basic Books.

Starr, P. 1992. *The Logic of Health-Care Reform.* Knoxville, TN: Grand Rounds Press.

Starr, P., and W. A. Zelman. 1993. A Bridge to Compromise: Competition under a Budget. *Health Affairs* 12 (supplement): 7–23.

Stauning, I. 1994. Women, Health, and Medical Technology. *International Journal of Technology Assessment in Health Care* 10:273–81.

Steinberg, E. P. 1985. The Impact of Regulation and Payment Innovations on Acquisition of New Imaging Technologies. *Radiologic Clinics of North America* 23:381–89.

Steinberg, E. P. 1989. Technology Assessment: A Physician's Perspective. In *Quality of Care and Technology Assessment,* ed. K. N. Lohr and R. A. Rettig. Washington, DC: National Academy Press.

Steinberg, E. P., and A. B. Cohen. 1984. *Nuclear Magnetic Resonance Imaging Technology: A Clinical, Industrial, and Policy Analysis.* Publication no. OTA-HCS-27. Washington, DC: U.S. Government Printing Office.

Steinberg, E. P., and S. Graziano. 1990. Integrating Technology Assessment and Medical Practice Evaluation into Hospital Operations. *Quality Review Bulletin* 16:218–22.

Steinberg, E. P., J. E. Sisk, and K. E. Locke. 1985. X-Ray CT and Magnetic Resonance Imagers: Diffusion Patterns and Policy Issues. *New England Journal of Medicine* 313:859–64.

Steiner, C. A., N. R. Powe, G. F. Anderson, and A. Das. 1997. Technology Coverage Decisions by Health Care Plans and Considerations by Medical Directors. *Medical Care* 35:472–89.

Stolberg, S. G., and J. Gerth. 2000. In a Drug's Journey to Market, Discovery Is Just the First of Many Steps. *New York Times,* July 23.

Sturdevant, R. A., and D. Stern. 1977. Accuracy of Physicians' Predictions of Cholecystography Results. *Medical Care* 15:488–93.

Sullivan, L. W. 1989. *Report to Congress: Volume and Intensity of Physicians' Services.* HCFA publication no. 03287. Washington, DC: U.S. Department of Health and Human Services.

Teays, W., and L. Purdy, eds. 2001. *Bioethics, Justice, and Health Care.* New York: Wadsworth.

Technological Change in Health Care (TECH) Research Network. 2001. Technological Change around the World: Evidence from Heart Attack Care. *Health Affairs* 20:25–42.

Temin, P. 1980. *Taking Your Medicine: Drug Regulation in the United States.* Cambridge: Harvard University Press.

ten Have, H. A. M. J. 1995. Medical Technology Assessment and Ethics: Ambivalent Relations. *Hastings Center Report* 25 (5): 13–20.

Teplensky, J. D. 1990. The Adoption of New Technology under Conditions of Changing Uncertainty: A Competitive Analysis. Ph.D. diss., University of Pennsylvania.

Teplensky, J. D., J. R. Kimberly, A. L. Hillman, and J. S. Schwartz. 1993. Scope, Timing, and Strategic Adjustment in Emerging Markets: Manufacturer Strategies and the Case of MRI. *Strategic Management Journal* 14:505–27.

Teplensky, J. D., M. V. Pauly, J. R. Kimberly, A. L. Hillman, and J. S. Schwartz. 1995. Hospital Adoption of Medical Technology: An Empirical Test of Alternative Models. *Health Services Research* 30:437–65.

Thacker, S. B. 1987. The Efficacy of Intrapartum Electronic Fetal Monitoring. *American Journal of Obstetrics and Gynecology* 156:24–30.

Thacker, S. B. 1988. Meta-Analysis: A Quantitative Approach to Research Integration. In *Modern Methods of Clinical Investigation,* ed. A. C. Gelijns, 88–100. Washington, DC: National Academy Press.

Thier, S. O. 1988. New Medical Devices and Health Care. In *New Medical Devices: Invention, Development, and Use,* ed. K. B. Ekelman, 3–12. Washington, DC: National Academy Press.

Thomas, C. 1992. Certificate of Need: An Idea Whose Time Has Come—Again? *State Health Notes* 13 (138): 4–5.

Thomas, C. 1993. *Certificate of Need: An Overview of 1992 State Legislative Activity.* Washington, DC: Intergovernmental Health Policy Project, George Washington University.

Thomas, L. 1974. The Technology of Medicine. In *The Lives of a Cell: Notes of a Biology Watcher.* New York: Viking.

Thomas, L. 1977. On the Science and Technology of Medicine. *Daedalus* 106: 35–46.

Thomas, L. J., Jr. 1988. Federal Support of Medical Device Innovation. In *New Medical Devices: Invention, Development, and Use,* ed. K. B. Ekelman, 51–61. Washington, DC: National Academy Press.

Thompson, J. D. 1967. *Organizations in Action.* New York: McGraw-Hill.

Thompson, M. S. 1980. *Benefit-Cost Analysis for Program Evaluation.* Beverly Hills, CA: Sage.

Thompson, M. S., and A. B. Cohen. 1990. The Feasibility of Willingness-to-Pay Measurement in Health Services Research. In *Costs and Benefits in Health Care and Prevention: An International Approach to Priorities in Medicine,* ed. U. Laaser, E. J. Roccella, J. B. Rosenfeld, and H. Wenzel, 27–34. Berlin: Springer.

Throckmorton, D. C. 2001. Future Trials of Antiplatelet Agents in Cardiac Ischemia. *New England Journal of Medicine* 344:1937–38.

Thurow, L. C. 1984. Learning to Say "No. " *New England Journal of Medicine* 31:1569–72.

Tieman, J. 2002. Calling in the Feds. *Modern Healthcare,* pp. 6–16, November 4.

Torrance, G. W. 1986. Measurement of Health State Utilities for Economic Appraisal: A Review. *Journal of Health Economics* 5:1–30.

Torrance, G. W. 1995. Designing and Conducting Cost-Utility Analyses. In *Quality of Life and Pharmacoeconomics in Clinical Trials,* ed. B. Spilker. Philadelphia: Lippincott-Raven.

Truog, R. D., W. Robinson, A. Randolph, and A. Morris. 1999. Is Informed Consent Always Necessary for Randomized, Controlled Trials? *New England Journal of Medicine* 340:804–7.

Tucker, B. P. 1998. Deaf Culture, Cochlear Implants, and Elective Disability. *Hastings Center Report* 28 (4): 6–13.

Tye, L. 2001. At McLean, MRI Scanner to Investigate Drug Addiction. *Boston Globe,* May 16.

United Network for Organ Sharing. 2001. *UNOS Online: The Organ Transplantation Resource.* Available at http://www.unos.org.

University HealthSystem Consortium. 2001. *About UHC.* Available at http://www.uhc.edu.

U.S. Congress. Congressional Budget Office. 1991. *Rising Health Care Costs: Causes, Implications, and Strategies.* Washington, DC: U.S. Government Printing Office.

U.S. Congress. OTA. 1976. *Development of Medical Technology: Opportunities for Assessment.* Publication no. OTA-H-34. Washington, DC: U.S. Government Printing Office.

U.S. Congress. OTA. 1980. *The Implications of Cost-Effectiveness Analysis of Medical Technology.* Publication no. OTA-H-126. Washington, DC: U.S. Government Printing Office.

U.S. Congress. OTA. 1982. *Strategies for Medical Technology Assessment.* Publication no. OTA-H-181. Washington, DC: U.S. Government Printing Office.

U.S. Congress. OTA. 1984a. *Medical Technology and Costs of the Medicare Program.* Publication no. OTA-H-227. Washington, DC: U.S. Government Printing Office.

U.S. Congress. OTA. 1984b. *Federal Policies and the Medical Devices Industry.* Publication no. OTA-H-229. Washington, DC: U.S. Government Printing Office.

U.S. Congress. OTA. 1992. *Does Health Insurance Make a Difference? Background Paper.* Publication no. OTA-BP-H-99. Washington, DC: U.S. Government Printing Office.

U.S. Congress. OTA. 1993. *Pharmaceutical R&D: Costs, Risks, and Rewards.* Publication no. OTA-H-522. Washington, DC: U.S. Government Printing Office.

U.S. Congress. OTA. 1995. *OTA Closes.* Press release, October 6. Washington, DC: U.S. Government Printing Office.

U.S. Preventive Services Task Force. 1995. *Guide to Clinical Preventive Services.* 2d ed. Baltimore: Williams and Wilkins.

Utterback, J. M. 1974. Innovation in Industry and the Diffusion of Technology. *Science* 183:620–26.

Vale, V., C. Donaldson, C. Daly, M. Campbell, J. Cody, A. Grant, I. Khan, P. Lawrence, S. Wallace, and A. MacLeod. 2000. Evidence-Based Medicine and Health Economics: A Case Study of End Stage Renal Disease. *Health Economics* 9:337–51.

Van Hout, B. A., M. J. Al, G. S. Gordon, and F. F. H. Rutten. 1994. Costs, Effects, and C/E Ratios alongside a Clinical Trial. *Health Economics* 3:309–19.

Vang, J. 1986. The Consensus Development Conference and the European Experience. *International Journal of Technology Assessment in Health Care* 2:65–75.

Vaughan-Sarrazin, M. S., E. L. Hannan, C. J. Gormley, and G. E. Rosenthal. 2002. Mortality in Medicare Beneficiaries Following Coronary Artery Bypass Graft Surgery in States with and without Certificate of Need Regulation. *Journal of the American Medical Association* 288:1859–66.

Viscusi, W. K. 1989. Prospective Reference Theory: Toward an Explanation of the Paradoxes. *Journal of Risk Uncertainty* 2:235–64.

Wade, N. 2000a. Reading the Book of Life; Now, the Hard Part: Putting the Genome to Work. *New York Times,* June 27.

Wade, N. 2000b. Reading the Book of Life: The Overview; Genetic Code of Human Life is Cracked by Scientists. *New York Times,* June 27.

Wade, N. 2002. Gene-mappers Take New Aim at Diseases. *New York Times,* October 30.

Wagner, J. L. 1979. Reimbursement Shapes Market for Technology. *Hospitals* 53:91–94.

Wagner, L. 1993. Kaiser, Blues Team up to Expand Assessment Program. *Modern Healthcare,* September 13, p. 8.

Waitzkin, H. 1979. A Marxian Interpretation of the Growth and Development of Coronary Care Technology. *American Journal of Public Health* 69:1260–68.

Wakker, P., and M. P. Klaassen. 1995. Confidence Intervals for Cost/Effectiveness Ratios. *Health Economics* 4:373–81.

Warner, K. E. 1974. The Need for Some Innovative Concepts of Innovation: An Examination of Research on the Diffusion of Innovations. *Policy Sciences* 5: 433–51.

Warner, K. E. 1975. A "Desperation-Reaction" Model of Medical Diffusion. *Health Services Research* 10:369–83.

Warner, K. E. 1978. Effects of Hospital Cost Containment on the Development and Use of Medical Technology. *Milbank Memorial Fund Quarterly* 56: 187–211.

Warner, K. E. 1979. The Cost of Capital-Embodied Medical Technology. In *Medical Technology and the Health Care System: A Study of the Diffusion of Equipment-Embodied Technology,* 270–302. Washington, DC: National Academy of Sciences.

Warner, K. E., and B. R. Luce. 1982. *Cost-Benefit and Cost-Effectiveness Analysis in Health Care: Principles, Practice, and Potential.* Ann Arbor, MI: Health Administration Press.

Webb, D., J. F. Culhane, S. Snyder, and J. Greenspan. 2001. Pennsylvania's Early Discharge Legislation: Effect on Maternity and Infant Lengths of Stay and Hospital Charges in Philadelphia. *Health Services Research* 36:1073–83.

Weeks, J., J. O'Leary, D. Fairclough, D. Paltiel, and M. C. Weinstein. 1994. The Q-tility Index: A New Tool for Assessing Health-Related Quality of Life and Utilities in Clinical Trials and Clinical Practice. *Proceedings of the American Society of Clinical Oncology* 13:436.

Weingart, S. N. 1993. Acquiring Advanced Technology: Decision-Making Strategies at Twelve Medical Centers. *International Journal of Technology Assessment in Health Care* 9:530–38.

Weingart, S. N. 1995. Deciding to Buy Expensive Technology: The Case of Biliary Lithotripsy. *International Journal of Technology Assessment in Health Care* 11:301–15.

Weinstein, M. C. 1979. Economic Evaluation of Medical Procedures and Technologies: Progress, Problems, and Prospects. In *Medical Technology*, DHEW publication no. (PHS) 79-3254, ed. J. Wagner, 52–68. Washington, DC: U.S. Government Printing Office.

Weinstein, M. C., H. V. Fineberg, A. S. Elstein, H. S. Frazier, D. Neuhauser, R. R. Neutra, and B. J. McNeil. 1980. *Clinical Decision Analysis.* Philadelphia: W. B. Saunders.

Weinstein, M. C., J. E. Siegel, M. R. Gold, M. S. Kamlet, and L. B. Russell. 1996. Recommendations of the Panel on Cost-Effectiveness in Health and Medicine. *Journal of the American Medical Association* 276:1253–58.

Weinstein, M. C., and W. B. Stason. 1977. Foundations of Cost-Effectiveness Analysis for Health and Medical Practices. *New England Journal of Medicine* 296:716–21.

Weisbrod, B. A. 1991. The Health Care Quadrilemma: An Essay on Technological Change, Insurance, Quality of Care, and Cost Containment. *Journal of Economic Literature* 29:523–52.

Weisbrod, B. A. 1994. The Nature of Technological Change: Incentives Matter! In *Adopting New Medical Technology*, ed. A. C. Gelijns and H. V. Dawkins, 8–48. Washington, DC: National Academy Press.

Welch, H. G., and E. S. Fisher. 1992. Cost-Containment Efforts in the Public Sector: Oregon's Priority List. In *Technology and Health Care in an Era of Limits*, ed. A. C. Gelijns, 63–75. Washington, DC: National Academy Press.

Welch, H. G., M. E. Miller, and W. P. Welch. 1994. Physician Profiling: An Analysis of Inpatient Practice Patterns in Florida and Oregon. *New England Journal of Medicine* 330:607–12.

Wenger, C. K. 1992. Exclusion of the Elderly and Women from Coronary Trials: Is Their Quality of Care Compromised? *Journal of the American Medical Association* 268:1460–61.

Wennberg, J. E. 1984. Dealing with Medical Practice Variations: A Proposal for Action. *Health Affairs* 3:6–32.

Wenneker, M. B., and A. M. Epstein. 1989. Racial Inequalities in the Use of Procedures for Patients with Ischemic Heart Disease in Massachusetts. *Journal of the American Medical Association* 261:253–57.

Wenneker, M. B., J. S. Weissman, and A. M. Epstein. 1990. The Association of Payer with Utilization of Cardiac Procedures in Massachusetts. *Journal of the American Medical Association* 264:1255–60.

Wheeler, K. E., T. Porter-O'Grady, and C. T. Barrell. 1985. Technology: A Strategic Factor in Hospital Planning. *Health Care Management Review* 10:55–63.

White, J. 1999. Targets and Systems of Health Care Cost Control. *Journal of Health Politics, Policy, and Law* 24:652–96.

White, J. B., and R. L. Rundle. 1998. Big Companies Fight Health-Plan Rates: Employers Demand HMOs and Hospitals Cut Costs. *Wall Street Journal*, May 19.

Whitted, G. S. 1981. Medical Technology Diffusion and Its Effects on the Modern Hospital. *Health Care Management Review* 6:45–54.

Wilkinson, R. 1987. MR: Profits Climb, Bad Debt Drops. *Hospitals*, November 5, pp. 58–63.

Williams, A. 1985. Economics of Coronary Bypass Grafting. *British Medical Journal* 291:326–29.

Winslow, R. 2002. GE to Offer New MRI Technology. *Wall Street Journal*, May 20.

Woolf, S. H., and C. Henshall. 2000. Health Technology Assessment in the United Kingdom. *International Journal of Technology Assessment in Health Care* 16:591–625.

Wortman, P. M., A. Vinokur, and L. Sechrest. 1988. Do Consensus Conferences Work? A Process Evaluation of the NIH Consensus Development Program. *Journal of Health Politics, Policy, and Law* 13:469–98.

Young, Arthur, and Company, and Emergency Care Research Institute. 1981. *A Profile of the Medical Technology Industry and Governmental Policies.* Report to the National Center for Health Services Research, U.S. Department of Health and Human Services, Hyattsville, MD, contract no. 233-79-3011. Washington, DC: Arthur Young & Company.

Youngblood, J. P. 1989. Should Ultrasound Be Used Routinely during Pregnancy? An Affirmative View. *Journal of Family Practice* 29:657–60.

Zaltman, G., R. Duncan, and J. Holbek. 1973. *Innovations and Organizations.* New York: Wiley.

Zweifel, P., and F. Breyer. 1997. *Health Economics.* Oxford: Oxford University Press.

Contributors

Alan B. Cohen is Professor of Health Policy and Management, and Executive Director of the Boston University Health Policy Institute, as well as Professor of Health Services in the Boston University School of Public Health. He also directs the national program office of the Robert Wood Johnson Foundation's Scholars in Health Policy Research program. His research has focused on medical technology adoption, cost containment and health policy, comparative health care systems, and the evaluation of health care programs. He presently serves as co-investigator of an evaluation of the Robert Wood Johnson Foundation's Pursuing Perfection program. For nine years, he directed the School of Management's Health Care M.B.A. program. Prior to joining Boston University in 1994, he held faculty positions at Johns Hopkins University and Brandeis University and spent eight years at the Robert Wood Johnson Foundation, where, as vice president for research and evaluation, he directed staff operations in the design of national program evaluations and in the management of programs in the areas of health care financing, state health policy, quality of care, and medical malpractice reform. Earlier, as a senior analyst for a Cambridge, Massachusetts consulting firm, he directed or participated in evaluation studies of federal and state programs in the areas of health statistics, health planning, Certificate of Need, and health professions training. Cohen is a Member of the National Academy of Social Insurance and a Fellow of AcademyHealth (formerly the Academy for Health Services Research and Health Policy). He received his B.A. in psychology from the University of Rochester, and his M.S. and Sc.D. degrees in health policy and management from the Harvard School of Public Health.

Ruth S. Hanft is currently Adjunct Associate in the Center for Bioethics at the University of Virginia. Her experience spans thirty years in government, academia, and the private sector. Before retiring in 1995, she served as Professor of Health Policy and Management at the George Washington University, where she held a joint appointment in the schools of business, public health, and medicine. Between 1977 and 1981, Hanft was Deputy Assistant Secretary for Health Policy, Research and Statistics, and later, Deputy Assistant Secretary for Health Services Research, Statistics and Technology, in the U.S. Department of Health and Human Services. Her responsibilities included supervision of the National Centers for Health Services Research (NCHSR), Health Statistics (NCHS), and Health Care Technology (NCHCT). Earlier in her career, Hanft served as a policy analyst in the Office of the Assistant Secretary for Planning and Evaluation in the U.S. Department of Health, Education, and Welfare. She is a Member of the Institute of Medicine, a founding Member of the National Academy of Social Insurance, a Fellow of the Hastings Center, and a former officer of the International Society for Technology Assessment in Health Care. Hanft holds a B.S. in industrial and labor relations from Cornell University, an M.A. in political science from Hunter College of the City University of New York, and a Ph.D. in public finance and health administration from the George Washington University.

William E. Encinosa is a senior economist in the Center for Organization and Delivery Studies at the Agency for Healthcare Research and Quality (AHRQ), where he conducts research on competition, regulation, and quality in hospital and HMO markets. His recent publications on managed care include: "The Economics of Regulatory Mandates on the HMO Market," "Competition among Health Maintenance Organizations," and "Adjusted Community Rate Reforms to Promote HMO Participation in Medicare + Choice." His current research looks at managed care's impact on hospital quality, risk selection in Medicare HMOs, risk adjustment of HMO capitation, pharmacy benefit design, and the costs of medical errors. Encinosa is also in charge of AHRQ's three Centers of Excellence on Health Care Markets and Managed Care. Prior to joining AHRQ, Encinosa was a Robert Wood Johnson Foundation Scholar in Health Policy Research at the University of Michigan. He holds a Ph.D. in economics and an M.A. in mathematics from the University of Florida.

Stephanie M. Spernak is Associate Professor of Health Services Management and Policy in the School of Public Health and Health Services at the George Washington University Medical Center. Her research areas include identifying factors (patient, provider, organization, government) that influence decision making, behavior, and outcomes in the health care domain. Spernak holds a J.D. from Georgetown University and a Ph.D. in applied social psychology from the George Washington University.

Shirley A. Stewart is a hospital executive with Hospital Corporation of America, currently assigned to Lakeside Hospital in Metairie, Louisiana. Previously, she served as CEO of Tulane University Hospital & Clinic in New Orleans. Stewart also was a Pew Fellow in Health Policy at Brandeis University's Florence Heller Graduate School, where her research focused on the diffusion of medical technology. Her diverse and extensive experience in hospital management includes executive leadership roles in for-profit as well as nonprofit institutions and in community hospitals as well as academic medical centers in several states, most notably West Virginia and Louisiana. She holds a B.A. in business and economics from Berea College (Ky.), and an M.A. in economics from Tulane University.

Catherine C. White is an independent consultant with extensive experience in health policy analysis and research. She has served as a research associate at the George Washington University and at the Institute of Medicine. White has directed and participated in projects for federal and state governments, health care foundations, educational institutions, and health care payers. Much of her research has focused on the costs and financing of health professions education, particularly graduate medical education, and on other health professions workforce issues. She received her M.G.A. in applied management and her B.S. in economics from the University of Maryland, University College.

Index